Wushu Were Here

Training Shaolin Kung Fu in China

This edition 2020

Contents

Preface

Keep true to the dreams of your youth.

Friedrich von Schiller

In 1980, I was a gangly nine-year-old attending a state secondary school in South Wales. For reasons still unknown to me, we became a teacher short in my year group and in place of a substitute teacher, my class was separated and scattered through adjacent classes. I was moved a year ahead.

When you are nine, the year above is a different planet; boys are bigger and girls are hotter and they all seemed more worldly. Some even used to skip off school to visit the local fleapit. Their steady diet of zombies and aliens was in no means impeded by film classification or age restrictions. Eager to fit in, I jumped at the opportunity to tag along. Concerns about making it past cinema officials were reassured when one guy turned up with his eight-year-old brother in tow.

This bunch of prepubescent reprobates rolled up to the matinee performance of The Big Brawl, which starred some Chinese guy called Jackie Chan. By today's standards, it's not a great film, but it had a massive impact on me. I left that cinema with one thought in mind; I wanted to do some of what that little Chinese guy did.

Being only three when Bruce Lee died, I had missed the initial wave of Kung Fu mania that Warner Brothers were now attempting to surf with Jackie Chan, but VHS lending libraries meant I was soon abreast of Bruce's work too. Enter the Dragon taught me another important lesson; Kung Fu wasn't just for Chinese, other people could do it too. Maybe even a gangly kid from South Wales.

David Carradine's TV show, Kung Fu, put another idea in my head, that of an ancient monastery in China. My two thoughts became one and I knew, not only did I want to learn Kung Fu, but I wanted to do it at the Shaolin Temple. Safely ensconced in my tiny little mind the idea didn't die, but sat there waiting for the right conditions to germinate.

Cold and lonely for many years that idea was starved of attention and nearly lost the fight for survival with little to maintain its ambitions. During its hibernation, university, jobs, houses, cars and relationships all pushed the little idea aside. Never quite forgotten, the dream clung to life as I tried several styles of martial art and eventually achieved a black belt in Lau Gar Kung Fu. Then one day my Kung Fu brother mentioned he would have liked to train at Shaolin.

With rapier-like wit, I replied, 'I've wanted to go to Shaolin since I was knee-high to Grasshopper.'

It was wasted on him. Being two years younger than me had made a massive difference in our formative years and rather than David Carradine and Kung Fu, he had been raised on Sho Kosugi and Ninja films. Nevertheless, within the depths of my mind something was stirring. The long-dormant childhood dream awakened and began to stretch toward the light intent on flowering. Shaolin was not only real, it was calling me.

At Zhengzhou airport the school bus will pick you up and bring you to International Kung Fu Centre. There you will book your accommodation, training and food and next day you will start your Shaolin kungfu/taichi/sanda training. It's very easy.

Xiao Long Website.

The midday sun penetrates the pollution haze and seers through the airport windows like a greenhouse. Were everything not so dusty it would probably glint in the heat. The journey has taken its toll on our two intrepid heroes. Staggering bleary-eyed into the foyer Victorian Dad has tired and irritable written all over his grizzled face, while I, confused at the best of times, have the frozen expression of a startled bunny. At this point, I'm just glad we don't have to make our own way to the school.

One reason we chose Xiao Long from the many Kung Fu schools in Dengfeng is that they are, by their own admission, set up to cater for foreign students. Included in these appealing nicetics is airport transfer. There is a bus service to Dengfeng and there are always taxis waiting at airports to take advantage of the weary and unwary. These options aside, we settled on the simplicity and thriftiness of the school's transportation. In my own strange little way, I am looking forward to being met by a guy holding a board with my name on it. I believe it has been documented that little things please little minds.

The arrival gate in Zhengzhou contains several people holding boards with names on. None of these names are in English. Nonetheless, I am approached by a number of placard bearers, but they aren't for me. I am even approached by people who have no board at all. However, Shi Yanlin, the guy I had been emailing for the last three months, and confirmed all details with two days previous, is conspicuously absent. My immediate suspicion is that he's not going to show, but my sense of better nature prevails and I reason he must be delayed. After all, I had given him my arrival date, time and flight number, and he had emphatically assured me he would be there to meet us. Let's face it, if you can't trust the word of a monk, who can you trust?

With this in mind, I leave my good friend, Victorian Dad, prominently positioned near the terminal doors and stroll around the foyer. I take particular note of anyone with a shaved head or holding a placard. There is no sign of my man.

As other passengers are collected by their nearest and dearest and go about their business, the crowd begins to thin. If two, six-foot, westerners with shaved heads had stood out previously, we are now getting further into sore thumb territory by the minute. We are so blatantly out of place it's painful. This makes it particularly difficult to determine if anyone is looking for us as everyone is looking at us.

My hopes are momentarily built up by a likely looking fellow in a flat-cap. Cigarette dangling from his lip, he nervously approaches and mumbles, 'Tagou?'

He has obviously taken one look at us, put two and two together and come to a lucrative conclusion. Tagou is the biggest school in Dengfeng, with over 13,000 students, and one of three that officially accept foreign students. It's also a school that didn't make the final cut in our selection process, primarily due to the expense and size. Nevertheless, I can see what he did there and I have to admire the guy's initiative. Hoping to benefit from his entrepreneurial spirit, I reply, 'Bu Tagou, women yau qu Xiao Long Wu Yuan.' (Not Tagou, I want to go to Xiao Long Martial Arts School).

His eyebrows raise and his mouth follows with a sneer. Apparently, this was not what he wanted to hear. He wanders back into the crowd.

There's only so long even someone as naive as myself can give another the benefit of the doubt. It's about an hour before I accept the absurd reality that I have been stood-up by a monk. Biting the bullet, I turn to Victorian Dad, 'Let's get a cab.'

In true Boy Scout style, we are prepared for exactly this situation as I have the school name, both in pinyin (Romanised pronunciation) and Chinese characters, written on a little card. Something that amazes the ubiquitous gaggle of cab drivers clustered outside the terminal. Encircled by slavering cabbies, I suddenly understand how a lightly grilled lamb chop must feel. There's no need for them to try concealing their delight. We all know VD and I are a meal ticket.

I keep my eye on the card as they pass it between themselves like a bizarre game of piggy-in-the-middle. I've been warned of a scam where drivers keep hold of potential passengers' directions, using them to negotiate a higher fee. I'm almost disappointed when the card doesn't disappear and I am denied the opportunity of pulling an identical card out of my sleeve with a, 'Ta da!' As ever, being prepared for an eventuality is the best way to make sure it doesn't occur.

Mocking my homemade card, the drivers bicker among themselves, probably arguing over which of their number is to make the kill and retire off the proceeds. Nothing in their attitude towards us is reassuring. My particular favourite moment as they pass around my little card is one guy reading it upside down. They continue to joke with each other as the ritual haggling begins.

My limited Chinese includes numbers, we covered them in lesson one. Should my basics let me down, I have a contingency plan in the form of a full set of fingers. Despite the fact we can all understand each other perfectly well when it comes to numbers, the cabbies insist on quoting me a sum, showing me the figure on their calculators and then getting the calculator to tell me the amount for good measure. This is my first glimpse of a talking pocket calculator. I guess that, having forked out on the calculators, they are determined to get the use out of them. I am to go through the same process all over China. The guy who sells talking pocket calculators must be raking it in.

Bidding starts at 900Yuan. I counter offer, the drivers refuse. We walk away. They call us back and counter offer. Repeat process until desired price difference is small enough to be insignificant or until one party gives in. The cabbies are only just warming up into the bickering and cajoling when, being the lightweight that I am, I can take the farce no more and cave in. We settle on 400Y, about £40 and at least 100Y over the odds. I know it's too much, but there is only so long I am prepared to argue over a tenner. As our taxi pulls off we are just glad to be underway.

I know we've been had, but our priority is to get to the school today.

Our enjoyment of the ride is in no way marred by our driver's belief he's in command of a tank powered by the sound of his horn. We are so enthralled that near-death experiences just add to the excitement and our jetlag is soon negated by adrenalin. Like two hyperactive children we point out sights. Hovels, shrines, even road signs showing the decreasing distance make our little eyes light up.

We are both particularly delighted by a rustic municipal road sweeper. The rickety truck tows a series of straw brooms attached to a centrifuge driven by the axle. This eclectic mix of traditional and modern is to be seen throughout China where ancient shrines nestle between designer clothes stores and Buddhist monks carry mobile phones. Not that they are reachable when you ring their number.

Using the shiny new expressway, we make the eighty kilometres to Dengfeng in about an hour and a half. Then the pantomime begins in earnest.

When our driver said he knew the Kung Fu school we wanted, he actually meant he had once seen a Kung Fu school, probably in a movie. So, we drive round and around Dengfeng while he points out different schools. I understand there to be over eighty Kung Fu schools in Dengfeng and our driver feels it his duty to show us each and every one. An hour or so later, the novelty of being randomly driven around these schools and asked if it's the right one is wearing pretty thin. Particularly when our driver insists each school is the right one and, when I reply in the negative, he looks at me in surprise repeatedly asking if I'm sure. Shrugging his shoulders, he sighs and asks for the card again. We go through the address together and he feigns inspiration saying, 'Ok,' and heads toward the next building that looks vaguely school-ish.

At various times during our exhaustive tour, we are taken back to schools we've already discounted and he even tries to pass us off with a restaurant, a primary school and at least one government building.

Our repetitive expedition of Dengfeng at one point intersects a police officer, who I think we could ask for directions. No, our driver has a better plan. Choosing to bypass the police officer, he befriends the next tramp we encounter by offering him a cigarette. To a casual observer they may appear to be merely standing outside a cardboard lean-to enjoying a smoke together. However, they are involved in a psychic exchange for our driver seems able to garner information from someone without actually engaging them in discussion.

In China, the offer of cigarettes is an accepted opening of negotiations. Almost exclusively a male activity, it is common to greet someone with a cigarette before starting a conversation. There are also different qualities of cigarettes, even fake ones, and offering a sub-standard cigarette can be seen as a slight. Businessmen may carry several different brands of cigarettes, offering the quality according to social standing. Being selective about whom he asks for directions means our driver doesn't have to offer any expensive cigarettes, or maybe he hasn't got any and therefore doesn't feel he can approach a more presentable looking information source.

Just after one of these impromptu smoke breaks Victorian Dad spots the Dengfeng branch of China International Travel Service. I point it out to our driver who looks upon this idea with the disdain it obviously deserves. Shaking his head, we continue our mystical progress. I'm sure in his mind he's thinking, 'Asking tourist information for directions indeed! Whatever will these crazy foreigners think of next?'

Personally, I think it's a great idea. Anyone who claims the best part of travelling is the journey has been sadly misinformed. Jetlag is doing nothing for my tolerance and I'm fed up of feeling impotent in a situation that's out of my hands. With daylight fading I'm beginning to get nervous so, when our driver next stops for a chat and a smoke, this time with a security guard, I leap out, run across the road and back down the street a couple of blocks to CITS. The staff look up in horror as I burst through the door and send for the manager in panic.

The portly manager shuffles from a backroom, cigarette dangling from his lips. Obviously not pleased at being disturbed, he fires off a string of questions too quickly for me to understand. Overwhelmed, I try to work out what he has asked, but I'm too slow-witted for his liking. Making a calculated decision that I'm not worth his effort, he looses a hollow laugh, returns his cigarette to his mouth, and ambles back to his crypt.

Fortunately, the girls have a better concept of customer service than their boss. Despite not speaking English, and struggling with my attempts at Chinese, they abandon their QQ conversation (QQ being the ubiquitous Chinese internet chat software) and let me use their computer. Upon seeing the website, they immediately recognise the school. It's about three hundred metres up the road on the left.

As ever with being lost, you only realise how lost you actually are as you get closer to your destination. The degree of lostness increases exponentially with proximity until a critical state is achieved. So much so, that you are at your most lost a matter of feet from the intended destination. We can almost see the school from where we are.

In a matter of minutes, we pull up at Shaolin Si Xiao Long Wu Yuan (Shaolin Temple Little Dragon Martial Arts School). The main gate is closed so our driver calls to the adjacent sentry box. The occupants look at each other, shrug their shoulders and give the universal hand gestures for 'not today thank you.' Our driver is having none of it. He hasn't come this far to give up now. Pointing to his passengers, he starts berating the security guards.

The guards continue shoulder-shrugging in a, 'not my problem mate' fashion, again motioning for us to clear out. This causes our driver to repeat his tirade at an increased volume. This does the trick. Mumbling amongst themselves, the guards begrudgingly press the barrier raise button.

With a wry smile on his face, our driver smugly drives us through the opening gate and I can't help feel proud of our man. This fare may not have gone as well as he would have liked, but now the end of his ordeal was in sight he is determined to regain his reputation as a true personal transportation professional.

While everything appears to be coming together, our experiences thus far have left me a little cautious. With VD once again on bag duty, I investigate the possibility we have located the correct school. I'm not convinced, as not only have complications to this point sapped my confidence, but the building bears no resemblance to the website photo.

Having escaped from him once already, our driver isn't prepared to let me out of his sight a second time. Possibly afraid of losing his fare or perhaps trying to prove his worth and justify the expense, he accompanies me inside.

Our delay in getting from the airport, and trouble locating the school, mean it's now dusk and reception is closed. We also seem to have arrived during a power cut as there's not a single light on in the building. This is where our driver comes into his own. Wandering off down a corridor, he returns with a small child in tow who points at me and, matter of factly, says, 'Gwailo', before wandering off.

I suppose I must look like a 'ghost man' hanging around aimlessly in the gloom like this, but I was under the impression Gwailo was a Cantonese expression rather than Mandarin.

The little fellow promptly returns with a young girl only slightly older than himself. Immediately discerning that I am indeed a Gwailo, she points to the furniture, commands me to, 'Zuo!' and sends the little chap on another errand.

Instinctively, I sit amongst the selection of solidly made wooden furniture. Realising I don't want to sit, I stand up again. I've spent the last day and a half sitting. Not convinced we may actually be in the right place, I check for clues.

Peering through the dark, I can just make out a particularly grand reception desk with positions for around eight staff. There is also the customary cabinet full of trophies, medals and photographs. The reception area was obviously designed to be impressive by someone who understood that a display of wealth involved things being bigger, shinier and heavier than your average thing. Nothing Freudian going on here then.

A generously proportioned head emerges from the shadows closely followed by a short, squat body with spindly, little arms and legs poking out of it. Were it not for the impressive expanse of hair, that serves only to make his head look even bigger, I would liken him to a potato man. It's certainly a lot more hair than I was expecting.

In lieu of the usual greeting of, 'Ni hao' (lit. 'You good?'), or more traditional, 'Ni chi fan le ma?' (Have you eaten?) In relatively comprehensible English he opens with a welcoming, 'You money? '

Bypassing his friendly query about my personal financial status, I hold out my hand for the shaking thereof, 'I'm Nick, I've been emailing you.'

'Yanni bu zai' (Shi Yanlin is not here).

That explains why this chap looks nothing like the website picture.

'I am Shibu Shifu. I am his friend. 'To prove this, he hands me a business card, 'This Yanni's personal card.'

Observing correct etiquette, I accept the flimsy business card with both hands, pretend to study the basic information it contains and carefully tuck it away. I'm not sure how possessing another person's business card is supposed to reassure me of anything, after all I've never met Shi Yanlin and I've now got his personal card. Although having my hands on Yanni's business card more than makes up for not being met at the airport as promised.

Using 'Yanni' as an abbreviation of Yanlin indicated this chap is in a privileged position of friendship with Shi Yanlin. Although evidently not close enough to be privy to our visit. Shi Yanlin, the Shaolin Monk I had been in communication with via e-mail, and who had guaranteed meeting us at the airport, is not currently at school. He isn't even in China. When pressed as to Yanlin's whereabouts Shibu casually mentions that Yanlin is in Europe touring with the Shaolin Monk show.

This new information slowly snuggles itself into my tired and muddled mind and an explanation of today's events dawns on me.

I suspect any hint of an apology will be a long time coming. Shibu ignores any implication of error at his end. Rather than asking if I'm ok, or if I need anything after the journey, he neatly sidesteps any social niceties and returns to his favourite subject, 'You pay now'. It's not even couched politely.

Singularly unimpressed by our welcome, I'm not prepared to hand over the cash that easily. Having established this actually is our school, I stall for time and retrieve VD. Other than flexing his luggage guarding skills, VD has been unable to contribute a great deal so far. Mostly being left to stand around and despair at my endeavours, which have left me looking organisationally inept. So, I feel it's time for him to add something more than moral support to the equation.

Attempting to pay off our driver, I find him reluctant to retire. I'd have thought he'd be glad to see the back of us, but he's formed an emotional bond. More likely, he's just enjoying the show and trying to get the details straight in his head in order to tell the story better at home this evening. I can imagine his family gathered around the table, when he announces, 'You'll never guess who I had in the back of the cab today.' Either way he's not keen to depart. I'd like to think it's my magnetic personality. Steering him toward his car, I hand him the previously agreed 400Y.

He's still surprised that, not only have we found the right place, but that this is it. Raising his hands like a boxer, he asks if I study Kung Fu. Upon my confirmation, he displays a level of amazement rarely seen outside the matinee performance of a children's magic show. I have to wonder why he thought we had been driving around Dengfeng, the Kung Fu capital of the world, looking for a Kung Fu school all afternoon. I rise above the sarcasm welling inside me and thank him for his trouble. He walks away still shaking his head in disbelief.

Our driver obviously had us nailed as trouble from the start and quoted accordingly. If our journey turned out to be more complicated than anticipated, I suspect the extra trouble has been compensated for in the margin he allowed himself. He must be laughing up his sleeve at the unfeasible amount of money we have given him, but, in all honesty, I am glad to do it. It would have been so much more difficult without him and, now we have finally arrived, I would say he was worth every penny

Throughout the known world, taxi drivers are traditionally enforcers of a Country's Entry Tax and at least our driver was prepared to put in some legwork for his fee. The journey hasn't exactly gone without a hitch, but I have to accept some responsibility for that one. My Chinese isn't exactly great and I could have been better prepared. As we say in the old country, 'the school of life teaches expensive lessons.'

International students live in a large building towards the rear of the school. Each student lives in a shared room with one other. The rooms contain a shower, toilet, sink and are fitted with an air-conditioner and telephone.

Xiao Long Website.

Childe Roland to the Dark Tower Came.

Robert Browning

Shibu leads us through a curtain of plastic slats at the side of reception, to be violently assaulted by a nauseating smell of stale urine. It's an aroma that's to become a frequent companion as the entire office building smells like a municipal car park stairwell. Desperately trying not to inhale, we trundle our luggage through the darkened building and down a flight of steps that must double as a urinal. An eternity later we emerge into the comparatively fresh air of a litter-strewn courtyard teeming with grubby children.

Momentarily relieved, we gulp down great lungful's of what passes for air in the ebbing light. Our brief pause is enough for many of these urchins to surround us calling out, 'Hello, hello', in a singsong fashion.

This makeshift welcoming committee from the soap-dodger contingent of the lollipop club makes it difficult for us to keep up with

Shibu Shifu who is striding into the gloom. A burst of speed scatters small children in our wake and we catch Shibu at the entrance to another building. Pausing long enough to say, 'You wait', he disappears inside.

Exposed and vulnerable at the doorway, the pursuing throng gather reinforcements and we are swarmed by a seething mass of dirt monkeys. Many in the process of liberally distributing junk food snacks over their faces, they encircle us and stare while maintaining their mantra, 'Hello, hello.'

Attempts to continue the conversation past, 'Hello', are either met with an embarrassed giggle or further, 'Hellos'. Under normal circumstances, I would play along, but I am so tired and frustrated that I can barely raise a smile let alone feel cognisant enough to speak Chinese. Also, there's something about grubby faces and snotty noses that offends my sensibilities. It brings out my paternal instincts and I fight the urge to run amok amongst them with a tissue. Even if I had enough tissue to wipe all these faces it would be an endless task. Like painting the Severn Bridge, no sooner had you got around them all, but you'd have to start again.

Shibu's bulbous head pops out of the doorway and says, 'Ok, go', instantly disappearing back inside. I assume he means us to follow him and not to go back home. Escaping the ravening horde before it turns into a scene from Lord of the Flies, we haul our luggage up three dark flights of stairs. On tracking him down in the corridor we are, again, told, 'You wait.'

If there's one thing that gets my goat it's being pushed around and I'm really beginning to resent Shibu's attitude toward us. Not only is he markedly unprofessional, he is downright rude. My tolerance is held in check by the thought that his incompetence is merely due to cultural differences and he's doing the best he knows.

As if he'd read my mind Shibu, in his broken English, explains that if we had notified the school in advance that we were coming they would have prepared a room. I rethink that bit about 'understanding' and 'cultural differences' and decide he is an idiot. Correcting him would be pointless and only complicate matters. My frustration coupled with my jetlag have me biting my tongue in an attempt to maintain cordial communications. If he pushes his luck much further with the blaming me for his school's incompetence I may well be forced to give him some home truths. I'm holding back at this juncture as it may prove strategically unwise to provoke our only contact. Otherwise I could cheerfully disembowel him.

A young girl, wearing a pink overall, scurries past carrying a couple of sheets and Shibu bustles us into a room telling us to, 'Wait'. The room we are shoved into looks like it has been subject to several explosions and a riot. Every stick of furniture is broken and the floor is littered with clothes, mouldy food and broken stuff. I say 'stuff' as much of the wreckage is unidentifiable, it may well once have been 'things'. A glance into the en-suite bathroom sends a shiver through my entire being. The five Chinese guys who occupy this room, take one look at us and walk out. Feeling uncomfortable to be forcing strangers out of their room we return to the corridor.

Shibu has done his disappearing trick again. I'm slowly losing the will to live. We hover around like two lost souls. The corridor itself is open on one side and overlooks the courtyard we walked across so we hang over the balcony watching the shadows milling below.

Ten minutes later Shibu emerges clutching some crumpled paperwork. The forms are several generations of photocopied photocopy and would be barely legible in daylight. In the dusky light I have no chance of reading it. God only knows what I have put my name to. We also sign a copy of the school rules, the few I can make out basically say we will not drink alcohol, smoke, 'engage in any sexual misconduct' and essentially do as we are told. The rules aren't a big deal, as I wasn't expecting to do any of the above anyway. We're not given a copy for ourselves so I can't remember what they are exactly, but I'm sure I won't get to break any exciting ones.

Formalities complete, we hand over the cash along with our passports so we can be registered with the local authorities. Snatching the notes from our hands, Shibu backs into a corner and squats down. Crouching protectively over the readies he checks them intently. Like Gollum nursing his 'precious', Shibu counts and recounts the money.

The school fee was quoted in US Dollars and, though Shi Yanlin had told me any cash would be fine, I brought the quoted currency to minimise complication. The fuss Shibu makes of counting the money over and over again just confirms I made the right decision. Although, it has to be said that none of his actions so far have filled me with confidence. Particularly since I recently discovered even Chinese monks are of dubious reliability.

By this time Pink Overall girl has finished her preparations and Shibu shows us to our room. It's immediately obvious why it didn't take Pink

Overall long to make up the room. She did nothing more than cross the sea of litter, henceforth known as the floor, and place a folded sheet on each bed. A quick glance leads me to believe she has left us a wafer-thin mint on the pillow, but closer inspection reveals it actually is the pillow.

On the plus side we do have a 'proper', sit-down, western toilet. It has no seat or cistern lid and doesn't flush, but it is a real toilet. VD's priority was a sitter. Without wishing to go into too much detail, his diet and lifestyle mean his colon has a full-time job trying to remove toxins from his body. A sit-down toilet, rather than a squatter, is a weight off his mind. VD's life is ruled by his motions to such an extent that his bathroom antics almost cost us the first flight of our journey.

The first leg was Birmingham to Paris where we enjoyed a slap-up egg and b. Prior to hitting the Imodium in preparation for the journey, VD required a comfort break. The toilet in Birmingham airport has a large LED display which gives information regarding the exact second the toilets will next be cleaned. There aren't any speakers so that you can hear boarding announcements, but in these situations, it is more important to prioritise the available information and obviously precisely how long it has been since the facilities were serviced wins every time.

Over the tannoy system came the announcement, 'Passengers Edmunds and Stew travelling to Paris, you are delaying the flight. Immediate boarding please or we will proceed to offload your baggage.' Cue two bald blokes running along the concourse toward the plane as baggage handlers search the hold to remove our luggage.

Last year I went to Italy with my friend Dave who has a completely different view of departure times. He is so paranoid about missing a flight that we were first in the queue, hours before the boarding gates opened. It was like going on holiday with my dad. VD on the other hand has a total lack of concern about getting on the plane choosing to see scheduled boarding times more as rough guidelines for when to visit the toilet and/or bar. Previously frustrated with Dave's chronic cautiousness, I'm now considering switching camps.

Determined not to fall for the same thing on at Paris, we made an effort to locate our departure gate and double check flight times before anything else. While were enjoying the French civility of a nice cup of tea, the departure gate was changed without notice and thus Paris witnessed a repeat performance of our Birmingham antics, but with French dialogue.

After the airport debacles I'm amazed to be in China at all. Victorian

Dad hitting the Imodium before we had even left Birmingham was not a good omen. Neither was nearly missing two connecting flights. Now we are here, I'm beginning to think the Gods were trying to tell me something. Perhaps we should have taken these incidents as a sign from above and not pushed Fate. One hears of people whose lives were saved by the smallest detail: a missed bus, a traffic jam, or other minor incident that resulted in them not being where they should and cheating death as a result. I too could have had a version of these stories, only a lowbrow version regarding VD's bowel movements.

At Beijing I was so terrified of falling asleep and missing the connection that my prevailing memory is of VD and I suffering continual neck-jerking micro sleeps in the too-cosy warmth of the departure lounge. All so that I could visit this train wreck of a room.

As I stand agape, we are joined by another unlikely looking character. Shibu gestures at the tubby figure lurking behind him, 'He your Shifu', and in case we aren't familiar with the term adds, 'He your master, you go him'.

Shifu (using the characters for father and teacher) means expert or 'qualified worker' and is the traditional honorific title of a Kung Fu teacher. We are later informed that Wan Shifu is better known as Shifu Fatso, and not for the irony.

I give the creature peering out from an unruly mop of hair the conventional small bow with right fist wrapped in left hand and say, 'Shifu nin hao.' He gives a sheepish grin and hides behind Shibu again. He is as delighted with the prospect of training us as I am with our welcome.

Continuing his best efforts to cement my resentment, Shibu plays his joker and lets slip the term 'quarantine.' I'm sure this wasn't mentioned in the small print. The gist of the ensuing conversation is that everywhere other than China is backward and has lots of hideous diseases and illness. Therefore, anyone coming from outside China must undergo quarantine to ensure they don't infect this idyllic paradise.

The schools primary concern at this time is H1N1 or Swine Flu. However, there are all sorts of flaws in their well-intentioned plan. Not least of all that the Chinese Government learnt its lesson quickly with SARS a few years ago and has since installed IR scanners that detect flu like symptoms alongside the customs officials at the international airports. We have already passed through these when we ran the gauntlet of Beijing's security. Although, there was a slight technicality there too.

Boarding the plane at Paris, I found a young girl in my seat. She wanted to sit next to her friends so I swapped places and sat in her allocated seat at the other end of the plane. Not a problem for me. Not the sort of thing you'd usually mention, and indeed I didn't think much of it until we landed at Beijing and had to fill in a questionnaire. The form asked basic personal questions, name, age, etc. There were also questions about personal health and one about where we had sat on the plane. Not wanting the complication of my ticket not matching the entry form, I put my original seat number and hoped the Chinese girl I'd exchanged seats with did the same so that there were no paperwork discrepancies. I also hoped there wasn't an outbreak of anything serious that the authorities might need to trace in order to contain.

The health checklist wanted to know if we were feeling any symptoms associated with Bird Flu (H5N1), these include: tiredness, sore/dry eyes, sore/dry throat, headache, achy limbs, in fact all the symptoms of a long-haul flight. I doubt in any other passengers admitted to these either.

The more paranoid passengers were wearing cotton surgical masks, but they are of negligible benefit in a sealed environment with recirculated air. They also become ineffective when damp which occurs overtime with the wearer's breath condensing on them. As a consequence, they were useless long before the flight landed. In Beijing I noticed that the cool kids were wearing designer masks as a fashion accessory.

Here in Dengfeng they don't care about Beijing and their fancy-dan scanner. Quarantine was quarantine for everyone. As such we are to be locked in a rubbish dump to ensure we are not disease ridden. Our next question is obvious, 'When can we start training?'

'You stay room three day time'.

Not the answer I was hoping for, but it could be worse. Working through my priorities, the next question has to be, 'How do we get food?'

'Roommate go bring for you.'

The statement is so illogical that my mind begins to prolapse in its presence. I'm unable to formulate a retort. A more cynical person might think this was a ploy to get out of feeding and training us for three days or, now they have our money, even a calculated effort to get shot of us altogether. I wonder why we were not told about this small detail until after we'd handed over the cash.

Our last meal was on the plane and I'm beginning to feel a little peckish. Packing away some sustenance would help recharge my energy levels and buck me up considerably. I ask where we can get food. Shibu mumbles to his fat mate, who grunts back. This agreed, Chubby shuffles off and Shibu motions to his departing form, 'You go him'.

We follow the fat one to the courtyard and wade through a veritable sea of grubby children to a shack at the side of the square. Barging a path through the massed sugar addicts, I duck the single watt, bare lightbulb swinging hazardously at head height and side-step the kids strung-out on the floor.

The shop carries a fine line in gaudily packaged junk food, all of which looks fundamentally evil and, I am willing to bet, would come under the European definition of a biological hazard. It will certainly do me no good to eat it. In the absence of anything I can readily identify as edible, and rather than make a rash decision I live to regret, I decide my waistline can afford to skip another meal and just get a bottle of water. VD opts for a 'Love Burger'.

Escorting us back to the room our Kung Fu trainer, Wan Shifu, says, 'Ok, go sleep'.

Questioning him about the quarantine and breakfast situation, is obviously a social faux pas. Fear and trepidation run amok over his face before he swiftly closes the door behind him. I hear him legging it down the corridor.

Our Shifu's act of closing the door reveals a fist-sized hole clean through it. This implies I am not the only person to have ever been frustrated in this room.

Unfolding my bed sheet, I discover it has been thoughtfully pre-stained to save me the inconvenience of doing it myself. With no viable alternative, I lay it out on the bed and sit my fat arse down. Doing so I give a double take as the bed surface didn't give as much as I had expected. Closer inspection reveals the bed is actually a plank. VD looks at me sheepishly, 'Yeah, I fell for that one too.'

While it sounds like an innuendo, the Love Burger proves even less appetising and a total misnomer as it contains neither love nor burger. Dressed like a conventional beef burger in a folded, paper sleeve unwrapping the Love Burger, reveals a large, brioche type bun. Separating its clam shell exposes a tiny grey cube at its centre, glowing like a radioactive unformed pearl. VD's verdict. 'That's disgraceful.' I'm satisfied that opting to stay hungry was the right choice in this instance.

We sit on the edge of our beds facing each other, too swamped to know where to begin.

The excitement has worn off and jetlag is catching up with me. The anti-climax combined with the frustration has me physically and emotionally drained. Deflated, I look around the room we have been dumped in and are expected to stay in for the next three days. I'd anticipated the conditions being a little basic, but not quite so dirty. Bare wires hang out of the walls and the floor is covered in the previous occupant's rubbish: old food, cigarette ends, empty packets, bottles and broken weapons. There's a certain irony in the fact our quarantine conditions are more likely to make us ill than to allow us to recuperate. I'm not sure the school is on the ball enough to identify, let alone able to deal with, any virus we could have brought with us. It has to be said that, so far, the trip isn't exactly going to plan.

I take back what I said earlier, travelling was better than arriving. I tentatively broach the subject, 'Dude, what are we doing here?'

I've known VD for some years now and he, in turn, knows me well enough to see that I am not a happy little bunny. This gives him the perfect opportunity to offer moral support and he attempts to placate me with pleasantries. I must say his attempts are half-hearted at best and his efforts might have been better spent convincing himself first. He tells me 'it's not as bad as it could be', that I'll 'feel better once we start training' and 'we should just get some sleep and come up with a plan in the morning.'

If we were still in possession of our passports I would all for walking out and finding a hotel, but I concede the point: it is a long way to come just to give up now. I let pride get the better of me and agree that we may as well wait until the new day. Thus satisfied, VD promptly passes out and commences his merry snoring routine. It's a sound I am to become reassuringly accustomed to during our stay, but at this juncture it's not helping.

I suppose it could be worse. At least we have actually made it to the school, not like a guy from my Chinese language class back home. He came to China to learn Kung Fu without any real plan and ended up drugged and robbed in a Beijing teashop before getting the next available flight home. Actually, at the moment I'm not sure that would be worse than this.

Resigned to spending at least one night here, I attempt to make the most of it. With the night drawing in, I huddle under my sheet, thankful I have my pyjamas for warmth and to minimise physical contact with the sheet itself.

Lying on my cold plank I feel decidedly dodgy. It's probably just a combination of tiredness and adrenal fatigue. I haven't slept for over thirty hours and must have passed being able to. I really don't want to be ill here or God only knows what quarantine will turn into. Between that, and wishing I'd listened to the people who'd told me not to come in the first place, my thoughts are in turmoil. The room and general attitude of the school have upset me to the extent that the events are playing on my mind.

Running through various scenarios I resolve to stick it out until we see the training. If we haven't settled in by then I can bail. I recall passing a sign for a hotel a little way down the road, which I'm sure I can get back to. If they won't have us, I have my laptop with me so I could locate another hotel or even book flights to Beijing. Feeling much better with a contingency plan, I manage to get a few hours sleep. By the time Victorian Dad surfaces from his slumber around mid-morning, I'm in a better frame of mind and ready to face the next challenge China throws at us.

Our school provides foreign students with hotel-style apartments in which there are such modern facilities as air-conditioning, television, drinking trough, telephone and internet, also an independent bathroom.

Xiao Long Website.

The suns rim dips, the stars rush out, at one stride comes the dark.

S. T Coleridge

Faced with the prospect of spending the entire day within the confines of a small room, we don't exactly rush to get up. Personally, I'm glad of the lie in. Not only do I need the rest, but it gives me chance to collect my thoughts. It shows how tired we are that we choose to stay in a bed that is a glorified plank with a sheet on it. My memory-foam mattress now heads what I'm sure will become a long list of things I will stop taking for granted when I get home.

Normally of a morning, I have a nice cup of tea and read for an hour in preparation for getting up. Lying in this bed, looking at the state of the room and being completely tea-less, is depressing. In the gentle, early light, the room looks more manageable than it did last night, but is still filthy enough to feel uncomfortable. After the long journey, and a poor night's sleep, I am in dire need of a wash and some activity. I am literally itching for both and the first step, if we are to consider spending time here, is to make this room bearable. At the least, it will give us something to do.

With the student body at training, I explore the lonely building in search of a mop or a broom. My initial idea of asking a Pink Overall proves a non-starter. Locating a Pink Overall girl is easy enough, and she is armed with a mop, but this is as good as it gets. When I approach, she puts her head down and refuses to acknowledge me. Asking to borrow her mop doesn't prove productive either. Emitting a shrill shriek, she maintains her focus on the floor, and runs away clutching said mop tightly to her chest. I really must take a shower as soon as the possibility presents itself.

Hunting along the corridor, turns up a deceased relative of a mop in the communal DVD room. The toilet of which is nothing but shattered shards of porcelain. It puts our room into perspective. With no other option on the cleaning equipment front, I remind myself that beggars cannot be choosers and accept this rancid offering.

Thus armed, we begin to give our room a once over. Moving the furniture aside uncovers dozens of supermarket carrier bags. Archaeological excavations also reveal our room was once the site of an ancient battle for we turn up an impressive collection of weapons. Among the countless broken parts, we unearth three reasonable Dao, a staff and a couple of serviceable Jian.

The larger debris cleared: mouldy food, empty packets and broken weapons, we use a piece of cardboard box to shovel the smaller detritus: dust, nutshells and cigarette ends. Setting to with the mop isn't the most hygienic way to go about the task, but at least now we can actually see the floor.

Floor visible, we draw our attention to the rest of the room. There is a chair, a table and three beds, each with a bedside cabinet. The surfaces are covered in a layer of dust and grime thick enough to grow potatoes in. Forget writing your name in it, you could carve your name in this stuff.

A good selection of randomly dotted hooks adorn the walls and a rope with a few clothes pegs runs the length of the room. Given the walls' condition, the rope might be holding them up. Sections of wall have been used as target practice for darts and one wall looks as if someone has tried to tunnel through inspired by the Shawshank Redemption. I can sympathise with their inclination.

There's a stale, toilety, sweaty smell lingering in the room, and our cleaning disturbs a lot of dust. We do the obvious and open the window to let some fresh air in and some smell out.

The school sits at the foot of the Song Mountains, which rise majestically in front. Our room looks onto the training field at the back of school, which is also home to the rubbish dump. The field is dry earth and the dump smoulders all day. Opening the window merely lets in more dust and smoke. We soon close it again. We also open the door, but anyone walking past obligingly closes it for us.

If the room needed attention, the bathroom is a more daunting task. It's actually a health hazard. A biological disaster area that should be contained by the United Nations. The lack of window and broken light mean we have to work in semi-darkness. Which may not be such a bad thing.

Chinese plumbing is too narrow to flush toilet paper through, this is where the carrier bags prove invaluable. We fill five with used toilet paper from the floor, in the process uncovering a toilet seat. We fill another four bags with debris from the counter before locating a sink.

We mop the stagnant water, but with no window or extraction fan the smell is going to linger for a while. Using a broken sword discovered behind my bed, I replace the toilet seat and VD has a bash at repairing the cistern. Hanging VD's industrial hand gel on a handy wall hook gives a personal touch making the place a regular home from home.

Unearthing the sink, I am pleasantly surprised to see hot and cold taps. Closer inspection reveals only the cold is plumbed in. There no pipe to the hot tap and no hole in the wall where it could be run. The shower has the same set up; there is a mixer control, but again no hot pipe to it, only a cold. This implies that a hot water pipe was never intended to be fitted. Unless it all comes through the one pipe, there may not be any hot water in the building.

The pipe situation is academic as the shower doesn't work anyway. Ironically, it does leak. Turning the shower on merely increases the rate of drip from the pipe and adds to the pool of water. The puddle doesn't flow away as the drain is at the opposite corner and the floor is angled away from it. As a further conversation piece, where most drains have a grill over their opening, this one is just a hole in the floor.

I dump our growing pile of overstuffed carrier bags around an already overflowing bin in the hallway. A quick glance out of our window tells us very few other inmates follow this refuse disposal procedure.

Directly beneath our window is a two metre strip of ground to the brick wall segregating the school from the training field. This gap is over a foot deep in rubbish.

Achieving as much as we can with the room, I reward myself with a wash. The water that glugs from the tap is so cloudy it looks like milk and there is no sink stopper, but needs must so I run my flannel under the tap and have a Whores Bath. VD turns his nose up at my effeminism and simply applies another layer of deodorant. Using the last of my bottled water, we brush our teeth and, unable to find the promised 'wash gargle things' supposedly included in the welcome pack, cut the empty bottle in half to fashion a crude mug.

With impeccable timing, Shibu Shifu breezes in just as the room is coming together. Ostensibly his visit is to drop off a timetable, but he also hands us a glossy brochure. Given that we have already paid up, it's a bit late in the day to be hitting us with the sales material. The brochure shows many fantastic views of a school and facilities. These pictures were either taken at a different location or heavily edited. They bear no resemblance to our current environment. The timetable is another photocopy of a photocopy and is so faint as to be illegible. So I ask him to go through the times so I can write them in. As he does, I realise they don't equate to what's there anyway. The amended timetable says:

5.30 Warming exercises
7.00 Breakfast
8.15 Training
20 minute break between classes
11.50 Lunch
2.30 Training (Buddhism/Chinese once a week)
20 minute break between classes
5.50 Dinner
7.00 Training
8.00 Free Training
9.30 Lights out

Having already given us more attention than he intended, Shibu is edging for the door when he makes the mistake of saying, 'Ok?'

He probably meant it as more of a statement than a question, or at most a rhetorical one. I answer anyway, and not with the response he wanted. I point out the problems with the bathroom only for him to look at me like I'm a pathetic whinger. For the sake of appearances, he pokes his nose in anyway. Finding all well, he attempts a quick getaway. I press the point and, with a sigh, he agrees to get the toilet checked out or, as he puts it, 'Ok, ok' and makes good his escape. Something about this guy doesn't fill me with confidence.

Impressed by the brochure quality, VD puts forward the theory it's nothing less than the Welcome Pack. It's difficult to believe that, with the loosest artistic license, a four-page brochure could be described as a pack, let alone said to contain a welcome. Based on our reception so far, I'm not holding out much hope for a seasonal fruit basket.

Every now and then, in seemingly random timing, the loudspeakers around the building kick in with a Shaw Brothers style fanfare followed by garbled chants. Cross referencing them against the timetable, I am unable to reconcile the two. I therefore conclude the announcements are a disorientation technique to reduce confidence and prevent free thought. They are certainly beginning to take their toll on me.

Basic ablutions performed and an impact made on the room, I'm feeling a bit happier and take the opportunity to settle myself down and deposit my thoughts on paper. The peace is short lived. A deranged dominatrix storms into the room accompanied by two in-bred, embarrassed looking tramps. Holding out her hand she demands 10 Yuan.

The school staff are generally an understated bunch, however, this lady stands out as being rather brassier. From her knee length, high-heeled boots, low cut blouse and leather hot-pants adorned with straps and metal hoops she exudes an 'In your face' attitude. She has obviously heard of Power Dressing and taken the concept past the boundary of common decency. Her face is longer and more sharply featured than the other Chinese here, and her large hooped earrings with her long hair piled up on top of her head accentuate the imperiousness.

It's a shame the whole impression is spoilt by her accomplices. They make a terrible pair of evil henchmen. The scene is further let down by our inability to communicate and we are reduced to charades. The ensuing parlour game antics bring no light as to what the 10Y is for, other than it's not a film or a book. The Madame doesn't look the type to be trifled with so I hurriedly fumble for the cash. The interlopers are astonished that I actually stump up the readies and openly laugh at me. I do hope I haven't just purchased a tramp.

Regaining their composure, the two men produce a carrier bag of miscellaneous, used toilet parts and a hammer. A person who thinks a hammer is the only necessary tool for repairing porcelain doesn't inspire confidence. Although, I can now say I have met him. I'm tempted to offer a broken sword to expand their kit.

The 'lady' points at the bathroom and shrugs, so I demonstrate the problem with the toilet, shower and light. Meeting with a blank stare, I resort to flicking the switch and pointing at the light. Giving a withering look, she attempts to educate me on its correct operation. The incredulity on her face when the light doesn't come on is truly spectacular. Amazingly, I am not too incompetent to operate a light switch. She then explains that the light doesn't work. The two guys set about the toilet in the dark. While they are giving the toilet what for, she stands over them eating peaches and gesturing to random parts. She is obviously the technical expert of the bunch.

The toilet repair is a classic demonstration of Chinese hive mentality. They seem unwilling to do anything as an individual. I don't know if this is a vestige of Communist thinking, or an example of Chinese altruism, but it takes several people to perform the most fundamental of tasks and, while they are bickering, anyone passing can feel free to join in with their own views on the matter. Thus, a dominatrix, a cleaning lady, three Shifu, a few students and a small child all help illustrate how it should be done.

Hearing the excited cries of encouragement, I take a peek over the enthralled crowd. Bizarrely, the maintenance guys seem apologetic about their ability and are fully prepared to take any proffered advice without fetching the offending busybody a clip around the ear. Goaded by his audience, I witness Henchman Number One liberally laying about the toilet with his fine adjustment hammer. Varying the position and velocity of his blows according to their audience's whim, it's like a crazy TV game show. I'm not giving him a car if he gets it right.

Shaking his head, VD asks, 'So how many Chinese guys does it take to change a lightbulb?'

I shrug, 'If they get it working we may regret being able to see what's there'.

Taking advantage of the disturbance, our Shifu sneaks into the room. I try to engage him, but he keeps his head down assiduously avoiding my gaze with his unruly fringe. Rummaging in his pocket he produces a handful of keys and tries each in the door in turn. None appear satisfactory. He grumbles and switches his attention to the toilet repair, but his heart obviously isn't in it. After only a brief interfere, he loses interest and waddles away.

Based on my impressions of Chinese organisation so far, I refuse to believe this maintenance team was arranged at such short notice. Their arrival directly following Shibu's assurances must be nothing more than a coincidence. The maintenance call was more likely placed by a previous occupant and their memoirs will state no one responded.

After their departure, I feel I have done the maintenance men a disservice. Inspecting their handiwork reveals they have repaired the flush mechanism and fitted a lid with a button to the cistern so we don't have to reach inside the tank to flush it. The light and shower still don't work, but, given the choice, I would have prioritised the toilet. With the bathroom taking shape, my contentedness is raised another notch and I don't much mind cleaning up the peach stones. The drawback to getting the room serviceable is we now have nothing to do. A lot more could be done to make the room habitable, but without a bulldozer it's just going to have to do as it is.

Now we are moving forward, I am feeling a lot happier, conversely, Victorian Dad is really getting umpty at his confinement. I am content to relax with a book until it's time to go into action, but VD really is champing at the bit. He is far too agitated to sit and, instead, paces between the corridor and window watching the other students training. Peering through the window bars we can see Chinese students training on the dry-earth below. There are about twelve different groups, working forms, acrobatics, flexibility and weapons. It's like a low budget version of Hans Island. It's all going on out there, which only serves to make us feel worse about our confinement. Just to rub it in, the sounds of training, 'Heys' and 'Ha's', all around us are a constant reminder of what we're missing.

I'm sure once we get a taste of training he won't be so keen. The Chinese have a term 'chi ku' or 'eating bitter' that is often used in reference to Kung Fu. The idea being that nothing worthwhile comes without hard work and discomfort. It's similar to the western idea of taking your medicine. Eating bitter manifests itself in Kung Fu as physical and psychological discomfort. That said, almost anything would be better than staying in this room.

The hallway is open on one side, like a long balcony, from which we can look down on the courtyard where more students are training. I watch the sea of red tracksuits for a while, but the novelty wears thin. I want to train Kung Fu not watch Kung Fu. VD is constantly hanging over the balcony like a fat kid salivating in a sweet shop window. Torturing himself in this way is only serving to further infuriate him. Any passing Shifu sends him back into the room and closes the door forcing VD into another shift at the window until the coast is clear.

Interrupting a walk-past visit, I look up from my book, 'What's that noise?'

'Just the toilet tank filling.'

'It can't still be filling up surely?' Further investigation reveals that while the toilet does indeed now flush, it doesn't stop.

Removing the toilet tank lid, we fiddle with the mechanism until it stops. Just like we did prior to the repair. I wish I had a hammer. At least it keeps VD occupied while he develops a technique of wiggling bits inside the toilet tank, but, with this method perfected, he is soon back on pacing duty.

Personally, I don't think that wearing a groove in the floor helps. I know it's boring and infuriating, particularly as they are taking no notice of us whatsoever. We have been abandoned in our room and told to stay there for three days. If I'm struggling with quarantine, there's no doubt VD sees our confinement as a form of punishment, but his curmudgeonly traipsing isn't helping my disposition either. The trouble with Accountants is, just like Posties, you never know when they are going to flip out. He must be getting withdrawal symptoms from lack of adding up. Maybe I should set him a few sums to do. Either way, I have to get him out of quarantine soon, for my own safety.

In an attempt to occupy ourselves, I suggest we stretch our stagnant limbs and go through some forms. Utilising one of our newly acquired dao, that hadn't been on toilet service, I run through my form. Although I don't have a great deal of energy the activity does us good.

I'm glad I didn't come here alone. We are struggling with the isolation as it is, I'm sure we would be more exploited if we didn't have each other for moral support. There has been no sign of the other students. No one has even stuck their head around the door to say, 'Hello'. Victorian Dad has attempted to start conversations with anyone passing, but so far no one has responded with anything more than a token gesture.

Later I realise this is partly a result of high student turnover and become guilty of the same thing. While I was prepared to walk out immediately as a result of our warm welcome, it transpires a lot of people do just that. Certainly, during our time about 70 percent of new students don't last their first week. From the school's perspective this is a result as they never refund fees.

This is where VD's cabin fever comes up trumps. Hanging over the balcony like a caged walrus, he accosts any by-passers. After a few false starts with non-English speakers and any passing Shifu telling him to go back in the room, he manages to waylay a Malaysian guy, Shaun, who comes up with the goods. He tells us where the canteen is. It's the big pink building with six-foot high golden characters across the front, declaring to the world Can Ting (Food Hall). As it was dark when we arrived, I hadn't spotted it, but now it's pointed out to me, I can't help feel a little sheepish.

Shaun, also tells us how to get a uniform and advises that we keep the window closed so as not to develop a sore throat from the smoke. But it's the topic of quarantine that's most interesting. When pushed reference our quarantine period, Shibu said, 'Everyone three days, everyone same.' Spoken like a true communist. Except it's not true. Shaun reveals quarantine varies significantly from person to person and can be up to two weeks. Also, if you have been in China for any length of time before coming to school, if you miraculously uncover this rule, and are prepared to argue the point, then you don't have to quarantine. Everyone who has actually been quarantined properly wishes they had booked into a hotel for a few days instead of serving their time here. Indeed, if we had been informed about quarantine beforehand we would have had a weekend in Beijing or Zhengzhou first.

Nevertheless, with Shaun's information on how the school operates, not all of which is flattering, we have a much better idea of where we stand and can began to formulate our plan of action. Our main issue is that the school doesn't have the slightest interest in us, so it's left to us to forge our own way. The mixed information regarding the nature of quarantine leaves plenty of scope for interpretation so we hit the dining hall regardless. If we can get each other's food, we may as well get our own and have done with it. The worst that can happen is they send us back. VD takes little persuading that quarantine, with regard to us, is not going to happen and eloquently agrees, 'Forget this, let's go to dinner.'

The big, pink canteen building has another of those plastic slat curtains at the entrance. I assume it's a fly-screen, however, all it does is prevent any fresh air getting in. Walking through the slats is like hitting a wall of nausea. I can see a theme developing with these curtains. Holding my breath, we navigate through the soap-shy multitude and push our way up the congested stairwell. I'm turning blue by the time we glimpse other westerners, but fortunately the air is a little less pungent up here.

Shaun must have been keeping his eyes peeled as he spots us immediately. He shows us the technique for getting food and where to sit. The proven method is to barge through a massed throng of grubby children and point at food. Even if you can speak Chinese, it's so loud and chaotic in the canteen that the food guys can't hear you behind their glass screens. Food is ladled onto those metal trays with the sections stamped into them, like you see in prison films. Clutching these protectively to our bosoms, we barge our way back though the, now glowering, grubby children to our designated seating area.

There are separate tables set aside for foreign students. They are higher than the other wooden tables and similar to the metal picnic benches you get in cheap fast-food bars. A handmade, laminated sign proclaims 'Foreign Students'. As the sign is in Chinese I doubt many foreign students can read it. Therefore, I'm adamant that the signs are as much to explain what we are, as to reserve the seating. The kids are fascinated with us. It's like being in a zoo. I can picture a family on their day out, their little boy looking at us and turning to his mother saying, 'What are those strange creatures sitting in the big seats mummy?'

'Hold on dear, let mummy read the sign and I'll find out'. Mother reads the sign and exclaims, 'My word! They are foreign students'.

Child in wonderment, 'Oh! They do look funny! Can we take a closer look?'

Sensing her child's interest, the parent strikes a more cautionary note, 'They are very dangerous and carry lots of diseases as they are not as civilised as us. Let's go and look at less unsettling sights'.

The meal is much better than I had anticipated and I make the mistake of saying so. VD agrees and we have an entire conversation regarding food quality. There was a choice of noodles or rice and, as I haven't eaten for over a day, I stick with the plain rice reasoning that I'll have the noodles next time. The boiled rice, cabbage and steamed bun are just what the doctor ordered, but nothing to drink. I could really do with a cup of tea to wash it down, something I was expecting to be able to get hold of in China. Again, I appear to have been misinformed.

Out of the room, and with some food in him, VD is also a lot happier with his lot. After finishing our meal, we sit around to postpone going back for as long as possible. This isn't easy as the canteen isn't a pleasant environment. Without external windows the main hall receives no natural light and the electric lighting is very harsh. Being completely tiled, combined with a lack of soft furnishings, make it very echoey. Smell aside, it's like being in a waterless swimming pool and certainly not conducive to relaxing in.

Hoping for a little social interaction, we are sadly disappointed. When Shibu handed me the timetable, he said, 'We eat very quickly here.' He wasn't kidding. No one hangs around. While the westerners feel the need to flock together, they are non-communicative. They all sit in the same area, but there is negligible fraternisation. The majority turn up to meals alone, eat quickly and quietly, and leave alone.

Exiting the canteen is a hairy experience. Within minutes of getting their rations the Chinese students convert the place into a death-trap. They spill more food than they eat and the floor is awash in noodles and watery soup making the tiles treacherous underfoot. Self-consciously, I mince my way along with narrow little steps trying to maintain my dignity. Maybe it's part of the training to improve balance. They'll have me walking on rice paper next.

We step through the plastic slats into total darkness. Still operating on a different time zone, I'm already disorientated. Despite China being a geographically vast country and spanning four international time zones, the whole country operates to a single Standard Time (GMT+8) all year round. The darkness only adds to my confusion. It was broad daylight when we went in twenty minutes ago yet the sun has set while we were eating. Without experiencing the transition, my body has lost its frame of reference and left me even more dazed.

In the courtyard, we begin what is to become a daily ritual: stopping off at the tuck shop for a 'Da ping shui' (a big bottle of water) with which to carry out our basic ablutions before tentatively feeling our way back to our room,

Lights out is at 9.30. On the dot, Shifu Fatso, bumbles into the room. 'Ok. Go sleep', and quickly removes himself before we can respond. If he's supposed to be checking us for hideous diseases, it's a poor show on his part. He probably remembers I tried to engage him in conversation yesterday and has now developed a cunning plan to avoid putting himself in such a predicament again.

Victorian Dad is already demonstrating his ability to sleep anywhere and instantly. It's a quality he shares with Napoleon Bonaparte. I swear his head hadn't actually touched the pillow before he was comatose. Still feeling the effects of our journey, I'm about ready to get my head down anyway.

The induction process has left a lot to be desired, but I'm more content now we have established our presence and are making progress toward training. I fold my wafer-thin pillow in half and put my arm underneath to raise it to a suitable height. As my eyes adapt, I notice VD has assumed a similar sleeping position with his doubled-up pillow resting on the crook of his arm.

I lie on my sheet-covered board listening to his snores serenading the flies waltzing overhead. I take it as a good sign.

The price includes pickup from the airport or train station, accommodation, three meals per day, uniform, one weapon per month and a small arrival pack.

Xiao Long Website.

China has a long literature that instils official rectitude, and a long record of dishonest and greedy functionaries.

Peter Quennell

Day two of our isolation finds me in a better mood. Yesterday's room cleaning was therapeutic and quarantine also gave us chance to acclimatise to the time zone difference, but the best way to deal with jetlag will be to get into the training routine as soon as possible. To get into the swing of things we have less of a lie in and get up with the intention of joining breakfast at 7am.

Normally, I wouldn't dream of facing the new day without a nice cup of tea, but under the current circumstances, it's just not on the cards so I read my book in bed without a drop of the trusty invigorator. It really is quite astounding the unforeseen privations I am being forced to endure on this little adventure. I entered into this trip fully prepared to rough things a little. Sleeping on a plank and not washing is one thing, but no tea is simply barbaric. Whenever calamities like this happen around the world one never imagines they will happen to oneself. There, but for the grace of God my friends.

Breakfast is the same as last night's dinner: a handful of rice, a steamed bun and some boiled veg. Spotting a lady ladling murky dark liquid, I help myself to a bowl expecting tea, but alas it's not. The liquid horror is worse than no tea. Resembling a thin black bean soup, the lukewarm gloop tastes of old dishwater. No wonder the kids 'spill' so much of it on the floor, I'm tempted to do the same with mine. I make a mental note to avoid it in future.

As hungry as I am, I'm not sure this humble repast was worth breaking quarantine for. I understand the reasoning behind quarantine, but the way it's implemented here makes it completely redundant. We are either in isolation or we're not, there is no middle ground. Even after seeking clarification, we are unsure if we are allowed meals or to leave the room and much of this conflicting information came from the same people. Shibu Shifu told us not to come out of our room or get into contact with anyone and then sent us to a tuck shop seething with little kids that we had to push through. It's simply not a viable form of quarantine. That this is not immediately apparent to our Shifu defies logic. Similarly, we can cram our way through three thousand other people to get food, but not eat there. It makes no sense.

Kung Fu mythology has a long tradition of testing the character and determination of potential students. Nowhere more so than Shaolin Temple. The tests were often more character based than physically demanding and involved assessing the applicant's will and suitability for training. Huike cut his own arm off before Damo accepted him as a disciple. Other trials tended not to be so extreme and were carried out by surreptitiously observing candidates while their resolve was tested. It would be easy to read something like this into our situations here. Being tested by the school, or even a cosmic force judging our dedication. If we are being put through a modern day equivalent, it's certainly testing my patience. Surely, travelling halfway way around the planet to get here must count for something? Completing the journey at all must have earned us some kudos. Everything we have done in China so far has been a chore, but we would be kidding ourselves if we thought there was any hidden significance behind our isolation. Quite simply, China operates on well intentioned, but misguided, bureaucracy and it's a pain in the arse to get anything done here.

After a very short discussion, we agree to view quarantine as more of an initiative test. In preference to facing three days of completely pointless quarantine we decide to wing it.

Breakfast done, we explore the main building with the intention of collecting uniforms. Theoretically included in our fee, we have been assured by the Shaun we will still have to pay for them. He also related a few tales regarding arbitrary pricing.

At reception I go to the nearest person at the desk and in my best Mandarin utilise the phrase I have been practicing all morning, 'Wo xiang mai yi jian zhifu.' (I want to buy a uniform.)

The pregnant pause from my audience has me in no doubt as to how my performance has fared. I wait for the ensuing tumbleweed to roll past then resort to the mime that I should have spent the time practicing. After an eternity, I see a little glimmer of light behind her eyes. Shaking her head, she points to the person next to her, 'Oh, a uniform! Why didn't you say so? You need to ask the next person along about that.'

The process is repeated as I am passed from one person to the next. Each one thoroughly enjoying every second of my charades so much they feel the need to make me start from scratch for their benefit. By the time I reach the third person along I am beginning to perfect my little song and dance routine about a lost orphan looking for his clothes. It's the feel-good hit of the season. The result of this latest, and I may add award winning, performance is to once again be passed to the next counter along. My heart drops when I see the barely sentient creature slumped across the desk with his head on his arm. From his expression it is difficult to tell if he is unconscious or a partially reanimated corpse. There is a convincing argument for both options.

He looks up at me blankly, I turn back to the lady who directed us to him and give her a stern, but quizzical, look. She's smiling innocently. He looks annoyed at being disturbed. I wonder if it's a wind up, but I go through my now flawless series of motions regarding the uniform anyway. After deigning to watch my one man show he turns to the women I have just been to, shrugs his shoulders, and laughs at me. Seeing the blood begin to trickle out of my ears the lady next to him anticipates that they have pushed me about as far as is wise and attempts to save her colleagues life. Using the same phrase I had opened the proceedings with and have been repeating for the last fifteen minutes, she tells him I want to buy a uniform.

Sulking at being denied the opportunity to tease the foreigners as much as his colleagues have, Idiot Boy shrugs his shoulders and begrudgingly begins to carry out his job of work. Glowering, he makes a chopping motion on his wrist, which I deduce to mean he would rather kill himself than deal with me or maybe at this price he was cutting his own hand off. Frustrated at witnessing so many reruns of my solo artist performance, Victorian Dad steps in and, nodding vigorously, repeats, 'Yes, yes.'

We are quoted 60Y (£6) for a uniform. It sounds reasonable so we buy three each to save going through this farce again; two to wear in rotation, as one is washed, and one for emergency situations. While a uniform is supposed to be included in the initial price, I lack the vocabulary to debate the issue. Also, we are not really in a position to argue as we are pushing our luck being out of quarantine in the first place. Besides, the whole farce isn't worth the frustration for £6. The school staff and indeed the entire population of Dengfeng, if not China, all know westerners have more money than sense and no stamina for haggling. The Chinese have long mastered this approach to getting their own way and obtaining the hard-earned from foreigners. One has to put haggling into perspective otherwise life becomes a constant battle over pennies.

Exerting as little effort as possible, the guy takes my two, one hundred Yuan notes and puts them through a note counting machine. I give him the benefit of the doubt that it's more to do with policy than his inability to count to two. He then begins filling out forms in quadricate. I'm sure that's not a word, but I mean the one after triplicate. Watching this guy filling in forms is excruciating; he has managed to take lethargy to a whole new level. He doesn't look particularly worse for wear, so I don't think he was on his stag-do last night, but his energy levels would make a dead sloth look hyperactive.

After much ado with the Village Idiot, chitties get stamped and passed around, we are given a copy ourselves and quite firmly told to sit. Taking advantage of the big furniture, we wait.

Everything here is done in the most complicated fashion possible by the most disinterested people imaginable. People immediately try to make you someone else's problem, get bored and walk off mid-conversation or go back to reading their paper in the hope you'll disappear. It wouldn't be so bad if you weren't half way through a transaction at the time. I can only imagine the selection process these people went through to get the job. I certainly can't begin to imagine the applicants who didn't make the cut. The job interview must run along the lines of:

Employer: 'Do you have any skills that could be of use in a work environment?'

Applicant: 'No',

Employer: 'Do you have any intention of carrying out a role in an acceptable fashion?'

Applicant: 'No',

Employer: 'Do you have any interest in working whatsoever?'

Applicant: 'No',

Employer: 'Excellent! I'm happy that you will be able to maintain our current standards of customer service. When can you start?'

I'm just glad we didn't have to go through this frustrating procedure when we were tired and hungry. If my tolerance was any lower there may have been some unpleasantness. Excited to be getting closer to actually training we are prepared to put up with more than we normally would, particularly if it's going to get us out of that room sooner.

Eventually, two young ladies arrive and escort us to the uniform store. One of which is struggling under the weight of a huge bunch of keys, like a tiny medieval jailer off for a busy day torturing. I would say all she is missing is a hump, but all the staff here have the hump, if only metaphorically. They all seem really put out at doing their job. Maybe they didn't notice this minor detail in the job description when they applied for the position. After opening the door, she follows us in, locks the door behind her and stands guard with her back against it while her accomplice kits us out.

The uniform store isn't your typical gentlemen's outfitter. The large, unfurnished, room is piled high with black bin bags with tracksuits spilling out and liberally scattered over the floor. I was expecting a fairly standard, 'We got two sizes; too big or too small' type arrangement, but the lady without the keys takes one glance at us, rummages through the mounds of clothing and gives Victorian Dad a tracksuit size 180 and me a 190. Much to her disgust, rather than take her word for it, I try the jacket on. It's a bit roomy, by about 5cm I reckon, so I ask if I can try a smaller size. While the previous look would have curdled milk, this one could curdle a cow. I'm sure she's thinking, 'Stuck up laowai. Thinks he knows what fits him better than I do. I've looked at tens of laowai and given them uniforms. What does he know? In order to teach him some manners, I'll cut him dead with my cow-curdling death ray.'

However, I'm made of sterner stuff than your average pre-curdled bovine and settle in for the Mexican stand-off.

In return she ignores the proffered jacket and maintains the stare. Never tolerant of being pushed around, my limit was reached earlier by the Village Idiot and this poor lady will now have to bear the brunt. Using my Iron-shirt technique, I bounce her death-stare right back.

Huffing, she snatches the jacket and excavates another from the pile. It has 185 written on it in biro; the label inside reads XXXL. Given that I'm a size Large in the UK, this tells you all you need to know about Chinese clothes sizing. In the interests of common decency, I pull the trousers on over my shorts. They fit about as good as a misshapen piece of polyester ever will. Maybe that's what she was so sulky about? It's not that she'd lost face when I questioned her judgement, but that the uniforms are so misshapen and crappy it doesn't really matter what size you're given.

The girls exchange a glance between themselves, which plainly implies an impolite definition of my good self. Think what you like ladies, now that I have my new togs the game is most definitely afoot.

The teachers speak English, which is really rare in china.
The foreigners will be coached by the master trainer Xiu Xu
Yong (buddhist name Shi Yan Lin) who is one of the first
class kungfu master from the shaolin temple with big teaching
experience on foreigners.

Xiao Long Website.

Energised by our success we make an excited beeline back to the room for a dressing up session. Purchases clutched tightly in my sweaty little hand, I'm feeling rather smug. The whole transaction went a lot smoother than anticipated and we are a step closer to getting out of quarantine and into training. I can almost taste the bitter already. Our excitement is palpable as we throw on our new outfits. Superman would be impressed at the speed of our transformation from civilians into Xiao Long students. It's rather an anti-climax to have to wait until the next training session.

Our cynicism regarding the school bureaucracy led us to budget far more time for uniform acquisition than proved necessary. As a result, we have bags of time until lunch. I'm far too restive to read, so join VD for a hang over the balcony. I'm amazed by the athleticism on display, especially considering the participants' age. Some students are little more than toddlers. Since my initial bout of abject despondency, our situation has continually improved, albeit due to our own efforts, and I am pretty much back to my usual irreverent self. VD, on the other hand, is becoming apprehensive regarding our ability to train at this level. He expresses his concern at the other students' relative youthfulness, 'Dude, all these guys are half our age!'

Sensing his discomfort, I attempt to console him by correcting his inaccurate observation, 'No mate, much more than that, some of those kids are only four or five.' It doesn't seem to help.

In a beautifully poetic moment, a strapping French student in his mid-twenties, practically crawls up the stairs behind us holding an IV drip that's plumbed into his arm. Ever the people-person, VD optimistically plays his 'Alright there?' card. As can be imagined, the guy isn't 'alright'.

The guy mumbles that he has only been training a couple of days. Not long out of quarantine, he has now been sent to his room after collapsing from exhaustion. Pierre staggers down the corridor. VD turns to me with raised eyebrows. A spectre of impending doom closes in.

Being dressed for action makes time move very slowly and isn't helping VD's disposition any, so I continue to accompany him at the balcony. Watching the sea of red tracksuits going through their paces is frustrating, but eventually it's time to toddle off to lunch. So concerned is VD by the perceived trials lying ahead of us that not even a serving of boiled rice and cabbage can raise his spirits.

According to our timetable, afternoon training begins at 2.30, but we are so excited we turn up at 2.15. Like a pair of eager little bunnies, we limber up on the steps.

Around 2.25 other foreign students begin to trickle forth in dribs and drabs and sit on the entrance steps looking stupefied. Now we are dressed the same as everyone else, we are still conspicuous as our uniforms are so clean they positively shine and, even with our jetlag, we are much brighter of eye and bushier of tail. Some guys, notably the teenagers, seem to have given up on any form of personal hygiene altogether.

Surveying our fellow students littering the steps reveals a varied group. Ranging from a couple of eight-year olds to us at nearly forty years old. VD is right. We are by far the oldest here. There are around twenty of us foreigners all together. The greater part are European, but others are from as close as Korea and Uzbekistan and as far afield as South America. Attempts to engage any in conversation are unsuccessful as they are all basically zombified. We later learn that most students take a nap after lunch and these guys are still groggy.

This lack of sentience must be why no one mentions how dashing I look in my shiny-new polyester ensemble. I appreciate we are all wearing the same thing, but I happen to look rather good in a uniform. The jacket is red with white flashing on the shoulders, which matches my eyes, and has the school name stencilled across the back and left breast pocket in white paint. The trousers are black with a two-inch white stripe down the outside seam. It's what the well-dressed man about town is wearing this season. I notice some guys have school t-shirts as well as tracksuits. I guess that's what the wrist slitting action the Village Idiot mimed so adeptly was all about. He must have been asking if we wanted long sleeves. I really must hone my charade skills if I am to survive here.

We are working on the premise that if we just blazon this out we won't attract attention. Just like carrying around a sheet of paper so no one will ask what you are doing. This turns out to be the logic on which China operates. Because we are there and in uniform no one asks why we aren't in quarantine. We blend right in with the others as everyone looks a bit lost. We also have the advantage of turning up in the evening and then being isolated. As a result, the other staff and students don't know exactly how long we have been here.

Slowly the Shifus appear and form a huddle where they hold a competition to see who can look the most disinterested. For the most part this involves shuffling their feet and spitting. Shifu Fatso wins this event hands down as he doesn't even arrive until halfway through their contest and then can't muster the energy to join in. The other Shifus collect their students and head off to the gym leaving five of us behind. Shifu Fatso calls to this remainder and, with a grunt, points to a spot in front of him. He shows an initial surprise that his class has doubled in size, by gaping open mouthed, but lacks the language skills and, moreover, the motivation to query our presence. So it looks like we are going to get away with it.

There are five in our group altogether: Juha, Knobby, Julie, Victorian Dad and Myself. Working solely on initial impressions Wan Shifu's class isn't exactly the cream of the crop. VD turns to me, 'Looks like we're relegated to Gimp Squad.'

I have a vision of the other Shifus eyeing up VD and myself as prospective candidates. 'Those two old guys can go with Fatty, he'll take anyone.'

This is of course what happens to Shifu who can't be bothered to turn up to Shifu meetings. They have their decisions made for them and get dumped on.

Not happy with us tagging on the line, Shifu reorganises us in height order. This simple procedure takes a little doing as he just points and waves his fingers around while grunting. Ultimately, he ends up physically manhandling us into the desired position before we work out what he's trying to do. Having lined us up, he gives a feeble wave of his hand saying, 'Goh Rhuh'. These two words take a little decoding as no one else moves. Shifu Fatso's gruff command is such a reasonable impersonation of Watto from the glorified toy advert that was the last Star Wars movie that I'm tempted to counter with a Watto impression of my own, 'What, you think you're some kind of Jedi, waving your hand around like that?' I resist the temptation as it would only confuse the issue further.

As an instructions, 'Go run', is certainly concise, however, with this curt command lacking in detail, and potentially open to interpretation, I hang back to let the others set the pace and lead the way. We follow their example and run circuits while Shifu Fatso leans on things. He is a champion leaner, and very versatile. He can lean on anything. Seriously, there is no end to the inanimate objects our Shifu can rest his corpulent frame on. Every time we complete a circuit he's leaning on something different. Which isn't as amusing in real life as in the film Drunken Master. After twenty minutes or so, Shifu Fatso wants to expand his repertoire by leaning on something in the training hall. He calls to us, points to a spot in front of him, where we assemble, and then points to the training hall, 'Go'. We troop up the stairs and demonstrate our new trick of lining up in height order.

The training hall reserved for foreign students is on the top floor of a three-storey building. The ground level houses a multigym and the first and second floors are large bare halls with a couple of dusty, threadbare mats and a few punch bags mounted on the wall. The ground floor weights gym only has windows on the front wall so gets precious little natural light. Whereas, both long sides of the training halls are all window which serves the dual purpose of making it really warm when the sun hits and really cold the rest of the time. They also let in the smoke and dust. However, expanding on Dengfeng's unique bouquet, the gym not only smells of shit and smoke, but throws in a hefty dose of stale sweat.

In a variation of 'Go run' around the school, we now 'Go run' circuits of this greenhouse. Judging from the pace the others set this isn't going to be a race. The gym proves an unorthodox obstacle course. Not only do we have to avoid the other classes in progress, but also the debris that has accumulated around the periphery. Empty plastic bottles, food wrappers, broken weapons and chunks of fallen masonry litter the perimeter along with a small, forlorn pink plastic, waste-paper basket. It may get used now the floor is filling up. A further running hazard is provided by sections of rumpled, threadbare carpet that send mini mushroom-clouds of dust around our ankles as we stomp over them.

After a dozen circuits, Shifu motions to the wall. A handy pipe runs the length of the room which our group places their legs on and commence to stretching against. Again, we follow suit. Looking along the line, I am heartened by the poor flexibility of our group. Julie has ten years of ballet under her belt and it shows. However, Knobby and Juha's efforts do a lot to restore VD's confidence in our abilities.

Further vague instruction from Shifu see us line up in single file at the side. Once again, we hang back to let the others demonstrate before copying their movements. Shifu Fatso makes no attempt to instruct us so, as Julie has been here the longest, we follow her lead back and fore the gym attempting to refine our mimicry as we go along.

The movements are variations on stances, punches and kicks and are the building blocks of Kung Fu. Performed repeatedly like this they serve to build flexibility, strength and agility and develop muscle memory. These basics are termed Jibengong which means, 'foundation work' and involves drilling the moves over and over. So far, they've been fairly staple Kung Fu basics and not too different to the things we have already done in our own Kung Fu.

Rookie mistake of the day was not bringing any water. Training in the heat and the dust dehydrates us very quickly. The instant Shifu Fatso announces a twenty-minute break I run to the tuck shop for a couple of bottles of water. When I return Knobby has commandeered VD and is giving him the skinny on the school.

Knobby is an eighteen-year-old dance student from the UK who, in order to protect the guilty, I shall refer to by the name the other students have affectionately given him. Knobby has done a couple of months of Tae Kwon Do, but is 'technically a blue belt' and has come to China to improve his gymnastics. Why he came to a Kung Fu school, and not to a gymnastics school, he doesn't elaborate. Knobby has been at Xiao Long a week already and didn't have to serve quarantine, as he spent the previous month at another Kung Fu school in China. Xiao Long is not living up to his exacting standards and he constantly compares the two schools only to find Xiao Long wanting. His major criticisms being the relative expense of Xiao Long with its hidden extras and the fact he is forced to train and not allowed to do his own thing as he was at the other school. Fortunately for our school they now have Knobby to put them straight. Curiously, in preference to specialising in his expressed field of interest, he is taking all the disciplines and correcting the other students as he goes. His volunteer work as an unofficial martial arts school inspector really is exceptional.

Most of Knobby's advice tends to be biased to say the least and doesn't appear entirely factual. This includes the Shifus' nicknames. Our Shifu is obviously Shifu Fatso, but Shibu Shifu is allegedly Elvis Presley because of three moles on his face. I don't get it.

The second session follows the same basic formula: laps of the gym to warm up followed by drills of punches, kicks and stances. All too quickly it's time for evening meal and we are dismissed to get ourselves another serving of rice and boiled cabbage.

English is the common language among the foreign students, but with such a diverse group it's few people's first language. Knobby, being the only other Brit, joins us for dinner. In true British style, he starts by complaining about the weather. Observing we are unwilling to slander such a pleasant season, he moves on to criticise the food, principally that it's vegetarian. I don't have the opportunity of correcting him that it isn't vegetarian, there simply isn't any visible meat in it, because he is now into his flow.

The first thing anyone attempting to disparage vegetarianism does is to reference Adolf Hitler. True to form Knobby continues his tirade against vegetarians by throwing Hitler into the mix. Just for the record, and I mean this in no way as an endorsement of the man, Hitler was not a vegetarian. Hitler was prescribed a vegetarian diet to cure his flatulence. Hitler was, in fact, a farter. It's amazing what you can learn from the History Channel. I don't share this with Knobby. He already knows everything he needs to know without being burdened by facts. He is also able to breathe through his ears so there is no pause in his diatribe to allow any retort.

For evening training we convene in front of the building and, when Shifu Fatso deigns to turn up, arrange ourselves in front of him. He glances along the line to make sure we are all present and says, 'Go gym'. He then takes a step back and grunts something that sounds like 'Sugar'. We take a step forward, clap our hands three times and give the traditional Chinese martial artist greeting 'baoquan' or 'hugged fist.' (A small bow from the waist with left palm cupped over the right fist). In response Shifu turns his head to the side and holds his palms out toward us.

We are now formally dismissed to train unattended until 9pm. For VD and I, the free training session is a bit awkward as we haven't been taught much to practice yet. After a brief recap of the walks we covered in the day, we do our own thing. Utilising weapons unearthed from our room, VD works on his staff form and I work my Dao. Being Wushu weapons, as opposed to the Kung Fu weapons we normally use, I struggle to get the feel of the form. The Wushu weapon simply doesn't respond the same as a conventional sword. The Wushu Dao is flexible for three quarters of its length and thin enough to be folded over on itself. That's not to say the blade isn't dangerous. It may be flimsy, but the thin metal edge is as sharp as an opened corned-beef tin. This is probably why their former owners abandoned them in the first place.

I try to make my movements as controlled and precise as possible insuring to lead with the cutting edge. This is difficult with a floppy blade as it wobbles all over the place.

I had been forewarned that foreigners training in China tend to be very dedicated, even to the extent of training harder than the Chinese students. I've seen little evidence of this at Xiao Long. So far, the contrary is noticeable to such an extent that I'm embarrassed at the lack of work ethic in my compatriots. Hardly any students do any real training in the evening session preferring to sit around and chat, or in Knobby's case hold court. By 9pm the majority have already drifted away and those of us remaining amble to our respective rooms.

It's not until we get back that I notice the condition of our clothing. The layer of dust and grime covering everything here has already worked its magic and, simply as a result of being in contact with China, we are filthy. With this realisation, I feel a pang of guilt for judging the others so harshly earlier. To quote the great Spike Milligan, 'People in glasshouses should draw the blinds prior to removing their trousers.' In an attempt to minimise the contamination of our room, I decide I will have two sets of clothes on the go: a set for training and a set for lounging. We enter and leave this world smeared in shit, I see no good reason to live in the stuff during the interim.

I'm feeling distinctly grubby. Given the training environment, it's hardly surprising my shiny new uniform has already developed a lived-in look. Rolling on a rubbish strewn floor and running through dust and smoke, the debris cling to our sweaty clothes and become ground in. It's difficult to be particularly fastidious about personal hygiene here, but I can't continue changing underwear and T-shirt without attempting to wash them. Other options include constantly discarding clothes and buying new or continuing to wear them and developing scabies.

Weighing up the alternatives, I peel off my clothes and rinse them in the sink with cold, soapy water. Hanging them on the window bars to dry gives the room a rustic feel that was so needed. They'll get a bit smoky from the fire, but will soon dry in the heat. This way I can run an alternating washing/wearing system until they cease to be serviceable and then throw them out and work another pair into the routine. One advantage of the polyester uniform is that it will dry quickly.

Even so, my clothes are not going to survive long with this treatment. In anticipation of the conditions, I packed a bunch of Sunday clothes to train in; they're most holey. It's mostly promotional t-shirts from brands I've never heard of and other items on their last legs that I'm intending to wear into the ground and discard as I go along. Given the conditions, it's certainly not worth wearing anything decent although, with clothes so cheap in China, it's hardly worth lugging any here at all. A side effect of clearing out my tired wardrobe is that I will mostly resemble a threadbare tramp during our stay. That said, being constantly surrounded by filth means everyone gets to look like a ragged vagabond pretty quickly.

A spot of basic flannel work and a change of clothes has me feeling almost human again and I'm all set to hit the plank. Which is just as well, as no sooner do I open my book than Shifu Fatso blunders into the room for this evenings rendition of his outstanding, 'Ok, go sleep' routine.

It's the fastest he's moved all day. No sooner are the words out of his mouth than he's turned off the light and made a sharp exit. Before I can arrange my thoughts to respond, the situation has passed. I'm left sitting up in bed, open mouthed and holding my book in the dark. At this point I would normally turn to VD for the moral support of a raised eyebrow, but he's not letting his complaints about the bed interrupt his sleeping pattern and is already snoring merrily away. As we have to be up early, it's probably a good time to turn in anyway.

A whole set of bedding, wash gargle things, daily necessities
shall be provided, as well as quality services offered by
full-time living service personnel to give foreign students the
warmth that gives a home.

Xiao Long Website.

Our thrill of being involved in the training is not so noticeable in the early hours of the a.m. Yet to catch up with the eight-hour time difference, I've been awake for hours already, but am still not exactly keen on moving from my pit. Lying on my plank, listening to the tannoy system churn out synthesised classical music, I'm thinking, 'The alarm will go off any minute. Any minute now, I'll have to get up.'

There's a clatter from Victorian Dad's direction, 'Dude, alarm didn't go off!'

I vault from the bed, like a young gazelle startled at the watering hole. Pawing at my pyjamas, I lunge toward the light switch.

VD is slower out the gates as his brief burst of sentience subsides and he sits on the edge of his bed bewildered. While he is pondering his existential plight, I hop frantically around the room trying to get both feet into one tracksuit leg. Having mustered the energy to stand, VD sleepwalks around the room bumping into the walls and furniture as I attempt to cover my pallid frame by furiously throwing clothes into the air until some stick to me. VD's shambling approach pays off better than my mad panic. We are neck and neck to the post.

With no thought of facing the basic levels of salutariness that a splash of cold, murky water can provide, we dash into the unlit corridor. The darkness doesn't curb my stampede until I sprawl out on the floor having introduced myself to the rubbish bin. Composure regained, I recall that the waist-high, pink-plastic barrel is positioned just outside the DVD room. In my exuberance I have missed the stairs.

Running my hands along the wall, I locate the stairwell and galumph down the stairs at a considerably reduced rate. We burst out into the courtyard expecting Shifu Fatso waiting and having to face the resulting punishment.

The initial adrenalin surge melts away as we stand around like a pair of gormsters shivering in the chilly morning air. Desperately huddled in our thin tracksuits, we watch the silhouettes of Chinese kids going through their paces as the other westerners gradually materialise around us.

The school's frugal approach to the electricity bill means not only are there no lights on inside the building, neither are the lights on outside. The courtyard is as black as my anguished soul. This gives us the perfect opportunity to hone our ninja skills as we stumble around, bumping into people, looking for our relevant groups. If the other students seemed barely sentient yesterday, it's nothing compared to the wee hours. It's like a George Romero movie.

True to form, Fatso is the last Shifu to appear. When he's located us, we line up and are put through basic warmup stretches. As usual, Shifu just grunts and we copy the fumbling efforts of the others as they stretch up and down, followed by press-ups, squats and lunges. Not a great warmup, but it's better than nothing and it does give our eyes chance to adjust before he barks, 'Go run!', and indicates for us to follow the other groups disappearing in the darkness. I don't know what he's so sulky about, we were the ones waiting for him.

We run in formation to the front of school, out the main gate and down Dayu road. I can just make out the shuttered-up shops along the pavement. Obviously, nothing is open yet and it's still too early for any real traffic, although our pre-dawn activity is still a little on the hairy side as the occasional vehicle we do encounter is taking full advantage of the clear road to attempt the world land-speed record. Fortunately, most traffic tends to be Heath Robinson affairs of an agricultural nature, generally a cultivator bolted to a homemade trailer. Not only do these contraptions have low top speeds, but give plenty of warning of their approach for, despite not having lights, their spluttering two-stroke engines announce their presence long before they come into sight.

Shifu Fatso bumbles along behind until we get too far ahead, then shouts, 'Stopah!' We wait for him to catch up and tell us to, 'Go run' again.

The sun's first blush is already filtering through when, not far down the road, we are halted at a crossroads. Shifu points to a pagoda way up on the mountain and, once again, proclaims, 'Go run'.

Spying the pagoda peeking out from the trees, VD turns to me with despair in his voice, 'We're gonna need a bigger boat.' My hope that it's a very small pagoda, and quite close, is soon dashed. I am forced to agree. The splash of primary colour sitting amongst the verdant mountainside does indeed seem rather distant. The other students know the procedure so we follow them up the dusty road. Along the way we are sporadically presented with interesting roadside displays in the form of mounds of rotting garbage and a delightful open sewer. All of which have me gagging as I lurch, semi-consciously up the hill, with a dissolving septum. I'm sure the smell of napalm would be preferable.

Passed some unmanned kiosks, over a bridge and along the side of a river we come to the Song Yang Jing Qu (Songyang Scenic Area) national park.

Inside the park is a whole new world. With dawn breaking over the mountains, we are presented with a glorious brightening and our thin polyester tracksuits soon warm up as we run towards the rapidly rising sun. The park is spotlessly clean, even the rocks and shrubs seem shiny in the early light and the air is a pleasure to breathe. A well-constructed wide stone path marks our route where it's every man for himself to the peak. There are a number of locals, primarily the older generation, taking their early constitutional. Puffing and panting my way up the stone steps, I pass many a smiling old lady swinging her arms energetically on her way back down. I dread to think what time they were up this morning. Frankly, it puts us to shame.

On reaching the pagoda, I pause to catch my breath and admire the view. A handful of oldsters have beaten me to the top. Looking rather smug, they sit around, hogging the available seats, coughing and spitting on the ground as if marking their territory. Their attitude to the white guy in a Shaolin tracksuit varies from bemused to disinterested. This is probably a regular activity for them and they are used to seeing knackered foreigners.

Running in the fresh dawn air has certainly woken me up and the scenery has done a lot to improve my spirits. Altogether, it's a pleasant experience. From the hill top, Dengfeng is laid out at my feet, but even as the town is just waking up, it's barely visible through a smoggy haze. Possibly a bigger problem in this neighbourhood than the traffic and industrial air pollution is the coal-fired heating and cooking. Outside every building is a mound of ash and a few compressed coal-dust briquettes. Flatbed Sanlun Che shuttle back and forth replenishing stocks throughout the day. Hanging over the town like a gloomy shroud, the coal dust is equally visible in the stuff that's coughed up.

The return journey is considerably easier with the assistance of gravity. I arrive at the crossroads where Shifu Fatso, like a faithful hound, waits exactly where we left him. He is so pleased to see me that he lines me up in height order on my own to await the group. Once we are all present, he walks along the line asking us in turn, 'You money?'

Some of us do, some of us don't. Shifu visibly deflates, gives a crestfallen grunt, shrugs his shoulders and says, 'Ok, go school.'

Inside my vacuous mind is a faint tinkling sound as the penny drops. It's seven o'clock; breakfast will be over by the time we get back. We march back to school at the hurry-up in the vain hope there will be a morsel of food left, but there's just no way it's going to happen. Our Shifu looks so dejected that I almost feel for him.

Reaching the school, we line up to be dismissed and Shifu delivers his best received line to date, 'Go Dengfeng.'

Not only is there a God, but the fellow is smiling down on me. 'Go Dengfeng' is the answer to our prayers. We can get a late breakfast in town and pick up a few creature comforts we are sorely missing. In preparation of such an event I have taken the precaution of writing a little list with Chinese characters and Pinyin. It contains: a kettle, tea, cups and a mirror. The kettle will serve a dual purpose. Not only will we be able to drink tea, something one would have taken for granted in China, but it will also provide hot water for our ablutions.

A quick wash and change and we are ready to rock. However, leaving the school premises is a complicated affair. Granted the freedom of the city by Shifu Fatso, we now discover that we need a permission slip. Shifu Fatso won't provide this, and refers us to Shibu Shifu. We go to Shibu's room in search of him.

Outside Shibu's room we bump into some other guys already waiting. They are all holding scratty pieces of paper and inform me to write out the pass myself and Shibu will sign it. It really doesn't matter what we write as Shibu can't read English and neither can the gate guards, so you just need the time in and out and the date. Like true jobsworths the guards will not let you through without a slip of paper, but any old scrap of paper will do. I head back to our room to rustle up stationery. On my return, the guys have relocated to the DVD room. Before jumping to any assumptions, I ask what's happening. They tell me Shibu had appeared and told them to wait here. I join the queue. As we are waiting, a cry goes up that Shibu has been spotted at the building entrance. We stampede down the stairs like a herd of Boxing Day bargain hunters and surround Shibu to prevent his escape.

Realising he has been cornered, Shibu resigns himself to his fate and, with a sigh, begrudgingly collects all the bits and pieces of paper and signs them. We then enjoy a strange party game where Shibu holds up the pieces of paper, one at a time, for crowd members to identify and claim their own. Everyone is excited about getting a pass and we jostle around him like kids in a sweet shop. All in all, it's a streamlined procedure by Chinese standards.

At the front gate, a dozen of us mill around the two guards and force our bits of paper into their hands. They don't seem fussed about inspecting the slips, but refuse to let anyone out without one. As long as they can say they did their job they don't feel obliged to do any more. Just to be contrary, I take advantage of the confusion, pretend to hand in my pass and slip out amongst the crowd. You never know when a pre-signed pass could come in handy. I see it as my 'get out of jail free card'.

We are just out the gates and heading down the strip when one of the Taiji guys catches up with us, 'Hey guys, can I tag along with you?'

'Sure, we are going to eat and to buy a kettle.'

'I know just the place, I'll show you.'

Seattle, for that's where he's from, guides us straight down the road to the spot where we lined up after our run this morning. On the crossroads of Dayu Lu and Shaoshi Lu is Jinjian Fandian, a small café known amongst the foreign students as the Breakfast Place.

The purchase of breakfast at the Breakfast Place isn't as streamlined a process as one might expect from a fast-food establishment. Seattle kindly demonstrates the procedure. Just inside the door is a lady selling pink tickets, back out on the pavement is another lady cooking chaodan (omelettes) and youtiao (fried dough sticks), who will take a seemingly random amount of tickets in exchange for her wares. Back inside queuing at the kitchen counter gives the opportunity to swap more tickets for baozi (steamed, filled dumplings) and helping yourself to a drink from fridge involves another queue at the bar counter to pay with cash. Packed into the room are a number of tables, the centre of each proudly displaying a collection of disposable chopsticks and a roll of toilet paper, which I dearly hope is to be used for the wiping of hands.

Once seated, Seattle, who has been at the school a couple of months, gives us a more balanced perspective than previously supplied by Knobby. Essentially, he says our school isn't great, but is as good as any other in Dengfeng and it's cheaper.

He also mentions he is later going to visit a local bathhouse where, not only can you wash in warm water, but they also serve beer. VD is absolutely delighted at the prospect of a beer and can't wait to get directions to this earthly paradise. Sitting in the Breakfast Place stuffing my face with fresh, food that isn't rice and cabbage and with the prospect of a bath on the horizon my world has taken a distinctly rosy hue.

Out of the blue, Knobby plants himself at our table announcing that the school is rubbish because they shouldn't make him train when his knee hurts. A voice from an adjacent table suggests he buys a knee support, which stuns him into a momentary silence.

Seattle continues his tale of a forthcoming meditation course being held by the monks, but Knobby is straight in there with a few disparaging words on meditation and its adherents. A personified Imp of the Perverse, Knobby just says the first thing that comes into his head, which in this instance is a nonsensical tirade against meditation. Obviously, no fan of toilet humour, Seattle is hit by the realization that we are assuredly a bunch of imbeciles. His eyes betray him for a split second as he suddenly remembers a previous appointment. Turning to a group of Xiao Long guys at another table he asks, 'Hey, do you guys know the supermarket in town?'

'Ya, for sure.' It transpires they do.

'Would you show these guys the way?'

'Ya, for sure.' I think that means they don't mind.

Thus, we are neatly palmed off on a quartet of German guys who gracefully accept their charge. Seattle gives his best regards and makes good his escape.

With my social senses tingling, I get the distinct impression we've been dumped. I can't blame the guy for protecting his bolt-hole. No one deserves to have their sanctuary ruined through being friendly to someone who proceeds to be a social liability. VD is much thicker skinned than I and feels Seattle had honestly forgotten his previous engagement. Knobby didn't notice anything at all as he was still prattling on without pause for breath. There are times when I envy people like Knobby their complete obliviousness to external stimuli. Life must be so much simpler without being hindered by societal constraints.

We cram into the back of a Sanlun Che with the emphatic Germans. These three-wheeled motorbikes with a covered compartment on the back similar to a Tuk Tuk, are Dengfeng's defacto mode of transport. Jammed in, I can't see anything of the journey to remember landmarks for the way back.

The seven of us disgorge onto the dusty street in the centre of town at the supermarket. It's just as well we have the German guys otherwise we would never have found the place. Even when it's pointed out, I don't immediately realise what it is. To a casual observer the supermarket is nothing more than an escalator disappearing under street level. As a stroke of luck, it's opposite a western style burger bar, called Dico's (pr. Dikeshi in Mandarin), which is unusual and prominent enough to use as a landmark for our later rendezvous.

Descending into the subterranean world reveals a perfectly reasonable supermarket. Surrounded by items both familiar and foreign we are able to fulfil the majority of our requirements.

Struggling to locate a couple of items on our list we recruit a staff-member to assist. There are so many staff around the store that we really are spoilt for choice. The place is ridiculously well staffed. Not only are there groups of three or four distributed around the place, but each aisle has a person manning it in case of any queries. However, ask them about the next aisle and they don't know. It's not their business. Their aisle is their kingdom and they do not trespass onto another's territory lightly.

Approaching a group forces their spokesperson into action. Pressured by the presence of her peers she escorts us to the relevant aisle.

Unable to furnish us with a teapot, the supermarket does produce a small shaving mirror, a kettle and a couple of mugs. All of which have their boxes opened by their aisle guardian to prove the relevant item is enclosed, before we are allowed to put them in our basket. Allegedly market stallholders aren't above pulling the old switcheroo on unsuspecting purchasers, especially day-trippers, and this could be their way of demonstrating they are above this kind of underhand stunt and also act as a justification for their pricing. While the establishment is expensive in Chinese terms, the prices are displayed clearly and there is no doubt as to what one is getting for the money.

With no viable alternative in these desperate times, I resort to a pack of instant white tea and a further moment of extravagance sees the purchase of a couple of hollow-fibre pillows. The pillow supplied by the school is wafer thin and packed with straw which my face finds disagreeable. An extra pillow will also make it more comfortable to sit up in bed. An activity which I am indulging in a lot of late.

The supermarket has done much more than provide us with a few material goods, it reassures us that most anything we could need is easily accessible. Previously warned that many items considered basics in the west simply weren't available in China, it's comforting to realise it's certainly not the case here. Looking around, we should be able to equip ourselves with most necessities without much ado.

A member of staff stands behind the checkout watching our purchases being rung up. At one point there is a price query and I take her to the aisle where we picked up the item in question, a packet of green tea, where she checks the price on the shelf and returns with me to the checkout. Goods packed and paid for, we are directed to this same woman who unpacks our purchases, checks off each item and tears the receipt before allowing us to repack and part company. This ensures we haven't got any items in the bag that haven't been paid for. It's her job to check receipts, so that's what she does. Even though we are the only people in the shop and she stood next to us during the entire transaction. It's a fine example of Chinese logic in action.

Buoyant after our success, we have plenty of time for a wander around town before lunch. Knobby had turned his nose up at the knee supports in the supermarket preferring to shop around. VD and I are happy to just scope the place out as Knobby drags us from one unlikely shop to the next, rejecting any proffered knee supports out of hand. He seems disappointed when even the least promising shop has them in stock. His attitude is such that I am not convinced he really wants one at all. Dengfeng isn't exactly a hive of metropolitan activity and has limited retail opportunities. While the goods on offer are slightly different to the versions we are used to, we are not exactly in a position to be picky so if you really need an item, you have to do the best with what's available. Knobby's random meanderings also mean we cover enough ground to get our bearings.

We had arranged to reconvene with the German guys at a café with the intention of refuelling there in preference to another rice and cabbage at school. We troop through an unassuming doorway with a small brass plaque bearing the legend Qin Xin Yuan and up the stairs.

The QXY café is unsure whether it is a restaurant or a burger bar. This confusion is apparent in its décor, range of comestibles and the attitude of its staff who don't know what their job description entails other than it doesn't involve dealing with customers. They have no interest in us at all. It's another overstaffed joint with far more staff than tables and we are the only patrons. The majority of the workforce stand around as object d'art.

There have been significant changes in China since its days of zero unemployment and I wonder if this current trend for overstaffing is a remnant of that period or government initiative to curb the increase in unemployment since the advent of the open market policy.

The café's stance regarding customers and the serving thereof makes ordering difficult. Despite an abundance of bodies they are not keen to get the transaction underway. I approach the counter and order a couple of specials. Half an hour later we are presented with an eclectic selection of food based on the Chinese idea of what western food might look like. Nonetheless, it's a welcome substitute to the meal we are currently missing at school as it fulfils our primary requirement of not being boiled rice and cabbage.

As we are taking the opportunity of gorging ourselves the German guys appear beaming like a bunch of cheeky cherubim and carrying a large round box with a ribbon around it. They have multiplied since we left them and are now much more awake. I nod toward the box, 'Have you bought a hat?'

'No, is huge birthday cake. Is no birthday, but is huge cake so cheap.'

The German guys think it is hysterical to have bought a birthday cake without a birthday to accompany it. Personally, I feel they are milking the point somewhat. While these are a cool bunch of guys, I became prejudiced against the German sense of humour on the plane journey here. A German guy sitting several rows in front of me was in serious danger of a cardiac arrest with his uncontrolled hilarity at the Mr. Bean show that was playing. It says something about the world condition that Rowan Atkinson has achieved his greatest success with his most puerile role. The experience cemented my view of German humour. Although, as it is a British show, I'm probably not in a position to criticise another nation too much for enjoying another fine British export.

The extra bodies, baggage and big cake means we need two Sanlun Che for the return journey. We leave the German guys chuckling away with their cake.

Returning to Xiao Long, we just saunter back in through the front gate. The guards don't even register our existence, let alone book us back in. I was all set for a bit of a showdown with the guards about not receiving a pass from me when I left, but now I'm convinced they never actually booked us out in the first place. It's just another example of the futility of Chinese bureaucracy. My 'get out of jail free' card might not be so useful after all.

Crossing the courtyard, we are spotted by the group of Pink Overall women who sit in the doorway spitting seed shells on the floor all day. Our supermarket carrier bags have piqued their interest and they begin to jabber excitedly amongst themselves, pointing at us and our purchases. Obviously not much has happened since we left this morning as 'Men go to supermarket' is breaking news. At this rate we may make the front-page of the evening edition.

The dominatrix's eyes settle on my pillows. Acting as spokesman for the group, she tugs at my sleeve, 'Duo xiao qian?' (How much money?)

When Adam Smith described Britain as a 'Nation of shopkeepers' he had obviously never been to China. The Chinese are fixated with the price of things and love nothing more than to say they could have haggled a much cheaper price.

Prepared for the inevitable loss of face regarding by business acumen I show them the price label on the pillow. From the outraged gasps and animated chatter that ensues, I assume the answer was exactly what they wanted. Now they can assure each other that they would have got it cheaper and, by inference, foreigners are stupid with no grasp of monetary value. Especially me, Mr. Saville Row, who's far too up himself to put his dainty little face into the school's straw pillow and has thrown away good money on a new one because it has stuffing in it.

Back at the room, we proudly array our new utensils and hot beverage making paraphernalia on the spare bedside cabinet and put the kettle toward earning its keep.

The scorching around the shattered electrical socket initially had me concerned for our safety and the wellbeing of our new kettle, but reasoning the risk of agonising death is worth it for a cup of tea, I gingerly plug the kettle in and let it loose on its inaugural outing. Thankfully, it doesn't blow up and boils like a good 'un. Although, given the milky gloop that chugs from our tap attempting to pass itself off as water, I don't envy the kettle's life expectancy. I'm dubious about drinking the stuff even after boiling.

As there is no light in bathroom, we hang our mirror from one of the many random hooks on the bedroom wall and, using a mug as a shaving bowl, shave our grizzled faces at the desk.

Shorn of a couple of days' stubble, I'm feeling almost human again and brace myself for the task of putting the instant tea to the test. 'Have some tea?'

'Yes, indeed.'

My snobbery proves unfounded as it is the very fellow. Its invigorating powers are soon at work and all is well with the world.

Putting the carrier bags aside for future use I realise they are the same as those we found in the room. Comfortingly, this implies we did the right thing in giving the Meishen Yishang Maoyou Xiangongsi our patronage.

Kettle possession changes our lives. Feeling the benefits of a sated appetite and a stubble free chin, we turn up to afternoon training, full of the joys. Even the soul sucking laps of school can't do much to dampen our enthusiasm and, after break, we are pleasantly surprised with even more variation in the training as, rather than 'Go run', we have 'Go gym.' Shifu takes all three groups to the ground floor training hall which houses a well-equipped weights gym.

I maintain that the best way to injure someone is to let them loose in a gym unattended. Shifu Fatso obviously doesn't share my concerns. He motions towards the machinery with his trademark grunt and settles himself down for a bit of a nap on the bench press machine while we are left to our own devices.

For the majority this means striving to cripple themselves in the operation of unfamiliar, heavy machinery. To further complicate matters, not only are the machines fairly elaborate as gym equipment goes, but there are no operating instructions on them and, despite the failing sunlight, we are expected to train with the lights off.

I'm enjoying myself working around the machines I don't normally have access to. With no supervision most students disperse into little groups and natter amongst themselves until the two little Korean kids ferret out a football and start kicking it around the gym. They are soon joined by Knobby, who somehow manages to be a bad influence on a pair of prepubescent delinquents.

Disturbed by the racket, Shifu Fatso awakes and seeing the potential carnage all around him determines to set a good example with the health and safely. To this end he gets a Mongolian guy to stand on the leg press machine while he presses him along with the full weight stack. A couple of reps fulfil his required energy expenditure for the day and, satisfied with a job well done, he settles down for another kip.

A couple of guys take it upon themselves to shift the ball players to one end and we all continue with our own thing until, in a brief moment of awakening, Shifu Fatso realises there is precious little training going on and dismisses us for dinner.

Arriving at dinner early makes all the difference to the dining experience. Not only can we traverse the floor without jostling through the massed throng, but also without risking life and limb on spilt food. We are even able to converse without shouting across the table at each other. The ladle guy sees us coming and hurriedly opens the serving window to provide our ration of the usual, and looks pleased to do so.

At evening training Knobby sees me practising my forms and asks me to teach him Lau Gar. It's strange to me that anyone from Britain would go to China to learn Britain's most popular martial art. Even more so to ask me for Kung Fu tuition when surrounded by accomplished masters. I agree anyway, and then carry on doing my own thing, knowing full well that his interest will disappear within a nanosecond and come to nothing.

I seem to have developed a taste for the high life as, throughout the session, I can't wait to indulge in the luxury of a whore's bath with warm water on my flannel. It's amazing the impact these small differences make. Now we have some basic amenities and are actually training, I am much happier with life.

Washed, changed and sitting up in bed with my new pillow and a cup of tea certainly changes my perspective. I'm so chipper that VD is getting annoyed at my bonhomie. He turned his nose up at the idea of pillow purchase, but seeing me lording it up gives him a change of heart and he decides he would like one after all. So content am I, that I magnanimously launch one at him. His wife had previously told me he is asleep before his head hits the pillow and, as if to prove her point, no sooner than I have socked him with one than he is out like a light and sawing wood like a grizzly bear.

Revelling in my newfound comfort, I'm put out when Shifu Fatso bowls into the room and disrupts my repose. It looks like the 9.30 lights out is among the rare timetable slots that run on time. It's so uncharacteristically punctual of our Shifu that I'm a little alarmed by his alacrity.

'Wah huh?' From his wide-eyed exclamation I deduce he is surprised to have come face to face with the Queen of Sheba. It's probably the pyjamas. Once over the wonderment, he realises it's just me enjoying the high life and, lifting his jaw from the floor, orders me to sleep.

I was aware of school policy regarding lights out, and that we would be locked in at night, when we settled on this school. My research led me to believe it's a fairly standard policy in this type of establishment however, now it's actually happening, I resent being sent to bed. I guess our Shifu is supposed to be checking our wellbeing and not just telling us to go to sleep. Again, this is a flawed concept as, not only is the old language barrier an issue, but Shifu daren't ask how we are in case he is then required to do something in the form of corrective measures. Although, I would have to be pretty sharpish to get a word in before he hits the switch and disappears.

I get my head down on my new pillow and drift off content with a successful day.

When heaven is about to confer a great responsibility on any man, it will exercise his mind with suffering, subject his sinews and bones to hard work, expose his body to hunger, put him to poverty, place obstacles in the paths of his deeds, so as to stimulate his mind, harden his nature and improve wherever he is incompetent.

Meng Zi.

Waking up before the crack of dawn isn't such a hideous prospect now there's a cup of tea on the agenda. If anything, the instant tea is even more potable in the early hours and gently brings me around to the idea of facing the day's rigours. Sitting up with my new pillow and hot brew, I'm gradually gaining consciousness as the tannoy crackles to life with a tinny recording of a bugle, followed by a synthesised piece of classical music.

As pleasant as our new luxuries have made reveille, waking to the tannoy music is disconcerting. It reminds me of a scene from Kubrick's 'A Clockwork Orange'. I appreciate the film doesn't do justice to the book, but the tale essentially centres around the individual's freewill versus the state. An irony that isn't lost on me as I arise to the bugle call in a Communist Government approved school.

This morning Shifu Fatso marches us to the back of school, past the training field with smouldering bonfire, and out onto the road where we Go Run circuits of the block. We go through the usual stance work and stretches before punching and kicking our way, in formation, up and down the pavement forcing the occasional commuters into the road.

It seems perfectly usual for people here to claim any public place for their own use. In doing so, it's given that any passers-by may take an interest. I suppose the logic is: if you don't want people to see what you are doing, don't do it in the street.

There must be limited entertainment opportunities in Dengfeng as the populace will usually stop and watch anything, but today's commuters are uninterested. I suppose these activities must be such a common sight that locals have become immune. They must have seen some hideous sights if our group of misfits can't pique their attention.

Breakfast is followed by the ubiquitous laps of school before we head up to the gym where Shifu Fatso takes a more hands-on approach to our stretching. He begins by lining us up an arm's length from the wall with our hands on the pipe and our heads down. He then works along the line pushing down on our backs to loosen the shoulders. Starting with small bouncing movements, he gradually becomes more vigorous, jerking our joints past their comfort zones until he finishes with a sudden, wrenching shove. We go through the same procedure in a variety of positions: touching toes, Gong Bu, Pu Bu, Front splits, Side splits, etc. all with the same manhandling.

This type of repetitive, bouncing stretch is referred to as Ballistic Stretching and is exactly what current sports technology theory advises against. While it's always unwise to force muscles and tendons beyond their range of motion before they're fully warmed, it is particularly so with Ballistic Stretching. Repeated activation of the stretch reflex can tighten muscles and cause micro-trauma, which heals with a scar. Being less pliable, scar tissue actually tightens the muscle reducing flexibility and can be more prone to pain.

Luckily, our morning warming exercises, and a good ration of Go Run between sessions, ensure our muscles are kept warm and loose throughout the day. The current weather helps too, it would be much more difficult to keep limber in the winter months.

Pointing at Julie, Shifu grunts, points to the other side of the hall and lifts his leg. Julie must have a psychic connection for she immediately knows what to do. Moving to the front of the line she stands at attention and brings her hands together in front of her waist. Tapping the back of the right hand with the left palm, she places her left foot forward and extends both arms out to the sides with fingers upright.

Swinging the rear leg up to the front and landing it forward she works her way across the hall. We slot into line and follow the leader back and fore. After half a dozen lengths, Shifu gives another grunt and we line up behind Julie for her to start a different walk, this time swinging the leg across the body to slap against the opposite hand.

The next variation is to swing the leg across the body and back around to slap against the same side hand. So far these leg swing walks have been fairly standard, but then there's one I haven't seen before. Turning sideways on with arms outstretched, we step across with the rear leg. The front arm folds across chest to palm block behind while the rear arm presses overhead palm upward with the front foot swung up to meet it. Finding it difficult to coordinate this one I make a mental note to practice it at the evening session.

Laying us down on the disease-ridden carpet, Shifu works along the row of prone victims. Pressing his clenched fists along our spines, he teases our vertebrae apart with his knuckles. Recognising what's going on, Juha is able to go one better. Crossing my arms in front of my chest, he is big enough to pick me up from behind by my elbows to stretch my spine and crack my back.

Pairing us up, Shifu indicates that we should perform a handstand against our partners. I launch myself at VD using the method shown me by my school PE teacher all those years ago. Mr. Robinson must have taught me well, I've still got it. Supporting myself on my hands with VD holding my legs straight in the air, it doesn't take long to realise why it's been twenty-eight years since I last did this. I'm far too tired and hungry for the rush of blood to the head to do me any good and it's an eternity until Shifu tells us to switch. Red faced and light headed, I brace myself just in time to catch VD's bulk as he slams into me. We are not the ideal group for handstands, but I'm pleased with what I manage.

Lining up once more, Shifu motions for us to hold our arms in the air with palms flat and fingers pointing behind us. He then walks along the line supporting our waists as we reach backwards until our palms are on the floor. Leaving us to hold the position he moves to the next person in line. There's no thought of instruction, he just gets us to reach for the sky and pushes us into a back-bridge. Although, in all fairness to the guy, his technique works. I would never have attempted the bridge without building up to it, but he had me doing it before I knew what was happening.

I lack the flexibility in my arms to hold the position for long and soon collapse, with a thud, but it's an achievement nonetheless. Lying in a crumpled heap on the filthy floor, I'm amazed I managed the back-bridge at all.

Shifu Fatso pauses to pull his thinking face, until his eyes light up and a huge grin spreads over his little face. Like a small child who has just remembered it's his birthday, he has realised it's time for Power Stretching.

Supine on the floor, with the rest of the group holding my shoulders and one leg down, Shifu straddles me and reaches for my other leg which I obligingly raise for him. This warrants a raised eyebrow which I take as a compliment. Perhaps VD and I aren't the liabilities he was expecting.

Grinning to himself, Shifu attempts to put my leg behind my head from a variety of angles. Power Stretching is carried out differently to the jerky motions we've just been through and almost conforms to the currently recommended stretching format. Static Stretching involves a slow, continuous movement lengthening the stretch as the muscle relaxes. Although, no matter how hard I try to focus and breathe into the stretch, he's not doing it slowly enough for my liking. Shifu doesn't seem interested in the complexities of stretching. His sole concern is to push my foot over my head or, at one point, into my mouth. It's the happiest I've seen him.

With muscle and tendon being forced through their limits, attempts to relax into the stretch only go so far. I am soon seeking sanctuary in the pain. Focusing my qi, as my Sifu at home taught me, I'm quietly pleased with the results. Not only am I getting a good range of motion in my stretch, but I'm not making a complete spectacle of myself in the process. Recognising my efforts, Shifu Fatso gives me another raised eyebrow. Repeat with the other leg, then it's payback time as I get to hold down one of the people who were just enjoying themselves at my expense.

Actually, Power Stretching a pretty cushy session. Not because it doesn't hurt or that I'm particularly flexible, but while we get twenty-five minutes of sheer agony, with five people in the group it means we get another four times thirty minutes of holding someone else down and laughing at them. The other groups in the gym are also enjoying a good old Power Stretch and the room is filled with much hilarity as they photograph and film their friends crying in agony.

Shifu Fatso is revelling in the stretching much more than is healthy for a grown man. From his tirade of obscenities, I can only assume VD agrees. Shifu may not understand what VD is saying, but there's no doubt he gets the gist and positively delights in the reaction. I feel Shifu is unkind to revel in VD's torment this way. Looking down on his tortured face I make a mental note to bring the camera next week.

Observing the scenes going on around me I am reminded of training with Master Yau at the Temple Gym in Birmingham. I can almost hear him saying one of his stock phrases, 'Why you pull that face? That face help?'

Of course pulling faces doesn't help, but Master Yau is able to explain what one should do to work through the discomfort. I don't know whether Fatso assumes a level of understanding on our part, doesn't understand the complexities himself or, more likely, just doesn't care. Either way he lacks the vocabulary to explain and contents himself with the hands-on approach.

After her turn, Julie continues to stretch at the side before launching into front splits. Shifu Fatso notices this and, with a 'Huh', stands up. Lifting one foot directly over his head, he grasps it in his hand and holds a pose. I'm not sure what he's trying to illustrate, but if nothing else his little display implies that the training here pays off, especially if its effects have lasted with someone so obviously out of shape. Julie has ten years of ballet under her belt, so her fitness and flexibility put the rest of our group to shame. Her physical ability exceeds ours by so much that I don't understand why Julie has been put in Fatso's group. Anywhere else her fitness and flexibility would be impressive. At a Shaolin martial art school, she only stands out for not being Chinese.

As beneficial as I'm sure Power Stretching is, it feels so good to stop. Wringing out the muscles removes the lactic acid and refreshes the blood supply giving the body an overall feeling of looseness that lasts the day. Looking like recruits from the Ministry of Silly Walks, we wobble off to lunch, where we enjoy another serving from the 'varied' menu.

Knobby's comedy skit for lunch is based on our dismissal procedure. After a training session we line up in front of our Shifu and salute (xing li). This involves taking a step forward, clapping our hands three times and, with a small bow, giving the traditional Chinese martial arts greeting 'baoquan'. Knobby's question is, 'Why do we have to give him a round of applause, he hasn't done anything.'

This etiquette is another school convention that hasn't been explained. They may expect an amount of basic knowledge from martial arts enthusiasts and for us to know this already, although it probably just hasn't occurred to them.

As it happens, I once had the symbolism explained to me. The baoquan varies among different schools as an indicator of lineage. For more recent styles, the common explanation of the salute is that the fist shows martial ability and the hand covers the fist to show civility.

The People's Republic of China standardised the Wushu salute in 1986 based on that used by Shaolin. The right hand is clenched in a fist and the left palm held vertically. They meet at chest height about 30cm from the body, with elbows bent and arms forming a circle. Feet together, the posture is erect and eyes focus on the person being saluted.

The modern PRC definition states the right fist demonstrates the pledge to cultivate martial arts and promote friendship. The wrapped fingers of the left hand symbolise uniting Wushu across the four directions. The left-hand thumb is bent out of humility. (A Chinese person pointing to themselves with a straightened thumb means 'I'm number one!' Even if you are number one, proper etiquette demands you be too humble to admit it, unless you're Bruce Lee). The first clap thanks the teacher for their training, second acknowledges classmates and the third is in appreciation of martial arts culture.

After lunch training starts off the same Go Run, but after drilling walks with the group, VD and I are taken aside to start learning the first form. Xiao Hong Quan (Young Hong's Fist) is an introductory Shaolin form and shouldn't be too acrobatically taxing for us.

Excited to start learning the form, we get carried away with training and turn up ten minutes into dinner. Too late we discover the canteen has been ransacked by a Mongol horde.

Dumbfounded amongst the destroying furniture and liberally scattered food, we must look so pathetic and forlorn that someone feels sorry for us and locates the ladle guy. He sorts us out some leftovers, which we devour amongst the devastation. A few little kids are still hanging around looting the debris and one is practicing a spear form in the middle of dining hall. The moral of this tale must surely be: never turn up to the canteen late. Other than being stone-cold as opposed to lukewarm, the leftovers are practically indistinguishable from a normal serving, but it's a lesson learnt: you can call me anything you like, as long as it's not late for dinner.

Evening free training session is more viable now that we have something relevant to practice and I spend some time getting to grips with the side-on leg swing before recapping the section of Xiao Hong we covered today. Fortunately, Julie is there to give us some pointers.

Dividing her training between Kung Fu and Mandarin, Julie has more energy than the rest of us and usually makes evening training. Julie has been here the longest out of our group, a month, so knows most of the form already and confides she has learnt the majority of it from other students and not our Shifu. She also spent time in Beijing before arriving at the school, but still served quarantine, as she was not informed of the get-out clause. We avoid the subject of our own quarantine.

Knobby has been here a week longer than us, but doesn't know any of the form yet. Primarily as he is more concerned with performing for the troops than training, although I do catch him glancing over at us from time to time. Juha rarely turns up for evening sessions preferring to listen to Finnish Death Metal in his room.

By 9.30 we are in bed ready for Shifu Fatso to tuck us in. It's been less than a week and we are already slipping into the routine and becoming friendly little Kung Fu automatons. I've even put my book down in anticipation of lights out. We are too exhausted to get up to much anyway and an early night is the only way to stop our tiredness compounding on itself and wiping us out completely.

To make the whole training process reasonable, scientific and abundant, the school shall adjust teaching and training contents and develop entertainment activities, and so on.

Xiao Long Website.

I had previously underestimated the invigorating properties of instant tea. Lying bed, my trusty cuppa has stimulated me enough that I am finally able to identify the crackly tune being piped through the tannoy system. The recorded bugle calls are followed by a synthesised version of Beethoven's 'Ode to Joy'. It's among the best known pieces of music in the world, but I have been so disorientated the last few mornings that I couldn't place it. Interestingly Beethoven's works, a Chinese favourite since the 1920s, only had their Cultural Revolution ban lifted 1977.

Now I have named that tune, I can't help feel it's a little inappropriate to our surroundings, particularly at five o'clock in the a.m.

Today's warming exercises are performed on the pavement at the back of school and are a variation around the standard theme. Breakfast offers no variation at all, but morning assembly brings a curious sight. Shifu Fatso not only arrives fairly punctually, but carrying a basketball. We are even more surprised when he comes out with a new phrase, 'Goh pahk'.

My immediate thought is he's off on his hols and wants to prepare his luggage. Gesturing for us to follow, he troops us out the back gates, along the training field and up the road to Wulin Yuan (Martial Circles Park), a public park on the corner of our block. We've run around the outside of this park during morning warming, but I hadn't really noticed what it was in the dark.

This end of Dengfeng is so recently developed that there are still oddments of building rubble and materials littered about. Built in 2005, the local park is shiny new, but already showing signs of wear around the edges.

Wandering through the park, I recognise some scenes as those featured in the school brochure which might explain why I didn't recognise the school when we pulled up. Shifu conducts us through the landscaped garden, past the lake and to the basketball court where Shibu, Sanda and Yuan Shifu's groups are already lounging around. Most students are content to bask in the sunlight, but having a basketball and a basketball court some try to get a basketball game together.

Declining the offer to play, Victorian Dad takes the opportunity to reconnoitre the area and leaves me to run around dementedly trying to put a ball in a hole. Sometime later he appears from the opposite direction clutching a couple of ice creams. I instantly recall how VD has always been the bestest Dad of a Victorian nature and promptly arrange a substitute so I can take to the bench. Only teaching him the phrase, 'liang ge' (two of) was a genius idea that is already paying dividends. Go Park is turning out to be a lot more fun than Go Run.

VD's ice creams start a flurry of activity as everyone tries to borrow money off each other and pump him for directions. The pleasant sensation of stuffing chilled lard into my fat face makes me a soft touch for a couple of Yuan. I just hope no one makes the connection and capitalises on it in future.

Generally, one should be careful with Chinese milk products. Not only because of the recent melamine contamination scare, but also because of the Chinese inability to understand the concept of refrigeration. Purchasing ice cream, and other dairy products, from roadside stands carries a high risk of dysenteric illness as a result of improper storage, but supermarkets are often little better as they have been known to turn the refrigerators off at night to save electricity. Indeed, many small, independent convenience stores never even power their fridges and merely use them as snazzy storage cabinets.

In spite of these health concerns we all end up with an ice cream. I would be willing to place a small wager the ice cream guy will be there again next Saturday. Unless a bout of bacilli induced dysentery finishes us off for good, he is pretty much guaranteed the repeat business. Indeed, our quest to ignore common sense and jeopardise our personal health could turn out to be a nice little earner for him.

As I sit in the sunshine enjoying my ice cream, a little kid, of about three or four walks past with his parents. Heeding the call of nature, the little fellow brings his needs to the attention of his parents who encourage him to dispel in the path. Not even over a drain or into a bush. Even a dog would have found a tree. The kid stands in the middle of the public park relieving himself onto a pedestrian thoroughfare and his parents consider it perfectly acceptable behaviour. I'd go as far as to say they take pride in their offspring's activities. When he is done, they take his hand again, and continue down the path leaving a little puddle as a memento of his visit. It isn't enough to put me off my ice cream, but it's disconcerting nonetheless. I would have expected the Communist ethic to be more respectful of communal places. It's no wonder the park requires a veritable swarm of Parkies just to keep the place up to scratch.

Relishing the calorie content of my lard-cone, I sit back and watch the basketball only to be dumbfounded by the Shifus' skill level. They are hopeless. When the ball comes toward them they freeze in horror and go completely blank. I even see Shifu Fatso try to bounce a ball he's holding in both hands and fumble it. Don't get me wrong, I'm not a natural ball-sports person. I'm ok at ping-pong, and other hand-eye co-ordination activities, but I'm too gangly and lack the synchronicity for sports involving anything below the waist. However, you would expect these guys to have co-ordination by the bucket-load. Maybe it's because all they've done their whole lives is Kung Fu. Yuan Shifu is the only one with any ability for anything other than Kung Fu, he also has better English and is more switched-on in general.

Most students are glad to lounge around in the sun, but some have brought cameras intending to use the park for a photo opportunity. As soon as the Shifus spot the cameras they clamour to have their photos taken. Sanda Shifu is an avid photographic subject. He darts around sitting next to people, putting his arm around them and demanding his photo taken. He has his photo with me twice, despite having never spoken to me. It's a level of physical intimacy I'm not entirely happy with and results in some amusing pictures of me in half-feigned uncomfortable horror.

Jiandao Shou, (scissor hands), was popularised in 1970s Japanese camera commercials to the extent that East Asians are still unable to lift a camera without all and sundry getting their first two fingers in on the action. It's so contagious that we foreigners are soon addicted to it too.

The fun and games wears thin quickly for me and I'm glad when Shifu Fatso rounds us up. Lining up for the march back he says, 'Go four tonne class.'

No one moves. I know 'Fo' is the Chinese word for Buddha, so I guess we have to go to Buddhism Class, but I don't know where it is. Everyone is equally puzzled, despite the fact they must have been to Buddhism Class before. Seeing no signs of movement, Shifu Fatso expands on his instruction. He places his palms together in front of his chest and says, 'Om, om, om. You know? Om, om.'

The group look at him blankly which encourages a painful encore. Unable to take it anymore, I enquire, 'Is that Buddhism Class, Shifu?'

'Yes, Buddha'. A look of relief crosses his face, 'Buddha Class go, twenty minute', and with that we are dismissed.

Buddha Class takes place in a small unassuming room, next to the toilet, at the side of the training hall. All the foreign students, barring a few abstainers on religious grounds, are merged into one group and line up outside the door in order of time spent at the school. Once Yuan Shifu has prepared the dusty little room, by lighting the incense and turning on the cassette player, we file into the room and assume our positions from left to right in a semi-circle.

Yuan Shifu hands incense sticks to the first half-dozen people who take it in turn to approach the altar, bow before the image of Guanyin and plant their incense. The remainder of us address the altar, bow and return to our positions. Shibu Shifu then hands out sheets containing the chants printed in phonetics. Sheets in hand, we proceed clockwise around the room joining in as best we can. There's a slight technical problem with the chanting as the phonetics barely work in English, a language spoken by, at best, half the group. The mix of nationalities in the room pronounce the sounds differently so we end up with a disjointed chant as we stumble over the words. Constantly out of synch, we are unable to create any real resonance.

A single lap sees us back at our starting position where we sit down for a bit of a meditate. The first few positions are marked by faded, round cushions, which are taken up by the most senior students. New guys get to sit on the floor strewn with bits of pointy masonry fallen from the ceiling. I could feel the debris under my feet as we walked around the room and as I crouch to the floor manage to quickly brush a space amongst the chunks to sit in. I don't get them all and the tiny ones I missed make me wish I had one of those cushions. At least the incense, a staple of Buddhism that carries prayers to the heavens, is masking a little of the odour from next door.

Buddhism class is a bit of a misnomer in that there is no actual teaching about Buddhism. It's really more of a meditation session. This is fine and dandy for VD and I. Having attended meditation classes through our martial art with the BKFA (British Kung Fu Association) we have a reasonable understanding of what's occurring. Thankfully most appear to be in a similar position, but a few are left bemused by the whole event. Without instruction, all they can do is copy the external actions of meditating. As there is no way to see what else is happening they just sit cross-legged and bored.

I'm a big fan of the old meditating as it's indoor work with no heavy lifting. Ironic then that it was this very sitting quietly that, according to legend, was the basis of Kung Fu in the first place. The claim being that Kung Fu was created from a series of exercises designed to increase the Shaolin monk's endurance for the prolonged meditations which are an integral part of Chan Buddhism. Giving rise to the Shaolin expression, 'Chan wu he yi' (meditation and martials arts are one).

The word Chan, is short for 'Chan Na', the Chinese phonetic translation from the Sanskrit term 'Dhyana' meaning meditation. Western thinking tends to regard meditation as a devotional, religious exercise. Chan simplifies the concept to simply being fully aware of the moment. The aim being to clear the mental noise that inhibits complete awareness and silence the internal dialog caused by our minds constantly processing sense perceptions and making assumptions from them. In the moment, these subconscious thoughts are subdued, delusions dissolve and what remains is what is. To a lesser extent this end can be achieved in any act that consumes the moment. Thus, sitting quietly or practicing Kung Fu can both be acts of meditation.

Chan meditation practice is a deceptively simple process. Ideally one sits cross-legged or in a lotus position, although seated on a chair is acceptable, in a quiet place with fresh air and little chance of being disturbed. The 'bai hui' point on top of the head is aligned with the pelvis base so that the spine is erect. Hands are cupped in front of the waist with the little fingers resting on the 'dantian', just below the navel. Males place the left hand fingers on the right fingers and the reverse for females. Thumbprints should be lightly touching.

The range of focus is withdrawn into oneself and the process of breathing is calmly observed, with attention given to each inhalation and exhalation. Concentrating on the breath flowing through the body clears the mind. Any thoughts that do creep in should be let go.

Sitting in my own little world, I'm obviously not focused enough as I slowly become aware of a disturbance in the force. Narrowly opening my eyes to investigate, I see Knobby gurning and generally larking about with South American guy. I nearly get annoyed with them, but remember something Delam, my meditation teacher, told me, 'You should thank fools for giving you the opportunity to practice your patience'. Personally, I would prefer to kick them up the arse. However, Buddha teaches us to rise above our emotions. Instead, I acknowledge the thought and, disassociating it from emotion, let it pass like a floating cloud and return to my natural state of an empty mind.

About thirty minutes later, we stand up for another wander around and bit of a chant, then it's back to the old meditating. I tend to lose track of time while meditating and before I know it, it's time stand up, bow at the altar and file out.

Lined up to be dismissed, Shibu tells us off for messing about in Buddhist class. This isn't aimed specifically at Knobby and SA guy; the whole group is held accountable. One of the Germans takes exception, 'Why tell us all? Tell people who do it.'

Knobby sullenly mumbles something about 'unfair' and 'not his fault'. Being a child, Knobby is physically incapable of sitting quietly for any length of time and probably would have done better with some instruction. South American guy, on the other hand, despite being old enough to know better, refuses to acknowledge any fault on his part. Taking the rebuke personally, he gets in a pre-emptive defence, 'I don't know man. I'm not a damn Buddhist'.

Whenever he gets corrected for anything his immediate response is to go on the attack. I'm amazed he hasn't been thrown out of school some time ago. What I don't get is: if you are so opposed to the Buddhism class, why go? There's a fat, sulky American girl in the other group who is partial to a good pontificate about her religion and why she doesn't attend Buddhism class. However, in all fairness, she doesn't attend the class.

We are also told off for eating outside school. Shibu is adamant our levels of illness are a direct result of dining out, cautioning us that, 'You get sickness. Only eat school or fast food or you get...' he pauses to choke back a laugh and attempts to pronounce the word diarrhoea.

Not only is it a difficult word for him to pronounce, but the very thought of it creases him up with embarrassed laughter so that, rather fittingly, the word explodes from him in small bursts.

Frankly I'm impressed it's in his vocabulary at all, although it's probably a term he gets to hear on a regular basis from his students. It's likely the most commonly spoken English word at school. Personally, I'm not convinced outside catering is the cause of all our woe, but Shibu is determined to give us graphic, semi-comical descriptions of places we shouldn't eat because they are not as clean as the school and what the result will entail. With these delightful images in mind we are dismissed for lunch.

At afternoon training Shibu Shifu turns up with a football and takes all the foreign students out onto the dusty field, next to the bonfire, at the back of school. Some students choose to abstain and just sit and observe the antics. The rest of us split into two groups and knock the ball about a bit. I've always been terrible at football, being completely uncoordinated from the waist down, however the Shifus take lack of ball-skill to a whole new level of sporting incompetence. Shifu Fatso turns up while we are playing and joins in the game with another dazzling display of ineptitude. He is so comically amateurish as to be embarrassing to watch. Topping his basketball demonstration, at one point, he attempts to kick, and misses, a ball he's holding in both hands. Considering that football was allegedly invented in China around 4,700 years ago, with a game called 'cuju' (kickball), created to teach soldiers about cooperation and vigilance, I can't help feel they haven't moved on much since.

Throughout the day I have been shocked by the Shifus' sporting ability. I was expecting them to be supermen, but today I have seen them attempt to play basketball, football and table tennis and they are absolutely hopeless. So much so that this is the only time we can get our own back. Even the novices amongst us can run rings around them. These fun and games are a pleasant enough diversion, but it's not what I came here for and is merely using up my time and energy. I could have stayed in Blighty and been rubbish at football. If this happens again next week, I won't join in.

Lined up to be dismissed for dinner, we announce our intention to visit the temple tomorrow. The formal invitation to the group only brings one other forward: Juha. Julie has already visited the temple and Knobby dismisses the temple out of hand saying he has no interest in it. One of Knobby's wonderful gifts is his unerring ability to dumbfound. Just when I think I've seen it all, along comes Knobby to offer a remark or action so inane as to bring tears of wonder to my eyes. I just don't understand why anyone would travel half way around the world to learn Kung Fu and not go the extra ten minutes up the road to its fabled birthplace. At the same time, it's fine with me. I'm satisfied we have done the right thing with the invitation and am equally happy with the outcome. Julie is cool and would have been welcome, but I'm glad I don't have to spend my day off being entertained by Knobby. I'm sure the pilgrimage experience would have been marred by someone constantly telling me it was 'boring' and demanding to be the centre of attention through the medium of toilet humour.

I have no such concerns with Juha. The Finnish giant, on leave from the army, is a diamond geezer. A good few inches taller than me, and considerably wider, he towers over the Chinese students. He doesn't speak any Chinese and fell for the website hook, line, sinker and little rowing boat so he's understandably a tad disillusioned in the whole affair. However, with typical Nordic stoicism, he makes light of conditions in his room, lack of shower, broken light and toilet, saying the Finnish Army provides better living conditions when he is on exercises in the woods. He doesn't bat an eyelid at spurious charges and merely shrugged his shoulders at spending three days alone in quarantine.

It's not like he's on his own in this situation, but he certainly has the right idea: the only way to survive here is to treat it as a bit of a joke. It's just the way China operates and getting all worked up about it doesn't help. It really is the perfect place to practice Buddhist detachment.

However, he does complain about the food. Being a big lad, Juha needs his nourishment. Used to a level of nutrition that's simply not available here, he struggles to maintain his energy even more than the rest of us. I'm not familiar with Finnish cuisine, but, judging from the size of Juha, it must be highly nutritious stuff. I joke he is a tank for the Finnish Army, but Juha doesn't get it and claims he is the smallest of his family and friends. I can only pray Britain never has a diplomatic upset with Finland.

In anticipation of our grand day out, I approach Shibu and ask him to sign a pass ready for the morrow. Our intention is to be up and away as soon as possible in order to make the most of our time. Shibu is having none of it, repeatedly insisting, 'Tomorrow I sign. I be there. It my job.'

My experience with Shibu to date suggests the process is unlikely to be as streamlined as he claims, but, getting nowhere with badgering him, I have no option than to take him at his word. Defeated, I take my leave to capitalise on the optional free training session and practice the new form. It's the only training opportunity I have had today and I intend to make the most of it. Reaching the gym, it's apparent the Shifus aren't the only ones winding down for the weekend; there are very few in attendance and none go the distance.

Practicing in the big, dusty hall on my own is a surreal experience, but leaves me satisfied that at least I got some training in today. The plaintive cry of the tortured bugle trapped forever on tape echoes through the empty hall to curtail my fun. I'm disappointed to quit the gym, but respond like a good little, track-suited Pavlovian dog. Turning off the light behind me, I head down the stairs. A quick wash and brush up sees me tucked up nicely just in time for our Shifu's visit and I'm out like a light.

Shaolin, Shaolin - How many heroes admire you.
Shaolin, Shaolin - How many amazing stories mention you.
Your superb martial arts are unique.
Your power shakes the four corners of the world.
Established long ago in ancient times
Shaolin's glorious reputation
a thousand years old mysterious temple.
Everybody yearns for Songshan Valley
the fascinating home of martial arts.
Your world famous reputation will last forever.

Theme song from the movie 'Shaolin Temple'.

Sunday is the day we've been waiting for. Our day off gives us the opportunity to visit the Shaolin Temple itself. The fabled birthplace of Kung Fu and Chan Buddhism, Shaolin is a Mecca for Chan Buddhists and martial artists alike and essentially why we came to China in the first place.

Until this week, VD and I were not practitioners of Shaolin Kung Fu. Our Kung Fu style, Lau Gar Kuen, is from Guanxi Province, but, as one of the Five Ancestor Styles, it originated in Shaolin making the temple our spiritual home.

It's often claimed that all Kung Fu originated at Shaolin and all martial arts derive from it. Though denied by many historians, this creation myth has become so deeply ingrained in the national psyche as to have blurred the line between fiction and historical fact. The commonly touted, and contentious, expression, 'Tian xia gong fu chu Shaolin, Shaolin gong fu zhu tian xia' (Shaolin is the source of all martial arts, but Shaolin is still the best) has done much to cement this claim and today Shaolin is generally regarded as the home of martial arts.

Many countries, including China, have a martial history dating back thousands of years, significantly predating the Shaolin Temple. Therefore, Shaolin is probably not the birthplace of all martial arts. To quote the 1919 Jingwu Association Anniversary book, 'Self-defence, being natural to everybody, the art is known to all people on the globe almost since the birth of humanity.'

If martial arts developed independently over the world, Shaolin has another claim to fame as the place where spiritual and martial came together in Chan Buddhism. Being officially recognised in 1983 as the National Key Buddhist Temple, gave credence to Shaolin's previous self-proclaimed title of, 'No. 1 Famous Temple under Heaven'.

Our aim to be at the temple gates when they open at 7.30am was vetoed by Shibu Shifu last night. Used to getting up at 5am, we have a fantastic lie in, but are left kicking about for an hour after breakfast until the official sign-out time.

I'm embarrassed to report that, yet again, I let my faith in human nature get the better of me and took Shibu at his word. At 7.55 I present myself, along with my pre-filled slips, on the steps of our building where Shibu assured me he would be.

At 8.05 I go back upstairs to the DVD room in case I've misunderstood his explicit instructions. A handful of students are already waiting there, but no Shibu. Combining forces, we split up to cover more ground, and run through a repeat performance of Thursday's logging out farce.

Once cornered, Shibu is both baffled as to why anyone would be looking for him and simultaneously affronted we haven't waited where he said he would be, despite having told several of us different locations. Rather than get involved in a complicated debate, I just push the notes at him. Begrudgingly Shibu collects everyone's notes and pretends to read each intently before signing.

It's 8:25 before we are out the gate. There is a bus service, but it only departs from town when it reaches capacity. With time in short supply the better option is a cab. Juha and VD bundle into the back as I get in next to the driver and say, 'Shaolin Si'. With a grunt and a nod, we are off.

It's too easy. I'm not used to things going to plan and don't want to end up with egg on my face if I can't organise something as simple as getting us ten minutes up the road. At this point my track record isn't particularly impressive. To nip any potential misunderstanding in the bud, I get out my pad and write down the three characters for Shaolin Temple. Waving it at the driver gets another grunt and nod, 'Shaolin Si, ok.'

Either he's not impressed with my second-rate calligraphy or he's offended at the suggestion he doesn't know where the town's most famous landmark is. Of course, he knows Shaolin, it's a must in the Dengfeng taxi drivers' Knowledge. Not only is Shaolin the biggest tourist attraction for miles, but we are three westerners with shaved heads, wearing Shaolin Temple school tracksuits. Heading away from town there are few other places we could be going. I shut up, let him do his job and enjoy the ride.

The Shaolin Temple dates back to AD495, when Emperor Xiaowen ordered the construction of many Buddhist temples for the Indian monk Buddhabhadra (known in Chinese as Bato). Named after its location, the Songshan Shaolin Temple is situated in the forest of the Shaoshi Mountain in the Songshan mountain range. The 'shao' refers to Mount Shaoshi, 'lin' means forest and 'si' is Buddhist temple. Thus, the name means Buddhist temple in the woods of Mount Shaoshi.

The little temple managed quite well, quietly minding its own business, until AD527 when another Indian monk came along. Following years of reclusive meditation Damo (Bodhidharma), in a sudden flash of inspiration, invented Chan Buddhism.

Descended from a warrior caste famed for stick fighting, Damo would have understood the importance of physical exercise and what we now call Yoga. Aware of the interconnectedness of body and soul, Damo was dismayed at the monks' level of personal fitness and set about instructing them in stretching and breathing techniques. The monks were likely amenable to these ideas as the same theory is central to the Huangdi Neijing or Yellow Emperor's Classic, an ancient Chinese medical text written at least 500 years earlier. Similarly, China also had a long martial history dating back to the Xia dynasty (around 2000BC). Damo's techniques evolved to incorporate indigenous Chinese fighting arts and holistic medicine to become Shaolin Kung Fu. Shaolin's golden period came in the Ming dynasty (1368-1644). Scholars and government officials came to Shaolin on retreat to learn Buddhism and, in turn, contributed their knowledge of medicine, martial arts, painting and poetry. Under these conditions Shaolin culture flourished and, absorbing these influences, evolved and became famous throughout China. This period spawned many fantastic tales, which have become folklore and commonly appear in martial arts history, fiction and cinema to this day.

Tales of the monks' abilities spread and the temple's wealth grew along with its fame as it gained more land and disciples. However, its fame and wealth became a two-edged sword for Shaolin was seen, not only as a rich target to bandits and warlords, but also as a potential threat to the establishment. As a result, Shaolin Temple has been destroyed and rebuilt many times during its long history.

1928 saw a devastating attack from the Nationalist army, commanded by the warlord Shi Yousan, which destroyed 90 percent of the monastery in a blaze lasting over 40 days. This fire practically demolished the temple and many priceless manuscripts from the library were lost in a catastrophe from which Shaolin has still to recover.

The Temple's land was appropriated by Communist forces in 1948, but the most recent assault took place during the 1960s Cultural Revolution which targeted religious orders. The monks who hadn't fled were jailed and the monastery purged of Buddhist materials, leaving it all but barren.

In the late 1970s Deng Xiaoping's 'Reform and Opening' policy officially made martial and monastic practices acceptable again and a handful of monks drifted back to eke out a meagre existence in the ravaged complex. Then, in 1982, Jet Li's movie 'Shaolin Temple' exploded on Asia and a deluge of sightseers and wannabe students flocked to the area. Shaolin Village sprang up overnight to cater for their needs and Kung Fu 'Folk Masters' appeared out of the woodwork opening their own schools in a bid to capitalise on the renewed interest.

As Jet Li remembers on his official website:

'When we arrived in the area in 1979 to start filming the first movie, the temple and the grounds were very dilapidated. The Cultural Revolution had only ended a few years before. There was nothing left inside, and the exterior of the buildings hadn't been kept in very good order either. There were only three monks living at the temple. One was the abbot, one the gatekeeper, and the last one was the caretaker/cook. As far as we knew, none of them had any particular martial prowess and nobody in the area practiced wushu.

After the movie came out, though, the temple gained fame throughout China and the world. By the time we returned three years later for more filming, the place had changed completely. All the roads within a four or five kilometre radius of the temple were lined with signs promoting Shaolin businesses of all kinds: Shaolin cola, Shaolin beer, Shaolin cigarettes…and school after school of Shaolin martial arts.'

This tourism resulted in an increase in Shaolin's revenue which was reinvested in the area but, with no real figurehead to give direction, development was haphazard at best. At this stage Shaolin was in danger of becoming a victim of its own success as, without regulation, Buddhism, the original purpose of Shaolin, was forced to take a back seat and the area became little more than a tourist trap.

In 1999, the venerable Shi Yongxin, was inaugurated as Shaolin's 30th official Abbot and set about putting Shaolin back on course. Under Shi Yongxin the temple experiencing rapid change, reclaimed the Shaolin name as a brand and cleaned up the area in a bid for UNESCO World Heritage status.

The reclamation process saw the burgeoning village that had sprung up around Shaolin demolished in 2001 amid a controversial forced relocation programme and the whole area landscaped. Similarly, many temple buildings erected since the 1980s were rebuilt in a more historically accurate fashion according to photographs taken by the Japanese during the 1920s occupation.

However, not all the renovations have been retro fitting: modern visitor facilities have been added and the new Zhengshao Highway improved accessibility by halving the journey time from Zhengzhou to Shaolin to around two hours. In fact, the very road we are on now.

A laminated picture of Chairman Mao hangs from the rear-view mirror. Deified with a halo of light beams emanating from his head, he smiles at us benevolently like a fat Buddha. Our school is only fifteen minutes from the temple and, courtesy of the new road and the driver's guardian angel, it's an uneventful drive.

Later than intended, but with the day still brightening, we pull up to the new visitor reception area. Until recently this was the Shaolin Village, but since the renovation cars are not allowed beyond this point and even the sounding of horns is banned.

An old hand with the day-trippers, our driver voluntarily vacates the taxi and takes our photo in front of the monk statue next to the big rock declaring this to be Songshan National Park.

The visitor centre is a modern courtyard with shops around the perimeter and ornamental flower beds. At the far end are shiny, yellow turnstiles and a ticket office. Few shops are open as we arrive, but the ticket office already has a swarm of people around it.

As an example of Shaolin's appeal to the masses, the entrance price to the grounds is 100Y, around £10. Not particularly expensive in the grand scheme of things, until compared to the prices of everything else in China. For frame of reference, entrance to the Forbidden City in Beijing is 40Y. And in this neck of the woods Y100 is considered a pretty penny.

A surly youth plucks my ticket from my hand, presses it against the turnstile's panel and motions me forward. I'm not sure China has got the hang of automated self-service.

I am just through the gates when I'm approached by a random Chinese guy. Cutting a dash in his cheap nylon suit jacket and jeans, he points to his camera and then to himself. Assuming he wants me to take a photograph of him with his girlfriend, I say, 'Sure' and reach for his camera. No. He hands the camera to his girlfriend, puts his arm around me, and adopts the classic 'V' sign favoured by East Asian photographic subjects. I join in with the scissor action and pose self-consciously with this stranger and, not a little baffled, say, 'Xie xie' (Thank you) and turn to walk away.

'No, no!' The guy's girlfriend also wants a photograph with me. Slightly more comfortable with the woman's embrace, I reward her with another dazzling, but confused, smile.

As a special bonus to their sightseeing trip of ancient cultural monuments this lucky couple get to take home a photograph with today's special attraction: a befuddled foreigner. I can imagine the proud pair showing off their holiday snaps when they get home, 'This is me at Shaolin Temple, and this is me with a dim-witted white bloke.'

I amble away feeling a little surreal about the whole thing. About four metres from the scene, another woman comes up to me, proffering a camera and wanting some of the same for her family album. This pretty much sets the scene for the day. Eventually I become a little blasé about the whole thing and just join anyone having their photos taken. It will add an extra dimension to their slideshows when they are presented to family and friends. 'Aunty, who is this funny looking man with his arm around you? He looks like he's constipated'.

Snubbing the electric stretch golf-cart, in favour of soaking up the atmosphere we set off down the tree lined avenue. At regular intervals are phone booths each dignified with a sitting Buddha on the roof, like a bizarre Bat Phone. I wonder if Buddha is sitting at the other end waiting for his red phone to light up.

The recent renovations have made a fantastic difference to the overall ambience. They've certainly made a good job landscaping, one would never guess that until recently there was an entire village here, but wandering a little off the track you can still discern the odd house-brick peeking from the dry earth.

There are a handful of shabby convenience food stalls scattered along the way. I can't begin to imagine how tacky it used to be with the flight simulators and video game arcades. Although, I see the threadbare camel has survived the cut and still offering his services as a unique Shaolin photo opportunity. He's not getting many takers though. I'm reassured that I'm a more desirable photographic subject than a flea-bitten camel or at least a cheaper alternative.

Prior to the relocation, much of the land around Shaolin was occupied by Tagou Kung Fu School and they still have access to the dry earth fields at the roadside. Through the trees, we catch glimpses of large squads of Tagou students going through their paces. Some visitors stop to watch, but it has little interest for us. It's the same thing we see and do at school. They even have similar tracksuits to ours.

We also pass the Shaolin Zen Hotel, which looks lovely, particularly compared to our school, but the exorbitant rates and short class hours meant it didn't make the final round of our selection process.

Rounding the bend, we come face to face with the classic, postcard image of the red gatehouse known as the Mountain Gate. A pair of stone lions guard the broad steps to the famous brass studded doors. Above the doorway the golden calligraphy written by Emperor Qing Kangxi in 1704 proudly proclaims, 'Shao Lin Si.'

Despite being early, and out of season, there are still enough people around that we have to wait to get a clear shot for a photograph. The electric golf carts shuttling a steady supply of people down the path already make it feel more like a tourist attraction than a monastery.

Predictably, Shaolin sees a lot more visitors during the summer months and sight-seeing and photo opportunities are limited by the sheer multitude. Out of season and early morning is definitely the way to go.

Either side of Maitreya, the Welcoming Buddha, the doorway is guarded by Buddha's protectors, the Generals Heng and Ha. Manifestations of Vajra, the blue and brown monsters tower over any visitors. Given their unique skills they are likely personifications of Kung Fu techniques. They're certainly an impressive pair to have on your side in a fight.

A less formidable guard protects the turnstile. A disinterested young monk, preoccupied with his mobile phone, takes our tickets and presses them to the machine panel without raising his head. It's not unusual for monks to use current technology, but it's inappropriate in a customer-facing role. I console myself with the thought he may not be an actual monk, probably just a guy in a costume hired to take tickets. The automated turnstile is friendlier with its welcoming, 'Qing jing.'

In the Mountain Gate rear wall is a statue of Wei Tuo. Positioned with his back to Maitreya, Wei Tuo, is the guardian of Buddhist monasteries as mentioned in the Golden Light Sutra.

A tree lined walkway (the Forest of Stele aka Beilin) slopes gently upward. Between the ancient trees are stele dedicated to the temple by notables with a thousand-year-old Maiden Hair tree at the top of the rise.

At four stories, the Drum and Bell Towers, originally built in 1300, are the tallest buildings in the compound. Rebuilt to their former grandeur, with a new drum and bell installed they are currently closed to the public. Outside the Bell tower, the original bell's shattered corpse reminds us of our mortality. Nearly two metres tall and cast with inscriptions over its surface, it's still impressive in death. Before the Bell Tower are steles depicting Li Shimin's gratitude for his rescue and his decree to the Shaolin Temple enabling the monks to consume a non-Buddhist diet and train martial arts.

Kimnara Hall is dedicated to Shaolin's patron saint, whose Sanskrit name, Vajrapani, translates as Thunderbolt Wielder. One of the earliest Bodhisattvas of Mahayana Buddhism, he is the protector and guide of the Buddha and symbolises the Buddha's power. As protector, Kimnara has appeared and saved Shaolin several times. The latest being in AD1351 during the Yuan Dynasty's Red Turban Rebellion. With the monastery under siege, a lowly kitchen worker leapt into the oven and emerged as a giant wielding a long fire poker. He fought off the bandits and the monks realised the kitchen worker was Kimnara in disguise.

Another story, told on a stele erected by Shaolin Abbot Zuduan (1115-1167) during the Song Dynasty, references a Tang Dynasty legend of the Shaolin monk Sengchou (480-560) who gained supernatural ability after praying to Kimnara and being force-fed raw meat.

These tales may well be metaphoric, but Kimnara has certainly influenced Shaolin for over 1500 years. He is credited as the originator of Shaolin's famous Staff method and many Kung Fu forms include a stance of Kimnara astride a mountain in tribute to the deity.

The Kimnara hall and statues, destroyed in 1928, were re-created in 1984 and now houses a golden statue of a fiery red haired Kimnara draped with a yellow robe. According to the Lotus Sutra, Kimnara is a manifestation of Guanyin. To illustrate this, the statue has a tiny Guanyin over his head. In front of the hall, a Ming Dynasty stone tablet bears the four guises of Kimnara from the Lotus Sutra.

Wenshu (Manjusri) Hall is dedicated to the Bodhisattva of enlightened wisdom and contains the Stone of Damo's Shadow. Damo meditated for nine years leaving his shadow etched into the wall of his cave. The rock was cut from the cave and moved to the temple for safety. Peering through the condensation on the glass case, I can just make out the image of the man himself. It's more difficult to make out in the flesh than in the photographs I've seen and I'm not sure I understand the process that left these marks.

Waylaid by another family photography event, I turn around to no VD and Juha. Bored waiting, they've wandered off leaving me lost in the grounds of Shaolin Temple. I'm sure there's a song in there somewhere. The Chinese just can't get enough of me today. I'm still at a loss for a plausible explanation of people wanting to treasure the memory of our meeting. I'm unsure whether to take it as a compliment or an insult. In my opinion, VD is far funnier looking than I and Juha is a giant, but they are not getting a look-in on the photographing front. Juha is typically unperturbed by everything, however, I detect some sour grapes from VD, especially when he puts forward the theory I am being mistaken for the Elephant Man.

Constructed according to the traditional format, the monastery compound isn't large and is already crowded with rubberneckers. The seven main buildings along the centre line were prioritised for renovation, but many side buildings are so recently rebuilt they aren't open to the public yet or are just shells sadly void of contents.

Moved along by the crowds, we pass the closed buildings and stare through narrow doorways into empty halls. Pausing to read the few information boards adds little. They mostly say the same thing: the building's name and when it was rebuilt. Combined with being reopened to the West, China's internal travel policy has only recently been relaxed and the Chinese are struggling with the concept of tourism. Specifically, with determining the middle ground between making money and providing something in return.

The highest level of the compound contains some of the more famous buildings. Of these I particularly want to see the Baiyi Hall which, along with a brass statue of Guanyin (Avalokitesvara) the Bodhisattva of Compassion, houses murals dating from the Qing Dynasty depicting historical Shaolin scenes. The north wall shows Minister Lin Qing watching the monks' training. Allegedly, Wugulun is pictured in this mural. He's the guy in middle with the moustache. Other walls show monks being instructed with weapons, the story of the thirteen monks saving Li Shimin and the story of Kimnara defending the temple against the Red Turban Army. To protect these ancient artefacts, a barrier has been placed in the doorway. Little of the iconic works can be made out from the gloomy interior.

Opposite is Dizang Hall which originally contained statues of the Ten Kings of Hell. Ransacked and left with a collapsed roof during the Cultural Revolution, the hall was restored in 1979. The walls are now embedded with jade murals showing scenes from the scriptures. In a strange yin/yang fashion the front wall depicts disciples listening to Dharma talks by Amitabha while the north and south walls show Dizang (Ksitigarbha) the Bodhisattva of Hell Beings. The Hieronymus Bosch style visions of Buddhist hell are fascinating but, with no concept of Buddhist mythology, the pantheon of Buddhas and demons is a mystery to me.

It's the last building along the centreline that VD has set his heart upon seeing. Qianfo Dian or Thousand Bodhisattva Hall. Built in 1588 during the Ming dynasty this building is also known as the Pilu Pavillion as it contains a wooden alcove housing a brass statue of the Bodhisattva Pilu (Vairocara). Pilu embodies the Buddhist concept of emptiness and the mural along the side and back walls depict the 500 Arhats worshiping Pilu. Originally designed to house idols and scriptures, Qianfo Hall was used for Kung Fu practice when the Qing government repressed the monk's activities. The indented floor bears the scars of four hundred years of stomping monks.

I also want to see Chuipu Hall, the home of Xilai Chapel, but it's the surrounding rooms that interest me. The outer rooms contain 236 wood and plaster life-size statues of monks depicting Shaolin martial arts and historical scenes, including the Eighteen Luohan movements and the rescue of the Tang Emperor's son, Li Shimin.

I've seen parts of the display in books and TV shows and they make for an impressive sight. There's so much knowledge represented in this hall that there is a Shaolin joke which goes, 'Spending five minutes in Chuipu gives you Kung Fu.'

The rooms are closed. I guess I'll have to learn Kung Fu the hard way. Instead, there is a monk selling miscellaneous Shaolin knickknacks from a table and one room has become a weapons shop. I ask the monk about the hall with the figures. He just shrugs his shoulders and motions to the unimpressive array of tat before him. Under the auspices of Shi Yongxin the Shaolin merchandising machine has gone into overdrive. Among the many gaudy gewgaws available is a range of Shaolin food products. Faced with the tacky charm, I can't resist a tub of Shaolin cookies. They'll make an excellent novelty gift.

Jaded by the crowds, hawkers and impromptu photo calls, we step through an archway to a whole different world. Ciyun Dian (Clouds of Loving Kindness Hall), or the Listening Courtyard, is completely silent. The bustle on the other side of the wall seems a million miles away. Renovated in 1984 the courtyard was expanded to include the Stele Corridor (Beilang), a covered walkway around the perimeter containing a collection of 124 stone tablets presented by various emperors and notables since AD500. The most recent stele features the lyrics to the theme song from Jet Li's film Shaolin Temple which is responsible for defining Shaolin's present incarnation.

With no crowd to carry us along, we are able to peruse the stele at our leisure. The tranquillity is such we fall into a reverent silence. Sat with our own thoughts, a trio of monks materialise. Spanning three generations, the novice and master observe the senior student practising Guandao before joining the master who is enjoying a cigarette break.

Shaolin's turbulent recent history means it is effectively missing a generation. With the temple being reborn in the 1980s the majority of the monks are relatively young, so you don't see any wizened, old, white-bearded guys like in the movies. As a matter of fact, the head abbot, the venerable Shi Yongxin, is only a couple of years older than me.

It's a scene we are privileged to see. The monks' day-to-day activities normally take place out of sight in areas either side of the central axis like the training grounds, dormitory and meditation hall. This group may also have come to Ciyun Hall for the tranquillity and I'm flattered they are comfortable enough with our presence to carry on with their own thing.

At the courtyard's centre is a shrine to Guanyin, the Bodhisattva with a thousand hands and eyes, to which I offer incense as a thank you for letting us light upon this magical place. Without Ciyun Hall my memory of Shaolin Temple would have been very different. Juha remains as enigmatic as ever, but VD's words echo my thoughts. Ciyun Hall is undoubtedly my favourite part of the temple grounds and one I am sure to return to.

Feeling much calmer, we exit the main temple where the crowds around the Mountain Gate have built up considerably during our chill-out time. Normally a reserved people, the Chinese are mad keen on being photographed. Jostling for position, they are fully prepared to make a spectacle of themselves as long as it's captured for posterity.

Many others are surging around the bustling stalls of tat in the vain hope of a bargain. Evidently most tourists have already been collared as they are wearing 'fozhu' prayer necklaces. These huge beads draped around the neck in a semi-comedic fashion are the Shaolin equivalent of a Kiss Me Quick hat. Many tourists are more interested in us foreigners than in the site itself. They should do a T-shirt, 'I went to Shaolin and all I got was a lousy photo with a laowai.'

If these antics seem disrespectful, I have to consider my own presence here. Fighting the urge to run amok amongst the stalls and throw the money-changers out of the temple, I face the dilemma that sooner or later confronts all sightseers. While tourism defiles the sanctity of the monastery, without tourist revenue the temple would not be enjoying its current reconstruction and I probably wouldn't be here.

Only the holy person can understand the way,
then one may attain wisdom and bliss.
Using the whole to see the principles, you may understand the way.
We must spread Chan like rays of sun all over the world.
All the branches of Buddhism celebrate the same root.
Clarity and stillness are deep as the sea.
When you abandon attachments, four true face emerges.
Only virtue is never ending, your pure heart never changes.
When your heart is still, its brightness will dispel the darkness.
Your true nature is the highest, if you are loyal, upright and kind,
you will receive happiness and peace.
Always remember your Buddha heart.
Following the spirit of Huike, this is the way to Buddhahood.

The Shaolin Generation Poem by Abbot Fu Yu (AD1260).

Doorways either side of the Mountain Gate lead to smaller compounds. To the right is the entrance to the Shaolin post office where you can send letters with a Shaolin postmark. On the left is the Shaolin Pharmacy Bureau. The disciplines of Buddhism, martial arts and medicine developed alongside each other at Shaolin and, like Chan and Kung Fu, Traditional Chinese Medicine is also regarded as a treasure of the Chinese nation.

Built in AD1220 by Abbot Zhilong, the pharmacy was closed in the late Qing Dynasty around 1860 due to frequent warfare and only reopened in 2004. Now a registered company, the Shaolin Yaoju is a research institution for the preservation and development of Shaolin traditional medicine alongside modern medicines.

As with most recently renovated parts of the temple, the Medicine Courtyard is a plain affair. The only feature is a brick pedestal in the courtyard proudly displaying an imp-like figure engraved with medical terms. Frozen forever in an imbecilic grin, patches of his brass body are worn shiny from millions of molesting hands. Not to be left out, I give his belly a quick rub as we pass.

Curiously, the covered walkway around this courtyard contains nothing but a punch bag. Apparently keen to vent some frustration, VD says, 'Hold my coat' and lets loose. Juha needs no encouragement to get in on the action himself. As he lays into the bag, an old lady wanders over and, delighting in his antics, kindly accompanies the Finnish fist thrower with, 'Heys' and 'Hahs'.

I leave the old lady to enjoy the show and investigate the Medicine Hall. Inside, a couple of bored looking monks stand behind a counter in a barren room. I've got to say it's not the most interesting Chinese Pharmacy I've ever been in. It has none of the jars of horrors that my local TCM doctor loves to display. There's not even a plastic skeleton or a waving cat. However, they must be doing something right as the Medicine Bureau now seeks to expand the promotion of Chan Medicine by building a charitable hospital in Dengfeng.

Interest in the punch bag exhausted, and with no other old ladies to entertain, there is nothing else here to keep us amused. But Shaolin is more than the main temple complex. Many significant locations are scattered amongst the forests and hills. With its vast age and turbulent history some notable sites have been lost to posterity and others now little more than ruins, but some gems remain. The Pagoda Forest is more fortunate as it is relatively well preserved.

We fend our way through the souvenir vendors at the Mountain Gate and head half a kilometre west to Talin. Unlike many translations, the term Pagoda Forest derives directly from the Chinese name with 'ta' meaning pagoda and 'lin' meaning forest.

Pagodas were introduced to China from India along with Buddhism. 'Pagoda' being a Sanskrit term meaning 'grave'. According to legend,

Sakyamuni's disciples asked how to mark his grave after his death. In response, he pointed to the Buddhists' common articles of book, bell and bowl and his disciples based his tomb design on these items. Below the pagodas are underground chambers containing bones, scriptures and relics. Shaolin pagodas blend this design with traditional Chinese architecture by adding a pointed temple at the top.

Shaolin's early pagodas were built of wood and have not survived the passage of time and many others were damaged or destroyed during Shaolin's history. Estimates vary, but approximately seventy pagodas have been lost. Similarly, it's difficult to be precise about the number of remaining pagodas, official figures say 228 with another 18 scattered throughout the grounds. There is a story that Emperor Qianlong sent 500 soldiers to count the pagodas at Shaolin and was still unable to determine an exact figure.

The remaining pagodas are stone and brick structures of up to seven layers and carry inscriptions about the interred monk and his achievements. Smaller than pagodas for Buddhist relics, their shape and style vary depending on the fashion when they were built. Despite many pagodas being lost, Shaolin still has the largest group of ancient pagodas in China, with tombs dating from the Tang dynasty (618-907) to the present day. Spanning such a long period, the Pagoda Forest is a historical record of architecture, carvings and calligraphy across the dynasties.

With fifteen hundred years of history, everything at Shaolin has a story. This tree was planted by a certain notable character, that pot was made to commemorate a particular event, those signs were written by Emperor so-and-so. None of this information is available to the casual observer and all requires serious effort to unearth. I suspect that the majority of visitors are unaware of all but the most significant attractions.

Similarly, there are many historical and cultural gems in the Pagoda Forest, but I am only aware of the more famous among them. The oldest recorded pagoda belongs to the Tang dynasty Chan Master Fawan. This simple stupa on a two-tiered brick pedestal is dated AD791. There may be older pagodas in Talin, or scattered around the grounds, but many have been lost and a few are little more than a pile of rubble or an outline on the grass.

I particularly want to see the Yugong Pagoda. This seven-layered, hexagonal pagoda commemorates Fu Yu, an Abbot of Shaolin Temple during the Yuan Dynasty. Fu Yu expanded Shaolin knowledge by inviting scholars and martial artists to stay at the temple and was posthumously granted the title of Duke by the Yuan emperor in recognition of his life's work. He also wrote the Shaolin Generation Poem used to this day. Beginning with Fu, each of the poem's 70 characters is used as the first character of a monk's name to signify their generation. Monks' surnames are given as Shi. Therefore, all monks of a single generation share the same first character of their name. Thus, one can tell the generation of a monk from their name. (See Appendix).

As an example of Shaolin's sphere of influence, there are also some eminent foreign monks interred here. Another Yuan Dynasty pagoda, built in AD1339, bears a highly-regarded epitaph written by a Japanese Shaolin monk. While a Ming Dynasty pagoda, built in AD1564 celebrates an Indian monk.

The most recent pagoda belongs to Shi Suxi. Though never officially inaugurated, Shi Suxi acted as Abbot through some of Shaolin's darkest days and was among the few monks remaining after the Cultural Revolution. Constructed in 2006, his pagoda has been criticised for the images of cars, computers and space travel carved into its surface, although this is perfectly traditional as it relates events from Suxi's lifetime.

Being recently interred, Shi Suxi has living disciples so his pagoda is also rare in that people pause to pay respects and burn incense there. Unfortunately, his pagoda is near the shuttle bus stop. Covered in stalls and touts, this area isn't a particularly dignified or solemn resting place, although maybe Suxi likes the company. At least he can see that his efforts to keep the temple alive were a success.

Sadly, most day-trippers don't stray past this area. They just follow the road straight through the middle like a conveyor belt, so never get to appreciate the full extent of the Pagoda Forest. A little back from the road is a completely different world.

As sightseers tend not to linger here, the Pagoda Forest is quieter than the main temple complex and the hustle of traders, barely ten metres away, is lost. This is all the better for us, as we can enjoy the sanctity undisturbed. In the leafy glade, surrounded by the solemn tombs, one can feel a real sense of history with the past masters. So tranquil is the Pagoda Forest that the area feels suspended in time. It's hardly surprising that it was named a National Scenic Spot in 1996.

That said, things are not always so peaceful in Pagoda Forest. The temple recently posted warnings of fake monks lurking around the pagodas collecting money by demonstrating Kung Fu and telling fortunes. Extreme cases have involved fraud and extortion, but we see no such activity. There is a tired looking monk sitting next to a wheelchair piled high with prayer beads, but he certainly isn't bothering visitors. Anyone getting this far, with any intention of buying prayer beads, has already been collared. I assume he's not on commission as he's more interested in keeping to the shade.

He's got the right idea. Away from the crowds, the combination of trees and ancient monuments has a wonderful atmosphere. Nothing like the dusty scene in the Jet Li movie, when Henan was still recovering from the ravages of drought. The tombs are a very real link with history and being in their presence makes me both proud and humbled to be part of Shaolin heritage. It would be sacrilegious to be anything but respectful here. I could bask in it all day.

Awed by the experience, it's unsettling to step back into reality. Once more running the gauntlet of traders, my patience is wearing thin. Normally when faced with pushy sales I just say, 'Bu yao, xie xie', (I don't want any, thank you) and walk away. However, the sales force is so massed and insistent that any hope of maintaining reasonable manners is lost. I end up just barging past and ignoring them.

Opposite the Mountain Gate, the Shaoyang bridge, over the Shaoxi river, leads to Shifang Chanyuan (the Temple of Four Directions). Built in AD1512, the temple was originally a guesthouse for visitors not entitled to spend the night within the monastery walls and was among those destroyed in the fire of 1928 and rebuilt during the 1990s. Unlike many buildings from that surge of reconstruction, the Temple of Four Directions resembled the original architecture closely enough that it has been left intact. Built on the four cardinal directions, nowadays the temple is a bizarre wax museum with the four wings crammed with Luohan statues. There are hundreds of the fellows here and even one which is supposed to be Jesus; he's the bearded fellow carrying a lamb. While it's interesting, we don't know enough Buddhist mythology to understand the figures so gaping at statues of bald blokes soon becomes a bit samey and the curators are intent on keeping the foot traffic flowing.

Alongside the Temple of Four Directions, a rutted dirt road leads past a dusty, dry earth training field to a few shabby, grey concrete buildings. Haphazardly sprawled along the valley, Wangzhigou is all that remains of the infamous Shaolin Village. A shadow of the wretched hive of scum and villainy that it once was. The story is that the Emperor once pointed to the valley and asked what it was, it has since been known as 'the valley the emperor pointed at.' Next to the temple is a handy kiosk, where we purchase a ticket for the electric shuttle.

The souvenir shops around the tourist centre are a hectic muddle of tat. Samurai swords, Ninja trappings and Barbarian fantasy swords sit alongside jade Buddhas and mantra CDs. Some crazy guy tries to sell me a repeating sleeve dart which he demonstrates by putting a couple of rounds into a plank from across the shop.

None of the shops have fixed pricing and all expect punters to go through the whole haggling shenanigans, but haggling isn't practical amongst a dense crowd and there's little here that's worth buying anyway. I can't help feeling that the Shaolin merchandising machine is missing a trick. There is nothing individual in the shops and no actual Shaolin products.

We scan the stores, hoping for books on traditional Kung Fu, or a guide book to explain the sights in more detail, but only manage to turn up one 'coffee table' scenery book and a few postcards. Given Shi Yongxin's prodigious literary output, I expected copies of his work to be available here of all places.

All the tat on offer is available at much more competitive prices on the strip in Dengfeng. To get away from the crowds, we call it a day.

Wandering back to the big monk statue, a taxi driver spots us and, using his initiative, calls, 'Xiao Long?' Wearing the school tracksuit has its advantages.

On the journey back, I consider my impressions. Having heard of the recent changes at the temple, I was fully prepared to be disappointed, but it's not as bad as I'd been led to believe. Criticism of the Government's attempts to preserve Shaolin as a National Treasure have centred around claims that it's being turned into a Kung Fu Disneyland. I've never been to Disneyland, but I'm prepared to bet it's in a whole different league. Shaolin may seem like a disorganised and ill-planned theme park but, in Chinese terms, it's a streamlined, serene experience.

The current incarnation may be less tacky now that Shi Yongxin is at the wheel, but it still has a way to go. While the merchandising serves a purpose by generating revenue to rebuild the temple, the gift shops need regulating and ideally removing from the temple itself and limiting to the visitor centre. Not only are there too many shops selling the same things at arbitrary prices, but most items have no connection to Shaolin, Kung Fu or Buddhism.

Assisted by the Government, Shaolin's attempt to rise above

commercialism has, so far, merely resulted in a glitzier tourist trap and Shaolin is, again, in danger of becoming a victim of its own success.

My disappointment with aspects of Shaolin's revenue stream show me to be guilty of a fundamental error. I have set Shaolin on a pedestal. Fed by popular media and myth, my idea of Shaolin has probably never truly existed. Letting go of material objects is a basic tenet of Buddhist philosophy. A temple is just a place and, like my ideas, is transient. I shouldn't allow myself to be so easily deluded. Shaolin has evolved from being a place to being a concept, the true spirit of which lives in the hearts of its followers.

When Fatso comes to tuck us in, I tell him that we visited Shaolin today. I appreciate it's probably not a big deal for him, and I don't know what I was expecting reply-wise, but he doesn't fail to disappoint. 'Oh, ok, go sleep.'

I really need to work on my anecdote skills.

Sanda tournaments are one of the two sport Wushu disciplines recognized by the International Wushu Federation. The emphasis of Sanda is on realistic fighting ability. Trainer themselves trained many years Sanda and participated on different competitions. They pass their rich experiences on to foreign students. Due to this unique training, foreign students' bodies will get strong, kicks and punches will get remarkable fast and students will reach a high level of fighting ability.

Xiao Long Website.

Morning assembly isn't quite the shock to the system it once was. I'm adapting to getting out of bed at sparrow fart o'clock and standing around in the dark waiting for Shifu to show. Although, if I'm regaining consciousness more quickly of a morning, the same can't be said for our Shifu. He's even more lugubrious than usual. Lining up in front of him, he rejects our company with a shake of his head and sends us to join Shibu's group. Collecting us together to form an uber-squad, Shibu Shifu marches us to the front of school.

Fashionably late, we find the schools 2,700 Chinese students already assembled and part way through a ripping yarn narrated by a disembodied voice crackling over the tannoy. I'm sure it's enthralling, but I can't make out enough of the emphatic words to glean any sense from the speech. Not only is the PA system distorting the words, but they are drowned by the cacophony of hacking, spitting and other bodily functions from the less than appreciative audience.

Somehow, I've managed not to previously notice the huge TV screen built into the wall above the entrance. The light from the screen silhouettes the massed throng as it changes to school scenes and our Chinese counterparts launch into a tortuous rendition of the school song. We foreigners aren't the only ones who don't know the words.

The next scenes are live from the front steps where a lectern and a couple of microphones have been set up for a bunch of official looking gentlemen to speak very animatedly. The tinny tannoy makes it too difficult to discern any of this diatribe above the audience's farmyard impressions, so I have no idea what their beef is.

This formal assembly at the front of school turns out to be a regular Monday event, and one which our Shifus are keen to avoid. They don't attend in person, but just send us to the main building and wait around the corner for our return. Theoretically the Staff of the International Training Department are here to 'promote the Chinese martial arts culture, to strengthen international cultural exchange, and to satisfy the needs of foreign students.' At the moment all they're doing is unifying our disillusionment.

We stand around for half an hour without the faintest idea what's going on, until Shibu decides we've reached a satisfactory level of motivation. Leaving the Chinese students, to what I'm sure is a thoroughly entertaining morning, he marches us back to our courtyard and we split into our respective squads.

Back at the helm, Shifu Fatso marches us to the back road for a bit of Go Run. Showing utter disregard for the general public, we sprint lengths of the pavement before settling into stances and finishing off by punching and kicking our way up and down the street.

After breakfast, Shifu Fatso takes us to the field. There are about a dozen other classes already underway by the time we arrive and most space has been claimed. Wedged into a little corner by the road, at least we are upwind of the smouldering bonfire. We place our bum-bags, water bottles and tracksuit jackets on a rock and line up for an hour of walking up and down.

With Chinese fashion being stuck in a time warp, along with Chinos and Polo shirts, bum-bags are all the rage. As it's not viable to carry things in our pockets when training this defunct fashion accessory comes in useful and most students have them. By Chinese standards mine is very humble affair, but, being a fussy old lady, I only carry a couple of quid, tissues, Imodium, chopsticks and hand gel. The Chinese tend to go for the 'bigger is better' approach and have waist bags the size of small rucksacks. Ironically, this means something I wouldn't be seen dead wearing in Britain is too small and subtle here. Ideally it should be leather-look, about the size of my head and have a mobile phone holster. Then I really would be the shiz.

At break, I return to the rock for a drink, only to find everything covered in flies. The Chinese students are always meticulous about folding, and hanging up, their uniforms, even though they are completely filthy. A quick glance behind the rock reveals why, 'God, this place really is a shithole.'

Usually reserved with his comments Juha pipes in, 'In Finland we say, 'Paska reike'. Is same thing.'

I bin the water bottles and dash to the tuck shop to buy fresh. I am relieved when our next session takes place in the gym. And this isn't just me being precious.

After a few lengths of the usual, Shifu introduces a new walk to our repertoire. Again, in place of demonstrating himself, he says, 'Julie, Julie.' Having got her attention, he crouches into a rough Gong Bu with his fist out to one side saying, 'You know?' Upon Julie confirming she does know, he says, 'Ok, go'.

Julie moves to the front and makes her way along the hall in a tighter and more precise version of Fatso's demonstration. Watching Julie from behind is the only instruction we get. We follow her up and down, slowly refining our technique from her example.

For this new drill, we start at the attention position and step our right leg forward and out 45 degrees into a deep Gong Bu, punching with the left fist at 90 degrees to the centre line. Leaving the punch out and staying at the same height, we bring the left leg alongside the front leg and step it forward and out 45 degrees to the left, the left fist returns to the waist and we punch with the right. It's a simple enough procedure, but one which I have difficulty with. My problem is I'm automatically withdrawing the punch before stepping, a movement more characteristic of my martial art, Lau Gar Kuen.

Lau Gar Kuen originated at Shaolin, but went underground to be taught within the family. Since that time both styles have had hundreds of years to evolve. Lau has become more compact with the emphasis on practicality, while Shaolin, in accord with Chinese government guidelines, has become more Wushu based with the emphasis on larger, performance orientated, movements. That's not to say either style is better than the other, just they are distinct. The two styles are different enough that the techniques I have drilled for years are now too small and when I get home I am sure my Sifu will be equally determined to beat them back into me again.

At lunch, Knobby asks to borrow my laptop to show photos of his previous school to his new best friend. I haven't even seen the guy myself and have to admire Knobby for his ability to stay abreast of what's occurring. Without him there would be no grapevine.

Popping around to Knobby's room reveals, but for the five snoring teenagers, his room is in a similar state to ours when we arrived. Combined with the indeterminate debris and soiled clothing hung on the floor, the aroma of old socks is a little ripe to say the least. Suddenly Victorian Dad seems like the ideal roommate. I'm certainly glad I'm not sharing with this bunch of Herberts or my Shaolin experience would have a whole different perspective.

Sitting on the steps waiting for class is the closest to a social event we get. As my brothers stagger half-awake, blinking into the sunlight like albino cave dwellers, the party begins to warm up. Some are content to sit quietly as they slowly regain consciousness, but as the congregation enlarges so does the badinage. Knobby is entertaining his new best friends, while others are back and fore the tuck shops buying each other snacks and drinks.

Among us foreign students are three little kids who are here for the long term. I reckon they are about eight years old. There is an Uzbekistani lad, who is a delight, and two Koreans who are a proper handful. Apparently, the pair have an account at the tuck shop which keeps them permanently buzzing on artificial additives.

Julie is at Chinese class and Juha and Knobby line up with the Sanda Class, leaving just VD and I with Shifu Fatso. When we assemble in front of him, Shifu disparagingly shakes his head and points to the other group, 'Go Sanda.'

Sanda is Chinese kickboxing. Not knowing any better, we line up with the Sanda squad. Arranging us in single file, Sanda Shifu walks along the line looking each of us up and down, critically appraising his troops. A sullen piece of work, he specialises in scowling and spitting. If Shifu Fatso holds the Laziness Award, Sanda Shifu gets the Sulky Spitter Medal hands down. Although, for dedicated spitting, he would place a poor second to the dominatrix housekeeper. Whether we meet his exacting standards or if he just resigns himself to our company for a few hours I'll never know. Continuing to scowl he points to the gym.

We start with the same warmup and Jibengong as Shifu Fatso's Kung Fu class and we walk back and fore the hall swinging legs and waving arms. I guess basics are basics whatever the style. Sanda Shifu knows hardly any English and generally sticks to the phrases, 'Oh, my God' and, 'You are tiger'. So, just like our Kung Fu class, there is no real instruction, the newbies merely copy the senior students while Sanda Shifu prowls the periphery, sulking and spitting on the floor. It can't have always been this way. At some point someone must have taught something, but for now all we can do is muddle along helping each other.

Next is stretching. There's no easing into the splits here. From a standing position with hands at sides, we clap our left palm on the back of the right hand in front of the body and push our arms out to the sides at shoulder height with palms outward while extending the right leg with the toe on the ground. This is the basic starting position. From this stance we swing the left leg up in front of and then back through and behind. We should now be on the floor in a front splits position. Looking around the room, this is clearly not the case.

'Oh, my God, all bridge!' Of the dozen of us, one person can manage the full splits. Compare this to the Chinese students who, all bar the very greenest recruit, can instantly drop into a front or side split.

The Sanda drills are a slight variation to our other lessons as the moves are smaller than the Kung Fu and limited to punch and kick combinations that could be used in ring fighting. This is followed by unsupervised pad work for kick practice.

As we knock the pads about Sanda Shifu notices VD's turning kick. It's not an orthodox kick, but it works for VD and has proved effective on occasion. Moving me aside, Sanda Shifu steps in front of VD, who holds up his hands in a guard position. Sanda Shifu's eyes instantly flare open. Squaring up, he demands, 'You want fight me? You want fight me?'

VD calmly says, 'No thanks.' Sanda Shifu just as quickly returns to his normal chummy self.

Once Sanda Shifu has moved on, one of his students sidles over and quietly cautions us, 'Be careful him, he beat you.'

'Really? And I thought we were so close after our photo frolics together.'

At break, I visit the small toilet at the side of the gym. It contains a few squat toilets and a urinal in the same room. The thing of note about this urinal is that it isn't plumbed in. Rather than an attached pipe removing the discharge, it runs straight through a hole onto the floor. Needless to say, the floor in the toilet area is a little damp and anyone visiting the toilet brings it back on their shoes. This makes partner stretching an unsavoury experience. As I enter, a Sanda guy is making use of the urinal and standing right next to the outlet. I point out the absence of plumbing and the proximity of his feet, only for him to shrug, 'I don't care. I don't have to clean it.'

It's like I've just met the teenage me. The small mercy being I don't have to partner him for the stretching.

The open plan khazi also contains a small hand basin with a cold water tap. I have no intention of ever washing my hands here; it would mean touching the taps. Instead I use the hand sanitiser gel I carry in my little bum-bag.

Using the hand gel may get me strange looks, but being a valetudinarian is the only way to limit the risk of illness in these conditions. Our bodies are so weak from the high intensity training and lack of nutrition, we are particularly susceptible to attack from any number of bugs the locals are able to shrug off. That said, the locals all appear to be permanently ill. They are always coughing and spitting and, demonstrating the best of Communist intentions, determined to share their infections with everyone else.

Back in the gym, another couple of guys warn us about Sanda Shifu. Allegedly, he has a reputation for such antics, having previously kicked through a door and beaten up two western students he suspected of smoking in their room.

The Sanda guys are the most vocal of the foreign students. Mostly in their early twenties, they constantly bicker with each other and have an opinion on everything. Initially treating us like Methuselah's older brothers, holding our own with the training and VD's handling of Sanda Shifu, has given us a shred of credibility and the guys open up. Regardless of age and race stereotypes, we foreign students all have more in common with each other than we do with the Chinese. Our whole outlook is different to theirs and, with globalisation and shared history, we get along simply because we have a similar sense of humour.

Their general critique of the Shifus basically confirms my own impressions. Although I do notice, despite Knobby's previous claim, no one else refers to Shibu Shifu as Elvis. I'm beginning to wonder if he is actually the font of all knowledge he claims to be. I shouldn't criticise, people in glass houses and all that. He is travelling around China on his own which, while he has the advantage of not knowing he is a gormster, is a lot more than I was capable of at his age. In a way, I can't help envy his limited grasp of reality. Being a star in his own mind forbids him from playing it safe but, at the same time, his naiveté prevents him capitalising on the experience. Now that I have squandered my own, I can join in the complaining about youth being wasted on the young.

After break, Sanda Shifu demonstrates the full depth of his imagination by giving us exactly the same lesson again. While we are working the pads, Sanda Shifu again comes over to us. Forewarned, we are a little tenser in his company than previously, but needn't have been concerned. Pecking order established, Sanda Shifu is perfectly relaxed with us. During our kicks he spotted VD's tattoos poking out from under his shirt and come to investigate. Without any of the polite formalities one may consider appropriate, he pulls up VD's shirt to take a look, 'Oh, my God. Tiger'.

It's a stroke of luck for Sanda Shifu that VD's tattoos are neatly covered by his limited English phrases. It's a stroke of luck for VD that Sanda Shifu doesn't try to uncover any more of his tattoos. The Chinese concept of personal space is a little more familiar than we are used to and Sanda Shifu feels entitled to rummage the well upholstered illustrations in a manner even VD's wife would blush at.

We are both glad when it's time for our daily rice. The stretching, punch and kick drills, and pad-work are all useful training, but no different from the Kickboxing training we get at home. As such, we would rather skip this class and concentrate on the Kung Fu we came here for. At least we have the evening optional training class to get some Kung Fu in. I use it to practice the new moves we learnt this morning.

Back at the room, Shifu Fatso surprises us by turning up earlier than usual and with Yuan Shifu in tow. Sitting on the bed, Yuan asks a few vague questions, ostensibly to check how we are fitting in. Their concern may relate to the recent high dropout rate among the foreign students and, with Fatso's English ability, Yuan Shifu has been roped in to mediate. Yuan Shifu asks if we have any problems with the training. VD assures them it's all fine. I just laugh and, pointing at Fatso, say, 'He's mean to me'.

I think Fatso gets the gist, because a wry grin spreads over his face, but Yuan Shifu is visibly affronted with the thought that he wouldn't be as tough on us. His ever-present smile tightens, 'You want be my group?' he demands. 'My group very hard.'

I've seen Yuan's group. They are always sitting around chatting. In fact, none of the other groups seem to train as hard as ours. Their Shifus are content to spend time talking with them, whereas our Shifu's lack of English, and our lack of Chinese, makes conversation so difficult that it's easier for him to train us. So essentially, Shifu Fatso is the harder taskmaster. That's cool with us, it's exactly what we came here for. Initially, we were put out to have been lumped in with the perceived low achievers. This was particularly disheartening when we saw the calibre of students who made it into the other groups. However, Shifu Fatso has turned out to be a blessing in a very convincing disguise. We have already discussed our impressions of the other groups and it's an easy decision: we'll stay where we are and get some training.

From the huge grin threatens to split his head in half, I assume Fatso appreciates our vote of confidence. I've noticed he tends to be left out when Yuan and Shibu are joking around with the students in English, so our support must be reassuring and I feel we are starting to break ground with him.

Satisfied with their contribution towards international relations, the Shifus head for the door. Still grinning, Fatso nods his tousled head and ducks out with the traditional, 'Ok, go sleep,' as he closes the door behind them.

During the teaching, the school arranges Chinese for two class hours, and Chinese Geography, Chinese History, Buddhology, Cultural History of Martial Arts for one class hour per week.

Xiao Long Website.

Prior to heading out for our Go Run we plod through a basic warmup in the dark courtyard. Stretching up and down, I notice a squad of pink coated cleaning ladies enacting a similar routine. By the time we are ready to head out they are already jogging circuits. I don't know why they need to warm up; all they do is sit, huddled together in the doorway eating nuts and spitting shells on the floor all day. Which is odd considering they are supposed to be keeping the place clean. Again, the positions here are massively oversubscribed. There are two ladies per floor for our building, who are only responsible for the hallway and stairs. We are supposed to maintain our own rooms and, as students only return to the building between classes, we have little opportunity to untidy the hallway. This means the cleaning staff are unoccupied for most of the day. I suppose the nuts and nattering help fill the time.

Back from our run, the Pink Coats are already at breakfast. They have their own little room at the side of dining hall and have a different menu to us. It also looks like larger portions. I suppose they need their energy

101

for all that sitting and spitting.

Breakfasted up, we are on the steps waiting for class as our fellow students gradually trickle forth. Now that we have served our time, and they are used to seeing our faces, the other students are more social when we meet. There is little fraternisation outside classes as most students sleep whenever the opportunity arises. The high dropout rate, combined with the fatigue, means it's difficult to display much enthusiasm at times, especially to people who are unlikely to be here for long. That's not to say they are an unfriendly bunch. Overall there is a good sense of camaraderie which stems from the fact we are all in the same boat.

The other Shifus appear, collect their squads and whisk them away. Ours is a little tardier. When he finally turns up, he sends us for a refreshing dose of Go Run and adjourns for a cigarette. A dozen canteen laps later, Shifu rematerialises and sends us to Go Gym, but in a change to the normal procedure he halts us at the entrance to the building. Gesturing to the concrete steps he says, 'Go run'. In change from running round and around, we now get to run up and down. It's Tuesday, it's 8am and this is Power Training.

Having ran up and down a few times, Shifu fine-tunes his idea and orders us to run up and back one step at a time. After ten laps we go through the same procedure two steps at a time, then three, four and five as Shifu continually calls, 'Go fast!'

The steps are cracked with large chunks missing from the edges and are littered with empty packets and plastic bottles. If that weren't hazardous enough, there's also a liberal covering of spilt food and mucus membrane from a thousand cleared throats. Passing each other on the broken and uneven stairs at speed was dangerous in the first instance, but the risk element increases considerably with the number of steps.

I'm not as nimble as some and, after a few stumbles, I'm concerned of an imminent disaster. Easing up only makes Shifu encourage me to, 'Go fast' again. As an excuse to pause, I explain that my Mam told me not to run on the stairs. His blank expression tells me the concept is lost on him. As far as Shifu is concerned, it's a perfectly routine piece of training. He'll have us running with scissors next.

Like many superstitions, the idea of passing on the stairs being bad luck is probably based on a mixture of observation and common sense. Just as walking under a ladder risks something dropping on your head, passing on the stairs may cause one to stumble. The Chinese love superstitions and portents of luck or doom so I'm surprised our Shifu is unaware of the implications for a stair related tragedy. Chinese Mums obviously don't voice these health and safety concerns to their offspring.

Beginning to tire doesn't help our safety margin and the others soon share my reticence. Grumbling, they also compensate for the safety factor by slowing down.

The emphasis of modern Wushu is on speed, which is developed from fast-twitch muscle. These stair exercises are designed to develop the calf muscles which provide the explosive power when jumping or moving in and out of stances. Shifu explains this by jumping up a couple of steps and lifting his trouser leg to display his calf muscle. Pointing at the tensed muscle, he says, 'Huh, you know?' His calves are about a third the size of mine, but I've got nowhere near his power.

Upon our grumbled confirmation, he motions to the stairs. We then go through the same routine jumping up the stairs and increasing the number of steps every ten laps. Things aren't going too bad until Shifu gets us to clamber down the steps on our hands and toes. This exercise has now passed beyond merely dangerous and into the territory of biologically hazardous. A couple of close scrapes is all it takes for me to decide it's not worth the risk. Peeling off from the group, I step outside the building to stretch against the wall.

After a couple of minutes, Shifu pokes his fat head around the corner looking for me. Seeing that I am training he doesn't push me. I continue to stretch against the wall while watching the Chinese students doing aerials in the courtyard. These kids are fantastic. They cross the courtyard in a series of aerials before running back to the end of the line. Some kids are simultaneously wielding combinations of weapons and still make it look effortless. Pretty soon the rest of my squad have also defected and joined me as an appreciative audience.

Faced with no one to watch run up and down stairs, Shifu calls, 'Ok. Go gym'. We troop up the stairs for more Jibengong and Zhuang Gong (stance training). Calves exhausted on the steps, we spend the rest of the lesson crossing the hall punching and kicking in low stances.

At break, I hang out the window watching the schools Shaolin Monk show loading up a truck with their stage equipment. Frankly, I'm amazed they ever manage to vacate the premises let alone tour. During the packing, they perform several comedy classics including my particular favourite where one guy carries a ladder over his shoulder and abruptly turns around only to narrowly avoid hitting someone else with it. Bits of truck even fall off. They do everything except squirt water from their button holes and throw custard pies. I watch until the farce becomes painful. There's an entire show worth of slapstick material here in itself. I could have sold tickets.

Joining me at the window, VD is visibly alarmed. Nodding to the toilet, he gasps, 'Dude, someone's let a horse loose in there!' Orwell may have felt that latrines were an overworked subject in war literature, but the topic is in no danger of going out of fashion with my colonically controlled colleague.

I'd noticed the giant jobby earlier and have to say, 'Well, it certainly isn't eating what we are eating.'

I wish I hadn't mentioned food. It's another hour and a half until lunch and I'm already starving. Another session of Jibengong sees me ravenous and first in the queue for my rice and cabbage.

Knobby joins our table to inform us the French guys in Shibu's group have given up. Cage fighters back home, they found the conditions too demanding and moved on. I am reminded of the French guy we met on our first day. Other than being on his last legs he, and his friends, looked a lot younger and fitter than us. VD gives me the old raised eyebrows again.

Knobby then tops this information by telling us the new guy in our group has disappeared. This is news to me. I didn't know we had a new fellow in the first place.

After lunch, I am just about to wake VD for the afternoon session when Shifu Fatso bundles into our room announcing, 'Go Chinese.' Grabbing notebooks and pens we run out into the square just in time to see a group of our fellow students heading toward the main building. We catch up and follow them inside.

I had forgotten about the stairwell. It was evening when we first arrived at Xiao Long and much cooler. The early afternoon heat hasn't made the smell any more agreeable. Pulling faces and trying not to inhale, some go as far as pulling their tracksuits over their faces or hold their noses, but we are all contorting our features in some fashion. The Chinese students we pass look at us in amazement. Living at the school for the majority of their lives must desensitise them. Oblivious to the stench, they are puzzled by our expressions and I'm embarrassed to have been caught making such a fuss in their home.

The class is already underway. The teacher welcomes us and asks us to take a seat. I do my best to oblige by cramming my legs under the tiny, antiquated wooden desk.

Smart-casual in her dark jeans and plain blouse, the teacher has a more professional look than we are used to seeing. Other than a sequined edging around her pockets, there's a distinct lack of bling. I'm guessing she's in her late twenties, but her absence of disco trimmings means she's positively frumpy by local standards.

The teacher has filled the blackboard with standard phrases, which we copy into our books. She then works around the class getting us to read the lot out.

Today's lesson is about the seasons of the year and a few phrases regarding the weather. A guy who has been at the school a while suggests we don't need all these phrases as it can be summed up in two expressions: 'too hot' or 'too cold'.

I've certainly experienced the 'too hot'. It doesn't take much for a guy from the Valleys to feel uncomfortable in any kind of sunlit warmth. I'm not looking forward to the 'too cold' either.

We timed our visit to avoid the extremes of Dengfeng weather, reasoning that spring (March - April) and autumn (September - October) would provide the optimum training conditions. During these seasons, daytime temperatures range from 20C to 30C, but it can still be wet and miserable and nights can be bitterly cold.

Taped to the training hall walls are pictures of previous students. In one photo they have built a snowman in the courtyard and in another they are training in thick coats with hats and gloves on. It's an aspect of Shaolin living that I'm not eager to experience. I'm also not fussed with talking about the weather, I could have stayed in Britain for that.

The teacher's English is pretty good and she has a brave attempt at trying to teach us, but you gotta feel for her. The class of twelve has about five different nationalities in it and most have limited English. To further complicate issues, we are all at very different levels with our Mandarin.

It's another example of the school not being equipped to deal with foreigners. I even struggle to fit my legs under the desk which is not only designed for children, but Chinese children at that.

I have done a couple of years of evening classes and probably represent the average ability in the class. Several students have very little experience of Mandarin and even flounder with basic pronunciation. The classes are pitched around my level, so for a good section of the class the lesson is just out of reach.

The lesson structure means it's not particularly productive either. We get about ten minutes each per lesson. Left with time on his hands, and being starved of attention, Knobby begins to act up. Calling across the class when the teacher is speaking and throwing things at other students, Knobby does his best to live up to his nickname.

I was previously prepared to tolerate the chap in small doses, but his rudeness to the Chinese teacher is beyond the pale. Not only is he an embarrassment to himself, but I'm affronted on the teacher's behalf. It's obvious many students feel the same. Knobby doesn't understand he is an ambassador for the west and his antics are creating a bad impression of us all.

When no one rises in support, Knobby begins to quieten down, but it's the final straw for me. I resolve to distance myself from him in future. I also make sure to thank the Chinese teacher as we leave, 'Laoshi, xie xie.' Her beaming smile implies she appreciates the sentiment.

Victorian Dad has been more tolerant of Knobby than I. Whereas I am only prepared to entertain his imbecility for so long, VD has gone out of his way to help him. I have fallen for this with other Knobbys in the past and learnt the hard way. Knobby doesn't really want help, just attention. VD is just wasting his time by letting his own training be hijacked. However, he's astute enough to work this out for himself and today's Chinese class has merely cemented his opinion of Knobby.

I needn't have worried about distancing ourselves from Knobby. He is as fed up of us as we are with him. Our lack of enthusiasm for his antics has led him in search of a more appreciative audience. This shouldn't be a problem for him as the high student turnover means he has a ready supply of unsuspecting, new best friends.

After a frustrating afternoon VD makes the executive decision that Chinese lessons aren't for him. Adding it to the evening training as another class he is skipping. In future, he will pretend to go to class when ordered and head to our room for a kip. It makes sense. If he's not getting anything out of the class, he may as well utilise the time doing something useful to him.

Heading towards the canteen, VD reminds me of the noodle option we saw on our first day here. Working on the theory it's a weekly event, he gets me all excited for nothing. Looking forward to dinner got me through the day. Needless to say, there are no noodles. It's the same meal three times a day, seven days a week. It must have been a momentous occasion on the school calendar for the noodles to be wheeled out.

Taking my ubiquitous ration of boiled rice, boiled green veg. and steamed bun, I espy a Chinese student sitting at one of our 'reserved' tables. There's still plenty of space so I take a seat opposite him. His feigned nonchalance rises several notches as, scowling, he assiduously avoids eye contact. The giggles from the table of Chinese students next to me suggest he has been dared to sit here. Taking the opportunity to break the ice, I give him my warmest smile and say, 'Hello.'

His cool shatters. Eyes bulging in abject terror, he flusters about as the table next to us explodes into laughter. Head down, he slinks back to his friends. It would appear he has lost his bet. VD turns up just as the kid is skulking off. Always impressed by my social skills, he enquires, 'Something you said?'

At assembly there's a hole in the line-up where Julie and Juha should be. As Fatso is already present, they are clearly late and need a gentle reminder. This is where Knobby comes in.

All the pulling faces and dancing around behind Shifu's back has earned Knobby a reputation as a pain in the arse and Shifu now allocates him the crappy jobs. Subsequently, hc is now Fatso's official gopher. He moans about his newfound role, but I suspect he likes the attention. Collecting latecomers falls among his allocated tasks.

As we wait for Knobby to return with his charges, Shibu Shifu comes over to our group. Addressing VD and I, he asks why we haven't been to the office to register yet. I thought this had already been done, but I'm now getting the hang of how these things work. Reading between the lines, the registration process should have taken care of by Shibu when we arrived, but he neglected the task. He may have doubted we would last this long. Questioning him won't get me anywhere so I just agree we will go to the office and get registered at the next opportunity.

The Chinese government require foreign visitors to register with the local police within 24 hours of arrival in the city. Hotels, etc. will generally scan passports, visas and entry stamps at check in and complete the registration on their guests' behalf. The school has not been so officious with our paperwork and we are now in breach of the law. Given the high dropout rate, it's likely the school doesn't bother registering foreigners for the first few days.

With his usual flair for efficiency, Shibu has waited until the office is closed before telling us to go there. Our next opportunity will be after breakfast tomorrow.

With one thing and another, we haven't had a great deal of training today so I hit the gym and try to refine the movements we've learned so far. Being naturally uncoordinated, I'm primarily driven by embarrassment and have to put in the extra hours just to keep up with other people's average ability. Many of the Jibengong movements are so big as to be alien to me and I have to concentrate on each detail to drill them into memory. It's taking a lot of effort, but I'm already seeing improvements, particularly in my flexibility.

It reminds me of something our very own Master Yau once said to me (the way I talk about him you'd think the bloke never shuts up), 'You see books and films about the secret of Kung Fu. There is no secret to Kung Fu, just practice.'

Many students complain about the Jibengong, saying it's boring and they want to learn something different. It might be repetitive, but that's the whole purpose. More is going on beneath the surface. The continual repetition means not only do the movements become second nature to the point of being automatic, but over a period the body changes. Strength and flexibility develop and muscle and bones physically adapt.

It's a little late in the day for me to start remoulding my bones, I should have started at four years old, but even small changes can make a difference. As Master Yau is fond of reminding us, 'Never underestimate the importance of basics.'

By 9.25 I'm sitting up in bed waiting for the sound of Shifu Fatso's flat feet to flap their way down the corridor. VD is already out for the count and I'm dog-tired myself, but if I hit the sack now Shifu will probably wake me up in order to tell me, 'Go sleep'. I decide to go for it anyway. He should be able to see our light is off through the hole in the door.

Registering at International Kung Fu center is very easy, we can arrange all necessary paper work for you as well as visa extension.

Xiao Long Website.

I'm getting a serious case of déjà vu with the old morning warming and Go Run business, although at that time in the wee hours it's easier than thinking for myself. After breakfast we brave the main building stairwell only to find Reception unmanned. Actually, 7.30 is probably a bit early for the office staff. Having been up since 5.00 it feels like midday to us and we had forgotten the real world operates to a different time scale.

Morning training contains no surprises and we spend the majority of it following Julie up and down the hall. Julie is the only one in our group who knows what she is doing and the only one whose name Fatso knows, so she gets called upon to demonstrate a lot. VD, Juha, Knobby and I, just get grunts, nods or, if he's close enough, a poke. He hasn't so much as asked our names. Yuan Shifu, who isn't even our instructor, has picked them up, but, for reasons best known to himself, our glorious leader is uninterested. It's not as if our names are complicated and, as VD and I are both called Nick, there's a two for one bonus to be had straightaway.

If he were to struggle over the pronunciation I also have a Chinese name, Ning Jian that I received at my Mandarin class. Among the first

109

phrases I learnt at Mandarin class was 'Call me Ning Jian' (Ni jiao wo Ning Jian). Ning Jian translates as Peaceful Sword although, from the strange looks I get, I'm beginning to wonder if it's a euphemism for erectile disorder. Subsequently, I've ditched the Chinese name and stuck with Nick, which should be perfectly manageable for any nationality.

VD even went to the trouble of getting himself a Chinese name from a name generator we found on the internet. There was also the option of Star Wars and Porn Star names so we got those too, just to be on the safe side. We needn't have bothered, our Shifu is as interested in us as he is in the low cal. option. Also, if any other students have Chinese names they don't use them.

After lunch, we try Reception again. Our old friend, the Village Idiot, is now in residence. From the expression on his face as he is forced to peel it from the desk to respond, he is evidently as delighted to see us as we are him. I appreciate VD and I may not be the most aesthetically pleasant of sights, but there's no need for that degree of horror and despair.

He must have been expecting us, for after a minimal amount of explanation he motions to the seat in front of the desk and swivels the webcam around to face me. In all fairness to the bloke, he is taking to his new role of official photographer with all the efficiency and enthusiasm he gave to his previous position as uniform sales manager. I greatly admire his ability to completely ignore our presence throughout the procedure. It must be a special skill they get taught at Chinese Customer Service School.

Squinting into his screen, he curls one side of his lip. He isn't pleased with the result, but, shrugging his shoulders, decides it's probably the best he's going to get from the subject. He motions VD to sit for some of the same.

Photos taken, Idiot Boy fumbles among the contents of his desk, hands us a form and a pen each and motions us toward the seating area.

The required information is fairly basic stuff: name, date of arrival, etc. and the question boxes are in English as well as Chinese so it's the matter of minutes to complete and return the forms.

From the look on Idiot Boy's face, I deduce we have returned too quickly for his liking. Perhaps he was hoping to pass us onto the next shift. Huffing and puffing, he reluctantly accepts our work and skims the forms for errors. Triumphant, he waves the form in front of us. His efforts are rewarded. Vehemently tapping the page with his finger, he grunts,

'Huh, huh!'

Closer inspection reveals VD unwittingly put the date order the wrong way around. Chinese format is month followed by day and VD has used the format he's familiar with. So, according to his form, our visit to the school passed months ago. It takes a single second's work to correct this simple, schoolboy error and not, as our friend would have us believe, the end of the world as we know it.

Now recovered from his disturbed slumber he performs a sharp about-turn in his attitude to work. He throws himself into the task of belittling us with vigour and enthusiasm unbecoming in one so young.

Next comes my turn. Placing the forms side by side, he notices we are both called Nicholas. He asks if we're bothers. I don't know which of us is the most offended at the idea. 'No sir, we are not related.'

Unconvinced with my answer, he narrows his eyes staring alternately from one of us, to the other comparing our features for any family resemblance. A Chinese friend previously told me he had trouble telling westerners apart because we all look so similar. As baffling as I found that at the time, Idiot Boy appears to be under the same impression.

Exasperated, he returns to the form. Further pointing and paper tapping means I've also fallen for another old chestnut.

Despite officially converting to the Gregorian calendar in 1929 as part of the Republican modernisation, China still calculates age using the lunar calendar. To further complicate matters a Chinese child is a year old when born.

Thus, my date of birth and age don't add up, much to the despair of our friend who now thinks I am too stupid to know how old I am. Again, this is simply remedied with a pen stroke, but the Idiot Boy makes out it's a major catastrophe for mankind. The worst part, as far as I'm concerned, is that I've become a year older. Although it would certainly explain the way I've felt since we've been here. I'm surprised I've only aged one year.

Idiot Boy's initial reticence to deal with us completely evaporates as his sense of superiority kicks in. Like a schoolyard bully, he has sensed a weakness and goes all out to capitalise on it. Revelling in his newfound power has brought him to life better than caffeine ever could. He scours the form in more depth, desperate to spot further fault. 'Huh, huh!' More finger tapping means he's found it. In the box marked 'Country', I have put 'Britain'. This is markedly the wrong answer because Idiot Boy hasn't heard of Britain so, obviously, I am wrong.

For the benefit of anyone similarly geographically challenged, Britain is composed of four countries: England, Northern Ireland, Scotland and Wales. At least any three of the four object to being associated with their neighbours and would prefer not be part of the whole, but as it stands today they are.

I am from Wales (Weiershi) and well aware many people do not understand the concept of Wales as a country. I was not expecting the Chinese to be any better informed. Although the film Braveheart was received to great acclaim in China, and served to put Scotland (Sugelan) on the map, unfortunately Twin Town, wasn't quite such a big hit here, probably because it lacked the historical accuracy the Chinese love so well.

Anticipating the populace to deny the existence of my homeland, I prepared the catch-all term of Buliedian (Britain) as a backup. China opposed the name Da Buliedian or Great Britain, during the Olympics and insisted on Buliedian instead. Idiot Boy must have missed the Olympics as he's having none of it, insisting there is no country of that name whatsoever. Not prepared to compromise, Idiot Boy presses the point:

'Ni shi na guo ren?' (What country person are you?)

'Wo shi Buliedian ren.' (I am British)

'Yingguo ren ma?' (English?)

'Buliedian ren.'

'Ah, Meiguo ren!' (Ah, American!)

'Bu shi Meiguo ren, wo shi Buliedian ren.'

'Buliedian?'

'Shi de.' (Yes)

'Ah Faguo ren.' (Ah, French.)

'Bu shi Faguo ren, wo shi Buliedian ren.'

His expansive knowledge of foreign countries exhausted, he refuses to be beaten and comes up with the bright idea of starting from the top and running through the entire list again, 'Ah, Yingguo ren.'

I, on the other hand, am not prepared to repeat the whole performance; we could end up in an infinite loop. I just can't take it any longer. With a sigh, I give in, 'Ok, Yingguo ren.'

To my eternal shame, I concede to being called English. It hurts me inside to say it and, as the words leave my mouth, I can feel my mother's cold, hard stare burning into me all the way from the old country. If that isn't bad enough, I now have to suffer the smug look on Idiot Boy's face which clearly says, 'I won. I made you look stupid by making you admit you don't know what country you're from.' Thus, I lose 'face' and not him. If he had admitted there was a country he hadn't heard of, he would have lost face. I, on the other hand, am fully aware there is all sorts of information I know nothing about and, in the west, we accept this as part of the learning process. In China, it's a social faux pas to admit not knowing something so at least my concession has saved his pride from being dented.

Fortunately, everything else on the form is in order and, his superiority in matters geographical established, he shoos us away before we get the opportunity to usurp his position.

Being 'dui lian' (without face), bothers me not. I'm prepared to put up with most things for an easy life, but the time to leave Idiot Boy hasn't come a moment too soon. One look at VD's seething face is enough to tell me his general air of bemusement has been beaten once more and we are again left to practice the ancient and noble art of self-restraint.

I remember our first experience of Chinese customer service when we visited a travel agent in Birmingham's China Town. The guy stared at us open mouthed. Previously informed I am funny looking, I still wasn't prepared for the reception. It was as if he'd never seen a white person before.

When he had composed himself enough to speak, he refused to believe we wanted to book a flight to China. It came to a point where we were trying to force money into the bloke's hands. His reverse psychology sales technique may have worked on us, but it must have been too clever for the average punter as the shop had closed down by time we returned.

I've heard many senior BKFA instructors say our own Master Yau is very westernised by Chinese standards. Until we came to China, I hadn't really appreciated what that meant, but I'm certainly getting the picture now.

As painful as the registration process felt, it didn't take that long and we are back in plenty of time for class. Joining our comrades on the steps, I fall into conversation with Knobby's roommates. One tells me they are glad we turned up and have been keeping Knobby occupied as the five of them were finding it hard work. Apparently, he even talks in his sleep, so they don't even have any respite from him at night.

After the usual canteen laps, it's up to the gym for more basics. Seemingly happy with the way our Jibengong is coming along, Shifu

Fatso gives us another walk to learn. From Ma Bu we twist right into a Gong Bu, and then step through with the back leg into a Ma Bu facing the other way and then twist to the left. While Fatso lacks the necessary vocabulary to explain the movement, this is another core technique of Shaolin Kung Fu.

The power of Shaolin Kung Fu comes from the twist of the hips and Shifu isn't satisfied I am generating sufficient momentum to deliver an effective strike. To develop this, he sets me side on to the wall in horse stance and gets me to thrust toward the wall into Gong Bu hitting the wall with my open palm. Each strike sends a cloud of dry whitewash into the air exaggerating the power in my strikes. Carried away with my success, I experiment by varying my strikes to determine the most effective technique for creating dust clouds.

A great man once said, 'Boards don't hit back', but, having caused me no offence previously, this wall begins to take exception to me pounding it. My palms are soon enflamed and my wrist and elbow joints develop that all too familiar dull ache. A soreness I recognise from hand conditioning under a former teacher and haunts me during the colder months. This is when I remember my current Sifu, telling me 'Never punch something as resilient as a wall, always make sure your striking surface has some give.' I understand the principal behind the action Shifu is trying to develop, but, despite my best efforts, the wall is certainly winning this battle. I begin treating the wall with a bit more care for the sake of my manual dexterity. My Dad suffers with arthritis and I see no good reason to encourage the onset in myself.

Seeing my loss of enthusiasm, Fatso attempts to encourage me to hit harder. I explain my wrists hurt and he gives me a disappointed look, 'Ok, ok, go'. He motions us over to the punch bags. We assume the same position and repeat the striking process with a fist. When we get the hang of this to Shifu's satisfaction, he sends the bags swinging, so we have to adjust our timing to hit the centre of the bag and withdraw the strike quickly. Getting too cocky for Shifu's liking, he adds a further complication by spinning the bags before swinging them. Again, the slightest misjudgement is very unforgiving with the wrist bearing the brunt of the whiplash as the fist ricochets off the bag. The only option is to get good quickly because the alternative is too painful.

At evening assembly, Knobby continues his harassment of Shifu. He's been making fun of Shifu, pulling faces and the like, behind his back gradually getting bolder as Shifu laughs along, but now Shifu has had enough. Being made fun of in front of the other Shifus cannot be tolerated and he is forced to make an example of him. To teach Knobby a lesson, and regain face, he pushes him to the ground and tells him to do press-ups.

Knobby asks, 'How many?'

Shifu turns his head away in pretence of thinking, and says, 'Mmmm, wan hunnner.' Just in case Knobby hasn't understood, he holds up a single finger and then his fist twice to act as the digits.

Obligingly Knobby assumes the position and proceeds to knock out five or six press-ups before collapsing. It was a bit of a pointless target for the boy really, Shifu might as well have said a billion. We watch Knobby agonisingly squeeze out another couple of press-ups until Shifu gives up and tells him to get back into line.

Dismissed, the others disappear as we head to the gym to practice our form. It's a pretty poor turnout. While it gives us plenty of space, there's no one to turn to for help so we end up practicing the few moves we know over and over.

The only time Shifu Fatso is punctual is when he comes to tuck us in. Tonight, he hangs around like he's waiting for something and seems awkward he can't communicate whatever it is. When the uncomfortable silence gets too much he resorts to his familiar, 'Ok, go sleep' and closes the door behind him.

I get the feeling Shifu is warming to us. We may even be getting a margin of respect from him, simply as he has seen us wanting to train. Also, as all things are relative, Knobby's antics make us look a lot more dedicated and respectful than we actually are.

The buildings, shops, restaurants in front of the entrance of Shaolin is called Shaolin Village. All of these buildings are destroyed.

www.shaolin-wushu.de

I've been looking forward to this morning's run. Demonised by the other students, the alleged 10K up the mountain and back is not exactly a piece of cake, but has so much more going for it.

Despite the extra effort involved, and the generic grumblings, most of my comrades feel the same. A set goal makes it more satisfying than random circuits of school or pavement laps and it's a much friendlier environment for running. The air is fresh, there's no traffic and, if you could Photoshop out the coughing and spitting locals and the occasional pile of rotting garbage, every scene would be a photograph. Out here in the wilderness, the ever-present smell of smoke and sewers is only just on the edge of perception.

We also get to run at our own pace. Shifu simply gestures to the mountain, says, 'Go, run' and that's exactly what we do. It's almost liberating.

That said, it's still a lot of running. The level of fitness and ability among the groups vary wildly and some struggle more than others. Never the most athletically inclined, I'm pleasantly surprised that I slot neatly into the range.

VD put in some training in anticipation of the running here. Unfortunately, his conscientious pounding of Worcestershire's canal towpaths hasn't prepared him for Dengfeng's terrain, but he still prefers the Thursday run to the random circuits. He may be struggling a bit with the hills, but he doesn't half shift when his Imodium wears off. His alternative is to fully embrace Chinese life and just go at the roadside.

Heading back down the hill to the crossroads, I catch up with a guy from Shibu's group. Pleasantries exchanged, Martin assures me, 'You don't seem to be struggling at all considering your age'.

Should I be? I decide to take it as a compliment and not get too hung up on any implications. My age had never been an issue until I got to China, but I would hope I'm good for a bit longer yet, after all, my Dad still runs marathons and he's even older than me.

Martin is a cool guy and always good for a, 'Jiao you!' to any flagging students, so I take his comment as the gesture of support I'm sure he intended.

The day warms up quickly and South American Guy has taken off his T-shirt. Seeing him running down the road bare-chested Shibu is absolutely appalled, 'Put on clothes, put on clothes!'

SA Guy pretending not to understand only results in Shibu screaming louder. Realising the 'non comprendez' routine isn't going to work he sulkily dons his shirt.

Once everyone has returned, Fatso assembles our squad, ostensibly to march back to school, but I suspect he has something up his sleeve. Proving my suspicions well founded, Fatso repeats last week's spot quiz by working his way along the line asking, 'You money?'

Lesson learned, we are all able to reply in the affirmative. The huge grin threatening to split his head in half tells me this was exactly what he wanted to hear. He marches us across the road to the café on the corner that we know as 'The Breakfast Place'. Now familiar with the procedure, we line up to buy our meal tickets, but I notice Shifu Fatso heads straight to the kitchen. When he emerges shortly after with two steaming bowls, I realise his game. Fatso must have an agreement with the management. Frankly, I'm amazed there is enough margin in their prices to allow for Fatso's commission. I go to town on breakfast: fried dough sticks (youtiao), soya milk (doujiang), omelette (chaodan) and stuffed steamed buns (baozi) which comes to the grand sum of 60p.

Tucking into our hearty breakfasts of not-rice, we are joined by South

American Guy who gives his opinion of the Chinese, 'They are stupid man, they will never rule the world.'

He then gives an expansive list of personal affronts he has suffered at school, like not being given ice cream at meals. 'In the summer they give us gelato man, but now there is no gelato. Why should they say if we have gelato? They should give us the choice man!'

There's no doubt he's had it rough. He also has a list of grievances against former roommates, 'He was so selfish man. He wouldn't even let me smoke in the room!'

There's a certain paradox there that I don't think he's got the hang of. A further irony is that his complaints have now scored him a room to himself.

Having eaten their fill, the Shifus spare us any more of this self-righteous indignation. With a grunt, we are marched back to school and line up to be dismissed, but instead of the expected, 'Ok, go' Shifu informs us there will be no training until after lunch as we have to clean our rooms, or, as he succinctly puts it, 'Go clean'.

I resent being told to tidy my room like a juvenile reprobate, but after seeing the younger lads' rooms, I can fully understand where Shifu is coming from. It's probably an attempt to stop the inside of the building looking like the outside. As Victorian Dad and I are not actually teenagers any more, our room requires little effort to bring it up to Shifu's exacting standards. Fatso sees our room every evening, so we have no problem ducking cleaning detail. In preference to kicking around for a couple of hours while the others go about their chores, we intend to explore our immediate surroundings.

This plan is slightly complicated by Shifu Fatso who, despite giving us permission to decamp the grounds, won't sign the pass. He probably hadn't expected me to have pre-filled slips to hand. Taken aback by my preparation, he performs a set manoeuvre of his own. Waving his hand to shoo us away, he says, 'Noh' and walks off.

In search of Shibu, we happen across Taiji Shifu. He doesn't speak any English at all, so I wave my bits of paper and make a writing motion. Before we know it, we are free for the morning. I'm warming to Taiji Shifu.

Our school is on the expanding, western, edge of Dengfeng on the Dayu Road also known as Bei Huan Lu (Northern Ring Road). The 1999 temple grounds clean-up saw the tatty tourist trap, known colloquially as Shaolin Village, demolished, the land remodelled and joined to the new

118

highway via Dengfeng. Overnight the legendary Shaolin village became a myth.

The inhabitants were given the option of new premises on the edge of town or a cash settlement. Many chose to take the money and run. Others relocated down the road just outside the nearest town of Dengfeng to spawn New Shaolin Village. As a result, most buildings at this end of Dengfeng have sprung up since 2000. Considering the very recent construction, the buildings are already showing serious signs of wear. The result of hurried construction, inferior materials and poor craftsmanship are evident. Doors and windows don't fit and walls are cracked and crumbling. Even the pavements are such obstacle courses, that you need your wits about you at all times. I'm willing to bet there's not a lot of hope of suing the local government for compensation if you do come a cropper. The western fad of Personal Injury Lawyers doesn't seem to have penetrated China's logical approach to looking where you are going.

Dengfeng has always been the nearest thing to civilisation for Shaolin visitors. The veritable population explosion as the schools and associated services transferred was soon absorbed. At last count there were around eighty Kung Fu schools in Dengfeng with a combined 80,000 students. Unsurprising, much of the town exists to cater for this burgeoning industry. It might be a communist country, but the shops and schools are all here to cash in on the Kung Fu phenomenon.

Local planning has ensured that this area is more organized and less tacky than its predecessor, but lacks character. It's essentially a strip of shops and restaurants at the edge of town along the road leading to the Temple. The area nearest our school is primarily composed of weapon shops that all sell the same poor quality goods. Practically all the shops along the street are martial arts associated. Kung Fu shoes, clothes and weapons stores are interspersed with the occasional convenience store or restaurant, which also carry Kung Fu shoes, clothes and weapons.

Our school is right on the expanding edge of Dengfeng. New Shaolin Village is so recent that it's strewn with building rubble and at this rate of expansion will soon be absorbed by the town.

The first shop we come to is a general martial art supply shop with our dearest Sanda Shifu sitting outside spitting. He pauses to give us a friendly wave before getting back down to it. Word is, he can be found hanging out here whenever he is not teaching. I'm sure the owners are delighted to have a scowling nutter squatting on the doorstep covering their path with mucus.

119

One of the things that alarm westerners visiting China is the spitting. Our fellow students often comment on our Chinese counterparts' unsavoury habit. Not only do they consider it perfectly acceptable to expel their nasal cavities and tracheas onto the floor, but it can be done in any location with impunity, indoors or out. Banks, supermarkets, buses and hospitals. Nowhere is immune. There was even a guy on our internal flight hawking loudly for the entire journey. Fortunately, I wasn't within viewable distance, but the sound was bad enough.

Traditional Chinese Medical practice believes it unhealthy to swallow phlegm. This attitude is manifest by the Chinese population to such an extent that they take a great pride in their spitting. Proceeded by a crippling hacking and larynx scraping in order to remove as much of the offending product as possible, the progenitor of a particularly large or loud expectorate can be seen to swell with pride in the knowledge of a job well done and leaves their handiwork for all to admire.

Allegedly, since the SARS epidemic of 2002, spitting has declined in the cities, especially Beijing where the authorities clamped down during the 2008 Olympics. However, the habit certainly persists out here in the sticks as an ever-present part of China's rustic charm. At any Dengfeng gathering, regardless of gender, there is a clearing of throats that sounds like Godzilla gargling with a rabid bear.

I've heard stories about expelling the phlegm demons living in the throat and variations on that theme, but I've formulated a different theory regarding the constant spitting. In Dengfeng, I would hazard the population spit because they are inhaling filth all day. They are so habitually ill they don't register the build-up of phlegm as a sign of anything being amiss. It's simply a way of life. The SARS outbreak must have been difficult to manage as I can't imagine how anyone knew if they had the respiratory disease or not.

The acid test of this theory is to live in this environment for a while and see how long it takes before feeling the need to expectorate. VD suggests the medical term for this condition should be Dengfeng Lung.

Since we've been at the school my throat has been playing up. It started with a bit of a niggling scratchiness, but has got steadily worse. It's beginning to hurt now and the swelling is making it difficult to swallow. I can't imagine it's going to get better of its own accord as there's simply no respite from the smoke and dust. Our room is next to the rubbish dump with a permanently smouldering pile of plastic. We run along the roadside inhaling dust, smoke and traffic fumes. We train next to the bonfire, on a sun-baked, dusty field next to an open sewer. At night we sleep in a hot, dusty room with the window shut to keep out further smoke and dust. Is it any wonder I have a sore throat?

The dry earth and smoke pollution cover everything in a layer of dust that threatens to take over. The schools answer is to get a small child to brush the paths with a broken tree branch. The rest of Dengfeng follows the same approach, so essentially, they are just moving the same dust back and fore indefinitely.

We walk to the eastern end of Dayu Road. The stores become smaller and less interesting until they peter out all together at the junction of Taishi Road. We walk back checking out the stores as we go. Many shops appear unattended and it's difficult to work out if they are open or not, but essentially they are all much of a muchness and we soon exhaust the repetitive selection of ropey Wushu accoutrements.

Just down the road from the Breakfast Place I recognise the sign 'Rou' (meat). One of VD's beefs with school is the food, more so with the lack of it in the food. Desperate for food with nutritional content, we determine to get ourselves on the outside of some dead animal product.

Parting the plastic curtain, we peer inside to an enthusiastic welcome from the owner. Demonstrating my lingual prowess, I utilise the one word on his shop sign and say, 'Rou'.

I can't imagine why the Chinese consider foreigners to be barbarians. All I did was storm into a restaurant demanding meat. However, the Laoban is only too happy to oblige and takes us to a huge bubbling pot in the corner. Digging into the murky liquid with a long fork he fishes out an impressive brown lump for our approval.

Upon my confirming this is what I meant when I asked for meat he hustles us to a table and furnishes us with a pot of flower heads in hot water. Seconds later, he has hacked the meat into bite size chunks and ceremoniously plonks the heaving plate on the table between us.

Since the advent of western style fast-food outlets, high grade meat is becoming more difficult to get hold of in China, simply because the larger chains are dominating the top end of the supply market. VD is convinced this is dog, whereas my money is on donkey. It's too cheap to be beef, too dark for pork and too big for poultry. It doesn't really matter what it is, I'm going to eat it regardless. I don't know the word for donkey so I ask the guy if it's dog. He evades the question and tries to get us to order something else. Producing a menu, from which I can only make out one character 'mian', leaves me with limited choice. Noodles it is.

We've practically demolished the meat-mountain by the time the guy returns with two huge steaming bowls of noodles. The bowls are at least twice the size of our entire meal at school. We plough through these Brobdingnagian portions with little effort.

Thoroughly content after our repast we make the most of the opportunity to laze about and drink the 'tea'.

Discussing our next move, VD reminds me of a purchase we wish to make. Some years ago, I saw a magazine article about a five-volume set of books covering traditional Shaolin forms published by Tagou, the biggest Kung Fu school in Dengfeng. Since we are in the same neck of the woods as Tagou, I reason that said books might be available hereabouts. Not surprisingly, there is a book and VCD shop on the Dayu strip which specializes in Kung Fu merchandise. This has to be a good place to start.

Heading back up Shaoshi Road, VD spots a pretty monk bag through the grime of a particularly darkened shop window. The door gives to our touch. As if by magic, a beaming smile materialises, closely followed by a wizened old lady.

The shop is piled high with Kung Fu uniforms, all covered in dust. They are hung from the walls and stacked on the floor, there's barely room to move. We ask to see the bag and the owner dissolves into a mound of material, emerging seconds later with bag in hand. It's a brown satchel type monk bag with lotus embroidery. Happy with the product we ask the price. 30Y sounds like a perfectly reasonable amount and VD hands over the cash. Taken aback, our genial geriatric stands there looking at the proffered notes. Perhaps we were supposed to haggle.

Coming back to life, she rummages behind the counter and hands us a bracelet of Buddha beads each and a business card. It may be her way of appeasing her guilt at over-charging us, but it's probably more to do with the way I have with the ladies.

Reading the business card, I find this tiny establishment is the Caisheng Wusengfu Biaoyanfu Pifabu. No wonder she doesn't have the name on the shop front, the name is actually bigger than the premises.

Back on Dayu Road, we pop into said VCD shop. A middle-aged lady looks up in delight, 'Hello Shifu, you speakah English?' This is a turn up for the books. Without waiting for a reply, she takes my arm and drags me over to the rack where she gestures toward the display rack proudly announcing, 'Hali Botta.'

She must be under the impression that I am a teenage girl, for I believe that to be the social demographic the boy wizard appeals to. I attempt to clear up the misunderstanding, 'I was really looking for something more in the way of a Kung Fu movie?'

'Humpph!' Unimpressed she returns to her counter leaving us to fend for ourselves.

VCDs never took off in the west but are massive in Asia. A lower resolution than DVD, they compress a movie onto a single CD for a fraction of the price. They are also easily counterfeited.

The shop mainly carries instructional Kung Fu VCDs, but rummaging around we come across a mound of books amongst which is one I'm looking for. It's a bit on the battered side, and sleeveless, but I reason I can live with that and it should put me in a better position to bargain as they have obviously been kicking around for a while. I also uncover a VCD of Xiao Hong Quan. I put these on the counter and ask how much.

'One thousand, three hundred Yuan.'

Without thinking I reach for my wallet only to have VD stay my hand, 'Dude, that's not right!'

I'm so tired the crafty entrepreneur nearly caught me out. Perhaps she misheard me and thought I wanted to buy the entire shop. As I stand there, open mouthed, trying to formulate a simple, yet polite, sentence, she produces the old faithful talking calculator and gets it to repeat the exorbitant price in a worse accent than hers.

The shop claims to be tourist friendly as it has price tags on the stock, but I know I can get the DVD in Britain for under £7, so £30 is simply ridiculous, and the least said about the £100 book the better. If this is what she considers a reasonable price, then I'm not prepared to entertain the time it would take to badger her down. I say, 'No thanks' and walk.

We head back to school with the cheeky chancer following us up the street, 'Come back Shifu, I give you goodah price'. She must be under the assumption this is part of the barter process, but I really can't be bothered to go through the motions. Everything might be negotiable in China, but my time is more important to me. Ignoring her cries, we keep walking.

This afternoon Yuan Shifu's group is light enough that the remainder join us. There's usually someone missing from training. Our small group is quite resistant so far, but attendance at the other groups varies considerably. Being tired and hungry our bodies are low on resources which makes us vulnerable to illness, the most common complaint being food poisoning. If a group is particularly low on the ground, they get bundled into another squad which doesn't really give the Shifus a lot of incentive to preserve our wellbeing.

With so many of their number incapacitated, the conversation turns toward the basic principles of self-preservation. In the western world, we have the five-second rule regarding food that has been dropped on the floor. Essentially, it's ok to eat it as long as you call the rule and carry it out within five seconds. Matt, an old-hand at the Xiao Long lark, explains the rule still applies in China, with the slight modification that it also includes contact with the air. Personally, I feel he's overly generous with this estimate.

Following a session of Go Run and Jibengong, after break Shifu sends the combined squad to the weights gym. On arriving we find the door chained shut. Foolishly assuming Shifu has gone for the key we await his return. Cigarette finished, Fatso reappears expressing confusion as to why we are standing the wrong side of the door. Pointing toward the gym he says, 'Go.'

Playing along, I point out the great big padlock and chain holding the door handles together. Shrugging his shoulders, he makes shooing motions toward us and walks off. Not content to give up so easily, I rattle the door and, eager to join in the dissent, Knobby bangs on the windows.

Our combined racket is enough to rouse the guy who lives in the little room at the side of the gym. His dishevelled form emerges from the gloom and, reaching through the gap between the two doors, unlocks the padlock to let us in.

The halls tend to have a little room off to the side, generally with a crudely fashioned curtain draped over the doorway. In this little room resides an attendant whose job it is to live in a little room. True to form, Shifu Fatso instructs us to, 'Go train', and saunters straight for this room to hang with the light-sensitive troll within. A few of us set about the machines in the dark, but, again, most are content to just make themselves comfortable lounging on the equipment. Walking over to the Lat Pull-down machine, VD commences some Lat Pull-downs.

'Whaah!' The Gym Attendant has resurfaced and is pointing at VD. Presumably unhappy with the operation of the apparatus he repeats his indignant, 'Whaah!'

Knowing it's useless to ask for clarification, VD shrugs and walks over to another machine. Happy his social position is affirmed the Gym Troll returns to his cave.

I can't see why the shouty guy singled out VD; many others are using the exercise machines in a far less orthodox fashion. Some even appear hell-bent on crippling themselves in the process. Frankly, I'm amazed we make it through to dinner without anyone suffering at least a minor maiming.

The training session after evening assembly is called Free Training, where we get to practice unattended, although very few people do any training during the session. While I enjoy Thursday's opportunity of a good feed, the lack of training means I'm keen to get into the evening session.

Once at the gym, Knobby immediately starts his usual troop entertaining antics, but occasionally I realise he's watching me. After a while he comes over and asks for help with his form. Despite being here three weeks longer than us Knobby's blasé attitude to training has resulted in our overtaking him. He probably hadn't noticed before as most students don't last long enough for it to show, but he is now feeling left behind. I was previously disinclined, but if he's decided to buckle down then I am more than prepared to give him my time.

We appear to have broken more ground with Shifu Fatso. Perhaps as a result of having survived so far and been seen attempting to train, Shifu appears to be warming to us.

At Tuck-in, he displays this acceptance by asking about our personal situations. This show of interest betrays the things that are important to the Chinese. So much so that these common questions were among the first things covered at my Mandarin class back home. The format varies so little I can effectively go into automatic response, 'How old are you?

'I'm thirty-nine.'

'Are you married?'

'No.'

'Do you have children?'

'No.'

'Whuh, what have you been doing?' Shaking his head, he turns off the light and closes the door behind him. I wonder if he's been speaking to my mother.

Students also share a recreational room with T.V, DVD player and a computer with free DSL internet connection. All these facilities are to ensure comfortable living so you can concentrate on what you came for, training.

Xiao Long Website.

Today's morning warming laps of campus are curtailed when Shifu Fatso orders us to the gym. Following some basic stretches, we move on to body weight exercises. We have a hundred sit-ups, a hundred squats, a hundred reverse sit-ups. Continuing this imaginative theme Shifu Fatso finishes up by giving us a hundred press-ups.

Walking along the line, he watches the feeble efforts of his motley crew with disdain. I've done about forty by the time he gets back to me, but as he approaches I say, 'Jiu shi ba, jiu shi jiu, yi bai.'

Wide eyed, he exclaims, 'Whuh huh?' as a huge grin spreads over his face.

Fatso is obviously familiar with the joke. It's good to see some universal constants exist. It certainly goes a long way toward the bonding process. His reaction is priceless and I struggle to finish as I'm now laughing too much. Well, that's my excuse for not finishing my hundred press-ups anyway.

A slightly different tone of grunt indicates we should lie face down on the floor. He works his way along the prone forms manipulating our spines with his nicotine stained thumbs and walks up and down our backs with his dirty shoes.

A double grunt coupled with a wobbly finger sees us take turns rolling down the line over the top of each other. This isn't particularly effective as I only feel anything when it's VD or Juha's turn. Shifu picks up on this and, not convinced we are sufficiently decompressing each other, calls the two little Korean kids from Yuan Shifu's group to run over us.

Delighted with the opportunity to trample their bigger siblings, the pint-sized terrors put heart and soul into parting our vertebrae. They might not weigh much, but they certainly make up for any respect we were giving each other and are stamping more enthusiastically than I would ideally like. Seeing their enthusiasm for digging the heels in, Shifu, for once, shares my concerns and tries to reign them in before we end up in traction. The implications are lost on them. They are having far too much fun to listen so Fatso has to resort to being strict. They wind up having a paddy and pretending to cry. If I was glad of the lie down after the press-ups, I'm delighted to get to the canteen away from the theatrically wailing kids.

After breakfast, we Go Run kitchen laps, then Go Gym for lengths of the hall swinging our legs. Another few lengths in stances and it's time for Power Stretching. By this point I welcome the opportunity to lie down again.

I've never been particularly flexible and my first Kung Fu teacher, seeing my feeble efforts, told me not to bother stretching as it was pointless. He elaborated that flexibility was genetically inherited so, unless both my parents were ballerinas, I would never get close to the splits. My current Sifu, on the other hand, told me to stop making excuses and stretch because, while I may never achieve full splits, any increase was a bonus.

Shifu Fatso clearly subscribes to neither of these views preferring to grin at me while attempting to shove my foot into my mouth. Between the exercises and constant running, our legs are permanently exhausted and aren't able to put up much resistance to being forcefully manipulated.

One could never get away with treating students like this in the west, but, while this approach may be a little insensitive, I can't deny its effectiveness. In the short time we've been here, there are already visible gains in my flexibility not to mention my pain threshold.

After break, it's Jibengong and we follow Julie back and fore the hall punching and kicking in different stances. As our only instruction comes from copying Julie, it takes a couple of lengths to figure out each movement. This is not what our Shifu wants to see and he's baffled as to why we can't decode his grunts and follow the simple commands. Not knowing whether to laugh or cry at our incompetence, he comes out with a new phrase, 'Noh, what are do?'

Shifu's despairing laughs are mostly directed at Juha whose size and build are against him when it comes to Wushu and he becomes the focus of much of Shifu's attention. 'Noh Juha! What are do?' is heard so frequently that it is in danger of becoming our group's catchphrase.

At least he's picked up Juha's name, although Juha doesn't seem so pleased about it. The phrase is used so often throughout the session that even the stoic Finlander's good-nature must be wearing thin.

Not humiliating ourselves enough for Shifu's liking, he ups the ante by adding a new move to the mix. Pointing at Julie, he waves his arms around and points to the mat. I'm amazed at how she manages to understand him. It must be telepathy. The new movement means we get to follow Julie up and down the hall in an even more shambolic fashion.

From the attention position, we step our left leg forward with leg straight and ball of the foot on the ground. Bringing our hands up to waist height at the front we slap the back of the right hand with the left palm and extend the arms horizontally from the respective shoulders with palms outward and fingers upright. Turning the head to look at the right hand, the left arm circles down in front of the body while the right arm circles up behind and overhead. As the arms continue their paths, the torso twists to the right, the left arm rises to eye level and torso twists to the left as the arm continues overhead and drops down again behind the body and back to the starting position. Looking at the opposite hand to which we started, the movement is repeated from the other side.

This circling arm technique is inside many fighting systems, not just Shaolin Kung Fu, but the influence of Wushu means the movement taught here is much larger than most martial styles.

At its most basic level this is a shoulder loosening exercise, but the circling also contains a sequence of moves. Adjusting the distance and focus of the whirling arms changes their purpose. At mid-range the moves are strikes and blocks. Closing distance, the circles become joint manipulations or throws and, by extending the range, the techniques can be used against weapons like a spear or staff to overcome the difference in reach before closing in. Similarly, the technique can also be applied when holding weapons, most commonly with a pair of swords or sticks.

Windmilling the arms in large circular motions while twisting the body from side to side is also a good way to condition the body by stretching muscles and tendons. Done well, the smoothly circling arms are a mesmerizing blur, like Bruce Lee's Meizhong Quan as seen in Fist of Fury. I, on the other hand, look like I'm fending off a frenzied wasp attack.

I've always struggled with my coordination and immediately know what I'll be spending the evening's free training session trying to get to grips with. I'm just about getting myself untangled when it's time to hit the canteen.

With VD taking the opportunity to get his head down after lunch I head to the DVD room in search of the promised internet access. It turns out to be a little disheartening. The term 'DVD room' isn't exactly a misnomer. It's technically correct in that it is a room and it does contain DVDs. Although, a casual glance is enough to tell me that the shattered disks littering the floor are beyond hope.

On another table, sitting under a pile of books left by previous foreign students is the ravaged carcass of an old computer. So much for 'free ADSL internet connection'. It looks like I am going to have to come up with another plan.

Waking VD, he informs me that he has entered his Imodium down phase and will be relieving internal pressure in preference to training. This procedure was developed by his wife when she refused to use the public facilities at a music festival. It works on the simple principle of cork it up for three or four days then have a day off and let rip. I'm glad to be out of the way before blast-off.

VD isn't the only one pulling a sickie. As our group's sole attendee, Shifu Fatso offloads me with a, 'Go Taiji.'

Fair enough. I've done a bit of Taiji over the years so I'm happy to give the class a go and see the Xiao Long take on it. I wander over to the Taiji group and ask their Shifu for permission to come aboard. My approach terrifies him and, mumbling incoherently, he motions me into the line. It's always nice to feel welcome.

Continuing to eye me suspiciously, he waves us to the gym. Upstairs a senior student takes charge and I copy the others as he silently leads. Gentler than Fatso's approach, the Taiji warmup is thoroughly pleasant.

Taiji Shifu is really enigmatic, rather than actively participating he stands at the front observing. In order to teach the class, he relies on his students to pass on their knowledge to each other. I assume he must have once spoken to someone or else this wouldn't work.

I've previously noticed Taiji Shifu is also aloof from his fellow teachers. Whereas they joke around with their students and with each other, he remains apart. It occurs to me his earlier embarrassment was probably due to his lack of English as he was in danger of losing face when I spoke to him. Realising I'm not going to ask him any more questions his panic subsides, but, out of the corner of my eye, I see him giving me a wary look now and again.

Warmed up, we start to work through the form and I, again, copy everyone else. Shifu then motions some members to step apart and comes around us with his senior student. Being the new guy, I'm shown the first three moves and told to practice them.

I spend the next two hours repeating the first three movements of a 108-move form. Occasionally a senior student wanders over and gives me a few pointers, but essentially, I just repeat the same three slow moves. My limited experience of Taiji nevertheless allows me to understand what I should be doing and I try to follow the principles as I remember them, but it's still very hard going.

Sensing my dissatisfaction, one of the German guys pats me on the shoulder. He jokingly complains that after eight months he's less than half way through the form. He's doing Taiji full-time and estimates it will take him another year. I'm not prepared to spend the time working out how long it would take me to finish the form with one session a week. Even in my confused state I realise it's not viable. I was prepared to have a little dabble with the old Taiji, but I'm simply wasting the valuable time I should be spending on Kung Fu. Maybe on a future trip I'll go to Wutang and learn Taiji properly. The one thing I have learnt today was, here and now, Taiji is a nonstarter for me.

Returning to the room, it has to be said VD looks none the worse for the absence of Taiji in his life. 'Well, you didn't miss anything there, mate. You up to dinner?'

'Absolutely.'

VD is much chipper after spending the afternoon alternating between napping and detoxing. I have to concede, while he may be letting the side down on the attendance front, it's a cleverer idea to conserve energy than waste it on something you're not interested in. The training here isn't really any different to what we are used to, there's just more of it. So, the issue isn't so much that the training is hard as much as it's constant. You could stagger away from any one session having enjoyed a good work out, but we barely have the chance to recuperate before hitting the next session.

Even allowing for the amount of waiting around, Go Run and other general procrastination, it's still possible to get an awful lot of training in. We are timetabled for about ten hours a day, but with all the faffing about, we probably get closer to eight. At home, I manage a couple of hours a day at best, so there's no comparison. It's no wonder the Chinese students are so good. However, the system is heavy on numbers and low on quality so the training lacks fine detail relying on quantity to compensate.

The high dropout rate amongst foreigners is partly because we can't cope with the amount of training combined with the living conditions. One could never train like this and have a life. Training this many hours a day leaves no time or energy to hold down a job, have a relationship or even succeed at school. For the kids who live here this is their everything and they don't know any different. I have to wonder how they'll cope after they graduate and have to enter the real world.

Collecting VD has delayed my arrival so we play our foreign student priority card and barge through the malnourished urchins. The clamouring children politely clearing the way makes me wonder if they have been prepped or are just deferring to our age. Shoving his friend aside, a little kid of about six years old with a liberal dusting of dirt and a runny nose, reaches into the tray of chopsticks and helpfully hands me a pair.

Accepting the chopsticks, I say, 'Xiongdi, xie xie ni.' I porter them to the table then discard them and use my own. These kids look like they've missed annual bath night a several times in a row and, while I appreciate the grimy child's gesture, I am not putting anything in my mouth that he's handled. I try to ensure he doesn't see me, but the risk of offending him is offset by maintaining my personal wellbeing. In this environment, it's justified as our exhausted state makes us so vulnerable. We have to pamper our personal health in order not to miss out on training, the very thing we came here to do. I'm not paranoid, China really is out to get me.

Doing his canteen rounds, Knobby briefly joins us to share the news of a new arrival. Knobby's new friend is a backpacker allocated to Yuan Shifu's squad. I noticed him earlier and he looks far too much like Charles Manson for my liking. The crazy-eyed, beardy trains in huge walking boots and refuses to buy a uniform on the logic he's not going to stay at Xiao Long because he can't learn anything here. My immediate thought is, 'So why come?', but I'm not interested enough to ask. Curiously, this scary throwback didn't meet the strict entry requirements for Fatso's elite group.

My lack of success with the DVD room internet prompts me to instigate plan B. During our initial efforts to make the room habitable, we uncovered a broken electricity socket under the desk with what looks like the remains of an Ethernet cable dangling from the wall next to it. Buoyant with the success of my previous DIY projects I set about this socket with the aim of getting us some internet.

Cable ends trimmed with my trusty sword, I'm under the desk touching bits of wire together as VD sits on his bed telling me when the LED on my laptop flickers. I twist those two wires together and insulate them with a tiny strip of sword grip tape and move on to the next. Our combined tiredness means this simple task ends up resembling a Chuckle Brothers episode, but I manage to resist the urge for a 'To me, to you' session. I'm sure VD's making up when he can see the light or not just to frustrate me.

Performing this delicate surgical operation, I get a vision of VD's wife shaking her head in despair at us. It's the sort of response we generally elicit from her. Sorely tested for many years by VD's ingenuity in maiming himself, she has now given up expecting anything resembling sensible behaviour from him and hit the bottle in an attempt to blot out the embarrassment of it all. For no reason I can determine, she includes me in the same category. No wonder she had such a spring in her step when she dropped us at the airport.

I'm crouched under the desk, trying to jam wires back into a wall socket with a sword, when Yuan Shifu comes in to tell us to close the door. Puzzled by my position he asks what I'm doing. Perhaps he's concerned I'm tunnelling my way out. One complicated explanation later, he pulls out his mobile and makes a phone call to the lady responsible for internet access. Determining she is not in, he takes some details from my laptop and says he will organize internet access for us the next day. Quoting 40Y a month, he refuses to take the payment up front. I'm not sure what to make of this. It feels too simple to be kosher and the fact he's not asking for the cash now implies to me he doesn't want to be held accountable. I can hardly blame him. There are always so many links in the chain of command here that I wouldn't want anyone to have any leverage over me either. It's nice of him to try, but for this one instance we will just have to accept whatever fate brings. Besides, I'm sure there must be an internet café in town.

All this messing about with my wire has made us late for training, but a bit of a dash ensures we are there before our Shifu and we get away with it. I don't know why we bothered rushing, when he does arrive he just dismisses us to Go Gym.

While VD heads back to room, I hit the gym and spend half an hour attempting to coordinate my windmilling.

Hearing Wan Shifu bumbling his way down the corridor VD decides he can't be bothered to go through the motions of fraternising and feigns sleep. All psyched up to deliver his evening monologue, Fatso blunders into the room where half of his prospective audience have finished without him. Deflated, he pauses to think. Giving me a huge grin, he puts his chubby, nicotine stained finger to his lips and tiptoes over to VD's recumbent form. I'm bemused and slightly concerned to what he has in mind, but he contents himself with peering at VD and giggling. It's like he's never seen anyone sleeping before.

Worried he's going to stand there all night, I clear my throat to get his attention. He takes the subtle hint, 'Ok, ok, go sleep, ok.'

Hearing the door close, VD opens his eyes, 'How rude!'

I can only shrug my shoulders in response. Again, the vagaries of Chinese humour have passed us by.

The school building, with large-scale, functional facilities, beautiful environment and convenient transportation, covers 150 hectares. Set amidst a peaceful environment away from the usual noise of modernising China. It contains 27 tree lined training grounds, 3 training halls, 2 basketball courts as well as pagodas, traditional training vats and pillars and enough recreational areas to make sure that a lack of training space is not an issue.

Xiao Long Website

Di shui chuan shi
(Dripping water will pierce a stone.)

Traditional Chinese Proverb.

Properly morning-warmed and breakfasted, we line up for Fatso's inspection. Establishing we are all present, if not exactly correct, he gestures vaguely toward the back of school and commands, 'Go Park', leaving us to march up Chonggao road unattended.

Arriving at Wulin Park, I am surprised to see Shifu already there. I dismiss this curious enigma from my mind and get straight into kicking back. It's a standard Go Park routine: a spot of basketing the ball followed by sitting around nattering.

Amongst the freely given opinions sits a silent, elfin figure. As usual, the quiet one is the one worth listening to. Marta, from Poland, stayed at our school when it was based in Zhengzhou and is able to give a more considered impression Xiao Long.

In 1982, our headmaster, Chen Tongshan, founded Shaolin's first Kung Fu school since the Cultural Revolution. This school, based in his own home, was later left in the care of his brother and Chen Tongshan went to work at the Shaolin Wushu Xue Xiao which he took over in 1988. When the Shaolin reconstruction programme marked the Wushu Xue Xiao for demolition in 2001 Chen Tongshan combined this school with the Zhengzhou Songshan Shaolin Martial Arts School and formed the Shaolin Si Xiao Long Wu Yuan at the edge of Dengfeng. Named after the headmaster's son and martial arts movie star, Chen Xiaolong, the school now has nearly three thousand students.

Marta says living conditions were better in Zhengzhou and the training harder, also that many pictures in the school brochure and website are from the Zhengzhou school prior to the merger. This also explains why we didn't recognise the school when we arrived.

This gives everyone the opportunity to have a laugh at the school brochure. Although in all fairness the brochure doesn't actually claim the pictures are of our school or that facilities like the showers are operational. We learn that it's not unusual for schools in the area to utilise pictures from other sources or even from rival schools passing them off as their own.

Amid tales of the school's mismanagement, one guy mentions the trouble he had when the school lost his passport. VD's raised eyebrows remind me we haven't had our passports back yet. We handed them to Shibu Shifu when we arrived so that our presence could be registered with the local authorities. It's a bit of Big Brotherness we don't have to deal with in Europe, but in China, with its love of bureaucracy, it's de rigueur. While things have loosened up significantly since the fall of the Bamboo Curtain, Chinese authorities still aren't exactly renowned for their easy-going attitude to international travellers' paperwork. Beijing passport control is among the most stringent I've ever passed through. Passports and visas are minutely examined, after which came the comparison check where each facial detail was checked against the passport photo. They looked into my eyes, studied passport, looked at my nose, studied passport, looked at my ears; you get the picture.

I was expecting our passports to be photocopied and the originals returned, but it's now been two weeks with no sign. Visitors to China are supposed to carry their passports at all times, but as we rarely stray far from school there's no real urgency for us to have them at the moment. That said, I would still feel happier knowing where they are. I wander over to Shibu and ask him. He says he hasn't got them, but we can collect them from reception anytime. As it's currently closed for the weekend, I resolve to do so Monday.

It's not until we have had our park ration that I realise why Shifu Fatso was at the park ahead of us. After ordering us to, 'Go school', I notice him heading towards a line of scooters at the back of the park. Upon return my suspicions are confirmed. Shifu is leaning on his scooter waiting. An epitome of indolence, our Shifu is so lazy that he's not prepared to walk the five minutes up the road where he can sit around for an hour. Too idle to support his own weight, I've seen him lean on any number of inanimate objects, but he now turns up prepared in case there is nothing leanable on to hand.

After Buddhist class, we line up and face a telling off for our Buddhist class behaviour. Personally, I find their attitude a bit rich considering the depth of instruction supplied. Seeing the others meditate it's clear a few pointers wouldn't go amiss. While I have a rough idea of what's occurring, most are Buddha'ing blindly and without any form of guidance are likely to remain that way. It's no wonder they get bored during the session.

Shibu also feels our chanting needs work to bring it up to scratch and tells us to keep the lyric sheets and learn the words for next week. Happy to oblige, Oliver asks Shibu for a translation.

'Is no word, only', Shibu twists his fingers into a series of shapes and mumbles before continuing his explanation, 'Like evil woman you know, but good. Only mean only do good thing, not drink, not eat meat, mean nothing like evil woman, just', mumble mumble. While Oliver's English is pretty good for everyday use, I can't imagine what he makes of the explanation.

If Shibu's description leaves a little to be desired the lyric sheet is something else. The words appear to be phonetic, but not in any system I'm familiar with and, as phonetics don't cross cultures well, our mix of nationalities ensures we all pronounce them differently. I've already made a stab at a translation, but without the characters it's really hard work as I'm working from a best guess.

Being formally reproached seems to be a regular occurrence after Buddhist class as we are also reprimanded regarding our ablutions, 'Do not cold shower. You will get fever'.

One of the guys points out that the showers don't work. Another adds that we only have cold water so the alternative would be not to wash at all. Someone else adds that we are lucky when we can wash as often there's no water. Shibu is oblivious to these minor technical issues. He has done his job in passing on the shower advice and his remit covers nothing else.

Lunch time discussions are all about Shibu's cold water comments. We have all developed our own way of dealing with the shower situation, mostly by washing in the sink, but as many are teenage boys they are unconcerned with the mundane issue of ablutions.

Continuing the theme, Stefan complains that the water is off again anyway. With no shower and drinking bottled water, VD and I hadn't noticed. It's not unusual for large building complexes to save on the fuel bills by only providing hot water at certain times. Similarly, at times of shortage, the local government rations water by supplying different areas throughout the day. I have established that this is not why our shower doesn't work by leaving the shower turned on and placing a cup underneath. Despite sitting in a puddle the cup inner remains bone dry. Miss Marple would be proud of my sleuth work.

All this talk of bathrooms reminds me of our leak. Even though the shower doesn't work the pipe to it leaks constantly. The leak isn't hard to track down as there is only one pipe in the bathroom and no evidence to imply another pipe was ever intended to be run.

Judging from the stains on the wall and floor, this pipe has been leaking for quite a while. Water has got under the floor tiles, which have cracked and loosened, and must now be leaking into the building core. More disturbingly, ours is not the only leak around the building, potentially causing a serious problem in the future. As far as I can ascertain, this building is the newest at school, being only a couple of years old and all the bathrooms in our building have similar faults with the electric and water.

China's recent rate of expansion has led to many building projects being jerry built. Often referred to as 'Tofu projects' these rushed constructions suffer from contract corruption leading to skimping of labour and materials. Recent high-profile construction disasters, most notably Tuojiang Bridge in 2007 and the Sichuan school in 2008, were responsible for thousands of deaths and left China sensitive about its building track record. Given the examples of prematurely aging buildings around us I can see why. This is not a reassuring thought when I lay on my bed finding patterns in the ceiling cracks.

When we arrived, there was a puddle of stagnant water on the bathroom floor. I mopped it up, but it promptly returned. I rooted around the room, in the dark as the light doesn't work, and found the problem source. It looks like the pipe connection needs tightening. I appreciate I'm not a plumbing professional so I showed it to Shifu so he could get the considered opinion of a qualified plumber. He appeared to agree saying, 'Ok, ok, is no work'.

I stupidly expected this meant he would get someone to fix the leak. Over a week later, still nothing has happened. He must have thought I was showing off my expansive vocabulary by pointing at things and naming them.

We mop the bathroom floor between classes about four times a day to control the water level. In spite of our efforts the puddle remains a permanent feature which we have adapted to. VD put a rolled-up towel at the bathroom threshold to act as a barrier and we keep the door open, as much as we can get away with, to ventilate the stagnant smell. I am no longer disconcerted when I get up in the night and splash through an inch of cold water in the dark.

Fatso probably thought he'd wriggled free, but this afternoon, when he comes to tell us to close the door, I nab him and remind him about the leak. Confronted with his trademark blank look, I guide him to the bathroom and perform a little Gene Kelly impersonation in the hope he will cotton on.

Apart from an initial surprise at my nifty footwork, his expression remains as vacant as ever. Worried my impromptu floor show has pushed him over the edge and into a coma, I retell the saga without the theatrics. Touching the pipe, I show him my wet hand. He says, 'I know, I know, is no work.'

Third time round, I take his hand in mine and hold it to the dripping pipe. He agrees there is water on the floor and makes motions that I should mop it up. Exasperated, I give up on the Chinese and give vent in my native tongue, 'I have mopped it up. I am continually mopping it up. We mop the floor several times a day. The problem is not the water on the floor. That is a symptom. The problem is that the pipe is leaking. Why do you think I was showing you my wet hand?'

Bizarrely this approach seems to work. It's as if the conversation tone is more important than the actual words used, but now I'm more confused that he appears to understand. He agrees to get the leak repaired, or as he puts it, 'Ok, tomorrow.'

Just to give them a clue when, if, they turn up I will stop mopping the floor, but I know what will happen. Bearing in mind they didn't notice the puddle when they were standing in it attempting to fix the toilet, I guarantee that they will either fail to see a problem, completely oblivious to the fact they are paddling in a half-inch of stagnant water, or they will decide the problem is the water and mop it up. As far as they are concerned, job done. Not their problem if water comes back once they got rid of it.

Fobbed off by Fatso regarding the leak after being fobbed off by Shibu over our passports, my cynicism is growing in proportion to the bathroom puddle. The drip is a constant reminder of our frustration with the school. A visible metaphor of the system wearing me down.

Among the foreign students are two little Korean kids who are permanently hyperactive with fuel from the tuck shop. This afternoon one of the little tearaways turns up to training with a bandaged hand. I ask him what he has done. Before he can reply, his mate snitches on him, 'He cheating'. The boy is a genius. I just wish I'd thought of it first. If the others catch on, tomorrow's assembly could look like a scene from the Mummy's Revenge.

Most students filter off to their various classes and the Shifus lump the remainder together on the playing field. There are a few classes of Chinese students already underway. The ground is so hard-baked that some Shifus send their students for bowls of water. Running back and fore with plastic washing-up bowls they spill most of the water along the way, the remainder gets sploshed around in an attempt to dampen the dust. The water has evaporated before the next load arrives, but at least it's good exercise for them. Although I would have preferred to see them carrying a bucket in each hand with their arms outstretched as Gordon Liu in '36 Chambers', and countless other Kung Fu films, led me to believe was the done thing.

When Shibu appears with a football under his arm, I'm reminded of childhood PE lessons where a failed sportsman would kick a ball into a muddy patch of slag-heap and expect us to entertain ourselves with a game of 80-a-side while they nipped off for a crafty fag.

It's easy to fool yourself that certain things are part of the training, but the reality is the Shifus will do anything to get out of training us. When apathy strikes, they throw the groups together for a game of football, basketball or maybe some Go Park, they'll have us playing hide-and-seek next.

Sticking to my football avoidance resolution, I take a stroll and work on my form in the shadow of the wall. After a while, Shifu Fatso comes over to get me to join the footer. I explain that I came to China to learn Kung Fu and not to play football. I'm not sure he understands, so I change tack. Pointing at my bald patch, I explain that being Welsh I'm simply not built for this weather. My heritage means I am genetically designed for a wet and miserable outlook with bouts of unrequested singing. I certainly shouldn't be standing around in the sun without a handkerchief on my head. He doesn't get this either, but resigns to leave me alone as I'm too much like hard work.

No one from our group is playing football, but they aren't training either. I notice Shifu doesn't question them and I consider it curious he should choose to pressure the only person who is training.

While some are happy to participate in a casual kick-about, SA guy, despite referring to the game as soccer, takes his football seriously. Hacking away at legs and barging through with murderous intent earns him a caution from Shibu. Immediately he takes the offensive, 'What point if not win, eh? You have no passion in life.'

It looked like a fair cop to me. He was out of order and got called on it, but as usual he refuses to take his caution on the chin and some heated verbal ensues. Shibu takes him aside and calms him down, but his outburst has put a dampener on the mood. Taking his ball back, Shibu tells us to line up.

We collect our belongings at the side of the field and VD puts on his glasses. It's the funniest thing Fatso has ever seen. Pointing at VD, he chuckles away nudging the others to join in. I normally wear my glasses first thing in the morning, put contact lenses in after brekkers, and change back in the evening. Less reliant on his glasses than I, VD wears his sporadically. As such, I assume Shifu hasn't previously seen him wearing them and thinks he's put mine on for a bit of a jape.

I love these little pieces of humour with our Shifu. It makes him seem almost human, a little strange, but human. VD, however, is rapidly losing tolerance with our portly instructor and takes it personally. Not even his teatime dose of cabbage and rice can bring him around.

Already despairing of Chinese bureaucracy, I'm forced to eat my words with regard to Yuan Shifu. Yesterday's doubts have proven unfounded and Yuan Shifu is now officially our hero. True to his word, this evening Yuan Shifu arrives to internet us up. Phone in hand, he follows instructions from his invisible helper until we are connected. We are up and running with so little song and dance that I am beginning to wonder if he is really Chinese.

It's as if the Gods have granted us a bounty. Despite the school website claims of free internet access for foreign students, my expectations have diminished since our arrival so it's one of the more pleasant surprises we've had. It may be slow and erratic but, for a small monthly fee, we are, nonetheless connected. Contact with the outside world is a massive boon. On the downside, some websites we take for granted cannot be accessed in China. VD was hoping to stay in contact with friends and family through his Facebook page, only to discover it's among the sites Chinese officials have deemed inappropriate and blocked access to.

The commonly touted reason for this control is the Chinese Government's desire to restrict information to its masses. This is based on the fact information sites like Wikipedia and Youtube and social networking sites, such as Facebook and Myspace, are blocked and even the global search engine Google is restricted.

Referred to as the Great Firewall of China, these restrictions may, in part, be due to the Chinese government's censorship policy, but there are other reasons. One is the copyright and licensing issues for internationally produced media and another is advertising revenue. All the blocked sites have Chinese equivalents which endorse Chinese products. As a Google substitute China has Baidu, the nation's most popular search engine. The same company produces an online encyclopaedia along the lines of Wikipedia called Baidu Baike, while Youtube has Chinese equivalents in the form of Tudou and Youku.

China's recent embracing of Commercial Communism has created a massive and booming market place. With such a receptive audience, it makes no sense to advertise inaccessible foreign products, particularly when there are so many native products available to its populace.

Despite its limitations, internet access has given us a psychological uplift and briefly roused VD from his rancour. Not only can we contact friends and family, but we now have a source of information for our surroundings.

Having written off the DVD Shop on Dayu Road, we use our

newfound internet access to locate a local stockist of the Shaolin books. Now that I know to treat Chinese advertising claims with a shovel full of salt, internet based research becomes a chore, but VD comes up with a cunning plan. Working on the logic that since Tagou wrote and published the books they should know where they are available. He emails Tagou enquiring accordingly. Given that Tagou is close by, it would be extremely handy if they carry the books.

Carried away with our new toy we are still using the internet when Shifu Fatso arrives to tuck us in, 'Ok. Go sleep.'

I stall for time, 'Yes, Shifu, I am sleeping.'

A full gamut of emotions contorts his features as he wrestles with the concept of what I said. Slowly the realisation dawns that I am basically lying to his face. Astounded, he splutters, 'You no sleep, you computer.'

Without waiting for a response, he hits the light switch and closes the door behind him. Listening to his flat feet echoing down the corridor, I can picture him still shaking his head as he stomps along. It was worth it for the look on his face.

As it's Sunday tomorrow we can afford to live a little tonight, so I turn the light back on and continue with the internet, but after the initial euphoria of being online the connection proves so tediously slow we turn-in anyway.

Without ascending the mountain, we cannot judge the height of heaven. Without descending into the valley, we cannot judge the depth of the earth. Without listening to the ancient masters, we cannot know the excellence of learning. The words of saints though a thousand years old do not become useless.

Traditional Chinese Proverb.

One of China's five holy mountain ranges, the Song Mountains have any number of temples and retreats hidden away amongst their 36 peaks. This week's expedition is to Shaoshi Shan. At 1512m, the tallest peak of the Song Shan range is also home to Sanhuangzhai, the Three Emperors Monastery.

Nestled high in the mountain, the ancient walls of Sanhuangzhai are being renovated and expanded by Shi Dejian. Previously taught by Master Xingxing and Master Suxi, Shi Dejian and a handful of disciples seek to preserve a more traditional form of Shaolin Kung Fu known as Chanwuyi. Chanwuyi was originally taught at another temple complex within the Shaolin grounds called Yonghuatang of which Shi Dejian is the 18th generation master. Founded in the Ming dynasty by Zhengdao, Yonghuatang was destroyed during the Qing dynasty and is now nothing more than scattered, overgrown ruins.

Sometimes referred to as Wu Gulun, after the monk who maintained the style during the Temple's persecution, this Kung Fu is closer to Shaolin's original system. As a side note, the shrine to Master Wu Gulun stands outside the small village of Baiyougou. And Shigou temple, where Zhan Mo, Hai Fa and Wu Gulun hid and practiced the Kung Fu during the prohibition is still relatively intact within the Shaolin grounds.

Based on the movements of birds and animals, Chanwuyi is designed to exercise the body in harmony with the mind and to complement a holistic lifestyle embodying the three Chan Buddhist principles of Chan, Wu and Yi: meditation, exercise and medicine.

This is the living link between Chan Buddhism and Kung Fu; the practical application of Chan through moving meditation. The intention being to gain a state of mind immune from distraction and lose one's sense of self within the movements. Taken to its extreme, this philosophy permeates even the most mundane task and becomes a way of life, thus, forming the basis of the expression, 'Chan wu he yi', Chan and martial arts harmonise as one.

Throughout its long history, Shaolin Temple has often needed to be flexible in order to survive. In the rapidly changing world the current trend is for more flamboyant, performance orientated Kung Fu which, along with the recent introduction of competition Wushu, has forced traditional Kung Fu to take a back seat. While acknowledging the need for Shaolin Kung Fu to adapt and develop, Shi Dejian has made a commitment to preserving the essence of Shaolin's original style. Recommended by Master Suxi to be the next Shaolin Abbot, Shi Dejian chose to disassociate himself from the profit-making activities of the main temple and relies on donations for the rebuilding and maintenance of Sanhuangzhai.

After the predictable farce of getting signed out of school, VD, Juha and I still manage to arrive at the Temple reasonably bright and early. Everything is much more subdued at this time of day and the quiet warmth of the morning light feels apt. The stalls on route are still setting-up and the vendors take no interest in us, so we can amble past without harassment. It also means I can avoid the dubious distinction of constant photo calls from my demanding Chinese fan base.

Heading past the Mountain Gate, through the Pagoda Forest, we get to the Shaolin Suodao (Shaolin cableway). The half hour, 60Y, cable car ride is well worth the financial outlay as it cuts hours off the journey to the top of Shaoshi Shan.

The viewing platform around the cable car station has a sign demanding visitors to 'Look out', just to make sure the view doesn't go to waste. It's surely not a caution notice as I'm fairly positive they don't exist in China. Following the instruction, I look down the valley, but it's still too early to make out much in the hazy light. Other than the sign, the only thing of note is a scabby dog foraging the scrub.

A right turn at the mangy mutt takes us down an innocuous, scruffy little trail that, just around the corner, transforms into a stone path. There is no indication as to where this path leads. It's as if the route is deliberately hidden.

Along the narrow mountain path, we spurn a rickety shack selling canned drinks and ready comestibles. The cable car has saved us valuable time, but we are still left with at least a four-hour round-trip.

The day soon brightens and the narrow path along the sheer face affords spectacular views down the valley through the clearing mist. As the haze seeps away, the height becomes more apparent. I'm pretty pleased to see the path has recently been renovated and a guardrail added.

At one point, we are directly opposite the statue of Damo on Wuru peak. The tiny white dot gleams against the grey and green of the mountain like a lighthouse beaming peace over the valley. But that's for another day.

The trek around the mountain continues in a similar vein as far as the eye can see. It's not particularly difficult, but there is a lot of it and the steps cut into the cliff weren't designed for my big, western feet so I am mostly walking on the balls of my feet. Still Juha, who is considerably bigger than I, is managing so I'm not in a position to complain.

The craggy cliffs are a UNESCO protected part of the Songshan Geopark site. Referred to as 'the textbook of geological history', it's claimed the 464 square kilometre park demonstrates 36 million years of geological evolution. Every so often a handy sign points out a different colour of exposed rock seam and explains the geological detail relevant to that particular lump. It's probably interesting to those who like lumps of rock, but the few I read leave me stone cold.

Just to prove me wrong, at the cliff we come across a safety notice warning against falling rocks which advises, 'Do not stay here long.' I know when I'm not wanted.

One would think our current levels of fitness would have us sprinting up the mountain, but our training has left us so exhausted that old ladies are shuffling us out of their way and young girls in high heels are overtaking us while chatting on their phones. They are probably telling their friends what a bunch of Jessies these huge westerners are.

Winding around the cliff edge, the path offers tantalising glimpses of the monastery. Constantly just out of reach, Sanhuangzhai taunts us by peeking in and out of view, always seeming just around the corner yet never any nearer.

Staggering up the steep stone steps, we meet a seasoned old nun going the other way. With her sparsely toothed smile she gives us an automatic, 'Amitofo', as she passes. She's probably on her way to the shop for a pint of milk and a Toffee Crisp. It makes me feel even more pathetic in my fatigue.

An hour's worth of footslogging brings us to a hanging bridge which, as far as I'm concerned, is a death-trap over the bottomless gorge of doom. The rusty, creaking monstrosity suspended from two badly oxidised cables is exactly what I don't want to rely on the Chinese to maintain. And it's not just my vertigo saying that. At least I give VD a good chuckle as I take nonchalance to a new level by striding manfully, and not a little self-consciously, across the swaying nightmare. Back on the cliff path, the monastery still doesn't seem any closer.

By the time we hit the monastery another hour later I'm about ready for a cup of tea, but there doesn't appear to be anyone home. I don't understand where the people who passed us have gone. The monastery is deserted apart from a small group of builders chiselling blocks from the cliff face by hand.

Shi Dejian has recently taken part in a Hong Kong University study into how meditation affects the brain. He also has an extensive tour program for the promotion of Chanwuyi. I can't blame him for wanting to get away from the cacophony of building work at Sanhuangzhai, but a true test of his meditative powers would be to practice here during the construction.

The monastery is a little austere, but I suppose that's only to be expected when everything here has to be carried up the mountainside by hand. Under these conditions it must be much easier to keep one's Buddhist vows and spurn material possessions.

Screwed to the rock face a bilingual sign lists the monastery rules.

'Regulations for visiting the Sanhuangzhai Monastery:
1. Smoking, drinking, spitting and urinating at random are prohibited.

2. Eating meat, fish, egg, onion and garlic within the monastery is not allowed.

3. Please dress tidily.

4. Please do not litter.

5. Please do not climb, sit or stand on the cliff and walls to avoid accident.

6. Superstitious activities such as fortune telling not allowed.

7. The monastery has the right to refuse any visitor vist the Monastery.'

Only one building is open, Wuliang Sheng Dian (Hall of Infinite Saints). Cut from the grey mountainside, the solid walls deaden the sound of the work outside. Sparsely furnished, the hall contains an altar, a donation box and a shelf around three walls seating lots of gold Buddhas. Presiding over all is a solitary, weather-beaten old nun as motionless as the statues she guards.

Taking advantage of the low stools against the wall I rest my weary bones. Closing my eyes, I give the impression of meditating, but in reality, I'm just glad to take the weight off.

Rousing me with an elbow in the ribs, VD nods to the singing bowl guarded by the gnarly old nun, 'I'm having a go on that bad-boy.'

Not one to be left out, I follow suit for some singing bowl action. Sticking cash into the slot, we offer incense and prostrate before the Buddha just to have the old dear bang on her bowl. Unflustered, Juha looks on. He has a fantastic poker face, but I'm pretty sure he only tagged along out of curiosity and is probably wishing he'd stayed in bed. I can see his point.

The pounding of hammers and chisels as the monastery is slowly hacked from the mountain somewhat spoils the tranquillity for which this remote monastery is famous. There is little evidence of the Shangri-La I'd been expecting, it's more like trespassing onto a building site. Still, I'm sure it'll be nice once it's finished.

With so much of the monastery out of bounds, there is little to entertain us and watching workers slowly chipping bits of mountain into smaller bits of mountain manifests limited interest.

The trek feels a lot further on the way back. My tired legs plod on autopilot as I stumble along, stubbing my toes on the narrow steps. The surrounding mountains stretch into infinity and the only sign of human impact is the path snaking under our feet. With energy levels flagging, we are almost in sight of the cable car when VD digs his heels. Tetchy when tired, he's even more so when hungry and now demands feeding. Fortunately the chow shack we passed all those hours ago is just up ahead.

The best of the limited selection is a big pot of instant noodles. They come at a premium, but it's the simple law of supply and demand. As the shack owner has dragged his produce up a mountain, we must compensate his efforts. VD demonstrates his lack of taste buds and asbestos throat by wolfing his noodles down. That should give his IBS a little treat later. They're a bit too spicy for me, but I plough in doggedly. I hadn't realised how hungry I was. Within a couple of mouthfuls Juha starts to spontaneously combust, but, despite slowing, sticks to it as resolute as ever.

Sitting back with fiery noodles warming my innards, the energy is just returning to my legs as the cable car operator ambles along the path shouting, 'Shiwu fenzhong hou guanbi!' (Closing in fifteen minutes.)

Told off for being late back to school and punished with a few press-ups is one thing, but I'm really not keen on walking to the Temple from here. For once, the others share my view. I give Cable Car Guy the universal thumbs up, Juha necks his noodles and we dash to the station platform.

Snugly packed into our gondola and pleasantly aglow, I realise that our impromptu snack has given us all bright red, swollen lips. We look like a bunch of particularly unconvincing transvestites.

Suspended high over the valley, the cool air plays soothing tunes on my aching feet and I begin to relax.

The cable car shudders to a halt. A light mist is settling over the peaks and the light begins to ebb. Wreathing the mountainside, the thin fog is damp enough to feel like hazy rain and visibility is reduced to a few metres each giving an effect of sitting on clouds.

Our carriage sways gently in the breeze. The operator wouldn't finish his shift with us still airborne surely? Suddenly the supporting cable over our heads looks very thin. I wonder at our combined weight. The sign says four people max per car. Does that mean four Chinese people? Our collective weight is easily that of four Chinese people. I knew bringing Juha was a mistake. Motionless, we sit in silence avoiding each other's gaze.

The car jerks into life. We cover our relief with continuing nonchalance. Five minutes later we pause again. The process is repeated a dozen times. Stepping on to terra firma, I realise the pauses in our descent were for the gondolas to be put away for the evening. Perhaps if I'd been more in harmony I wouldn't have been so concerned.

Walking out of the mountain shadow, the day becomes warmer and brighter. Despite being late afternoon there are still sizable crowds at the Mountain Gate and the stall holders show no signs of flagging.

As VD is checking out Guanyin statuettes and Juha stocks up on Ninja weaponry, I glance around the array of Shaolin doodads. Pausing for just that little too long over the beads, the stallholder takes the opportunity to accost me. Thrusting a set of beads into my face she says, 'Sixty Yuan.'

I already have a bracelet given me by our friend in the clothes shop, so I'm not in the market for another, 'No thanks.'

'How much you want pay?'

'No, it's ok thanks.'

'How much, how much?'

As I don't really want them I take a punt, 'Ten Yuan.'

'No, no, no, fifty.'

I shrug my shoulders and turn to walk away, but she grabs my arm, 'Ok, ten.'

I'm reaching for my pocket when she renegotiates without me, 'Twenty.'

Rolling my eyes in despair, I start walking again. The beads hit me in the back as she grunts, 'Ten Yuan.'

Not a little confused, I hand over the cash and retrieve my new beads. I'm not really sure whether I have inadvertently discovered how to haggle or she very cleverly got me to buy something I didn't want.

'You very good, you come tomorrow I give you job.'

I'm still no clearer about what happened.

In the cab Juha remains deadpan. He's difficult to read, but after five hours footslog around a mountain to look at a building site I'm guessing his thoughts aren't kindly toward us. He's all set to go back to school until the subject of food is raised. Interest piqued, Juha is coming to town.

Apparently, a graduate of Mr. Toad's School of Motoring, our driver's chosen method of vehicle operation is to drive fast and brake hard, squeezing through the tightest space possible while continually sounding his horn. Like many of the western students, Juha hasn't ventured out of school much and has yet to become accustomed to Chinese motoring. His usually tranquil expression looks a little strained as our driver strives to educate him.

Visibly relieved to vacate the cab, Juha is less convinced when I'm lured down a narrow alley by a neon sign. Large PVC windows set into otherwise featureless, grey cement provide an aquarium style view of a small restaurant. The long, thin shop already has a few tables in full swing which is all the recommendation I need. A sociable bunch, the Chinese are even more so in the evening and the atmosphere is great. The other tables are full of life, chatting away and laughing. It's the very fellow for us. Tucked away in the alley, the place must be permanently in the shade and needs the sign and windows to function.

A small, family affair: the husband cooks, wife serves front of house and little girl does her homework at the counter. More up market than the average noodle bar, the fuwuyuan presents us each with a shrink-wrapped bundle. The package contains a small plate, rice bowl, glass and spoon stamped with a certification number stating they have been sterilized. Lacking sufficient facilities, the establishment must outsource its dishwashing to a dedicated firm.

Popping my package reveals the contents not to look particularly sterile. Now I'm beginning to get the hang of the way things work in Dengfeng, I give them a quick wipe with my hand-gel.

Order taken, the fuwuyuan gets on the phone and minutes later a scooter pulls up. The geriatric Easy Rider exchanges a bag of groceries for a handful of cash and putters back to the light.

Being the size of a cupboard, the restaurant kitchen doesn't carry a lot of stock and who would when the delivery system is so reliable? With fridges still considered a luxury item, the Chinese eat a lot of fresh food, simply because they buy it when they need it. Even fish and some meat are sold live, so it's not unusual to see someone returning from the shops with an incredulous chicken under their arm or a puzzled fish in a bag. Although eating out is so cheap it can barely be worth the effort of cooking at home.

Beaming at the mass of plates covering the table top, it's the first time I've seen the Herring Muncher so happy, 'You've cheered up, Juha.'

'Sure, is food.'

He's not wrong, just a little understated, it's fantastic. Once outside school, the food is even better than I'd anticipated. I'm no stranger to a Chinese meal, but the stuff here is a distant relation. I'm guessing most Chinese chefs in Britain were forced to flee their motherland in fear of their lives having been unable to maintain the minimum local culinary standards. The real McCoy is fresh and diverse and, although I don't know what most of it is, I'm stuffing my face as fast as I can drive the chopsticks. Chinese chefs can transform the simplest ingredients into a delicious dish. I wish one of them worked at our school.

The staff are also more attentive than we are used to; topping up my hot water and keeping the beer coming with a cheery smile. Having a more vested interest in their clientele, these independent restaurants tend to be more customer focused than the corporation wage slaves of large concerns. It's a level of service I'm more than happy to patronise especially as it's not reflected in the price. A few beers, a pot of tea, six bowls of rice and five dishes comes to less than £10 between us.

Seeing another customer emerging from a small side-room, Juha heads for what he assumes is a toilet. Returning from the cupboard he says, 'It is only a sink.'

Many smaller eating establishments do not have toilet facilities, which isn't an issue when the streets are so well catered with public conveniences. I ask the waitress, 'Zhi shi cezuo ma?' (Is that the toilet?)

'Ke yi.'

I'm none the wiser. 'Ke yi' means 'can do.' I tell Juha to go for it and block out any images that try to enter my mind.

This is Juha's first sortie into town and he is enthralled by the sights and sounds of Dengfeng life. The walk back to school gives him the opportunity to revel in the beauty of the everyday mundane. Amongst the scenes of routine life Juha is particularly enthralled by the eclectic traffic.

Weaving among the more generic vehicles are modified bicycles and mopeds carrying unconceivable loads and/or the entire family perched atop. My particular favourites are the congestion causing self-builds, assuming I'm not stuck behind one. And what's not to love about these homemade contraptions invariably based around a Walking Tractor with long Easy Rider style handlebars bolted to a piece of household furniture. Resembling props from a Mad Max movie, these Scrap Heap Challenge contenders only add to Dengfeng's post-apocalyptic feel.

The Two-wheel or Walking Tractor is a single-axle, self-propelled engine with an exposed flywheel which can pull and/or power various farm implements with the operator walking behind. Introduced during the Cultural Revolution, after large Russian tractors of the Great Leap Forward proved inappropriate to the conditions, China now has around 16 million of these tractors. The engines adaptability, combined with Chinese ingenuity, means they are used all sorts of capacities never dreamt of by their inventor. As far as I'm concerned, the more outlandish and downright wacky the better and these transportation death-traps rarely fail to delight.

Evening training finds me alone in the gym and I spend the session stretching my calf muscles loose. Our little excursions mean we miss out on a full day's recuperation that the other guys get from staying in bed, but it's such a waste not to see China while we are here that the trade-off is worth it, mostly. Combined with the quantity of steps, the small treads and my big feet mean I've been walking on the balls of my feet for most of the day and my calves are seized-up, solid.

While I consider myself relatively fit, today's jaunt perfectly demonstrates the adage, 'you are fit for what you train for'. It's an expression I've heard many-a-time and today's jaunt has brought home to me exactly what it means. With many of China's sacred sites being up mountains there's a lot of steps to be climbed and my training did not include a Stairmaster.

It takes a fair bit of stretching and pummelling to soften my rigid calves and by the time I get back to the room VD is flat out. Today's wholesome fresh air and exercise ensure I'm not far behind him.

In practicing Shaolin-style xiaohong boxing, a practitioner is required to manoeuvre his body in such a manner that his body goes spiralling to rise, that his arm tends to gyrate when being held out, that synchronicity of his hand and foot movements is required to second his body movement, that all parts of his being must work in unison, and that his force must be focused always on the target his attack is directed at. Mastery of xiaohong boxing is a must for all those who want a training in Shaolin kung-fu.

Shi Yongxin

Feeling our way in the dark, we tentatively march to the front of school and gate-crash the fun packed fiesta in progress. Shuffling into the back of the massed herd, I'm settling in for a session of being motivationally spoken to, when Shibu removes us from the farting and spitting throng. We were just getting to the good bit as well, I'll never know what happened now.

Our Shifus are as enthused with the Monday morning assembly as we are. I get the distinct impression they use us as an excuse to cut out early. I suppose they've heard the speech a few times already and, having so far proved immune to its magic, missing another one isn't going to make much difference.

Keen to be away from the school's watchful eye, the Shifus march us out the front gate and down the road. At the next junction after the Breakfast Place we are directed through the rather grand gates of another public park.

Even at this early hour, Songyan Park is chocka with people. Larger than the previous park we visited, it's also equipped with a wider range of facilities. There are tables for ping pong, Chinese chess and cards as well as areas for ball games and group activities.

Above all else, the Chinese are a practical people. Their homes, often small and basic, serve the function of a place to sleep. Logically, as they are out most of the time, they don't need anything bigger. Being a sociable bunch, they live in public places, congregating in parks, cafés and pavements, or any public space. It looks like they have all chosen to meet here this morning.

The park is well enough subscribed that all dedicated areas are occupied and visitors utilise any space they can. Marching along the path, we are forced to wend around small groups playing badminton, tennis and jianzi (Chinese shuttlecock) in the pedestrian thoroughfare. Larger than a badminton shuttlecock, the jianzi is weighted and players pass it through the air using their feet, or at least that's the aim. Box hedges border the flower beds in a vain attempt to protect them from the cloddish sports enthusiasts.

Dotted among the trees, people are enjoying all sorts of activities, even playing musical instruments or singing. The beautiful thing is that no one is in any way self-conscious, even if they are particularly bad at what they do. Perhaps as a result of their gregarious living, the Chinese, normally a self-effacing, modest bunch, have no embarrassment about performing in public regardless of ability. One guy, I initially mistook for a cat torturer, turns out to be molesting a violin with no regard for public decency. With his music stand set up beside the path, he mercilessly wrestles his victim through an excruciating series of scales. I've seen similar mercenary tactics used by Cardiff buskers to scare people into parting with their pocket change, but this guy has no cap on the pavement. This is for real. Yet his complete lack of musical ability causes him not the slightest hint of embarrassment.

His endeavours make me wince in pain and would bring tears to the eyes of a real musician, but the Chinese are a hardy bunch. Passers-by stop to listen and give encouragement and, regardless of being unable to play a note themselves, offer advice. Actually, given his ability level it makes sense for him to practice in the park. This way his family and neighbours won't string him up. He may be here hiding from them.

We pass a dedicated performance area just as a gaggle of old ladies playing Taiji fan are finishing their session. They are immediately replaced on the concrete square by a troop of ballroom dancers. It's six in the morning, and barely light, but the dancers are fully kitted out with ball gowns and dinner jackets as if they are on their way for a night at the Ritz.

Continuing into the park, Shibu halts us at a recreational area containing brightly coloured exercise equipment. The primary colours give the impression of a children's play area, but the majority of the users are seriously ancient. Motioning to the geriatric jungle gym, Shifu explains the schedule, 'Go train.'

With this instruction, we slot ourselves around the old people and set about the gym like chimps on steroids. With their morning ruined, the oldsters are determined to appear unphased by our presence and freeze into a stony silence. The equipment is deceptively complicated and we are forced to follow the example of the existing users in its operation. A fatally flawed strategy as most appear to be making it up as they go along. It's difficult to judge the exact age of the people around us. While most look like they should be deceased, they appear remarkably fit and flexible, even compared to us. With typical Chinese aplomb, many old fellas are smoking while they exercise.

Warming up casually, clustered in small groups is much more social than our normal routine and gives us the opportunity to fraternise without compromising what passes for training.

Ear-wagging the conversations around me, it's clear my own impressions of school are far less jaded than the majority view. Many were disheartened to find school life is nothing like that promised on the website. Remarkably, it seems we were misinformed by an advertisement.

Everyone has a story of being let down or extorted. A reoccurring gripe is the arbitrary pricing, particularly of things meant to be included in the package. One guy mentions he paid seventy-five Yuan for his uniform, I paid sixty for mine. Similarly, the taxi fare from Zhengzhou varies widely, even among those picked up by the school's 'free' service.

Despite the discomforts and frustrations with the management, we are generally in a jovial enough mood. We even try to out-do each other with how much we have been ripped off. I guess those who can't see the funny side don't hang around long. The mythical welcome pack is another running joke. We want to believe in it, but no one has actually seen one.

However, all our complaints have to be put into perspective. The real question is, 'What are you prepared to go through for the opportunity to be here?' The fact that, despite our moaning, we are still here says it all.

There are about thirty of us Foreign Students. Unlike the Chinese students, who are in age groups and advance through the school together, we are a mixed bunch with very different goals and fitness levels. About half a dozen are here for more than six months and three are under twelve years old.

Generally coy about their background, the majority have some martial arts experience and have come to Xiao Long to expand their knowledge, but a few have no experience at all, or have come to get fit or lose weight. Some want to be Kung Fu teachers in their home countries and, at the other extreme, one is a backpacker that just wandered in for somewhere to stay. None are particularly hardcore in their training and most don't last more than a couple of days.

The high dropout rate means a large portion of the foreign students are relatively fresh to school. Not yet used to the program of intense training and poor living conditions, they are mostly bewildered, tired and vulnerable to injury.

That said, while our amenities are basic, we still have it cushy compared to the Chinese students. Foreigners have better living conditions, different timetables and train in smaller groups. Though demanding, the training has been tamed down to suit the pansy foreigners. The bottom line is, despite being a Buddhist school in a Communist country, they are in it for the money.

The guys with military experience compare the school with their basic training camps. One guy even compares it to prison. I don't ask. There are complaints of mistreatment like been yelled at and thrown to the ground, but the worst I've seen is push-ups for being late. Not only does the school want the foreign currency, but we are also an unknown quantity. The Shifu may be a little unsure about pushing around people so much bigger than them with undisclosed backgrounds.

Ironically, almost all of us had expected tougher discipline and feel the lack of it regrettable. Although initial disappointment that the Chinese students train and live separately soon fades with the appreciation of the small perks this gives us.

With the day brightening around us the casual exercise and socialise becomes even more pleasant, but it's not what we signed up for. It's a poor excuse for a warmup; we spend far more time chatting than exercising.

Similarly, it's nice having a natter with the others, but it's all variations around a theme. These things in common serve to unite us, but the repetition will only serve to make us more jaded. Personally, I find the lacklustre training a bore. I would prefer to train properly and then have a break, so I'm glad when Shibu lines us up for the march back.

At the park gates, a group of old ladies are line-dancing on the pavement. Julie is absolutely mesmerized by them. I've got to admit, it looks like the most fun ever. I beg Shifu to let us join in, but he just gives me one of his embarrassed grins and mumbles, 'Go school.' This is doubly disappointing as it would also have been a much better warmup than we had.

Morning training follows the usual pattern of Jibengong, stretching and forms. After lunch, I visit reception in search of our passports. Finding no one, but our friend the Village Idiot in attendance doesn't exactly raise my hopes. He glances toward the plastic curtain as I walk through, but puts his head back down on realising it's no one important. He's not getting away with it that easily. I approach the counter and, standing directly in front of him, say, 'Ni hao.'

Receiving no response, I repeat my greeting in louder tones.

Raising his head from his arm, he gives me a disdainful look through bored eyes. Now I have his attention I strive to continue my momentum before he drifts off again. 'Wo yao women de huzhao.' (I want our passports). Not the most subtlety phrased request, but neither party involved are equipped to be lyrical conversationalists.

Shrugging he replies, 'Mei you.' (Don't have)

'Wo de huzhao zai nar?' (Where is my passport?)

Raising the bar for demonstrations of disinterest, he shrugs with his chin and returns his head to the crook of his arm.

Barely restrained myself from ripping out his clockwork heart and stamping on it, I walk away empty handed. Yes, he got the last laugh. I can see him looking smug like he's just done something clever, but he's not worth my time. I'll come up with another plan.

With Julie at Mandarin class and Juha and Knobby at Sanda, there's just VD and I at afternoon training. Looking at his depleted squad Shifu Fatso decides the two of us aren't worth his effort. Pointing toward the Sanda group he attempts one of his classic plays, 'Go Sanda'.

Having fallen for this last week and got nothing out of the lesson, I take a stand, 'Women bu yao qu Sanda. '

Not happy with this response, Shifu puts his hand on my shoulder and, with a grunt, attempts to push me toward the Sanda class. I shrug his hand away elaborating, 'Women yao lian Gong Fu.'

Victorian Dad quickly gets a grasp of the situation and joins in with the nay saying. Shaking his head, he purses his lips and says, 'No, no, no.'

Not particularly eloquent, but it has the desired effect. Victorian Dad is famously obstinate and being deprived of nourishment and sleep aren't helping his disposition any. Seeing VD set his face into stubborn mode, Shifu Fatso realises he is not dealing with an amateur sulker. Confronted with our combined resolution, Shifu weighs up the option of a real battle of attrition or doing his job. Predictably he opts for the path of least resistance. Chalk one up to the boys, it's about time we had a victory.

This battle of wills proves to be the best move we've made at school. Starting with the usual Jibengong, we are walking back and fore the hall in a series of stances when Chen Tongshan, the school headmaster, arrives.

Although his family have been connected with the Shaolin Temple for generations Chen Tongshan is not an actual monk. A traditional Kung Fu 'Folk Master', he was made an honorary monk (his monk name is Shi Yanshan) and named one of the Eighteen Diamonds of Shaolin for his work helping rebuild the temple.

Considered outdated and old fashioned, traditional martial arts were forbidden during the Cultural Revolution and many Kung Fu masters were forced into hiding or fled the country. This led to a surge of Kung Fu masters to areas like Hong Kong and helped awaken the west's interest in Chinese martial arts at a time when most martial arts were brought back home by soldiers stationed in Korea or Japan.

Now seen as part of China's intangible heritage and culture, martial arts are encouraged to the extent old masters are being tempting out of the woodwork and even from abroad to bring their knowledge back to its roots. Chen Tongshan was among the first to return to Shaolin and founded the Shaolin Xue Xiao, the first Kung Fu school opened after the Cultural Revolution. He returned texts to the temple that his family had kept hidden and brought Shaolin to the world through the Shaolin Wheel of Life show. As such, while many of Dengfeng's Kung Fu schools incorporate the name Shaolin, ours is among the few officially associated with the temple.

Approaching our small group, Chen Tongshan tells Shifu Fatso he wants to see us demonstrate Xiao Hong Quan.

Often described as the mother of all forms, Xiao Hong Quan is one of the oldest Chinese Kung Fu forms. Allegedly created by Li Sou in the Yuan dynasty (around AD1300), Xiao Hong represents the basic principles of martial arts of the time and contains the essence of Shaolin Kung Fu. By its very nature, Xiao Hong is the first form to be learnt and the one form you really want to get right. Unfortunately, the influence of modern Wushu means many contemporary versions are sadly lacking in martial technique. Of the 80 or so recognised martial arts schools in Dengfeng, none teach anything other than the officially sanctioned Wushu.

The Xiao Hong Quan taught here, as in most Dengfeng schools, is a simplified version of the original form. This often leads to confusion when the original version is referred to as Laojia Xiao Hong Quan (old frame) or even passed off as another form called Da Hong Quan.

We stand in front of Chen Tongshan and, in turn, demonstrate the form as handed down by Shifu Fatso.

Singularly unimpressed with our display, Chen Tongshan demonstrates how he would like to see Xiao Hong performed. His form is beautiful to behold and is the only traditional Kung Fu we have seen here. Interestingly, his form reminds me of Lau Gar's Master Yau. Solid without being hard, this is most definitely Kung Fu not Wushu. It's also nothing like our version.

Shifu Fatso has taught us the form in sections with very definite pauses. Even when performed at the specified ninety miles per hour, or as Shifu calls it, 'Goh fust', it just doesn't flow. The headmaster's version is much slower, but with a more confident, rooted power.

In a desire to define martial arts they are frequently split into the categories of internal and external. This generalisation sits awkwardly as traditional martial arts tend to contain both internal and external elements. However, the modern Wushu we are being taught here is solely based on the external.

Overtime, the Chinese martial arts have been variously called: Jiji, (striking techniques), Wuyi (martial arts), Guoshu (national techniques) and Gongfu (practiced skills). In 1990, the International Wushu Federation developed Modern Sports Wushu unifying these terms into Wushu (martial techniques).

During the Republican era (1912-1949), historian Tang Hao criticised the Chinese martial arts of the time as infected with 'flowery techniques and embellishments' at the expense of practicality. He could well have been talking about contemporary Wushu.

That's not to say it's not very good, but it veers away from being a martial art into performance based acrobatics. Wan Shifu, a former Wushu champion, is amazingly agile and supple, which is no less impressive given his shape. However, his version of Xiao Hong Quan bears little resemblance to Chen Tongshan's. Wan Shifu's contains a lot of speed and movement, but the applications he has given us are questionable. Chen Tongshan's form is not so fast, but more powerful and solid and the applications are self-evident. Again, his Kung Fu is most obviously traditional and not sports Wushu

Now that he's shown us how it should be done, Chen Tongshan proceeds to take us through the form picking apart everything Shifu has taught us. This does beg the question. 'Why didn't Shifu Fatso show us this in the first place?'

Unable to speak English, Chen Tongshan leads by example, asking Shifu Fatso to interpret whenever necessary to enforce a point or explain a technicality. This is where the training goes a bit pear shaped.

Chen Tongshan watches our movements until something needs rectification. Speaking to Shifu, he goes through the intricacies of a complicated hand transfer or weight transition with Fatso nodding intently. Taking this on board, Shifu turns to us and says, 'Go fast, ok?' I'm pretty sure there's something lost in translation here. Fortunately, our experience enables us to piece together most of Chen Tongshan's explanations and guess the rest. By the end of the session, while not entirely satisfied, Chen Tongshan seems happier with our efforts.

Training with Chen Tongshan is a privilege that is far too brief an experience. All too soon the lesson is almost over and Chen Tongshan briefly casts his eye over the other Shifu's groups before leaving.

During break, one of Shibu's group comes over to ask what we have done to warrant the headmaster's attention. Chen Tongshan's appearance is such an unprecedented event that most of the western students don't even recognise him. As word spreads, we become the centre of attention. One of Yuan Shifu's students tells us this is his second year at the school and the first time he has actually seen the headmaster.

This leads to a discussion about Xiao Hong Quan. Some of the guys have previously trained a Shaolin style and already know a version of the form. Each of the Dengfeng schools have their own versions, all with slight variations upon the theme. Regardless of previous experience, we all have to learn the Xiao Long standard. This wouldn't be such a chore were the training not so lacking in detail. With the school's primary focus being on Wushu, those who came for traditional Kung Fu or in search of meditation and spirituality are sadly dissatisfied. Which makes us all the more privileged to have been shown some of the real stuff.

That said, there is a philosophical experience to be had here, but, much like martial arts in general, it takes place on a personal level. The majority of the foreign students are relatively content within themselves and just get on with it. A few guys, on the other hand, are still finding themselves as people and making up for quality of personality with quantity. Unfortunately for them, we are all too tired to be interested in attention seekers.

We all had preconceived ideas of what the training would involve, foolishly believing publicity material, and have all been misled in some fashion.

Martial arts are about more than fighting, there is also the fight within oneself. The fight to get out of bed in time for training, to put yourself through the discomfort and to refine yourself through hard work. Kung Fu can't be spoon-fed, you have to work for it. This is where the eating bitter comes in. There's no vegetarian option. It's what my Dad would call 'character building'.

However, it also pays to train intelligently. One needs to be realistic about personal ability and identify aspects of training that benefit you as an individual. This involves being honest with oneself which is another of those easier said than done tasks.

Training with Chen Tongshan has added another dimension to our Xiao Hong form and given us a, much-needed, psychological boost.

At assembly, I explain the passport situation to Shibu who assures me he hasn't got them, but will get them for us.

We spend the evening training session repeating Xiao Hong Quan slowly trying to weave our new additions into what we have already learnt. Relearning a form to iron out imperfections is much more difficult than learning it properly in the first instance as built-up muscle memory has to be overridden. This requires a lot more repetitions than to ingrain initially. Before we know it, we are the last people to leave the gym.

Getting back late, it's not long before Shifu Fatso comes to tuck us in. It's difficult to tell whether our earlier standoff has affected our relationship. His natural state is set at grumpy and our, 'Ok, go sleep.' is delivered with his usual level of surly disdain.

The irony is our little rebellion possibly saved his bacon. Without it he would not have been present at Chen Tongshan's impromptu inspection and his absence may have been questioned. I give him an extra friendly, 'Goodnight Shifu', and I mean it to sting.

Men go abroad to wonder at the heights of mountains, at huge waves of the sea, at the long courses of the rivers, at the vast compass of the ocean, at the circular motions of the stars; and they pass by themselves without wondering.

St. Augustine

The great man is he who does not lose his child's heart.

Meng Zi

We've had a good ration of Go Run with our morning warming exercises when, after breakfast, Shifu Fatso takes us to the back of school for more of the same. My issue with Go Run is that we rarely get a goal or even a direction. Until now I have simply followed the route of senior class members. Today, however, I'm feeling a little mischievous and, fed up of being so casually fobbed off, decide to give Fatso a taste of his own medicine. When Shifu issues the usual command, I shrug my shoulders, 'Wo ting bu dong.'

Despite me saying I heard, but didn't understand, his response is to repeat his mantra louder, 'Go run.'

'Sorry Shifu, I can't understand. What was that?'

With each repetition, he becomes louder and his gestures more emphatic. Once he has reached an uncomfortable volume, I nod, 'Ok.'

As the relief registers on his face, I speed off in the opposite direction. It takes a few seconds for Shifu to recover from the shock before he starts shouting, 'Noh, stoppah, noh!' In true Forest Gump style, I keep going. Fatso continues to call and I only slow down when he sends Knobby to bring me back.

Returning to the fold, Shifu sulkily pushes me back into line. He knows what I've done, and he doesn't like it. Rather than fall for any more monkey business, he scales down his operation. Pointing to a car parked further along the pavement, he comes up with the idea of getting us to sprint to the car and back again, 'Go car.'

As the words leave his mouth, a car passes on the road next to us. There must be something in the air. Precedent set, the rest of the group need no encouragement to join in the antics. As one, we tear after the car leaving Wan Shifu standing at the roadside. 'Noh! What are do?'

Further such hilarity ensues and we end up doing a lot more exercise than usual as a result. Even Juha, who generally doesn't like to break into a sweat, is prepared to put himself out in the cause of annoying Shifu.

It may be mundane, but such things are necessary to reduce the monotony. Even Shifu gets the hang of it after a while, almost delighting in the ways we are able to misinterpret his commands. His face is so expressive that it's captivating to watch. He can run a full gamut of emotions in seconds: surprise, confusion, contemplation, understanding and, finally, laughter. With the Chinese love of physical humour, the only way we could improve our performance would be to slip on a banana skin. I think we're beginning to grow on him.

For the second part of the session, we head to the gym. Having had our fun, we mostly behave ourselves for Jibengong. Although, I notice Shifu Fatso's cheeky grin remains in place even as we are dismissed for lunch. He must be dying to tell his mates what idiots we are.

Entering the canteen, I'm still on a high from the morning's frivolity and allow my imagination to run away with me. From a distance, it appears roast potatoes are on the menu. I take a double helping only to have my hopes dashed. Of course, they're not roast potatoes. It was nothing but wishful thinking on my part. Yesterday's stale steamed buns have been given a new lease of life courtesy of the oven. I really should know better. That said, they aren't dissimilar to roast potatoes and give the meal a welcome variation.

Enjoying my post-lunch instant tea, I realise a slight technical flaw in my short term tea consuming future. The only problem with the convenient beverage is I didn't buy enough and have ran out.

Leaving VD to exercise his discretionary skills, I head to Chinese class via the tuck shop in the vain hope of getting a viable tea substitute. A benefit of our classes not coinciding with the rest of school is we can generally beat the tuck shop rush. With the shopkeeper's undivided attention, I show her the empty tea packet.

Predictably, I am out of luck. She takes the briefest of glances at the packet before confirming, 'Mei you', but offers an alternative in the form of a cold, green tea-flavoured drink. I settle for this compromise, fork over the readies and accept my change. The second I'm out of sight, I disinfect my hands.

At first, I felt this piece of traveller advice a tad extreme. Now I'm here, I can see the point. Advised that cash is among the dirtiest things one can ever handle, it only took one glance at the kids here to firmly cement that idea in my head. The tuck shop uses an old shoe box as its till. The staff throw the money into it and then rummage through for change. The shops make life easier for themselves by rounding up the prices and don't have to deal with coins so it's all paper money. It's also the most crumpled, filthiest notes I have ever seen. In fact, the money in circulation around the school is so well used I didn't even recognise the smaller notes as they bore so little resemblance to the shiny-new ones I brought with me. Considering the number of times low denomination notes change hands in this environment, it's a wonder there's anyone left standing. The Chinese kids must be immune to any contamination and, in the coming war, will walk all over us with accidental germ warfare.

To be on the safe side, I disinfect my hands after every cash transaction. I am also using a temporary wallet so as not to contaminate my usual one. Given the state of the kids, I dread to imagine the insides of their pockets. These may sound like extreme self-preservation tactics, but it's proving effective. At risk of jinxing it, so far, I'm one of the few not to have come down with a case of Mao's Revenge. Some guys barely make every other session.

There are six little shops on the edge of our square. The general store carries a limited stock. Amongst the mostly bare shelves are combs, toothbrushes, pots and key-rings. The four ram-packed, tuck shops are practically identical and the weapons store is decidedly nondescript.

While the tuck shops are completely interchangeable, after a painful transaction I decided not to use a particular shop again. Most of the westerners have a favourite shop or one they avoid although, ironically, we don't agree on which. In fact, the shops are so alike that I sometimes forget which one I'm boycotting.

The way to a small boy's heart, and thus his pocket money, is through his stomach. The tuck shops know this only too well. As these are the only vendors accessible to the kids, the junk fiends congregate in our square intent on satisfying their cravings. Capitalising on their captive audience, the shops are slightly more expensive than those outside the gates. As an example, a bottle of water outside is 6jiao and here is 1Yuan (nearly double the price). Which, given the number of times a day we visit the shop, soon adds up. Prior to every training session we all purchase fresh water and most eat from there several times a day too.

During breaks the shops are besieged. The kids are constantly eating junk. The calorie content of the stuff must be horrific, especially considering its nutritional value. These kids must burn about a million calories a day and are maintaining a constant sugar high. Within these walls, sugar is the opium of the masses. Particularly devout, our two little Korean Kids, are permanently hopped up on goof balls.

A repercussion of the kids coming to our courtyard to buy their crap is they discard their litter here too. Littering is the Chinese national pastime. No one bats an eyelid at dropping anything, anywhere. It may be a job creation scheme in line with communist policy of full employment. Again, it's typical of the Chinese mentality that everyone litters, there are no litter bins and the people employed to deal with the litter exert the bare minimum of effort.

Tea substitute in hand, I brave the main building stairwell and, holding my breath, get up the stairs as quickly as I can. Other deposits on the steps prevent an all-out sprint as I need to tread carefully. It's not so much that the clientele doesn't respect their school, but they don't know any different. The Chinese students even spit and litter in their own rooms.

Mandarin class follows the same format as last week, but concerns a visit to the doctor and covers illnesses, and injuries, we might expect during our stay. I appreciate the practicality of the lesson, but it's not comforting to think I might need these expressions. Our teacher follows up with a section on Doctor's orders regarding treatment and taking medication.

Several others must share VD's views regarding the viability of Mandarin class as he is not the only one opting out. Although it's not like any of the absentees could be said to be fluent. In fact, I'm surprised at how ill-prepared many of the others have been for their trip here, particularly in regard to the language. While I fumble through my phrase book attempting to converse in the local lingo most don't even try to speak Chinese, but as many don't ever leave the school grounds I suppose it doesn't matter to them. It also goes someway to explaining the mandarin class attendance.

The turnout is a double-edged sword. While we get more attention, the lesson was planned with a bigger class in mind. To fill time, we work around the class repeating the terms over and over.

Meanwhile, back at the room, VD has been productive. Returning to collect him for dinner, he affirms he has used his time constructively, 'Check out this bad-boy.'

Holding his phone in front of my face, he proudly shows me a video he's made demonstrating the softness of his bed. Watching his quality production, it occurs to me how haggard he looks. I hadn't noticed it in our daily grind, but his phone is devastatingly honest. I've heard the camera adds ten lbs, but this one also adds ten years. To cheer him up I tell him so, 'Man, I hadn't realised how rough you're looking.'

His surly grunt is all I need to assure me he appreciates the sentiment and is pleased by the constructive critique of his work.

By turning up early the canteen is much quieter and we are able to speak without need to shout over the rabble. Taking advantage of the lack of surrounding noise, I continue my joviality by attempting to converse with the Ladle Guy. To me, he's the most important guy in school. Previous interactions have been nothing more than hand signals. In the tranquillity before the storm, I can not only point at my rice and cabbage, but say the names as well.

Ladle Guy is well-impressed with my linguistic efforts and, along with a beaming gap-toothed smile, gives me a significantly larger portion than normal. I like Ladle Guy.

Buoyant, I plonk my tin tray before the steamed bun window. The lady tasked with guarding said vapoured comestibles stares at me blankly. It may be due to the long shifts, but I've noticed that staff often appear bored rigid. It's not just our school, the same can be seen in many customer-facing occupations: banks, supermarkets, etc. Manning their posts for long periods of inactivity has led them to develop a talent for zoning out. Unlike our friend Idiot Boy, at least she's upright.

I once worked long shifts in a factory and understand how to autopilot. Indifferently dispensing buns can't require much more acumen than a production line. I am forced to be more proactive in my bun acquisition. With my heart-warming smile, the one reserved for ladies bearing food, I turn on the old charm, 'Ni hao. Qing gei wo mianbao.'

The transition from vacantly stupid to hysterically stupid takes a nanosecond. One hand over her grinning face she points at me with the other spluttering, 'Mianbao, mianbao!'

Given that her sole purpose here is to dole out steamed buns it should be fairly obvious what I'm asking for, but she's hell bent on making it difficult for me. On top of todays' frustrations, it's too much for me. Pointing to the congealing mass of dough balls slowly merging into each other, I repeat my phrase and throw in a stern stare for good measure, 'Qing gei wo mianbao.'

Still laughing hysterically, she piles a dozen buns onto my tray. Score. I'm prepared to humiliate myself for food privileges. While we may have gotten off on the wrong foot, I must say I'm beginning to rethink my initial hostility to the bun flinger. She has grown on me considerably during our exchange and I've brightened up her day to boot.

The buns are exactly the sort of stodge I needed. All dinnered up, I check the word mianbao in my dictionary. The term more properly describes a bread roll baked in an oven whereas steamed rolls are called Mantou. Still, it should have been fairly obvious what I was asking for.

Further down the list of derivations is one I am familiar with: Mianbao Che or 'bread roll vehicle' for a little minibus, but there are many more I don't know. Perusing the expansive list reveals, by using the wrong tone, it's possible I asked Bun Lady for a tampon.

The Mandarin tones are a minefield for me. Standard Mandarin has four tones plus a neutral tone. In my book that makes five, but the convention is to call it 'four and another one'. This had me at loggerheads with the tones at our introduction. Over the years, people have commented on my musical ability. My attempts at Mandarin confirm their views well founded; I am truly tone deaf. I simply can't hear them. This is somewhat of a disadvantage as tone is all important in Mandarin. As an example, depending on the tone, 'wushui' can mean 'afternoon nap' or 'sewage'. At least I provide hilarity wherever I go.

It has now been three days since Wan Shifu's assurances of 'tomorrow' and the bathroom leak is still merrily dripping away. The water level builds up so quickly we have been forced to relent with the floor mopping. I have now grasped the concept that, in China, tomorrow never comes.

I had been warned to expect this kind of response. The Chinese consider it impolite to be negative and don't like to say, 'No'. The preferred method of dealing with unwelcome requests is to agree and then ignore them.

This avoidance strategy is another of our reoccurring gripes. The other day, when the guys were swapping anecdotal evidence, Mason, from Australia, was able to support their stories with a few yarns of his own. Working for a Chinese firm in Shanghai, he has direct experience of the Chinese work ethic and means of doing business, particularly the concept of Face. He said that when he first started in Shanghai his boss gave him a telling off for admitting he didn't know something in a meeting, 'Don't say you don't know, it makes you look stupid. Just make it up.'

Apparently, this is such a common occurrence that construction projects are regularly brought to a halt when the wrong materials or quantities are ordered as a result of someone put on the spot inventing information off the top of their heads. It puts our shower into perspective.

Adding the leaky pipe to my list of amateur DIY projects, Captain Bodge-it strikes again. Using the handle of a Balisong knife, I tighten the pipe joint and wrap sword grip-tape around it. Not exactly a professional finish, but it's the best I can manage. At this rate, I will soon have done more property maintenance here than in my own house.

Carried away with my plumbing endeavours, I don't notice the time passing until Knobby bursts in, 'Come on, you're late for assembly', and hurtles out again.

VD looks up from his repose and, with a synchronised shrug, we amble downstairs and line up next to Knobby. Unimpressed by the three-fifths of his squad in front of him, Shifu points at the space where there should be a Juha, grunts, then points at Knobby and says, 'Go.'

Knobby dashes back into the building to reappear shortly after puffing and panting. Three minutes later, a completely placid Juha shuffles into position next to me. The process is repeated and Knobby goes to get Julie. Once we are all present and correct, Shifu points at each of us in turn and then to the ground, 'One hundred, go.'

Unable to arrive in a timely fashion himself, he nonetheless expects impeccable punctuality from his devoted students. This well-deserved admonishment is the only way to teach us the evaluable and necessary lesson. In the true spirit of brotherhood, he includes Knobby in the press-up-athon.

'Why me? That's not fair!'

His protestations prove fruitless. Shifu makes it clear this isn't a democracy by pointing to the ground and repeating, 'One hundred. Go.'

Grumbling to himself, Knobby assumes the position and goes through the motions with the rest of us. I don't understand why Knobby gets the press-ups when he was the only one on time, but it's not like he does them properly anyway. None of us do, but I suppose the intention was there.

The appalling display of half-hearted press-ups over with, we do the clappy-hand thing and are dismissed for training. Julie and Juha promptly return to their rooms and Knobby heads to the tuck shop. Of the thirty or so western students about a dozen are in the gym and very few of those even attempt to train. Again, we are the last people to leave.

After this morning's fun, I'm prepared to give Shifu Fatso the benefit of the doubt regarding his apparent dislike of us. I'm sitting up in bed reading when he comes to tuck us in. Pointing at me, he mumbles the usual, 'Ok, go sleep', but has caught me in a saucy mood, 'Yes Shifu. I am sleeping.'

Struck dumb, he stands gaping at me. The look of constipation turns to astonishment as he splutters, 'You no sleep, you look book. No look book, you sleep.' He walks out shaking his head at these crazy foreigners who don't know whether they are sleeping or not. I, on the other hand, am elated with the result. Shifu's literal translation is delightful and I can see 'no look book' becoming a catchphrase. Although it's entirely possible that, like Zhuangzi's Butterfly Dream, I am asleep and just dreaming I'm reading a book.

Dengfeng Streets

One reason the school smells of wee

Buddha Phone

Kimnara, Patron
Saint of Shaolin

Shaolin Stalls

Inside Shaolin Temple

Shaolin Medicine
Courtyard

Wangzhigou

Sanhuangzhai

Listening
Courtyard

Dengfeng

Zhong Yue Miao

Zhong Yue Miao

Dengfeng Scenes

Songyan Park

Welcome Immortals Pavilion

Ancient Watchtower

Longmen Grottoes

Guanlin

Damo Cave

Path to Chuzu

Chuzu Nunnery

Courtyard Scenes

Luoyang Opera Stage

Many thanks to Nick Stew, Julie Desjardins, Louis Bailey
and Juha-Matti for sharing their photos with me.

He who is drowned is not troubled by the rain.

Traditional Chinese Proverb

Also for your convenience the school has two small general
stores, a weapons shop, doctor and a hairdresser.

Xiao Long Website.

I awake to the comforting drone of a grizzly bear sawing wood, but can't
shake the feeling something's out of place. As my fuzzy brain responds
to my spider senses, I realise it's colder and damper than I have become
accustomed to.

Shuffling out to the hallway reveals we have been on the receiving
end of some serious precipitation during the night. Something the whole
school was completely unprepared for. Rain has come through the open
balcony and flooded the hallway. Clothes and bedding hung out to dry
are now soaked and the pervasive covering of dust is now a puddle of
mud.

Torrential downpours aren't uncommon at this time of year.
Dengfeng summers are long and hot, running from April till October with
temperatures up to 40 degrees, high humidity and short spells of heavy
rainfall. July and August are the hottest months and probably best avoided

by those from more tepid climes.

In a way, it's a shame I missed the rain, I could have stood in it to wash. Even China's infamous acid rain, caused by rapid industrial growth and coal powered electricity stations, must be better quality than the gloop that chugs from our tap. Left with an obvious choice, I splash my way back to bed and reset the alarm.

A little after 6am, Shifu Fatso blunders into the room to tell us there's no training until after breakfast. Handily, I learnt the word for rain, 'xia yu', at last week's meteorological based Mandarin class.

It's nice of Shifu to come and let us know what's happening, even if it is an hour after the event. Actually, I'd worked out there would be no morning warming hence not going to assembly at 5.30. As Shifu doesn't mention this I wonder if he turned up himself.

Fatso's clumsy departure disturbs VD's angelic torpor. He raises his grizzled head to see what's happening. Surprised to see me sitting up in bed reading in the early light, he questions me regarding said event, 'Whuh?' He must have enrolled in evening classes at Shifu Fatso's school of vocabulary.

I explain the situation in words of limited syllables conducive to his befuddled mind, 'Rain stops play.'

'Result!'

I know how much he loves his Go Run and it breaks my heart to see his dismay at missing his morning dose. Barely containing himself from doing a little jig of sorrow, he plants his head back into the pillow. I swear his snoring continues at the exact point he left off.

With the light oozing through our threadbare curtains, I lie in bed looking at the patchy, whitewashed walls decorated in a patina of unthinkable stains, squashed insects and self-adhesive hooks. Unless one is comatose, there is little pleasure to be had staying in this room.

Already adapted to the routine, even VD can't keep his head down for long and joins me as I investigate a commotion outside.

Outside our window, we see the normally hard-baked training field is now a quagmire. The mud is so deep that a car parked overnight has sunk up to its axles. The attempted retrieval has already become a slapstick comedy involving more people than the task requires all working at cross purposes, randomly criticising the others, falling over and wandering off when they get bored.

Keeping the window closed to keep out the dust and smoke, has paid dividends with the inclement weather. Others are less fortunate and have woken to discover their rooms have turned into paddling pools and their clothes are soaked. This is one of the exceptional cases when training is postponed and some guys enjoy their lie in so much they don't even make it to breakfast.

Ironically, the total washout raises spirits all round. The extra hour in bed and the cooler atmosphere perks everyone up. More sentient than usual, we are able to be more sociable and there's some good-natured banter. The fun soon turns to criticisms of life in China and has me wondering what exactly they were expecting. China is not like the movies. It's brighter, louder and a lot more fragrant. Which is the polite way of saying it's dirty, crowded and noisy. Despite all this, the country has a strange charm. The hectic mishmash of two worlds colliding is delightful, but, as western influences snowball, this charm is being swept aside by globalisation and, in some respects, it's a case of 'last chance to see'. That said, our idealised images of China probably weren't shot here and may never have existed in the first place.

The subject of Kung Fu movies proves common ground. We all know the contemporary movies, but our varied ages mean we have different influences from our relevant generations. My interest in Kung Fu was initially sparked by the 70s David Carradine TV series, catchily titled, 'Kung Fu'. Now I'm actually at Shaolin, I feel slightly misled. There's not as much walking on rice paper as the show led me to believe. Filmed at a leftover Camelot backlot in Hollywood, it also looks nothing like our current surroundings. Although, just like Grasshopper, I'm sure I'll get plenty of flashbacks from this experience.

I moved on to 70s chop-socky flicks, mostly filmed in Hong Kong. Martin is a fan of 80s Hong Kong gangster films. This was around the time mainland China's interest in Kung Fu and Shaolin Temple was rekindled by Jet Li's film.

A couple of the teenagers are into the animated series Avatar the Last Air Bender and the two little Korean kids are heavily influenced by a Power Ranger type show. A real threat to the unwary they are forever making bizarre finger movements before launching a flying kick at anyone unsuspecting enough to get in their way.

A few know nothing of Kung Fu movies. Again, I find this strange. How can you be interested enough in Kung Fu to have travelled this far to learn it, but not have seen a single Kung Fu movie?

Conditions leave little option than to train indoors. In general, I prefer training in the gym to the field. Although, I'm not sure if inhaling the carpet dust is any better than inhaling the field dust and bonfire smoke.

Last night's downpour doesn't clear the air for long. By lunchtime the smell of ozone has disappeared, the puddles have evaporated and the bonfire has been restarted. School shows no evidence that it's ever witnessed any precipitation and we are right back to our arid conditions.

Juha was not with us for morning training, but it's not unusual to have someone missing. Actually, it would be more unusual to have a full complement. Heading for lunch we find our Finnish friend sitting on the steps. Wearing his civvies and nursing a heaving rucksack can only mean one thing. Juha is leaving. Persevering for the best part of a month, Juha is finally throwing in the towel to return to the Finnish army, saying it's easier and has better conditions. He may be pining for the fjords, but the real issue for Juha is the food. As far as I'm aware, Finland is not renowned for its culinary delights, but I'm still willing to bet it knocks spots off this place. Being a big lad, Juha needs a lot of feeding and simply isn't getting enough nutrition here.

For us pampered westerners, the lack of nutrition is a constant bone of contention. Used to a higher quality of food, and a lot less exercise, we are generally running on empty. We are all hungry, all the time. Most students refuel between classes at the tuck shop, but Chinese junk food is even worse than its western cousin. I'm desperately trying to resist the lure of the empty calories of sugar, E numbers and complex carbs. To quote the late, great Bruce Lee, 'When you are a martial artist, you only eat what you require and don't get carried away with foods that don't benefit you as a martial artist.' I appreciate the sentiment, but it's difficult to put into practice when there's little else available. Also, despite sharing his name with our school, Bruce Lee didn't train at Xiao Long otherwise he might have had a different perspective. The Chinese expression, 'Ur si la' (starving to death) may well be the school motto.

Shifu often asks me if I am hungry. When I reply in the affirmative, he pulls his 'disbelief' face and makes his surprise sound, 'Whuhuh!' Anyone would think I've just told him Buddha was a Catholic. I don't see why it's so hard to believe I'm hungry. Of course, I'm hungry. I'm a grown man living off a handful of rice, a steamed bun and a tablespoon of boiled cabbage three times a day while training from five thirty in the morning until nine at night. I could eat a horse between two mattresses, go back for seconds and find it none too much.

We get the same portions as the little kids. Bearing in mind I am four times their size and used to a more expansive diet, it's simply not enough for me. It doesn't seem enough for them either. Even the steady supply of junk food cannot adequately fill the void between meals as we occasionally see groups of students rustling themselves up a little rustic cooking on the courtyard or on the training field. It shows how hungry I am that I salivate at the sight of sweet potatoes roasting in a smouldering pile of litter.

One American girl told me she has no martial arts experience, but came to Xiao Long as she heard this was a good place to lose weight. While the Shaolin Slimfast is an extreme way of going about things, it is very effective. I've already lost enough body fat to give me a nice amount of definition. My six-pack is the most visible it's been for years. However, my body is now beginning to absorb the nutrition from my muscles, something I don't have an abundance of to lose.

The simple formula of calories consumed verses calories burnt means, as much as I try to ram food into myself, there isn't enough protein in the diet to maintain muscle mass. Warned about the food in China and, anticipating the lack of protein, I brought a tub of protein powder. Opinions vary, but working on the principle of requiring about 0.8 grams of protein per kilo of body weight, I need a minimum of 70g a day. I allow myself 30g supplement a day. Our diet in no way makes up for the deficit.

Attempts at cordiality with the Ladle Guy are paying off as he now recognises me. I think he appreciates my efforts as I get a big grin when he sees me. He's amazed at the quantity I put away and looks genuinely pleased that I go back for seconds and even thirds. I'm not about to tell him my repeat visits aren't due to his culinary expertise.

It's not so much 'eating bitter' that's the problem here as 'eating the food'. Victorian Dad can't bring himself to eat more than a single portion. His real love of food, and withdrawal symptoms from the lack thereof, coerce him to explore the opportunities afforded by the tuck shops. Enthused by his solo foray, he bursts in like an excited child and lobs a packet of crisps at me, 'Check out these bad boys.'

As instructed, I hold the dubious looking package up for scrutiny. The neon colours make my eyeballs oscillate wildly. The packet should carry a health warning simply on the grounds of garishness. The contents are even less appealing. Nevertheless, I put my prejudices aside and give them the old British try. I would compare the experience to eating cardboard, that's gone stale, 'They're certainly no Monster Munch.'

VD concurs and graciously consumes mine for me before settling down to his siesta. Washing my hands and face, it's amazing what comes off them, but trying to run my head under the tap isn't doing the job. I decide to get myself a trim. I look up the term for haircut and set off to the school barber.

Behind the tuck shops is a small square where a wizened old woman hand washes the students' laundry in a plastic bowl and hangs it to dry. Drunkenly stumbling between the dripping uniforms is a toddler playing with spear. The kid must be about eighteen months old, little more than a baby, as he's still wearing 'kai dang ku' pants, the Chinese equivalent of nappies, i.e. Trousers with no arse in them. Barely old enough to toddle, the kid is attempting to swing the spear around and even manages a few recognizable Kung Fu moves.

Distracted by the baby's Kung Fu, I almost miss a teenager coming out of a doorway at the corner of the yard. The kid is rubbing his totally hairless head and has a sullen look on his face. I assume this is the place. Peering into the windowless, unlit room, my path is blocked by a stern woman who pre-empts my query with a question of her own, 'Ji fa?'

For once my basic research has paid off and I am able to answer the question with confidence, 'Wo yao ji fa.' My intent confirmed, she motions me to a seat inside. Attempting to walk across the hair covered floor, I give her the benefit of an ad hoc Neil Armstrong impression as I lift my knees high to free my feet of the spongey layer. In every other barber shop I have ever visited, the barber has swept the floor as they went along. This floor, however, is about a foot deep in hair and may never have been swept in its life.

My success with her first question is my undoing. The follow-up question is well outside the scope of my planning. Admitting defeat, I shrug my shoulders, forcing the lady to mime. Apparently, she was giving me the option of electric clippers or a cut-throat razor. I'm dubious about the hygiene of the cut-throat and the lady can see I'm not sold on it. Clarifying her point, she explains if I have the razor I have to first wet my head in the bucket of hair and murky water.

The seat next to me contains a little lad receiving a head shave with a cut-throat razor. His barber takes this moment to send the boy for a vigorous dunking before continuing. There is so much hair in the bucket that my baptism would leave me hairier than when I started. I bottle it and demonstrate my bourgeois western extravagance by choosing the more expensive option of the electric clippers.

It takes longer to plug the clippers into the bulb-less light fitting than

176

it does to cut my hair. Minutes later, all evidence of my receding hairline is eradicated and my head is shiny-clean once more. Traditionally, Buddhists shave their heads as a symbol of material detachment. It also works from a personal hygiene perspective. The amount of training and limited sanitary conditions here, mean that short hair is definitely the way to go. In this environment, even my limited hair growth is beginning to feel grubby. Often used in literature to symbolise an abrupt change in lifestyle or the beginning of a journey, the early onset of male pattern baldness means shaving my head is no great hardship for me.

Unplugging the clippers, my barber attaches a hairdryer to the light fitting and gives my freshly buzzed scalp a blow dry. I've got to hand it to these guys, when you chose the premium service they treat you like royalty.

The haircut is more expensive due to the electricity used. A commodity that is worth more to them than their time. This is why the only light comes from the open doorway. This luxurious service sets me back the princely sum of 5 Yuan.

With time left before class, I have the chance to wash my head under the cold tap and check my email. With no response from Tagou, I set about a protracted internet search. Eventually my efforts turn up another bookshop in Dengfeng that claims to stock the required books. The website is a little hazy regarding their location so I email them for directions.

Rousing VD from his slumber, he looks at me and does a double-take, 'Didn't you have hair earlier?'

Waiting for afternoon training, we get to hear Knobby's introductory speech again. Nominating himself for the position of Official Meet and Greeter, Knobby now has another best friend. It's easy to spot the new guys at school, they have clean tracksuits and are friends with Knobby. Although, as the school does not attempt to assist with integration, Knobby is actually providing a useful service.

Today's new friend is a fat guy from the States who reckons he's 'connected' to the Mafia. If he is connected to anything, it's not to reality. The guy is at a complete loss here as no one is interested in his tales, not even his new best friend.

The problem for Knobby is that none of his new friends get put into our group. Even itinerant backpackers looking for a day's bed and breakfast get put into the other groups. I don't understand the selection process. Shifu Fatso has plenty of spare capacity, and most new guys are obviously not going to last more than a couple of days, but they are still allocated elsewhere. While few people make the grade to gain admittance to Fatso's group of misfits, it's not the kind of special I wanted to feel.

The improved mood of this morning's lie in has held and sociability abounds. Opening up, some guys confess they are amazed we have survived this long. Having seen us train we appear to have earned a margin of respect. Most of this credit is misplaced; it's not that we aren't aching or tired, but that we don't complain us much as them.

As a gesture of the high esteem in which we are now held, the young guys invite us to skip evening training and watch a film with them in the DVD room. This is where the grumpy old man really shows his age. I tell them I look forward to the event, but have no intention of turning up. I have no desire to sit around throwing food and breaking things. They don't remind us, so I guess we're all happy with this arrangement.

The film-night defectors make little difference to the number at training, although I do notice a couple of non-Chinese students who only appear to surface for the evening session. I'm not sure what they do all day otherwise. Come to think of it, the two little Koreans and the Uzbekistani lad seem to appear sporadically. I guess they must have some actual scholastic lessons occasionally.

Heading back to our room, I can hear the sounds of shouting, laughing and crashing coming from the DVD room. I'm reassured I made the right decision in not attending this prestigious event.

VD tells me the bookshop has very cordially replied to my query regarding their whereabouts.

'Brilliant. Have they given an address?'

'According to this they are in Dengfeng, China.'

'You don't say!'

While factually correct, I was hoping they would have been a little more geographically specific. At least it has established that they exist.

Considering the recent breakthrough with Fatso, I wonder if it's our inability to communicate that makes him feel awkward. In anticipation of his nightly visit, I prepare the phrase, 'Thank you Shifu, goodnight.'

Right on cue, Shifu marches into our room and grunts, 'Ok, go sleep.'

Looking up from my book, I let him have it, 'Shifu, xie xie, wan an.'

His face scrunches up as he tries to work out what I've just said. There's a pregnant pause as the cogs whirr into action. I'm beginning to wonder if I've got the tones wrong and insulted his mother. Eventually the dawn breaks over his scowl and his face cracks into a broad grin, 'Oh,

178

ok, ok.'

Still smiling, he plods out closing the door behind him. I feel we have broken new ground with him.

I'm woken in the early hours by the sound of slamming doors and running in the corridor. The slapping feet and inane giggle sound suspiciously like our beloved Shifu Fatso. Based on his demeanour throughout the day, I had already concluded he is not a daytime creature. It's now clear that he prefers the nocturnal world where he comes alive and runs, flat-footed, up and down the corridor tittering like a young girl. Something doubly annoying considering he's not long told us to go to sleep. Now I've identified the disturbance my mind can filter it and I'm soon drifting off.

At the foot of the 1494m-high Taishi Shan. A short ride southeast of the Shaolin Temple and 74km from Zhongzhou sits the squat little town of Dengfeng. Tatty and squalid in parts, it is used by travellers as a base for trips to surrounding sights or exploratory treks into the hills.

Lonely Planet guide.

We can always fool a foreigner.

Traditional Chinese Saying

Shifu Fatso doesn't seem any the worse for wear after his late-night shenanigans. By which I mean he's no grumpier or more dishevelled than usual. He takes us through our warming exercises with his usual aplomb, before sending us for a bit of Go Run. An hour and a half later, we are dismissed until the afternoon with my two favourite words, 'Go Dengfeng.'

So eloquently given the freedom of the city, we still have the palaver of signing out. Now familiar with the system, it only takes half an hour before we are heading down Dayu Road. The dusty road is already giving off a shimmering heat and the usual lethargic Sanlun driver is waiting in the shade of a tree at The Breakfast Place. Happily puffing a cigarette, the old fellow has his legs up on the handlebars leaning back into the trailer unconcerned by what the day will bring.

Seeing us approach, he makes no effort to clinch a sale, even going as far as to avoid our gaze. It matters not. This week we have decided to soak up a little local colour by walking to the town centre.

The main town serving Shaolin Temple, Dengfeng covers an area of 1220 square kilometres with a population of 630,000. The sprawling backwater was known in ancient times as Yangcheng and renamed Dengfeng after the Tang Dynasty Empress Wu Zetian's pilgrimage in AD688.

Typically low-rise, the ground floors are a business premises with accommodation above. Before the advent of supermarkets, Britain used to have small shops on most street corners. I wonder how the intrusion of globalisation will affect the way of life once shopping malls and supermarkets seep out from the cities.

On our way into town, we experience the transition from small, independent traders to the larger chain stores. Shops on the outskirts are little more than doorways with the proprietor sitting outside. Peering into the dark, it's often impossible to tell what they are attempting to purvey. My best guess is that we are in the junk district as the majority of shops seem to sell rusty old metal. It's like the guy lives in a mini-scrap yard with the goods arrayed around his mattress.

If trade is slow, these old guys are unconcerned. They are prepared to guard an ambiguous lump of rust all day on the off-chance someone, feeling their life incomplete without it, will pop in to buy said rusty lump. It's his house, he was going to be there anyway, so there's nothing lost.

Operating from such small premises means day to day activities tend to spill out onto the pavement. Obstacle courses at the best of times, the pavements are impassable on the outskirts as these entrepreneurs lay claim to the area directly in front of their shop forcing us into the road. Tasks that we in the west prefer to do in the comfort of our own homes, take place here for everyone to see: cooking, socialising, haircutting and manufacturing are the least of the occupations carried out at the expense of pedestrians. One old guy is welding an equally ancient bicycle together while his neighbour peels veg onto the pavement. As ever, even the most mundane of daily chores involve another group standing around gawking, pointing and explaining how it should be done.

The ramshackle buildings and permanent layer of dust, give Dengfeng a post-apocalyptic feel; as if the locals are eking out an existence on the remnants of a once a thriving civilisation. Whereas it's actually the opposite. These guys are an anachronism of a recent past that is rapidly being swept aside by China's hunger for retail products. Globalisation is hitting China like a truck, creating a society very different from the one envisaged, and fought for, by the youth of yesterday. The same people that have very different ideas now they are parents themselves.

Closer to the town centre, pavements become more pedestrian orientated and the shop fronts brighter and gaudier. Loud sparkly colours endorse the consumer dream, while billboards and posters promote lifestyle products endorsed by teen popstars. The advertising images look like posters for 80s Hong Kong action films. The guys wear casual jackets with shirts tucked into jeans while hot pants and knee length boots are all the go with the ladies. Which means the nouveau rich are aspiring to fashions that died about twenty years ago. It's like China is caught in a time delay. I'm going to need a DeLorean to get back home.

Among the everyday folk are very obvious attempts to mimic the adverts. Deng Xiaoping's ideology that, 'to be rich is glorious' has been taken to heart by the populace and they are mad keen to embrace consumerism. Anyone with any money wants to show it off so there are very visible signs of affluence: glitzy mobile phones, gaudy colours, ostentatious jewellery and designer labels with big logos.

I've noticed a lot of clothing with, what I assume are, unintentionally humorous slogans; usually misspelled or inappropriate English words. I guess the middle-aged lady has no idea what public statement she's making with, 'Sexxy Toy' emblazoned across her chintzy sweatshirt. It's so comedic I have to wonder what the Chinese characters on some of my clothes say about me. These flamboyant displays of wealth and outdated fashions make the women look like stereotypical hookers and the men like clichéd gangsters.

Most of the town are in on it, but there is a term for those who go too far. Jintuhao (golden local tyrant) historically referred to locally powerful landowners, but is now used to describe the ostentatiously wealthy. It implies they lack refinement and taste, and are domineering, crass and eager to stand out. Extreme examples from the headlines include solid gold phone covers and pet tigers, but you're unlikely to see that on the streets of Dengfeng.

The newfound wealth has created a two-tiered society which the Chinese call 'fu guo qiong min'. 'Rich country poor people' is used with a certain amount of irony and is very visible in Dengfeng where ramshackle noodle stands and street hawkers set up on the pavements outside glitzy designer stores. The boutiques confused identity is exaggerated by bizarre Europop style Christmas songs. As the words are in English I suppose they don't know it's a Christmas song and just like the tune. The garish mishmash of cheesy musical styles compliments the fashions well.

Not to be outdone, the street vendors have competing sound systems. One guy selling dodgy designer underwear from a suitcase, has a music system five times the size of his stock inventory.

Used as a cheap workforce by the west, a massive percentage of the world's consumer products are now manufactured in China and the workers are keen to embrace the products they supply. This is especially true of technology which the Chinese have taken to with a vengeance. Everyone possesses a mobile phone and wants everyone else to know they do. To service this demand the streets of Dengfeng are covered in phone shops and often several in a row.

This does beg the question of what will happen to China's workforce now they are developing skills and have aspirations of their own. The more they demand in terms of pay and conditions, the less cheaply they will be able to produce the goods that were outsourced to them.

At the moment our needs are a little more basic than electronics and fashion. We've been getting through toilet roll at an alarming rate. Intending to stock up on sundries at the supermarket, we are also in need of food that isn't lukewarm rice and cabbage. The deficit of protein in our diet leads to desperate measures as we entertain the idea of Dicos, the fast food joint opposite the supermarket.

Pronounced 'Dikeshi', Dicos is the Chinese idea of a western burger bar. Immediately we enter the plastic world, the six staff behind the counter freeze in horror. On the face of it, they are unused to customers, and overwhelmed by the upset to their normal routine. Foreign customers must be too much altogether.

Disturbed from their primary role of standing around chatting, they suddenly remember tasks they should be doing and push each other around in their haste to get underway. Serving laowai isn't high on their list of priorities. Approaching the counter, I see they are arguing.

'I'm busy. You serve them.'

'I don't know how. You do it.'

'I don't want to deal with big-noses, get new girl to do it.'

The argument culminates with the least senior staff member being physically manhandled to the counter by her colleagues. Terrified, the girl pulls a laminated menu from under the counter. Large chains, particularly western style restaurants, are usually better equipped to deal with foreign customers and can produce a picture based menu at the hint of a non-Chinese face. Stupid westerners can then simply point at idealised images of what they would like to eat.

Dutifully, we point at pictures, part with cash and are curtly told to sit. Selecting the least cluttered of the rubbish strewn tables, we set about making a little nest among the debris. The staff hide behind the machinery and watch in fascination as Victorian Dad clears the cartons, wrappers and partially consumed burgers while I wipe grease and ketchup from the seats with paper napkins.

We settle ourselves just in time for another willing helper to unceremoniously dump a tray of cartons between us and run to the safety of the counter.

With trepidation, I unwrap my burger. Just like western fast food, the stuff bears no resemblance to the artist's impressions on the menu. At first glance, our meals roughly resemble the comestibles I would expect from a low budget burger bar. That is, until I make the mistake of looking under the bun lid. Witnessing the unappetising mess first hand, one would think I'd know better, but I make the bigger mistake of putting it in my mouth.

Lukewarm grease spurts from the burger spraying the table and wall. This explains why the staff don't bother cleaning. I can't believe I'm still eating it.

Even VD, a consummate consumer of pernicious comestibles, blanches at his first taste. Setting his mind to the task in hand, his dogged determination reminds me of a bulldog chewing a lemon. His facial contortions as he forces his body to swallow have me mesmerised until a cockroach, of a size rarely seen outside the post-apocalyptic B-movie, nonchalantly saunters across the top of the seat behind him.

Sensing my penetrating stare, the armoured head turns in my direction, but I manage to look away in time. I've got no intention of getting into a fight with anything that size.

Glancing around, I find we are not the only clientele after all. We are just the only cash customers and are significantly outnumbered by our insect friends. I don't mention it to VD until we are ready to vamoose. I don't want to put him off his burger.

If these creatures are loose in the seating area, I dread to think what the kitchen is like. I have a feeling this will be our last visit to Dicos.

184

A side effect of school's basic fare is our systems have been given a detox. Used to an uncomplicated diet our bodies are taken by surprise by the Dicos assault. Waddling out of the restaurant, I can feel the gallons of over processed, undercooked lard swilling around. In pretty short time we are both desperate enough to make use of Dengfeng's public amenities. The quilted green army blanket covering the doorway has a greasy smear on either side where countless grubby hands have pushed it aside. Making myself as thin as possible, I endeavour to squeeze through the gap without making contact. In the process inventing the vertical limbo. The tiled interior lowers the temperature a few degrees from that outside, but doesn't compensate for the smell. Fortunately, this is going to be a quick visit.

High-stepping it over the sleeping forms huddled in their army overcoats, I head to the disabled cubicle. These are usually western style toilets. This one isn't. Not in a position to be picky, I put my Ma Bu training to the test. In Dicos' defence, at least I don't have to hold the position for long. This must be why it's called fast food. It's definitely my last visit to Dicos.

Waiting for VD, I am propositioned by an old lady intent on me trying her nuts. Unsure of where exactly this is leading, I err on the side of caution and reply, 'Wo bu yao, xie xie' (I don't want any, thank you).

I must look like I need mothering as old ladies are always trying to feed me. Even the old Chinese couple I sat next to on the plane, kept trying to palm their rations off on me. Although that may have been because they couldn't face the airline food themselves and didn't like to see it go to waste.

This little lady is not so easily deterred and I have not supplied the answer she wanted to hear. Just in case I'm too stupid to understand the concept, she continues to proffer the bag into my face. Finding success elusive, she picks out a nut and demonstrates how to eat it. Furiously mashing her gums together, she gives me a huge gap-toothed grin and, once more, shoves the bag into my nose. Repeated protestations proving futile, I pretend to be cross with her and snap, 'No!'

I have inadvertently uncovered the secret of Chinese comedy. Her weathered old face cracks and she convulses with laughter at this laowai's ready rapport. Struggling to compose herself, she manages to pause her laughter long enough to offer me more nuts. With Swiftian like wit, I dish out more of the same and start her off again.

VD cautiously wanders over. A tad perplexed, he asks, 'Dude, what you are doing to that crazy old woman?'

Caught red handed, what can I say? I have a way with the ladies. She then makes the mistake of offering VD a nut.

'Oh, don't mind if I do.' He fumbles around in the bag, extracts a handful of nuts and scoffs them in one go, 'Mmm, not bad.'

Reaching for the bag again, he is thwarted as the justified and ancient crone snatches it from his grasp, 'Hunh!' My old lady is not impressed by VD's lack of entertainment value. She's clearly fed a strawberry to a pig before. Clutching her paper bag, she potters off grumbling to herself.

Refuelled, and emptied again, we make for the supermarket. Not that I am easily influenced, but I have the hankering for nuts. Rounding the corner into the confectionary aisle, I am confronted a parent encouraging her child to squat. His kai dang ku enable him to go about his basic needs without the complication of removing clothing or inconveniencing his parent. Although, parental involvement seems to have no bearing on the choice of toiletry location. While bigger cities, especially around their economic centres, are fairly cosmopolitan, Dengfeng is out in the sticks. The sticks are a different game altogether; children and parents are without the slightest trace of inhibition. You really do have to be careful about putting your foot in it here.

It might not inhibit them, but it comes pretty close to putting me off. I return the chocolate nuts to the shelf and get a bag of boiled sweets instead.

My training shoes were already wearing thin and, like me, are now on their last legs. China adores high gloss flooring which becomes a death-trap when wet or dusty. My worn treads have become treacherous and I am in need of a new pair. Fortunately, the brand is readily accessible here.

Created by the Da Fu Rubber Company in the 1920s, the name Feiyue means Flying Forward. Modified over time, the 1958 design was based on the cloth shoes used by monks and in 1963 the double chevron design became the best-selling shoe in China with an output of 1.6 million pairs. Feiyue gained popularity with martial artists and athletes until they became synonymous with Chinese Wushu and recently their light weight and flexibility also made them popular amongst parkour practitioners. As such, Feiyue are the defacto shoe in Dengfeng. Most of the population wear them and most shops carry them. The issue for me is the size. I'm slightly bigger than your average Chinese bloke and the school shop has nothing close. Neither does the supermarket.

We pass a whole row of martial arts shops on the way back to school so I nip in to one and ask the proprietor for a size 46. Rooting through a wall of brown paper packages, she retrieves a pair of size 45 saying I'll have to buy them as it's the biggest size they make.

Demonstrating the benefits of Shifu Fatso's Power Stretching, I lift my foot up level to her face and point at my shoe, 'Feiyue do make a size 46, I am wearing a pair.' In spite of all evidence to the contrary, the shopkeep insists Feiyue do not make a size 46. With no shortage of martial arts equipment stores in the immediate area, I can afford to vote with my feet. I thank her and go next door.

In response to the same question this shop keeper rummages through a mound of shoes and excavates a pair of 47s.

'No, I want 46'.

Indicating his moped parked in the shop, he says he will go and get some.

'No problem, I'll come back Sunday.'

Despondent at not making an instant sale, he grudgingly agrees. I fully intend to go back Sunday, but try the next shop along anyway. They have a size 46 on the shelf. Expecting to pay 20Y, I am told they are 25Y because they are bigger. It's not worth the argument for 50p so I just hand over the cash.

The couple have a deal of confusion with my change, taking great pains rummaging through the notes to get it right, but I am soon out of the door carrying my shiny new shoes.

We're almost within sight of school, when I smell something wondrous. Outside the park gate is a guy selling hongshu (baked sweet potatoes). After the travesty of Dicos, I really fancy something plain and stodgy. This will be the very fellow. Handing over the requested amount the vendor hands back my money. Shaking his head, he points at a tear in the note saying it's no good.

A crowd will gather around anything in China. Sensing the potential of free entertainment, a group of little kids, who should probably be at school, materialise out of nowhere to form a rough circle around me. Quickly getting the gist of what's happened they point at me and laugh, 'Ni bei pian le.'

They are laughing because I've been tricked. Bless them. In a flash of clarity, I recognise the note as one I received in change from my shoe purchase. Click! The pieces slot together. Had I been more on my game I would have been alerted by the couple's furtiveness. While the people of Henan have a reputation throughout China as being untrustworthy, this is the first time I've really experienced it. Several guys at school have been duped with fake, damaged or random currency so I should have been more careful. It's only a couple of quid, but suddenly my new shoes have doubled in price.

I root out another note for the spud-seller and give the useless note to a grinning kid in recognition of his charitable mockery. Taking leave of the giggling finger-pointers, we seek sanctuary in the park. It's a lot more docile in the sleepy afternoon warmth and the paths less hazardous without the frantic activity of the morning exercise fanatics. Taking up a seat, we lazily set about our spuds.

The good-old, no-nonsense potato is exactly what I needed. Laying in to the stodgy goodness, my nutter senses start tingling and I look up to see a scruffy guy in the walkway conspicuously examining a padlock. Locking and unlocking it, he removes the key and holds it up to the light, nodding that it is good.

Scanning the occupied benches for any attentive parties, he repeats his lock inspection, but fails to pique any interest. His audience are a staid bunch and indifferent to his antics. I feign concentration on my spud and watch with peripheral vision as his act continues.

Biting the bullet, he approaches a well-to-do looking grandparent with his charge and attempts to sell him the padlock. It's a poor choice of target. This old fella isn't as green as he looks. Not wishing to purchase said padlock he tells Scruffy so, repeatedly, and at volume. For good measure, he throws in that he shouldn't be bothering people in the park and to depart forthwith. Beating a hasty retreat, the failed padlock purveyor mumbles back, 'Why not? It's a good lock'.

Confronted by another universal constant, the Nutter in the Park, I have to wonder, 'What was the good of going to Peking when it was just like Shrewsbury?'

Spuds demolished, we explore deeper into the park. It's much larger than I had appreciated in the early hours. The beautifully maintained plants and shrubs ease the temperature and external sounds making it another oasis from the outside world. Like the statues among the trees, the afternoon crowd are a casual lot. There are still scattered groups singing, exercising and practicing their hobbies, but fewer and less manically than the early risers and have more card playing and newspaper reading going on.

Following the tinny strains of a Christmas jingle to the far end of the park, we are brought to an abrupt halt by the Fairground Ride of Insanity.

Creaking around the track to the strangled strain of Jingle Bells are a selection of technicoloured, equine-esque creatures. Giraffes, unicorns and carriages pulled by reindeer wend their way through a psychedelic safari of deer, dinosaurs and Ultraman. To top off this eclectic collection of childhood ephemera, the carriages have laser pistols to shoot at Bambi on the way around.

Even with my limited experience of children's rides, I can see they've pulled out the stops on this one. The design meeting must have been a mammoth brainstorming session by a bunch of whacked-out stoners. Concerned that none of their target audience be left out, they spread their bases and went for a bit of everything.

If I'm awed, and a little frightened, by the mechanical monstrosity, VD takes a different perspective and expresses the exact attitude the designers were aiming for, 'That may be the best fairground ride ever.' The proprietor misinterprets our interest and follows the Carny Code by gesturing to a vacant carriage. We decline on the grounds that, assuming it would take our weight, my mind isn't equipped to deal with it.

Back in plenty of time for training, I excitedly crack open my new shoes. I can't get my feet into the things. Comparing them to my existing shoes, there are noticeable differences in the design and logo which leads me to conclude that they are 'jiade'. I have just purchased a pair of Fake-Yues. I'm not so much affronted at being conned, as I am amazed a product that retails for £2 is worth the effort of forging.

Not only was I stitched up on my change, but my expensive footwear is useless to boot. That particular store hasn't exactly lived up to my expectations as a valued customer. Combined with the dodgy note they gave me, I have come away sadly lacking in customer satisfaction. To save the shoes going to waste, I'll offer them to the other guys, but that shop, for the sake of a couple of quid, has lost my custom forever. I put my threadbare shoes back on.

Today our group is not the last to get going. South American Guy is making the most of his time in town and, despite his pass expiring hours ago, is still not back. Shibu keeps his whole squad standing in formation waiting his return.

When SA guy finally turns up, rather the worse for wear, we can hear the ensuing argument from the third floor gym. Showing no signs of contrition, he immediately goes on the offensive, 'Why should I come back on time man? You should give us more choice.'

Shifu Fatso watches from window scowling, but pushes Knobby away when he tries to peek. 'No! Go!' he points to the carpeted area where we are Jibengong'ing it and Knobby skulks into line.

With SA guy shouting back at Shibu, he must be concerned about losing face in public. Sending his squad up to the gym alone, he steers SA guy into the accommodation building to continue their discussion out of earshot.

Shibu's group slink into the gym and mill around dejectedly like lost sheep. Showing more acumen than I would have given him credit for, Fatso takes control and incorporates them into our Jibengong. Given their current state of mind, it's a shrewd move to keep them occupied.

At break I attempt to lighten the mood with the tale of my shoe fiasco. It's not a great success and there are no takers for my shoes. Juha's departure has elevated me to the position of resident yeti. The Fake-Yues are far too big for anyone else, so I can't even give them away. A lot of the Chinese kids tread down the back of their shoes and flop around in them. I'll do the same and wear them as bedroom slippers.

Still Shibu-less after break, it's the usual half-hearted session in the weights gym where all the talk is of South American Guy. Apparently, he has already had a few run-ins with school and, particularly, with Shibu. It's also not the first time he's turned up late or well lubricated. Guys that previously shared with him have further tales. It's a slightly different perspective to the version we got from the man himself.

Classmates are a random factor and part of the gamble of coming here. At the moment, it's a cool bunch, but the turnover rate means the mix is subject to change at little notice. Roommates are essentially the luck of the draw and, with the foreign students hailing from all over the globe, a little culture clash can be expected, but most make the best of it and try to get along. After all, as the outsiders here, we are all in the same boat.

Of course, there's a bit of griping or moving rooms. The surreal conditions make the slightest things disproportionately annoying. Poor nutrition, tiredness, lack of home comforts and close confinement all add up to frayed nerves. I'm sure the only reasons there aren't more fallings out is that people are just too tired and we have a common enemy in the shape of the school.

SA guy has managed to upset so many roommates that he now has a room of his own. To me that's more of a reward than a punishment. He does sound like a doozy, but I almost admire his gall while simultaneously being annoyed at the school for allowing him to get away with it. Given that he's obviously no fan of authority, I have to wonder why he came to a Kung Fu school in Communist China in the first place. On top of that, I don't understand how he has managed to avoid eviction for so long. I expected sterner repercussions for breaking the rules.

Evening assembly has a definite tension. SA guy is a no-show and Shibu appears perturbed. Being so rundown in such an enclosed environment, we are very sensitive to small shifts in atmosphere, so one person's actions affect everyone.

With everyone feeling the strain, I am again on my own in the gym and when I get back for beddy-byes even Fatso doesn't linger. VD and I aren't really party to the intricacies of the situation, but I hope it blows over soon so that we don't have to live under this cloud for much longer.

We live in illusion and the appearance of things. There is a reality.
We are that reality. When you understand this, you see that you are
nothing, and being nothing, you are everything. That is all.

Kalu Rinpoche

After breakfast, we assemble in front of our building for Shifu to tell us
to, 'Go run.' It must be his favourite expression. Having already had our
morning warming exercises, which mostly consisted of Go Run, we now
set off around the school for more of the same.

I am beginning to dislike this Go Run business. Every training
session begins with Go Run. Generally circuits of school, sometimes
there's a slight variation on the theme where we run sprints, or out on the
road, or in the gym, but it's all Go Run. I am rapidly coming to the
conclusion one can have enough Go Run. It's not the running itself I
object to, but it's often used as a substitute to training us. If we were told
to do a certain number of laps it wouldn't be so bad, but as soon as we
are out of view, Fatso takes the opportunity to disappear for a cigarette
leaving us circling the block in a holding pattern until his return.

Laps of school are particularly unpleasant as they take in the back of
the canteen. Navigating the mounds of rotten kitchen waste and cold
ashes is enough to put anyone off food for life. The rats are so used to us

jogging past that they carry on about their rodent pursuits unperturbed by the irregular flow of red tracksuits.

Without a set number of laps, we can't pace ourselves and without a goal the run is very unsatisfying. The others must be of a similar mind as, when the Shifus disappear, we slow to a comfortable jog and chat on the way.

Currently persona non-grata with his own squad, South American guy tags on to me, 'Hey man, what do you learn in China? I learn to run, eh?'

'Yes, but look how versatile you are now. We have learnt to run in all sorts of conditions. We run in the hot, in the cold, in the dark, in circles...... '.

'Yeah, man, I run up the mountain too.'

Apparently, I'm not the only one developing issues with Go Run which makes me feel less guilty about taking a stance. Putting my plan into action, I do enough laps at a reasonable speed to warm up, then peel off and stretch. I appreciate the need for a warmup, but there is only so warm that one can get and we are it.

When Shifu Fatso next emerges, I have one foot on the concrete table-tennis table and am pulling back on my toes. Initially surprised I am not where I was left, he doesn't bother me as I'm sort of doing something constructive and only partially skiving.

Not only does Go Run take up a good chunk of our time, but it also uses energy I need to conserve for the real training. Unlike the Chinese kids, we have a narrow window of opportunity here and I need to make the most of the available time. This concept is lost on our Shifus. They don't know any different because this is all they have ever done. They also have no idea what our home lives are like or what a big deal it is for us to be here.

In the west, few of us are able to take fifteen years out of our lives to dedicate to Kung Fu. These guys do nothing other than Kung Fu and have no lives outside the school. Along with most martial arts schools in China, Xiao Long students enrol at four or five years old and receive their entire compulsory education here. Shaolin Kung Fu is not designed to be learnt quickly and one should ideally start at a tender age when the body is still pliable enough to open the pelvis and develop the correct alignment.

Where conventional Chinese schools get two six-week holidays, the students here board all year-round and only see their parents a couple of times a year. Returning home for the spring holiday is the only time most of them leave the school grounds until they graduate at age 17.

This does beg the question of how the kids adapt to the outside world after being institutionalised for so much of their lives. That said, many head straight into another institution as a martial arts school diploma enables them to get into the army or police. A select few stay on as coaches or perhaps even make it to the big screen. Parents are prepared to sacrifice time with their children and struggle to pay the school fees with the aim of securing their children's future.

Chinese parents are not alone in seeing martial arts as a career move for their children. Among us foreign students are three full-time children. The eleven-year-old Kazak lad next door has been here for three years and the two Korean reprobates are younger still.

The Chinese students may be raised in the system, but it's surprising how the power of the establishment has sneaked up on me. In no time at all, I have adjusted to the Xiao Long regime and respond to the synthesised bugle calls disturbingly quickly.

After the initial couple of weeks, the body adapts to the lifestyle and one loses one's self within the Xiao Long alternative reality bubble. It's amazing how quickly the mind and body acclimatise to the training. My mind is essentially shutting down and giving all resources to my body. I don't have the energy available to think about what's going on if I tried. We are all too tired to make anything happen outside of class. When we have any spare time, like after meals, we stagger back to our respective rooms to recoup energy for the next session and most guys catch some shut-eye.

With so little happening outside our daily routine, the days merge together and I'm losing my comprehension of time.

Lined up at the field edge, it suddenly occurs to me it's Friday. It seems no one is immune to the Xiao Long time vortex as I have to remind Shifu Fatso that today is Power Stretching. Shifu doesn't immediately cotton on. Instead he looks at me thinking I've had too much sun. When the penny drops his face lights with glee.

Always a favourite with our Shifu, it's not a popular choice with the rest of the group. They grumble and glower at me as we troop up to the gym. I didn't remind Fatso about the Power Stretching because of a masochistic streak, but because it's making a difference to me. Also, I suspect if I hadn't we would have been palmed off with another Go Run style time-filler.

I'm happy with the way Power Stretching is paying off. My first

Kung Fu teacher told me not to bother stretching as flexibility was genetically inherited. After only a couple of weeks here I am very close to the splits already and, just for the record, neither of my parents are ballerinas.

Power Stretching is less comfortable than solo stretching, but by taking me out of my comfort zone it also seems more effective.

Holding me in position while Fatso contorts my limbs, one guy comments, 'This man not show pain.' While he overestimates my discomfort threshold, it's nice that something else I've trained is also paying off and Master Yau's words haven't gone entirely to waste.

Now our bodies are broken in, I'm comforted by the routine and have slipped into my own little niche, but VD is beginning to rage against the machine. While I'm paranoid about skipping any training opportunity in case I miss a valuable nugget of information, VD is determined not to train anything he doesn't see as worthwhile.

As with the laps of school, my technique is to go along with the flow for the most part and, when it suits me, to make my own way. VD, on the other hand, rails against the running which merely serves to make him less tolerant to the next perceived injustice visited upon us. When this next issue occurs, he has already wound himself up so much that he is unable to deal with it and storms off in a huff.

His tolerance levels aren't helped by our compulsory confinement. All this running about is thirsty work. No doubt as a result of the hard days training, toward the cocktail hour he observes a dryness. A feeling that could best be assuaged by getting on the outside of a pint of something cold and alcoholic. Unfortunately, not only are we imprisoned of an evening, but, even if we could get out, there is nowhere within reasonable distance to acquire such a beverage. With his blood/alcohol system so far out of whack VD's spirits are at an all-time low.

It's not so much not being allowed to drink, but that we are not trusted to go out and are physically locked in at night. With the front door locked and bars on the windows, we've just got to hope there's never a fire. I've got a good idea of what the school couldn't organise in a brewery, but I dread to think what they'd be like under the pressure of an emergency. Thinking about it, our only escape route would be to climb down the balcony.

After lunch, everyone returns to their rooms to get their heads down for half an hour. True to form, Victorian Dad is right there when it comes to catching up on his beauty sleep. He ought to be gorgeous by now, I can only assume he's doing it wrong. Although his face certainly looks slept in.

Along with my journal, during this time, I occupy myself reading. As such, I'm ploughing through my books at an alarming rate and am running low on reading matter.

In my early teens, I read James Clavell's 'Shogun', which rode the East Asia fad of the time. Just before this trip I chanced upon several of his other novels in a second-hand bookshop and, as one was based in Hong Kong, I decided that was close enough and bought the lot. The great big tomes with uncomplicated plots are the very fellows for long flights and dull evenings. Although I hadn't anticipated getting through them so quickly. Amongst the titles is a tale of Allied soldiers in a Japanese POW camp during the Second World War. This probably wasn't the smartest of things to read during our internment. Being tired, achy and hungry makes anyone tetchy and, without intending to belittle what those Prisoners of War went through, I'm beginning to see similarities between our lives. I resolve to read something a little more jovial next.

Dropping off the book I've finished in the ravaged DVD Room, I excavate the jumble of cast-off literature with limited success. The majority of the donated books are in German. This implies more German students visit here than any other nationality, or possibly that only German students can read or are generous enough leave their books behind. The Germans certainly make up the largest western contingent at the moment.

My quest for light-hearted reading matter amongst the ad hoc library is thwarted by the scant selection of English language books. The best available option is Ray Bradbury's Fahrenheit 451. I'm turning into an irony magnet.

Any thoughts of battling the censorship of an oppressive regime are quashed by the tannoy announcement. I poke VD in the ribs and gather our kit.

In front of the building, we wait for our Shifu to get his act together. Already assembled, Shibu's squad is a little light and he questions them as to the whereabouts of the remainder. Not satisfied with the response he sends them to collect those missing.

While the indolent loafers slowly surface and fall in to their squad, Wouter staggers across to Shibu to report he's feeling ill and won't be training. Wouter, from Holland, isn't one of the lead swingers and one look at him is enough to see he really shouldn't be up and about.

Shibu takes him aside, listens sympathetically, and steers him back toward the building. Next thing I know, Wouter is bouncing down the steps on his head. The Shifus cluster around his spread-eagle form and poke at him with their toes until someone notices the pool of blood blossoming under him. They then alternate between prodding him and pointing at the growing pool of blood.

This is exactly one of those moments where it's up to the foreign students to come together and protect their own. Breaking ranks, one guy runs for the school doctor and others tend to Wouter; compressing the wound and keeping him stationary. The doctor isn't up to anything more than applying a temporary dressing and diagnoses that Wouter should be taken to the hospital.

A short discussion results in a consensus that Wouter should not be left alone and two of his roommates agree to accompany him. The Shifus are initially against this, but are forced to concede in the face of our unified resistance. We can all see Wouter is in no condition to make any informed decisions and we don't trust the Shifus to do so on his behalf.

Not only are we concerned for our comrade's welfare, but I'm sure everyone has in the back of their minds that it could be them lying there. In a similar position, none of us would want to rely on the Shifus and the few phrases we learnt at Chinese class simply aren't going to cut it at the hospital.

Assured Wouter is in trustworthy company, we re-join our groups for training. With Shibu playing 'responsible adult', Fatso adopts his squad and takes us all out to the field. Fulfilling his obligation by taking Shibu's squad under his wing, Fatso sees no need to go any further and opts for a time filler: Touchy Knee.

Touchy Knee is essentially a game of tag. One person is 'it' and has to touch another person below the knee to make them 'it'. That person then tries to tag another while holding one hand to the area that was touched. You can't tag the person that just tagged you and running out of the area makes you 'it'.

Half the people don't join in. With no one's heart in it, Fatso takes us up to the gym and out of sight of any potential observers. Away from any prying eyes, the training remains lacklustre. Fatso struggles with the combined group and concern for Wouter is in the back of everyone's mind.

Dismissed for an early dinner, we are just in time to catch Wouter returning with his fractured skull stapled back together. Wearing a string-net skullcap that holds his bandages in place, he looks like a deranged Hip-hop gangster and we all queue up to have our photos taken with him. With no attempt to clear Wouter's blood, the soaked-in stain will serve as a constant reminder to us.

Sitting on the blood-dyed steps, we give our best gangster rap poses. Laughing through the pain, Wouter is able to see the funny side of it and explains the events that led to his mishap.

Informed that Wouter felt dizzy, Shibu decided the best medicine was to make him walk up and down the steps until he felt better. The consequences of which could have been anticipated by a child. Talk about being penalised for doing the right thing, I make a mental note to stay in bed if I'm ill.

Put out at the Dutchman's celebrity status, Shibu curtails our joviality by sending him to bed. As Wouter limps into the building Shibu adds his professional medical opinion, 'No train ten day.'

This arbitrary instruction is not what Wouter wanted to hear. He gingerly shuffles back down the steps to argue his case. Fair play to the guy for trying, but his best bet is just to do as he's told for a few days and then quietly slip back into training.

Not being allowed to train for any extended period is our greatest fear. Even the slackers amongst us live in dread of such an event. A day off now and again with a minor illness can be a welcome break, but anything longer is defeating the object of being here. While Shaolin is termed a Kung Fu Resort, it's not the sort of place to kick back and relax. If that's what you're looking for, I would recommend a beach holiday.

After assembly, I head up to the gym to work on my form. I'm the only person there. It's only Friday and everyone else is already winding down for our Sunday off. As I am stretching, the new guy sticks his head into the hall, takes one look at me, and flees. Whatever he's looking for I'm obviously not it. Actually, I don't understand what Gangster Joe is doing here at all. He's not in quarantine but, despite possessing the training uniform, he wears the jacket with jeans and I have yet to see him train.

Maybe he's so good he doesn't need to train. I, on the other hand, do. I've never been a natural and my Kung Fu has been particularly hard won. In my own inimitable way, I perfunctorily work through the form desperately trying to commit the movements into muscle memory. Repeating each move slowly. I attempt to build in some of the finesse Chen Tongshan was so keen on us having and that Fatso hasn't been giving us.

I appreciate there is a language barrier here and, although the school claims our teachers speak English, I should have been more prepared. That said, I'm not sure our Shifus have that level of understanding to pass on.

With no one to turn to for constructive criticism, I'm limited by my own experience. However, working my own interpretations into the form at this early stage is dangerous as I could easily go off on a tangent and end up with a form that looks nothing like the original.

Concentrating on the details, time goes quickly and, before I know it the tannoy announces it's time to return to my cell.

Reading back an email I've just written home, I discern it to be complete nonsense. I thought I was functioning ok, but I must be more tired than I realise. I suppose I'd better have an early night. In silent protest at the regime, I 'Go sleep' without being told to.

Shaolin Kongfu is not about violence,
but rather a way to pursue peace.

Shi Yan Zhuang

China's Three T's:
Tibet, Taiwan and Tiananmen.

Sufficiently morning-warmed and breakfasted, we assemble for morning training. Grumbling to himself, Shifu Fatso walks down the line inspecting his troops. The grim expression implies we are not a pleasant sight. The feeling is mutual. Finding all present, if not entirely correct, he growls, 'Go park'.

Along with Go Run, the novelty of Go Park is also wearing thin. What was once a pleasant interlude, is now just a nuisance. Another excuse for the Shifus to get out of training us. The park removes us from the school's mechanism and allows our Shifus to kick back while we entertain ourselves. Most students are happy with the arrangement, but for me it's a waste of time and energy I could be using to train. Given the option of frittering daylight, I'm sure I could put it to much better use. Eating and sleeping spring to mind.

Marching up the road we pass a few local lads sitting on the low wall surrounding the park. Much has been said about Chinese women being beautiful princesses that maintain their youthful looks for a long time before, like oranges, aging very quickly and turning into old fishwives overnight. However, I have heard little mention of the men in comparison. From my observation, the men, conversely, deteriorate quickly with a tendency to the early onset of middle-aged spread. In Britain men reach middle-age, give up, tie their trousers with a bit of string and gravitate to the garden shed. Chinese men seem to go through a similar process in their mid-twenties and eschew the shed in favour of spitting and chain-smoking at a roadside perch.

Arriving at Wulin Park we discover that Shifu Fatso has dematerialised. While we are left unattended, Shibu's group cluster around him at the side of the basketball court making small talk. Most of the other Shifus have a better level of English than our beloved Fatso and can fraternise more with their students. The eternal cynic in me suggests this is also an easier option than training them. Starved of attention, Knobby heads toward the happy throng with a gleam in eye. Butting into the group, he plays for the crowd by attempting to inform Shibu Shifu about the Tiananmen Square incidents.

There is an audible intake of breath. Some students freeze, but most are used to Knobby and ignore him. He ploughs on with relentless disregard. Not particularly well informed, he still insists on giving his version of events that happened when he was barely a glint in the milkman's eye. Singularly unimpressed, Shibu is simply not able to understand why anyone would concoct such an improbable story.

Fortunately, Knobby's explanation is too garbled to be convincing and, when no one rushes to his support, he loses momentum. It's just as well Knobby's reputation precedes him as he could well have become unstuck with this one. However, it's taken as more of his buffoonery and a diplomatic incident is avoided.

There are three things one shouldn't mention in China: Tiananmen, Tibet and Taiwan. Known as the Three T's, they do not fit well in polite conversation. Trying to 'educate' anyone about their own country is, at the very least, a thankless task. The Chinese are no exception. There is nothing to be achieved other than to become unpopular. Frankly, the Chinese look down on foreigners and their ways at the best of times. Telling them you know better, or that their country is in any way flawed, will only cause further isolation.

The current generation of Chinese aren't used to political debate and, unlike their western counterparts, do not openly criticise their government. I criticise my government all the time. Being British, it's my responsibility to be ill-informed and have a good moan about things I have no control over. Our government is on the list along with the weather.

The Chinese, however, do not subscribe to this mindset. The only concession I have heard to Chairman Mao being less than perfect was that he smoked a lot, and this was after my protracted diatribe regarding my own government's failings. I suspect the token dissent was a gesture of sympathy rather than solidarity. The official line is that although Mao made mistakes in his later years his achievements are primary. Such belief in their government is bewildering to an outsider. I'm mostly embarrassed by mine.

The majority of the Chinese population have no interest in politics whatsoever. There's probably not a great deal of point when your country runs a one-party state. This said, it does seem a more honest system than the British one which, at the moment, is little more than a popularity contest between liars and conmen in the pockets of big business. Even in our alleged democracy the government always gets in and immediately reneges on their promises. Given they have no intention of following through on their campaign manifesto, and I'm thus unable to make an informed decision in their selection, one has to wonder if the choice is worth having.

With my jaded opinion of British politics, I can't help envy the Chinese their pride in their country. Their superiority complex is more difficult to contend with. The conviction is ingrained to such an extent they resort to doublespeak to support their argument. An example of this would be the Chinese current bone of contention with United Nation policy in the Middle East. Seen as acts of a bullyboy state, they see no comparison with invading and occupying Tibet in order to 'peacefully' liberate them from their independence. George Orwell prophesised of this ability to hold two conflicting pieces of information and act on either without reconciling the discrepancy.

On top of this pride, decades of turmoil and insecurity have given the Chinese a healthy paranoia regarding their government. Not only will they not openly criticise, they are cautious about being with someone who would.

So, even if Knobby were convincing enough to fill Shibu in on the Tiananmen incident, Shibu still couldn't accept it as reality, much less acknowledge it in public. It makes me wonder what has been indoctrinated into me over the years. Just to be cautious, I'll try not to believe everything I think.

Nevertheless, Knobby's little display has unnerved the Shifu and left us feeling awkward, so we're all glad when our Go Park is cut short. On the bright side getting back to school early means I get the chance of a nice cuppa before Buddha Class.

Marching back, I notice a car parked under a, 'No Parking' sign. Not an unusual sight in itself, but a paradox occurs to me. Before coming to China, I had a vision of an Orwellian surveillance state, but it's practically the polar opposite. The populace has an arbitrary concept of regulation and enjoy an unhindered freedom in everyday matters. 'No Smoking', 'Keep off the Grass', and other polite notices mean nothing until it suits them. Even red lights at road junctions are seen as guidelines.

Any number of minor offences that would result in a police fine back home leave local law enforcement unconcerned. Unless a direct criticism of the Party itself occurs, the government maintain a fairly laissez faire attitude to the day to day activities of its population. Bizarrely, this flexible mentality towards rules means, in some ways, Communist China is less restrictive than Britain's wishy-washy nanny state.

Buddha Class sees me nearing the front of the line. I should soon be able to light a joss stick. I'm also getting the hang of the chant, but still can't manage without reading from the sheet. I've been working through the phonetics with my dictionary, replacing them with pinyin, and it's slowly beginning to make sense. Unaided, it's an uphill slog that could have been explained in half an hour given a competent teacher.

Done Buddha'ing, we assemble for our weekly telling off. Shibu's gripe this week is the trashed DVD room. It's a fair point. I've only visited the room briefly and it is in a frightful condition. Investigating the alleged internet access, and rummaging the ad hoc library, left me disheartened by our classmates. The hoyden have wilfully broken the computer and DVD player during their DVD/food fight. The evidence being a smashed computer and DVD player in a room littered in lumps of food and broken DVDs. Happy to criticise the manners of their Chinese counterparts, many western students have little respect for their surroundings either.

Shibu's threat of removing DVD room privileges is particularly hollow since the recent damage has removed the reasons for visiting it anyway. Personally, I am upset there is not more repercussion. Glancing down the line, I notice the perpetrators don't even have the decency to look embarrassed. Again, I am satisfied we didn't attend movie night. I've found it difficult to conceive that the other guys consider me a grown-up. For the most part I don't think of myself as an adult, then something like this happens. Now I feel really old and adulty.

Following our chastisement, Shibu reminds us against taking cold showers and casually announces, 'We are put hot shower for you.'

'Excellent,' I think to myself, 'now all we need do is wait for the shower to magically materialise.' I am not alone in having difficulty swallowing this. The others look around at each other confused.

One of the French guys is first to ask for clarification. However, Shibu is adamant a hot shower has been installed in the bathroom of the DVD room and follows up with instructions for the operation of said appliance, 'Always turn off. Not keep turn on'.

One shower between thirty of us is better than no shower each. Things are on the up. Reeling from the shower news we are dismissed.

After a swift lunch, I grab my soap and towel and investigate the promised shower. Miraculously, a water heater has indeed been precariously bolted to the wall. The plate has been removed from the shaver socket and the bare wires from an extension cable twisted onto the contacts. This cable runs across the room at neck height to just above the shattered toilet where the water heater is plugged into it.

From the dripping walls and inch of soapy, muddy water congealing on the floor, I deduce the shower has already seen significant use. Ok, the water doesn't drain and the place is a death-trap, but it's a shower nonetheless.

The shower must have been in planning for some time as it has appeared too quickly after last week's Buddha class discussion to be related. It also adds weight to my suspicion that there is no hot water in the building.

Inexplicably, not only does the shower exist, but it works reasonably well. A lazy jet of warm water dribbles down my body coaxing streaks of Dengfeng dust to join the muddy swirl. I hadn't appreciated how grubby I had become. It turns out I don't have a tan after all.

With nowhere to hang my clothes, I wash them under the shower too. If Shibu expects to me to unplug the shower from the extension after using it, he is going to be disappointed. I'm not prepared to touch the electric here at the best of times, let alone when I am dripping wet and ankle deep in water.

Walking back to our room wearing a towel around my waist with my wet clothes draped over my arm, I meet Yuan Shifu coming the other way.

Startled by my semi-clad frame, Yuan Shifu jerks to an abrupt halt and begins to convulse in shock. My initial thought is that he's having a seizure. He's obviously trying to say something, but is too outraged to formulate any words. Finally exploding into hysterics, he manages to stutter, 'Nick, no! Not do again.' I leave him standing in the corridor shaking his head and laughing.

As I hang my wet clothes on our window bars, VD enquires about the shower situation. Initially as sceptical as I, my vouchsafe convinces him. Seeing me shining like a slightly pink new pin, he is keen to get some hot-water action for himself. Determined to give the best advice I can, I add that there is nowhere to hang clothes in the room so he might want to take off anything he doesn't want to wash and leave it here. In fact, walking there in just a towel is probably a good idea.

Just when I was becoming inured to our ablution privations, the school pulls a small wonder out of the bag. Along with a giant leap in personal hygiene, the shower heralds a new era of laundry. Taking our dirty clothes into the shower is more effective than the cold-water hand wash in the sink. Filling the limited space on the window bars, we turn to the rope hung across our room. We are soon taken over with wet clothes. Under the current conditions they won't take long to dry, but the winter months could be problematic. All aglow with cleanliness, I head to training with a newfound enthusiasm.

There's a slight breeze this afternoon. It's not particularly brisk, but funnelled down the walkway and trapped in the courtyard, the wind spirals dust and debris around in a mini tornado.

A couple of Pink Overall girls walk past with a pink-plastic bin. Carrying the bin between them, they cross the windy courtyard and empty it onto the back of a flatbed motorcycle with predictable results. They don't hesitate from their task as the litter blows straight off the truck. One each side of a rubbish bin, they return to the building content that they have done what they were told and emptied the bin.

Leaking out into the afternoon light, it's clear who among my brothers have investigated the new-fangled shower. They have a pinkish glow, a certain daisy-freshness, that is noticeably absent from the teenage contingent.

The dust and litter spiralling in the eddying currents is mesmerising, but means alfresco training is not an option. Even inside the gym, the air is thick with dust that sticks in the eyes and throat. I burn through my water long before break and have a liberal coating of Dengfeng sticking to my perspiring limbs. The positive effect of the shower didn't last long.

The fumes from the burning rubbish at the training ground have been getting worse lately. The smouldering plastic gives off a thick, acrid smoke that sits heavily in the air. Returning from the tuck shop, I perceive a window has been left open and, given a prevailing breeze, the black smoke has invaded the gym to the extent I have trouble seeing from one side to the other. Long before the end of the session my eyes are watering and I have difficulty drawing breath.

Training under these conditions is ridiculous. Unsurprisingly, no one stays the distance. Staggering into the room with red-rimmed eyes, wheezing like an asthmatic horse, I ask if VD would care to partake of evening repast. Looking up from his phone, he reassures me I look terrible.

Struggling to swallow my tepid mush, it's clear that evening training is a no go. My throat has been a scratchy for a few days, but now it's swollen enough to restrict my airway. Being in no condition for physical exertion puts me in a difficult position. While I am not in a good way, I need to keep a low profile about my complaint. Even though it's perfectly obvious to me what's happening, from the school's viewpoint I have all the symptoms of the degenerate western diseases they are so concerned about. The last thing I want is to be put back into quarantine.

VD also has a sore throat, but isn't feeling it as badly as me. I guess his body is used to abuse by toxic substances. That said, he suffers more from the other end, so I suppose it averages out.

We have been quite fastidious since we arrived, but it is so difficult to be hygienic that at least one of us is suffering at any given time. It's just as well we have a bathroom to ourselves as, even between two of us, it tends to be a tad oversubscribed. I've mostly adapted to the conditions now and VD is sticking to his Imodium routine, which involves damming up the flow until we have a day off and then letting it run free ahead of our day out. This means, as I have long suspected, most of the time he is literally full of it. Possibly not the ideal spokesman for their campaign, the guy is, nonetheless, a walking advert for Imodium and I have suggested he seeks a sponsorship deal. Our discomforts are fairly typical of the personal complaints here. With the other students similarly disposed there is rarely a full turnout for training and no one can fart with impunity.

Rummaging through my expansive first aid kit, I come across nothing for a sore throat. Supplied by my nurse friend Dave, it consists entirely of complicated surgical dressings, which may look impressive, but I have no idea how to use. He supplied me with enough medical equipment to open my own A & E ward, but neglected to give me the expansive training required to operate it. My level of medical expertise prevents me from utilising anything more complicated than an aspirin and I am distraught my kit doesn't contain any. Fortunately, tomorrow is our day off so I'll have the opportunity to visit a pharmacy. A shower would help no end, but it's permanently engaged throughout the evening and I resort to the stand-up wash in cold water at the sink.

VD is spark out by the time I finish my ablutions so, rather than risk the slim chance Shifu Fatso will notice my red rimmed eyes and difficulty speaking, I turn the light off and get into bed.

When Shifu opens the door, he is most indignant that I am apparently asleep without being told to do so. Letting out a, 'Humph!' he firmly closes the door and plods off down the corridor.

My experience is that when undergoing severe physical labour the mind is not at all active. One thinks of the particular problem in hand or perhaps the mind just wanders not performing coherent thoughts. As to missing various phases of civilised life, one has no time to miss anything save food or sleep or rest. In short one becomes little more than a rational animal.

James Murray.

Food and Medicine are one and the same.

Traditional Chinese Medicine adage.

Last night's training session was the last straw for my throat. Difficulty breathing gave me a fitful night's sleep and my already tired body is feeling decidedly sorry for itself.

Having laboured through morning warming, I find breakfast too difficult to swallow and wind up back at the room for a cup of tea instead. My priority now is to self-medicate. The niggling pain, combined with my tiredness, makes me grumpy enough that I am disinclined to go through the usual procedure of running around to get signed out. A perfect opportunity to make use of my pre-signed slips.

Spotting us heading for the gate, the security guard begrudgingly vacates his little hut and stands outside in anticipation of a showdown.

Without breaking step, I thrust the slips into his hand and carry on. I don't know if he even looks at them, but I'm home free and about half an hour ahead of anyone else. The guard will be wondering what's keeping them. However, the Chinese obsession with paperwork means he will be satisfied his job has been carried out to the letter.

Today's walk into Dengfeng isn't a pleasant experience. Even at this early hour the pollution is visible. Compounding on my damaged constitution, the barrage of dust, smoke and vehicle fumes soon have my sinuses and larynx so tight that my head is pounding.

According to China's environmental ministry, Zhengzhou, the capital of Henan Province, is among the country's top 10 most polluted cities. It's about an hour and a half away and I'm suffering here, so I'm particularly pleased we didn't decide to stay at the Zhengzhou school. Suddenly those surgical masks that Chinese commuters wear don't seem like such a stupid idea after all. In fact, they don't look heavy duty enough. I wonder if I can get my hands on a full NBC suit at the local army surplus?

In the process of crossing the road, I pause at a narrow central reservation between the lanes. Tucked between the straggly shrubs is a small, mesh cage of chickens. This is a particularly creative use of public property. Although I doubt these unfortunate fowl will be fit for human consumption given their constant inhalation of vehicle fumes. It's not doing me any good and I'm just passing by.

It would be nice to do the traditional Chinese medicine approach, but what I really need at the moment is a quick fix that can be provided by bog-standard throat syrup and generic painkillers.

It's just after 8am and most of the small, independent shops are already open to serve Dengfeng's rush-hour commuters. Among the uninspiring, and often featureless, shop fronts the blue neon cross of a pharmacy is soon located.

Barely the width of the doorway, the narrow shop has three chairs against the side wall and a counter at the far end guarding shelves of boxes and bottles. The proprietor is already dealing with a patient and both look up in surprise as we enter.

Clearly bemused by our appearance, the proprietor excuses himself from his client to enquire how he can help us. Equally intrigued, his client is happy to take a back seat to enjoy the show as I bumble through my request.

A couple of words not covered in our Medical Mandarin class were paracetamol and ibuprofen. Looking up the names, I found them too much of a mouthful and opted for the more blanket terms.

'Wo sangzi teng, wo yao zhitongyao he xiaoyanyao.' (My throat hurts, I want painkillers and anti-inflammatory).

A blank stare is the stern reply.

Expecting such a response, I show him my prepared phrase. Nodding appreciatively at my beautiful calligraphy, he still isn't prepared to hand over the medication on my say so. He places his palm on my forehead, prods my windpipe with his fingers, whips a thermometer out of his breast pocket and sticks it under my armpit. Motioning me to a seat, he continues with his current patient and I watch the master in action.

Covering his counter in small squares of paper, the Quack reaches to the bottles behind him, and counts pills into the centre of each sheet. A blur of activity, the crazed octopus flicks his arms along the shelves magically maintaining a serene expression.

As the mound of pills on each sheet grows at a rate of knots, VD turns to me in alarm, 'That guy ain't well.

Folding the corners together, each parcel is given a twist and popped into a bag. Whereupon the patient cheerfully thanks the doctor and departs with his bulging bag of origami. Retrieving his thermometer, the Pill Monger shrugs at the reading and pulls a face that says, 'Western pansy.' Reaching for a box of tablets he cracks two out and directs me to take another two in four hours' time. Hoping for a one-stop shop, I am thwarted by his wares. It'll have to do for now and I'll look for a larger store to stock up.

The Chinese love of medicine ensures a larger Pharmacy is located within minutes. Conscious of the ever-present attention, I stride purposefully to the counter and, in my husky voice, wheeze my way through the prepared dialogue.

Predictably, the rehearsed phrase is, again, unintelligible to the shop assistant and I'm forced to resort to mime. Either my miming skills have significantly improved or else Chinese pharmacy workers are trained in non-verbal communication. Whichever is the case, the lady gets the idea in no time at all.

I like the image of a group of white-coated apprentices being trained in charades, but it's more likely my ailment is so common in these parts and the symptoms speak for themselves. So much so that it's a shame to bother a certified medical professional over such an obvious diagnosis.

Prodding around my swollen throat, she nods, bobs behind the counter and returns with a bottle of gloopy liquid with a picture of a flower on the label. It certainly looks like a viable candidate for the job. Not in a position to make an informed decision, I take her word for it.

My fingers close on open air as she snatches the bottle from my grasp. Shaking her head, she starts filling a sheet in her triplicate book. Tearing off the pink page, she motions me to an old guy sitting at the top of the room. I wander up and hand him my piece of paper. He takes a long draw on his cigarette and casually glances at the slip. Scrunching up his face, I get a thoughtful scrutinise before he rubber-stamps the slip and waves me away.

Approved, I return to the white-coated lady who signs the slip and directs me toward a guy manning a till by the door. This guy puts his cigarette down to receive my slip and I hand over the requested readies. He stamps the slip and I, once more, return to the original lady. She exchanges my slip for the medicine.

It's just as well I'm not critically ill or I would have died by the time I got my prescription filled. I wonder if this is a government sanctioned initiative to maximise production. With this process in place, the workforce are discouraged from being ill on the grounds it's too much like hard work. No wonder China's economy is experiencing such rapid growth. They are taking over the world while the west is in bed pulling a sickie.

Relieved to be finally done with the process, I head for the exit. A hand on my chest blocks my path. The security guard stationed at the door relieves me of my paper bag, empties my purchase on to the counter and compares it to the receipt. Satisfied that it adds up, he tears the receipt and indicates I should put it back in the bag. Another Jobsworth. Throughout the entire transaction there were no other customers and I'm certain he witnessed every second of my Melmothian wanderings which provided the closest thing to entertainment he will get today, yet he still felt obliged to carry out the particulars of his job description to the letter.

The bureaucracy involved in the simplest transaction here is insane. I can't even begin to comprehend how China competes in the global marketplace with such antiquated, labour-intensive systems in place. Along with the failure to understand public profile, their customer service is probably related to the Communist State. Until recently there were no public companies so the customer base was not in a position to vote with its feet, or vote at all, and labour-intensive production ensured full-employment. Similarly, staff had no incentive to go beyond the minimum effort.

It's unfeasible that this approach could form the basis for the fastest growing economy in the world. Just how they managed to become any sort of economic force at all is beyond me.

Among the many Chinese travelogues, I've read are two books written by people specifically travelling to Shaolin to train Kung Fu. One book was written while the guy was in China and the other was written by a guy sometime after he'd returned. The guy who wrote about his experiences insitu was particularly frustrated, while the one writing in hindsight visited some magical pixie land full of little cuddly bunnies. I've got to say I'm in agreement with the stroppy fellow.

While it may have been hard won, at least I have my medicine now. No sooner am I out the door than I break out my purchases and wash down another couple of painkillers with a good swig from the bottle. Not only is it quite pleasant, but it has an almost instant soothing effect. I can see me splashing out on another of these babies. I wish I'd bought two when I had the chance. I'll keep the packaging to simplify the repeat purchase.

Witnessing the amber liquid disappearing, VD's withdrawal pangs resurface. Deciding the cough syrup is close enough to the amber liquid he craves, he pulls the bottle from my hand and takes a good swig. Speaking as a connoisseur of fine liquor, he delivers his verdict, 'Mmm, not bad.'

As much as I value VD's opinion of my life saving fluid, its procurement was too laborious to let him guzzle the lot as a beer substitute. I wrest the bottle from the dirty winos grasp and slip it into my pocket. I'll have to placate him with some fodder until we can get some real booze.

It's still early enough for breakfast and we soon spot a tower of bamboo steamers simmering over a gas cylinder on the pavement. This alfresco kitchen keeps the heat down inside the shop, doesn't tie up valuable floor space and advertises better than a neon sign. Reasoning it can't be any worse than the travesty of Dicos, we give the Xiaochi Dian a go.

The Chinese equivalent of a Greasy Spoon, 'small eat shops' are a common sight. Often tiny, these hole-in-the-wall restaurants have a limited menu with breakfast joints typically specialising in two dishes: baozi and jiaozi. Essentially, the same ground meat and chopped vegetable filling served in different parcels. Jiaozi are a thin pastry envelope sealed by crimping the edges, like ravioli, and baozi are filled doughy buns.

Cramming ourselves into another room barely wider than the doorway, we take up stools at the shelf running along the wall.

While I prefer the baozi, VD is more of a jiaozi man so we order a bowl of each. They immediately materialise in front of us. There's no waiting around as the food is permanently ready to go. The steamer contains about ten pieces which are eaten by dipping into saucers of vinegar, soy sauce or chili paste. The only fly in the ointment is the pot of chopsticks. The limited facilities of such tiny premises can mean washing up tends not to be a particularly thorough affair. One look at the grubby, damp collection of old chopsticks festering in an old bean can is enough to know they ain't going in my mouth.

Nowadays many noodle and baozi bars provide disposable chopsticks, but these come with their own issues. China uses about 57 billion pairs of disposable chopsticks annually with the associated deforestation and waste disposal causing massive environmental impact. There have also been claims that the manufacturing process of disposable chopsticks makes them a health risk to use at all.

Using my own chopsticks whenever we eat out gets me some funny looks, but, as well as safeguarding my health and saving the planet, I'm saving the restaurant an extra expense so they'd probably prefer if more people did the same.

Despite Shibu's warnings to the contrary, I feel that food prepared in front of us is safer than the lukewarm stuff that's been sitting around for hours in the school canteen. The proof is in the eating. Hot, fresh and tasty our steamed breakfast is soon polished off and we order another round of the same.

Tradition states that Zhang Zhongjing invented jiaozi in the Eastern Han Period (AD25-220) to help poor people keep warm in cold winters. Similarly, baozi was invented during the Three Kingdoms period (AD220-280) by the military strategist Liang Zhuge to cure his soldiers' plague.

I don't know about curing plagues, but these geniuses' inventions have worked wonders for me. VD echoes my thoughts as he leans back from the table rubbing his sated belly, 'Best breakfast ever.'

It's amazing that some hot food and cheap medicine was all it needed to take the edge off our misery. I'm not exactly cured, but we both feel a whole lot better.

Our route passes the Dengfeng CITS who were such a success with locating our school when we first arrived. Hoping for a similar result, I decide to give them a shot with the bookshop. Again, the lady behind the counter doesn't speak English, but allows me to access her internet. Seeing the website, she nods and writes down the address for me. I can't make much sense of it, but will work it out later.

Continuing into town, we enter the territory of larger businesses. In keeping with their corporate images, shops and bank staff are assembled outside their premises going through their version of morning warming on the pavement. This is an image I'm familiar with from TV, but looks less dynamic in the flesh. To say their performance is half-hearted would be to exaggerate their enthusiasm. I would estimate that it's quarter-hearted at best.

Straying down an unassuming side street we light upon a collection of stalls. The ragtag canopied tables are a world away from the generic supermarket we have become accustomed to frequent. This sedate gathering has an entirely different clientele. Middle-aged and older this demographic are also more practically attired. Army surplus is all the rage in Dengfeng, especially among the older generations. With such a massive military force, I suppose there must be a lot of it kicking about.

There are also a few ancient oldsters in the traditional tunic suit. The Zhongshan suit was introduced as a form of national dress by Sun Yat-sen shortly after founding the Republic of China in 1912 as a visible snub to the dress code imposed by the usurped Qing dynasty. Worn by party members and government leaders as a symbol of proletarian unity, the suit is embedded in the western imagination by the image of Mao Zedong and often referred to as the Mao suit (although it was actually named after Sun Yat-sen, who was also called Sun Zhongshan). With the opening of China in the 1990s, the suit became less popular and increased western influence has seen it completely abandoned by the younger generation. Today the suits have effectively been replaced by contemporary suits with ties. However, some of the older folk are sticklers for tradition and the suits can still be seen on the street. With China evolving around them, these relics exist in a parallel world sticking to the clothing they have known their entire lives.

I wish I could have visited the China of the 70s and experienced the images of China I was brought up with: bicycles and Mao suits. With the pace of change, I'm just catching a glimpse of my vision of China as it fades from view into history.

214

Another popular item of clothing I find quite fetching are khaki canvas plimsolls similar to our Feiyues. They may be government issue as many of those wearing them seem to be in the employ of the local council. Meandering through the market, I spy a stall piled high with the things. Before I get chance to open my mouth the stall holder is asking what size, but is not pleased with my answer. Waving her hands, she repeats, 'Tai da le! Tai da le!' and sits back on her little stool.

I can't be, 'Too big' surely? I struggle with shoes in China. At 6 feet tall I don't stand out due to my height, there are plenty of Chinese guys here around my height. They must just have relatively small feet in comparison. Zhang Juncai, one of the tallest men in the world is Chinese, he must surely have bigger feet than me. I'll have to find out where he shops. Actually, it's a shame Juha has left. I could have brought him down to the shop just to see her face as his size 15 feet blocked out the sun. Although he may have given her a cardiac arrest so perhaps it's just as well he didn't get out much.

The market reveals little else of interest. Stalls of pots and pans, vegetables and baby clothes are all too domesticated for us non-householders. With the morning advancing Zhongyue should now be open to the public.

Back out on the road, I hail a Sanlun only for the driver to ask, 'Shaolin Si?' Anyone would think Shaolin is the only place westerners visit in Dengfeng.

As the main tourist attraction you should visit the Zhongyue temple at the outskirts of Dengfeng. The Zhongyue temple is in contrast to the Shaolin temple a taoistic temple. Various movies were shooted in this temple and many of the ignorant foreigners thought it was the Shaolin temple.

Shaolin-wushu.de

Shaolin is not the only famous temple in town. The Song Mountains are sacred to Taoists as well as Buddhists and at the other side of Dengfeng, at the foot of Huanggai Peak, is Zhongyue Miao or Central Mountain Temple. Established in the Qin dynasty (221-207BC), Zhongyue is said to be the earliest base of Taoism in central China.

One of China's five sacred mountain ranges, the Song Mountains represent the Earth aspect of the five elements. Formerly Taishi Miao, Zhongyue Miao was built on an existing Shenist site dedicated to the mountain god Taishi. Following a pilgrimage from the Tang Dynasty Empress Wu Zetian in AD688 Zhongyue began to flourish and the town was renamed Dengfeng meaning 'ascending to bestow honour'.

Throughout its long history, Zhongyue has been damaged and repaired many times, but it was during the Qing dynasty reign of Emperor Qianlong (1736-1796) the temple took on its current form. Renovated using the same design and architecture as Beijing's Forbidden City, most buildings are in the Qing dynasty imperial style and Zhongyue is sometimes referred to as the Little Imperial Palace. Heavily damaged during the Anti-Japanese War (1937-1945) the temple was extensively repaired in 1986.

Heading out of town along Sheng Dao Road, we pass a strip of small, dusty old shops selling joss sticks and paper offerings. The only sign of life, a solitary old lady peeling vegetables onto the pavement. The shops peter out and shortly after the driver indicates we have arrived.

At 9.30, it's already late in the day for us, but there is no one else in sight as we follow the wide path between two large Bagua symbols picked out in box hedging. The gradual incline leads to the gate where a few stalls are just setting up, and appear in no hurry to do so. On my guard against the vendors, I am almost affronted when they make no attempt at harassment. Life moves at a slower pace this side of town.

The traditional three-section archway proclaims, 'Central Mountain Temple. First among Famous Mountains.' To the right of the entrance is the standard little kiosk where I ask for, 'Liang zhang piao.' (Two tickets)

Thirty Yuan apiece lighter, we take a couple of steps to the left where the ornate paifang has been converted into an actual gate by means of a fence and turnstile. Rather than turn on the automated turnstile, the ticket lady nips from the back of her hut and we hand our tickets back to her for manual inspection.

Tickets checked and punched, we are into pleasant wooded parkland with Yaocan Pavilion up ahead. I'm sure I recognise this scene from an old Shaolin Temple documentary. If any Kung Fu movies were filmed here, passing Zhongyue off as Shaolin, it was probably because Shaolin wasn't as impressive or accessible at the time.

The mossy path between the ancient cypress trees, leads to Zhonghuamen (Gate of China). The two storey, red building with three arched doorways is a small scale version of the Forbidden City's, Tiananmen (Gate of Heavenly Peace).

Within the temple walls the atmosphere is even more sedate. The trees subdue the heat and dampen exterior sounds so that the place is quiet enough to feel deserted. Being a working temple, the grounds are well maintained by monks and volunteers. The few other visitors are also more respectful than the Shaolin crowd, quietly going about their devotions rather than just here to gawk. After Shaolin, their unhurried fashion feels more apt for a temple.

The central path continues to a 12ft bottle gourd, 'hulu', painted with

Bagua symbols. A popular symbol in many mythologies, for Buddhist and Taoists the bottle gourd symbolises longevity, health and good luck. The emblem of Li Tie Guai, one of the Eight Immortals, and Sau, the god of longevity, the gourd is also used as an allegory for the body as the container of the soul. I mainly associate the gourd with Drunken Kung Fu and am not surprised when VD wants his photo taken next to it.

Unfortunately, we have little understanding of Zhongyue's real historical artefacts. Carved with Taoist classics, inscriptions from notables and scenes of China's five sacred mountains, the hundreds of ancient stone tablets are wasted on us. The most well-known stele is by the monk Kou Qianzhi (365-448) who during the Northern Wei Dynasty was responsible for Taoism becoming the official state religion. Sadly, his reforms resulted in the persecution of Buddhists and embroiled Taoism in long, and often bloody, factional political struggles.

A little more within our realm of appreciation are the four metal warriors standing guard over Gushen Warehouse. Cast in the Northern Song Dynasty (960-1127), these three-metre-high figures originally stood at the four directions, but have been moved to the eastern part of the grounds. Devoid of weapons, which were sawn off during the Cultural Revolution, their poses look a little odd and they are certainly not pleased about it. Local tradition states the Iron Men can cure diseases and prevent disasters and children touch them to gain strength. I give them a good pat as I need all the help I can get. From the look on their faces my molestation couldn't get them much angrier

The gatehouse building doubles as a gift shop. Amongst the usual paraphernalia is a monk sitting behind a laptop. It's a poor idea getting monks to sell to the general public. Either they sully the idea of monasticism or else they are rubbish at selling stuff. In this instance, it's the latter as he doesn't look up from his laptop. The audio sounds like an English language tuition programme. The sentence he's listening to is pretty advanced stuff so, in the interests of cultural exchange, VD wanders over, 'Hello there.'

Looking up in horror, the monk waves both palms out in front of him as if surrendering. Mumbling unintelligibly, he's clearly embarrassed. Chagrined, we back off and leave him to it. Maybe he's just got the programme and was having a skip through it.

The courtyard of Lofty Saints is dedicated to the Five Taoist Great Mountains. Containing four palaces arranged according to the cardinal directions of Chinese geomancy, Zhongyue is at the fifth direction, the centre. In front of each palace is a large rock carved with the mountain's name. The south, Nanyue, is Hengshan in Hunan, the north, Beiyue, is Hengshan in Shanxi, east, Dongyue, is Taishan and west, Xiyue, is Huashan.

Working around the palaces, we are furtively accosted by a middle-aged lady. I noticed her and her friend watching our movements earlier. No doubt they have marked us as any easy target. While her friend keeps watch, she sidles up, 'Psst.' Opening her cupped palm, she reveals a golden slip like a small credit card in a red plastic sleeve, 'Taishan Laojun, wu shi yuan.'

Taishan Laojun or Laozi is a central figure in Chinese culture. One of the Three Pure Ones at the top of the pantheon of Taoist deities, he is also regarded as the founder of Taoism and author of the Daodejing.

'Look at that bobby dazzler!' Unable to resist the temptation of a shiny thing, VD gets to work. With her friend conspicuously keeping an eye out, she makes a token effort at the haggling process, but quickly accepts 20Y for the icon and dissolves among the trees. I have my suspicions this was not an entirely legitimate transaction. Assuming the icon is not endorsed by the temple authorities, is it still valid as a charm? I wonder what the Three Pure Ones' stance upon unofficial merchandise is. It's an ecumenical can of worms.

Running the perimeter is a gallery filled with statues of Taoist officials from other realms. As with the Luohans at Shaolin's Temple of Four Directions, the relevance of these mythological figures is lost on us, but the walls behind are decorated in a less ambiguous fashion. Covered in torture scenes Hieronymus Bosch would flinch at, I hope I don't wind up in Chinese Hell. I'll have to check if there's a Hell department set aside for buyers of knock-off effigies.

Attempting to glean some understanding, I try to decipher a placard. My pausing attracts the attention of a grubby, blue-robed old monk. Unlike the orange-robed and shiny-domed Buddhists, the Taoist monks wear their long hair knotted into a bun on top of their heads. This one is also a stranger to personal hygiene.

Quicker on the uptake than me, VD leaves me to the monk's attentions. Using a combination of gibbering and sign language, the soap-dodging cenobite demonstrates how to place my hands together into a yin yang symbol in order to supplicate before the figures. There are hundreds of the things and I'm not about to spend all day about it. My visible discomfort gives VD a good chuckle at my expense. Excusing myself, I make a sharp exit.

Guarding Junji Gate are the two Shang Dynasty (1562-1066BC) Generals: Fang Bi and Fang Xiang. Famous for their loyalty and ferociousness, they have become 'door gods' preventing evil from gaining entrance. At four metres high, these heavily armed sentries would be more intimidating without the gnarly old monk squatting between their legs and giving their vulnerables a going over with a paintbrush.

In this courtyard, atop a 3-metre-high platform, is Junji Dian (Great Hall) where emperors previously made sacrifices to the mountain. Based on the Forbidden City's Taihe Dian (Hall of Supreme Harmony), at 20 metres high and covering 920 square meters, Junji's vermilion walls and orange tiles make this the largest and most colourful building in the complex. Between the two sets of steps up to the Hall are the 'Bi', or path of god, the engraved dragon steps reserved for the Emperors use.

In front of the hall, an old couple heap paper money into an incinerator. Known as 'jin zhi' (gold paper), 'zhi qian' (paper money), or 'ming bi' (ghost money) the offerings are burnt in veneration of the deceased. Unlike Buddhists, who only burn joss sticks, Taoists also burn money and artfully folded paper, representing gold ingots and household items that may be useful in the afterlife. Offering material goods run contrary to Buddhist principles.

This custom was regulated in 2006 when China's Ministry of Civil Affairs, banned the more extreme joss items. Made of papier-mâché around bamboo frames and sometimes life-size, 'luxury villas, sedan cars, mistresses and other messy sacrificial items...' have all been blacklisted.

With all this cremating going on they probably need the trees to compensate for the carbon footprint. In essence, Taoism is all about yin and yang equilibrium and living in harmony with the environment, so maybe the trees are here for just that purpose.

Also like the Hall of Supreme Harmony, Junji Dian has a magnificent zaojing ceiling. A distinctive feature of classical Chinese architecture, these domes are constructed without nails from brackets projecting inward and upward from the base. Also known as 'spider web ceilings, they usually consist of different depths. The central, deepest, part is the round 'well', the middle octagonal and the outermost part, coming down to the ceiling level, is square. The whole design symbolises the ancient Chinese belief that 'Heaven is above and the Earth below' and that Heaven is round and the Earth square. The same theory is represented in old Chinese coins. Dominating the ceiling, a coiled dragon looks down into the hall, protecting the shrine of the Zhongyue Emperor Tianzhongwang, the God of Central Mountain.

Having run out of joss sticks, VD reaches for some on the table in front of a dozing monk. The monk doesn't bat an eyelid, but an old lady hovering nearby immediately up-sells him to a flashier incense.

Quoting 40Y, she begins explaining the procedure. Fully aware of how it works, VD becomes flustered by her explanation and puts his 100Y note in the monk's bowl.

Nudging the monk awake, the ancient entrepreneur points to the bowl, which the old fellow obligingly empties, and waves VD toward the altar. He is left with little option but to have an expensive prostrate with the bowl ringing away behind him. I make a mental note to lay in a stock of small denomination notes for future temple visits.

Stepping through the gateway into Zhongyue's last section, my first sight is of a young bloke in shirt and slacks blissfully cuddling a tree. I was under the impression that 'tree hugger' was a sarcastic term for new age folk and Zhanzhuan stance, but here is someone doing just that. He seems to be enjoying it too. They should really get a room.

This last courtyard is where it's all happening. Still sparsely populated and tranquil, there is a lot more activity here. Along with the arbophilliac, scattered between the trees, solo figures practice Qigong and Taiji and a solitary blue-robed monk sits in meditation.

Upon the platform is Yushu (Imperial Book Repository) a severe looking structure built during China's Republican era (1912-1949). In front, a small group of ladies are freestyling Taiji under the stern eye of a chain-smoking lady Shifu. They spiral, swirl and belch their way around the platform as she sings the mantra between puffs on her cigarette. The freestyle Taiji looks like great fun. I wonder if they learn a form first, learn moves independently or just make it up as they go along.

Practicing in this area looks like the done thing. Shaolin's swarm of pointing and gawking sightseers make meditating or practicing Kung Fu difficult, but we have no such qualms here. Under the shade of a cypress tree, we practice our own Qi Gong routines and I work my forms without anyone giving me more than a passing glance.

Our Qi Gong works well in this atmosphere and we are both buoyant as we dawdle through the grounds. Zhongyue may not be as well-known as Shaolin, but is well worth a visit. Less than half the size than at its peak in AD1013, the existing complex is still impressive.

The limited number of visitors, and laid-back attitude, means the overall atmosphere of Zhongyue is more pleasant than Shaolin. Even the admission fee of 30Y is very reasonable in comparison. I'd like to come back during a traditional temple fair (Miao hui) to see the temple when it's really bustling.

Outside, the stalls are now up and running. They carry the usual paraphernalia, but the temple atmosphere has leaked out through the walls. Even the vendors are laid back and the haggling and heckling is negligible. By twisting their arms, VD manages to pick up more joss sticks, sacrificial money and a bronze-ish Taishan Laojun figure.

The drawback of the quiet location is there are no Sanlun waiting. The walk back into town gives us the opportunity to explore the eastern end of Dengfeng.

At the edge of town, on the corner of Sheng Dao and Yangcheng road is Yingxian Gongyuan (Welcome Immortals Park). There is also a street vendor selling Yumi (roasted corncob). While I'm making another impulse food purchase, VD is accosted by a pair of ancient ladies. Something happens to ladies over a certain age, they are no longer bound by polite social conventions. The younger generations are limited to staring at his tattoos from a distance, or surreptitiously sneaking a peak, but such passive viewing simply will not suffice for the coffin-dodgers. With an old dear either side, VD is powerless as they grab his arms and trace the illustrations with their fingers, even going as far as to rub them to see if they'll come off. Through gap-toothed grins, they chuckle and point out their favourites. 'Oh, Shaolin Si, good', and the Buddha, 'Ah, Fo good', even gets a wrinkled thumbs-up. Happy to play along for a while, his sensitive side begins to show through as the old bats get more personal with his body surface and it's my turn to enjoy his discomfort.

Through Chaoxia gateway, a steep flight of steps leads up the mountainside to Yingxiange, 'Welcome Immortals Pavilion'. As the local planners have gone to the effort to be so welcoming to all and sundry, it would be rude not to make use of it. It's also just the place for a picnic.

Cracking out the provisions, we admire the view over the town. The grey urban sprawl springs up to the west and along the mountain ridge we can see the watchtowers built to protect the ancient town of Yangcheng (the former name of Dengfeng).

Dating back to AD120, the Qimu, Taishi and Shaoshi Watchtowers are collectively called 'The Three Watchtowers of the Han Dynasty on the Central Sacred Mountain'. Qimu Watchtower and its temple have been practically destroyed, but Taishi Watchtower, directly opposite Zhongyue Miao, is the best preserved and contains inscriptions and drawings from the Han Dynasty.

More urban/industrial than our side of town, there's little of interest as we head to the supermarket. Suffering a chemical imbalance as blood begins to reassert itself in his alcohol system, VD is on a quest for booze while I need to maintain my self-medicating and stock up on essentials like Snickers and instant tea.

Usually I like to sample the local produce when abroad, but have found that to be a mistake with Chinese chocolate brands. They all taste like stale cardboard. The only western brand I've seen so far is Snickers. They must have spotted a gap in market and were straight in there. It's not a brand I would usually turn to, but desperate times…

Clustered in a conspiratorial gaggle, the toiletry aisle assistants conspicuously ignore my trawl of the shelves and let me fend for myself. Scrutinising likely packets against my notes, I notice many every day products like razors and deodorants are security sealed or in locked cabinets. Not as compact or expensive as other items on display, these items are nonetheless singled out as being more pilfer-able than others.

Finally matching likely candidates for paracetamol and ibuprofen, I head to the liquor section to hunt down the local specialty 'baijiu', which translates as 'white alcohol'. Among the many baijiu brands on offer are a series of gallon containers at two Yuan each. That's about twenty pence for a gallon of liquor; significantly less expensive than water. A very brief discussion decides our eyesight is worth more to us than the financial saving.

It's an interesting 10 minutes spent deliberating which rotgut will be less damaging while still serving its desired purpose. We are just settling on something in a glass bottle for fifty Yuan when a little voice pipes in, 'Hello Nick.'

'Hello Shifu.'

Yuan Shifu has rounded the corner and spotted us perusing the booze. Instantly I'm transported back in time thirty years to the off-license where I was caught red handed by one of South Wales' finest also-rans who blackmailed me into playing rugby for the school as a punishment.

Overcome with concern for our wellbeing Yuan Shifu cautions, 'Nick, it is very strong.' My immediate knee-jerk reaction to authority kicks in. Remembering I'm no longer twelve years old and will buy anything I like. I stick it in the basket just to prove a point. Besides alcohol of this strength must be analgesic, so I owe it to my sore throat to get some in.

At the checkout, I receive the usual disinterest throughout the transaction. With our purchases piling up on the counter, I ask the checkout girl for a, 'bao', she laughs and pointing to my satchel explains it is a 'bao', carrier bags are, 'dai zi'. At least she had the decency to put me straight rather than just laugh at me. In general, the locals are pleased with my attempts at the language, or at least prepared to pander me when I'm spending money. And I do so love to spread joy wherever I go.

Back on the street the smell of charcoal barbecues fills the air, a sure sign the Night Market is warming up. A gregarious lot, the Chinese come out to play at night and though the night is young the street is already bustling.

More energetic than their daylight counterparts, the traders have given the street a magical transformation. The road has become a shanty town of plastic-sheet marquees sheltering plastic patio furniture and open-air food stalls. Referred to as Da Pai Dong, the name itself is synonymous with Hong Kong street vendors and originally meant 'restaurant with a big license', but the term is so well used it has spread to mainland China and covers most cooked-food stalls.

We've done a fair bit of trekking today and all this walking doesn't half work up an appetite. I've seen enough vintage Jackie Chan movies to know Kung Fu students are permanently hungry, but this is just ridiculous. I came here to learn Kung Fu and now spend every waking minute thinking about food. Still, it would be rude not to take advantage of the opportunity while we are on a roll.

Clad in aprons and sleeve protectors, the vendors announce their wares from practically identical stalls. With no way to make an informed choice, we watch other customers to get the procedure and then pick a stall at random.

In front of the makeshift tent a table is laid out with stuff on sticks. Green stuff which is clearly veg., pink stuff which is probably meat and some other stuff which could be anything. VD haphazardly points to everything and we take a seat inside. Flash-fried with rice, his eclectic selection is transformed into a steaming mound and presented inside a bag wrapped bowl.

With limited water to hand, washing-up takes a back seat in these places so the fuwuyuan places the bowl inside a polythene bag before serving the food. In place of washing up, she just changes the bag for each customer.

The smouldering coals and roasting food can't begin to cover the scent of the drains and overflowing bins, so I'm all up for making this a hasty meal. Furiously shovelling the smoky fare into my mouth, I drop a few grains of rice onto the table. Although I've been using chopsticks on a casual basis for many years, I lack the skill of a native. It's not a problem in the school canteen, but when eating out I am conscious whenever I fumble with an awkward piece of food.

I attempt to ignore the incriminating evidence, but they stare at me like the Tell-tale Heart throughout my meal. At least there aren't many other patrons to witness my clumsiness. The only other customers are five drunken Chinese guys on a table behind us. In their early twenties the guys are having a right old time of it. Clattering chairs and plates to the floor the revellers stagger over to shake our hands and repeatedly say, 'Hello', before ricocheting down the street.

Glancing over at their table is a real eye-opener. To say it looks like a bomb's hit would be offensive to explosive devices; it's a complete disaster area. Mounded with empty beer bottles, half eaten food, cigarette ends and packets the surrounding floor is no better. The fuwuyuan doesn't bat an eyelid and has the area ship-shape in a jiffy. I'm almost embarrassed we have left our table too clean.

Along the pavement, handcarts purvey more portable provender, mostly things on sticks or in a bun. Nosing through the small barrows we see a range of weird and wonderful provender much of which, apart from some fruit, are unidentifiable to me. Mainland Chinese like to joke about their gastronomical diversity with expressions on the theme of, 'they eat everything with four legs except the table'.

Over its vast history China has had more than its share of hardship, but the disastrous rural planning of the 1950s Great Leap Forward began a string of events which saw over two decades of suffering. Following a few already lean years, the use of Russia's failed New Agricultural Production Policy model saw millions of rural Chinese starve to death. Henan Province was particularly hard hit. Already, no stranger to drought, famine and disease, such brutal conditions led to a very practical approach to sustenance and everything that moved was fair game. The devastated countryside was picked bare in desperation and left all but barren. The ecosystem is still recovering from the impact, but has been assisted by a recent Government tree planting directive.

A thousand years of utilitarian eating have given the Chinese a taste for exotic dishes that, now food production has reached a surplus, are considered delicacies.

The environmentalist in me applauds the thrifty ethic of eating the entire animal and leaving nothing to waste. Something we in the west were more inclined toward until the 1950s advent of supermarkets with their shiny desensitised packaging made us squeamish toward natural products.

The all-encompassing fare also includes insects like centipedes, beetles and silkworms, but I haven't seen any on a menu until now. Amongst the stands of mysterious petits fours and curious hors d'oeuvres is a guy specialising in scorpion on a stick.

Three to a skewer, the impaled captives stand upright on the counter. Their macabre, slow-motion dance a sign of freshness. Not normally an adventurous eater, I still like to give things a try when the opportunity presents itself, but the pain-wracked scorpions wriggling in anticipation of immolation gives me a pang of conscience.

Less precious than I, VD orders himself up a horror kebab. Waved over a flame, the singed arachnids get insult added to injury with a liberal brushing of hot sauce.

They are much easier to look at now the stinger has stopped moving, but I'm not sure if they have actually deceased or are just paralysed by the red gloop. Either way, there can't be enough meat on the little guys to make them worth eating.

Delicately nibbling a tiny pincer, he shrugs and cleans the stick into his mouth. Considering each crunch like a Bulldog chewing a wasp, he delivers the verdict, 'It's like eating chili soaked splintered glass.'

That's all I need to know. I'm not a fan of chili, I've also eaten broken glass and didn't rate that much either, so I don't feel I've missed out. That said, it's the first time I've seen him not go back for seconds, which says it all as far as I'm concerned. I settle for a sugar cane from the next stall. It tastes like wood, but I still think I got the better end of the stick.

At the corner we take a right and walk up the block to the next corner where a gaggle of small children are watching TV through a shop window. Some even have little stools and snacks. It must be the cheapest babysitter ever.

Another right takes us to more market, but less foody with smaller stalls and heavier foot traffic. Swept along with the shuffling flow of bodies, it's difficult to take in the available wares. From carts to sheets

226

on the ground, the ad-hoc stalls cover an incredible range of items, but the clear favourites are blingy things and mobile accessories. Not being the blingy sort, most stalls have little interest for me, but there's a great atmosphere. With mopeds and carts whittling their way through the streaming crowd, this snapshot of everyday life feels like the real China.

VD nudges me toward a VCD stall where I promptly locate a triquel of one of my favourite Hong Kong movies, Mr. Vampire. The sequel was so bad I guess the third can't be any worse. Seeing me rooting through the dodgy disks, a passing child stops to help, and thoughtfully selects a copy of Harry Potter for me. I don't understand what people see to connect me to the boy wizard.

Next door an old lady is selling homemade insoles from a blanket laid out on the ground. Thinking to give my Feiyues extra cushioning for the sake of my aching old bones, I rummage through the mound. Coming to my aid the old dear asks, 'Duo da le?'

'Si shi liu.'

'Tai da le!', but passes me a pair of 44s. Close enough for my money. The insoles have got to be better than nothing and, at 10p, well worth the punt. Now it's up to the Wushu shop on the strip to collect my new shoes.

They are still not in stock, but the shopkeeper assures me he will be back in two minutes. Revving up his moped in the shop, he pootles out the door and down the road. In no time at all, he's back carrying a bin-liner full of shoes.

Lesson learnt with the last pair I bought, I sit down and try these on. The logo matches the pair I'm wearing and they fit perfectly. I get two pairs and in future will get all my gear here.

The decent food and basic medication combined with the Zhongyue Iron Men magic means I'm feeling positively perky for evening training, but bail when I see the smoke-filled hall. From now on I will be more selective about my training conditions.

Taking the evening off, we play cards and crack open the baijiu. Damn it's rough. The alcohol content is such there's little room left for flavour. A better way of Yuan Shifu putting me off the grog would have been to tell me what it tasted like. Back home I would use this stuff to clean drains, so logically it must have cleansing properties and is therefore medicinal. VD agrees and makes the most of the evil fluid by getting moister than an oyster before slipping into his ailing velociraptor impression.

By the time Shifu Fatso comes to tuck us in, VD is well into his swing and unwittingly provides the late night entertainment. I've seen our Shifu wide-eyed, but now his jaw drops. Frozen, he just gapes at the rendition of a walrus mating with a grizzly bear. Without lifting his jaw, he turns to me and points to the quivering beast.

I'm at a loss myself so just give him a shrug in a 'My word' fashion. He's still shaking his head as he walks out. I love that we entertain our Shifu so much.

By amending our mistakes we get wisdom,
by defending our faults we betray an unsound mind.

Hui Neng

Another Monday, another stand around bewildered as three thousand surly adolescents deliver a half-hearted rendition of the school song. It wouldn't be particularly inspiring at the best of times, but first thing on a Monday morning the intentions are wasted on me. Although, with my self-medicating keeping the pain in my throat at bay, I could probably join in if I knew the words.

Conscious of my sore throat and barking cough, I notice the majority of my fellow students are suffering similar symptoms. Our combined hacking and spluttering is becoming quite impressive, although we have a long way to go before entering the same league as our Chinese counterparts.

The rasping cacophony on parade indicates that the Chinese students have it far worse than us. Being teenagers doesn't help the sullenness and spitting. I suppose they have been exposed for longer or perhaps we are just more discreet about it. It must be endemic to Dengfeng in that everyone is permanently ill and so takes these symptoms for granted. Having never been without it, they simply don't know what it's like not to have a cough, sore throat, etc. It also explains why everyone here is constantly coughing and spitting. Oh well, when in Rome. At least I have the decency to expunge my lungs into a drain or grass verge and not directly on to the path or inside buildings. And they call us barbarians! Seeing how far my standards have slipped already, I wonder how long before I'm joining in with the rest of the heathens.

Most of us are adapting to this part of local culture like true natives. Fittingly for a former ballerina, Julie's technique is the most refined. Holding one nostril closed, she fires a fearsome snot rocket into the verge. You just can't buy that sort of class. In between coughs, I comment that China is slowly eroding our common decency. With an impish grin she agrees, however VD disputes the available evidence claiming, 'I refuse to be turned into a savage.' No answer is the stern reply.

Satisfied we have heard enough to be thoroughly motivated, Shibu again denies us the finale by removing us from the scene ahead of the final act. Marched through the gates and down Dayu road to the Breakfast Place crossroads, we line up at the foot of the hill. Holding his palm up for the rest of us to stay put, Shibu points to the lead guy just as a car comes around the corner, 'Go run.'

With the sun peaking over the Songyang Mountains, we take turns to race random vehicles up the hill. Most are such rattly disasters that they don't provide much of a challenge and loaded Sanluns really struggle up the hill, but motorbikes put up more of a fight. Were a fairly modern, or well maintained, vehicle to appear we would have no chance, but the odds are very much stacked in our favour.

Coiled like a nervous bunny in a carrot patch, I pray for one of those crazy lawnmower contraptions which should give me the least stressful outing. Almost as good, I get a flatbed Sanlun.

The driver has slowed for the corner and I've got the initiative. I'm off to a good start and it's going well until the driver realises what's happening. Revving the guts out of his engine, he catches me as my initial surge of energy burns out and I settle into my stride. Seeing me keeping pace alongside, he grits his teeth and wills his machine faster while trying to remain nonchalant. Staring straight ahead, he attempts to squeeze every possible ounce of power out of his dilapidated vehicle rather than face the indignity of being overtaken by a pedestrian laowai.

Depending on the load and condition, some of those mopeds and lawnmowers can really move. My competitor doesn't number amongst them. I turn my head and give him a great, big smile, but he resolutely refuses to acknowledge me.

The thought strikes me that, as I am obviously invisible, I could jump on the back and hitch a lift up the hill. The idea is immediately replaced by a vision of me sitting on the road amongst the wreckage. I ease up on the thinking and concentrate on the running. It's neck and neck as we reach the peak where Yuan Shifu is acting sentry. Smiling, he points me back down the hill. With a saddened heart, and a magnanimity befitting such sporting events, I wave my motorcycle friend farewell and return to the line.

I get a few equally exciting turns up the hill before Shibu decides the traffic isn't consistent enough to fully stimulate us in a true morning warming fashion. Reassembling the squad, he points back along the road, 'Go run.'

This must be Shibu's idea of variation as I now get to follow his students around a different block. More urban than our usual route, we pass a couple of small breakfast shops that are already open. I formulate a cunning plan.

Along the way, we slowly divide into two ability groups. I head up the less athletic division. On the return leg, I gain enough ground on the rest of our group to dart inside a small baozi shop unobserved. Served in trays of ten, I get two to go.

Food is the great leveller in China. Social animals, the Chinese are obsessed with eating and food is a guaranteed ice breaker on any occasion. So much so, that the traditional greeting was, 'Ni chi le ma?' meaning, 'Have you eaten?'

Clocking my uniform and laboured breath, the wizened old dear must have an idea of what's taking place and is delighted as I tuck the steaming bags into my tracksuit. Pausing to let the body of runners pass, I can hear the old dear's elated chuckling as I tag on the end of the group. The baozi smell, so good I barely manage to resist eating them as I run along.

The heat from the buns is a little unpleasant against my stomach, but the jacket is roomy enough that I can shove things inside without our Shifu spotting them. Otherwise I'm sure he would try to claim a percentage.

With us for the initial assembly, VD absented himself to go deal with some runs of his own. I join VD in the canteen just as he's tucking into his brekkers. His little face lights up as I bung the baozi at him. Best served piping hot, the baozi are still warm enough to satisfy his discerning palette and his rice and cabbage don't get a second glance. Happiness is a handful of warm buns.

At assembly, the Shifu have a bit of a con-flab, merge the groups together and march us out to the field. Scuffing their feet into the dusty surface, they mark out a rough square and, pointing at their handiwork, leave us to entertain ourselves with a game of Touchy Knee.

It's another a waste of time. As usual, half the group doesn't join in, but sit around chatting. We show willing for a while, but soon drift away too.

Working on my Xiao Hong Quan, my spider senses start tingling and I get the uncomfortable feeling of being watched. Turning around, I see a building full of dead eyes looking back at me. Backing on to our training field is the dormitory for another Kung Fu school, every window of which has half a dozen dirt-stained inmates wedged up against the bars.

There are a lot of Kung Fu schools in Dengfeng and this surly and unkempt mob are nothing like our boys; they have green tracksuits as opposed to our red ones. As far as I can make out from the name stencilled on the back, their school is called something like Zhongguo Song Shan Shaolin Si Wushu Xueyuan (Chinese Song Mountain Shaolin Temple Martial Arts Academy). It must get very confusing around here with so many similarly named institutions. No wonder the taxi driver had so much trouble locating our school when we arrived.

This bunch must really be starved of entertainment to want to watch me. My display can't be up to the standards they are used to seeing, yet they continue to stare silently. It's not even like they find the white guy pretending to know Kung Fu amusing. Surely there would be some indication if I were providing any comedy value. Gawking impassively, they are a tough crowd to please. Disconcerted by the hundreds of eyes boring into my head, I nonetheless attempt to give a good account of the old Xiao Long spirit. Their silence at my display speaks volumes. Once again, I'm glad when Shibu reappears to announce, 'Twenty minute go gym.'

Stretching on the pipe before class, I look down on the courtyard below. The Chinese kids' classes have already begun and a bunch of Chinese day-trippers are wandering around the school photographing everything in sight.

We often get excursion groups at school. The building next door houses a theatre stage with a mock-up of the Shaolin Mountain Gate. During season the school's Shaolin Monk demonstration team performs most days to coach-loads of domestic tourists. After a performance, the visitors often wander around the school taking pictures and being spellbound by the little kids.

It's the usual situation: two middle-aged guys pick up weapons from the many piles lying about the place and start to mock fight while their friends take photos. Feeling left out, another of their friends circles the group and, picking up two melon hammers, attacks them both from behind. This can only end in tears, but before I get to see the ensuing massacre, Shibu once again spoils the punchline by calling us to line up.

After lunch, I'm waiting for class when one of our fellow students approaches from the opposite direction holding a banana. My eagle eyes fix on the luscious fruit. My salivating maw must betray my interest. Looking very pleased with himself, Nikoli waves the fruit at me, 'There is new shop.'

I retrace his route in my mind, 'At the canteen?'

'Ya, is hole in wall.'

Within seconds I am wielding cash outside the canteen where a small window now acts as a serving hatch for a discreet fruit shop. Sticking my head inside, I see the room within is nothing more than the triangular space under a flight of stairs with a curtain hung up. A family of at least four people are living here with the fruit. On top of the crates is a thin mattress and, atop another pile of crates, a TV. It's a little awkward getting them out of bed and pulling them away from their Soaps. However, they don't let the fact they are selling fruit to the public interfere with their everyday lives. In typical Chinese fashion, they continue to hold telephone conversations, watch TV or slurp noodles while serving their valued customers.

There is a good selection of fruit but, as much as I would like an apple or a pear, I limit myself to a banana as it can be conveniently peeled. The yellow vitamin and mineral injection is just the job and, unlike our allotted food, actually tastes of something.

The supply of multivitamins I brought hasn't been hitting the spot and this fresh fruit is an invaluable dietary supplement my body has been craving. From now on I'll make sure I'm even earlier for training and get myself a piece of fruit.

Fatso doesn't show for afternoon assembly. In his absence, Shibu groups everyone together and sends us to Sanda Class. With no alternative, we troop up the stairs with the others where Sanda Shifu sets us to stretching.

While we are sprawled across the patches of carpet attempting the splits, Sanda Shifu gives us little attention. Prowling the perimeter like a caged animal, he notices something on the floor. A quizzical look crosses his face and bends over to pick it up.

Scrutinising the small object, Sanda Shifu turns to Martin and demands, 'What this?'

'A sea shell.'

Sanda Shifu tries the words on for size and decides on a second opinion. Holding the offending article in front of my nose, he asks the same question of me. It is indeed a shell, probably from a snail rather than an ocean dweller. Still unsatisfied, he goes around the whole group demanding each of us in turn. It's like he's daring us to say anything different from the last guy, but none of us do. Bored with the same unadventurous answers, he shrugs and throws the tiny shell to the edge of the hall.

I don't know what happened there, but it felt like a dangerous moment. Excitement over, we return to concentrating on not being able to do the splits.

Initially I assumed Fatso's absence was a cunning plan devised between him and Shibu as a way out of teaching us, but there's another purpose here. After the first session of stretches and drills, Shibu joins the class. He watches us work combinations on the pads before gathering us around him. Obviously impressed with what he's seen, he asks for a volunteer to go to Zhengzhou and fight the Chinese Sanda champion.

Victorian Dad and I have had some success in Kickboxing competitions at home, VD more so than I, and he briefly entertains the idea until reality kicks in. While it would be a nice experience, it's simply not worth the risk of jeopardising our training. The only way to minimise risks is to pamper ourselves when possible and not tempt fate.

The conditions are draining us to the extent that no one is near their top form and we live in constant threat of injury and illness. To nurse an injury here doesn't bear thinking about and a serious incident could drop one well and truly in the cachu. VD and I have enough commitments at home to have developed 'the fear' some time ago, so I'm not offended when I'm not pressed to participate.

There are other guys here, younger and fitter than us, who have much more chance than we do. There are also those who are not and don't. Knobby, who has now had nearly five Sanda lessons, thinks he is in with a chance against the Chinese national champion, and from there a shot at the world title. An inexhaustible fund of entertainment and fascination he announces, 'I'm getting quite good now. I could win'

234

Unperturbed by the well-meant words of caution, he tags along to show the Chinese students how to Sanda. For some reason, both Shifus are required to accompany them. Left unattended, we soon become the usual mothers meeting.

Marco, a Wing Chun practitioner, from Germany has been particularly unhappy with the training here. So much so that he is working his way through the disciplines. He started with Kung Fu, switched to Taiji and is now training Sanda. A good-natured chap, he is more upset with himself for coming than at the school.

'My father told me not to come to China. He said it would be no good. I should have listened. Maybe next year I will go to Japan and learn Karate or Samurai sword.'

This leads to a conversation about Japan's beautiful scenery. VD counters with talk of local sights and mentions Zhongyue Miao. None of them have heard of it. One guy, who has been coming to Xiao Long for the last three years, says, 'There's nothing to see in Dengfeng except Shaolin Temple.' Sadly misinformed, at least he's seen the temple which is more than can be said for many of the guys.

Training at Shaolin is fulfilling a life's ambition for me. My friends, who could never be accused of dismissing me out of hand, put it down to a midlife crisis. The reality is I really should have done it years ago and I need to make the most of the opportunity now I'm here. Seeing the way some of the guys train baffles me. They obviously care enough to spend the time and money travelling halfway around the world, but take no interest now they are here.

VD and I, on the other-hand, are struggling to fit everything we want to see and do into our schedule. Before we get chance to extol the virtues of the numerous worthy cultural spots nearby we are rejoined by Knobby. He's more reserved than we have become accustomed to and needs prompting before confiding he's decided against the idea of conquering the national Sanda circuit for today.

Slowly the others trickle back. Only Oliver was up to the mark. It's only an exhibition fight, but, as one of Dengfeng's three major schools, Xiao Long has to be seen to participate. Fielding a foreigner gives the opportunity to show themselves on a wider stage and still save face if they don't win. Still nursing his head injury, Wouter is in no position to fight but, as he is out of training anyway, offers to accompany Oli to Zhengzhou for moral support. As our Shifus show no sign of returning we dismiss ourselves for dinner.

Evening assembly sees Misfit Posse reformed and returned to the care of our beloved Fatso who gives us the type of half-arsed session to which we have become accustomed. For all the pretence of making us work, the Shifus soon drift away. Abandoned, we follow suit.

Back at our room, Yuan Shifu wanders past while we have the door open and comes in to tell us off for that very offence. For a nation that carries out all its daily activities in public view, the Shifus seem very keen that we should have our privacy.

As he is the most intelligible of our Shifus, I show him the website of the bookshop I have been looking for. He immediately responds with adamant certainty, 'I know that place, I make you map.'

Before he's even started drawing I know what's going to happen. A mere glance at the rough sketch confirms my suspicion. He is not directing us to the shop we are showing him. He is giving us directions to the VCD shop just outside the school. The one owned by the bonkers lady I have already given up on. I can't imagine why he thinks we need a map to a place we run past most mornings; it's just outside the school gate! This may be another example of being afraid to lose face by saying he doesn't know. Yet again I am being directed to a random bookshop, rather than the one I asked for. It's as if they have no grasp of specifics. I'm not looking for any old shop that once sold a book.

According any credibility to the picture on the website, it's clearly not the shop I am looking for. I thank him anyway. He closes the door behind himself. Two minutes later VD returns from the shower and leaves it open again.

All showered and daisy fresh, VD is sitting on the edge of his bed sans shirt when Shifu Fatso makes his evening visit. He gets as far as, 'Ok' before noticing the tattoos. Having a fair amount of body coverage, and a fair amount of body to cover, VD's illustrated form is a spectacular sight. Shifu Fatso obviously agrees, 'Whuh!'

Wide-eyed, he crosses the room and, without so much as a 'by your leave', starts inspecting the illustrated form, poking and prodding the porcine in the process. VD graciously tolerates the physical intrusion for a while before pushing Shifu away and donning a shirt.

Denied the viewing pleasures of VD's flesh, Shifu points at me and gives an inquisitive grunt. I hastily refute the suggestion I may possess any body art. Actually, I don't, but it's bound to figure into my midlife crisis soon enough because I can't afford a Harley.

Disappointed in me, Shifu forgets he's already given us an, 'Ok' once and we get another, closely followed by a 'Go sleep', as he closes the door.

Feeling not a little defiled VD exclaims, 'My word!'

'Personal space isn't a concept he's familiar with is it mate?'

My philanthropic good nature getting the better of me, I decide to help Shifu overcome his social inhibitions. Reaching for my dictionary, I look up the words for more personal body areas in order to tell Shifu about VD's other tattoos that require inspection.

During the night I'm woken by the sounds of arguing in the corridor, but I am too tired to investigate. If anyone wants my input into a domestic dispute they will have to bring it to me first.

Heaven must love fools for they made so many of us.

Monkey Magic

The self is the self's only enemy, and the self is the self's only friend.

Lord Krishna

Knobby's news service does the rounds at breakfast to fill us in on current events. Apparently, South American guy sneaked out of school and was spotted in a downtown bar by Shifu Fatso. Staggering back in the early hours, SA guy found Shibu waiting. True to form, SA guy dealt with Shibu by letting loose right back at him. It must have been the resulting row that disturbed my angelic repose.

I had a vague sense of an occurrence during the night. A hazy recollection of a phrase flickers in my mind, 'Don't tell me what to do, man. I am passionate, you are dead inside!' It's reassuring to have fractured memories pieced together.

As Fatso assembles our squad, I see SA guy in front of his squad doing push-ups with Shibu standing over him. It's a bit of a lame punishment considering that's what Knobby gets for just being Knobby. The situation also begs the question of what Fatso was doing in the pub, although it does explain why he is so tired and grumpy all day. I had assumed he was just a natural misery, but now have a suspicion he's permanently hungover.

Given that Fatso gets to hang out in a low-down boozer, and South American guy gets a few press-ups as punishment for the same, I feel I'm being penalised for following the rules here. VD is desperate for a pint and a promenade of an evening and would gladly do press-ups in exchange, but we follow the rules and lose out whereas SA guy flaunts the rules and, essentially, gets away with it. Seeing SA guy's method of dealing with the system, I realise I may have made a tactical error in maintaining composure. Aggressive defence is obviously far more effective.

The oppressive atmosphere continues throughout the morning and everyone keeps their heads down. Shifu Fatso is especially grumpy and constantly watches Shibu's squad out of the corner of his eye as they enjoy a double session of Go Run and press-ups. We are dismissed early for lunch and are finishing up by the time they are released. They are not a happy bunch of bunnies. Already losing tolerance with SA guy, being rudely disturbed during the night and then communally chastised and punished hasn't helped. Personally, I'm more upset with the system for letting him get away with it.

After lunch, I call in the tuck shop for a bottle of water. Recognising me, the shopkeeper proudly gestures toward her shiny-new selection of beverages. She has 'tea-flavour with strawberry milk', 'tea-flavour with wheat' and 'coffee-flavour with milk'. As she got them in stock due to popular demand, i.e. I once casually inquired, I feel obliged to try them. I buy a couple of each except the strawberry. Tea with strawberry milk is such a hideous idea that I have to read the packet several times to confirm what it actually says. I still can't believe the travesty.

The shopkeeper obligingly provides hot water from a flask and demonstrates the preparation procedure. Unwrapping the paper cup reveals a wide, telescopic straw, a sachet of flavoured powder and a pot of rubbery chunks. Adding hot water and stirring the lot together creates a sickeningly sweet, imitation tea, drink. The golden paper cup is emblazoned with a picture of a girl band who clearly enjoy the endorsement fee. This must mean I'm considerably hipper and/or gayer than I have been led to believe. The concoction isn't exactly what I had in mind, but is close enough to pass muster. Warm and soothing, I find the Xiang Piao Piao most pleasant. I make one for VD, but he's not so convinced. He opts out of Mandarin class so I take his drink with me.

Taking a deep breath before entering the building, I exhale gently as

I run up the stairs. Fortunately, the tea impersonator comes with a lid so I can still make pretty good time without spilling any. There's no doubt this is the best approach to the stairwell yet.

Spying my garish paper cup, Knobby shouts across the classroom, 'What are you drinking, Nick?'

I show him the label, 'It's a tea-flavoured drink.'

'That's disgusting! You must be sick to drink that.'

Knobby's verdict established, I return to my work. This week's class is particularly useful as it covers the more common Kung Fu training terms used at school.

My martial art at home, Lau Gar Kuen, is a Southern style and, as such, is taught with Cantonese terms, the language spoken in and around Hong Kong. Mainland China has many regional dialects, but has a unifying language of Mandarin. Mandarin uses a simplified form of the Cantonese characters, but they are pronounced differently enough to effectively be two separate languages. To further confuse the issue, the indigenous population of Dengfeng have a regional accent broad enough to be classed as a dialect in its own right, Dengfeng Hua. Although Dengfeng's recent growth has attracted people from all over China making it fairly cosmopolitan as far as the sticks go, and the accent is becoming less evident.

Some words used here are similar enough for me to be able to work out what's happening. For example, a Kung Fu teacher in Cantonese is Sifu and in Mandarin is Shifu, but many commands are completely different or worse, sound similar enough to be confusing. This is the list we learn:

Gong Fu	Kung Fu
Shang ba jie	Stretch up
Xia ba jie	Stretch down
Xia cha	Splits
Xia yao	Back bridge
Ma bu	Horse stance
Gong bu	Bow stance
Xu bu	Empty stance
San kai	Break up
Zhan dui	Line up
Bao shu	Count off
Wa tao	Frog jump

240

Fu wo cheng	Push-up
Zheng ya tui	Front leg stretch
Ce ya tui	Side leg stretch
Zuo	Left
You	Right
Qian	Front
Hou	Back
Xue	Study
Pao bu	Run
Ting	Stop
Zhen ti tui	Vertical kick
Xie ti tui	Diagonal kick
Ci ti tui	Side kick
Bailian ti tui	Lotus kick
Wai bailian ti tui	Outside Lotus kick
Tan tui	Spring leg
Shi zi tan tui	Ten character spring leg
Cai jiao	Slap foot
Liang qi jiao	Double rising foot
Taiji quan	Tai chi
Qi mei gun	Eyebrow staff
Dao	Knife (single edged sword)
Jian	Straight sword
Luohan quan	Fat monk Fist
Zui quan	Drunken Fist
Tang lang quan	Mantis Fist
Tao lu	Form
San da	Chinese Boxing
Sheng biao	Rope dart
Shuang jie gun	Double sticks (Nunchaku)
Shan zi	Fan
San jie gun	Three-section staff
Qiang	Spear

Terms commonly used during training indeed! If our Shifu gives us a verbal command at all it's usually an abbreviated instruction. As an example, 'Shang ba jie' becomes 'Shang' and then 'hou' meaning 'back' for us to change direction and perform the stance to the other side. Although our Shifu mostly gives a trademark grunt or random gestures and we guess what he wants.

That said, this has been the most useful Chinese lesson so far. We could have done with it at the beginning of our stay or, even better, included it as part of an orientation program given during Quarantine.

Heading back to the room to drop off my book and wake VD, I have to clamber through a knot of Pink Overall ladies crammed into the doorway of our building. There's about eight younger girls clustered around the dominatrix. Perched on tiny, dayglo plastic stools, they spit seed shells onto the floor while she holds court. Making a concerted effort to ignore me, not one makes the slightest attempt to move so much as an inch to make my manoeuvre any easier. Once entrenched there is no shifting them.

In spite of the army of cleaners and maintenance guys liberally distributed around the school, nothing is cleaned or maintained. Every doorway has a member of cleaning staff sitting on the step. Our building has a permanent group of Pink Overalls sitting in the doorway. It's as if the school employs people to sit around all day. Chatting, snacking and spitting over the steps, I can only assume it's a scheme to maintain low unemployment figures and assist the economy. By being employed, they simultaneously generate income and create work for themselves and others. If not a government endorsed program, the cunning devils may have come up with the idea in order to protect their jobs. They couldn't be so stupid as to accidently make their jobs more difficult surely?

I'm all set to fill VD in on the lesson he missed when I'm confronted by a hideous sight. Victorian Dad earned himself the sobriquet at a previous Kung Fu club as a result of his fizzog furniture resembling that of a character from Viz Magazine. (I refer to his wife as Victorian Mum as I feel it's politer than Mrs. VD.) Alarmingly, I discover he has been abducted and replaced by Victorian Potato Head. Seeing my dismay, he sheepishly explains the effort of maintaining the facial topiary under these conditions was far too demanding. If only he had mentioned his intentions earlier I could have grown some facial hair just to confuse our Shifu further.

Shifu gives VD's new streamlined face a double take and a customary, 'Whuh huh!' at assembly before sending us off for our stint of Go Run. Knowing the Chinese term doesn't make it any more palatable, education can be a curse sometimes. As we commence the warmup stretches, I determine to make use of my new vocabulary. When Shifu calls, 'Shang!' I helpfully supply him with the rest of the term,

'Shang ba jie, Shifu?'

His little eyes become saucers, 'Whuh huh?' Regaining composure, he gives me a beaming smile, 'Yes, Shang ba jie.'

Precedent set, this continues for the rest of the lesson. Whenever Fatso grunts a command, I say the term in Chinese for him. If I'm a bit slow he looks to me in anticipation so he can confirm my response and repeat the term I have given him. A more cynical person might suggest I am teaching our Shifu to speak Chinese, but he is enjoying it so much that I haven't the heart to stop. And I so rarely get to be teacher's pet.

One advantage of training on a rubbish dump is the amount of sharp objects protruding from the dry dirt. During the session, I collect a rusty screw in my shoe. The Feiyue soles are so thin as to be easily pierced, but this is the first time I've found anything useful in there. I stick it in my pocket and am thus tooled-up to set about another DIY project.

Coincidentally, one reason we get told off for having our door open is the metal plate which houses the door catch is missing a screw. This means the door is apt to spring open of its own accord. I know better than to try getting anything fixed by the maintenance guys. The chain of command from me, through Shifu and God knows how many other people, means it's just not going to happen in my lifetime. Also, the looks I get when I ask for something make me feel like a whinger. I can't begin to imagine the chaos and carnage that would ensue if the maintenance guys attempted to replace a screw. It's not worth the fuss. If I want anything done, I'll do it myself.

The open door doesn't bother us, but after dinner I set about fixing it because we keep getting told off for it. Besides, it gives me something to do. Cutting a plastic bottle cap into strips, I pack out the hole in the doorframe and remount the catch with my rusty screw. Necessity is indeed the mother of invention.

Something happens to British men over a certain age. With male pattern baldness and middle-age spread kicking in, they gravitate towards the shed, horde screws in a jam-jar and perform sub-standard DIY. I hadn't realized how quickly I'm turning into my dad.

I'm tightening the screw with a broken Dao as another Shifu passes. Raising his eyebrows in despair, he tells me, 'Guan men' (close the door). Satisfied with a job well done, I leave the door open just to be contrary.

At evening assembly, I wander over to Shibu to remind him about our passports. Seeing me coming, he attempts an escape but I corner him. His response is such that I feel he is being deliberately vague over the issue.

This elusiveness makes me uneasy. Since we have been here, I've picked up a few clues as to how things work. It hasn't exactly inspired me with confidence. The general tactic is to either ignore or deflect the issue until the enquirer gives up and goes away.

At assembly, Knobby lines up with a tea-flavoured drink of his own. Showing me his cup, he announces, 'The strawberry one is the best and anyone who doesn't think so is sick.'

Refusing to put the cup down inevitably results in another batch of token press-ups. I appreciate Shifu's attempts at discipline, but without enforcing the punishment it's not going to curtail Knobby's antics any. I'm sure most of us find Knobby's japery embarrassing, but unless Shifu puts his foot down properly he's only adding to the problem by providing the attention Knobby craves.

I'm briefly joined in the gym by Knobby, but he's only come to gripe about our Shifu abusing him. He's so vocal about his perceived mistreatment that I'm sure it's a guise for showing off about his own misbehaviour. The few others at training pay him no attention so he gives it up as a bad job and seeks out a more appreciative audience.

On his bedtime rounds our Shifu is a bit smilier than we have become accustomed and lingers a little. Perhaps this resurgence in friendliness it's a side effect of Knobby's monkey business making me seem more sensible than I really am. The difference between our acts of defiance, like our previous Sanda standoff, and Knobby's tomfoolery, is that ours isn't personal and not in front of other Shifus, so our Fatso doesn't lose face.

Combined with today's chipping in with the Chinese terms, we are gaining ground with our Shifu again. His wonderfully open expressions are as easy to read as a preschool primer and I'm warming to his childlike simplicity. Sharing this thought with VD, he informs me that he is of a similar mind. As I have yet to see any evidence to support this claim, I'll have to take him at his word.

A lot of foreigners do not get over this hard training. Within
one week the body has strong cramps and it revolts. Sometimes
the cramps are so strong that you have no chance rising the stairs.
Each step means pain and the body recovers only slowly. After
the first month the pain eases, but during the next training months
pain will still remain a little bit. During learning new techniques
and weapons 'new' muscles are stressed. Also effusion of blood
cannot be avoided.

www.shaolin-wushu.de

Gathered together before the dawn, Shibu's group find themselves in a
situation more familiar to us; completely surrounded by no Shifu. But
they need fear not, for our glorious leader comes to their rescue by
allowing them share our Go Run. It's not unusual for a Shifu to be absent,
particularly for morning warming, so we think little of it as we pound the
deserted roads in the eerie light.

The Shibu shaped hole is still there after breakfast and his group join
us again. From the look on their faces I can tell they are delighted with
the prospect. The group instantly trebling in size poses no great hardship
for our man. He simply sends us all off for an extra generous helping of
Go Run around the kitchen block.

Initial warmup suitably taken care of, Shifu takes us out to the dustbowl at the back of school for Jibengong. After basic stretches, we set about lengths of the field in various combinations of kicks and stances. Even with these simple movements Shibu's squad's experience shows through. For the majority, they are far more flexible and less clumsy than us. It's motivating to see how the moves should be done and trying to imitate them is a better level of tuition than we usually get.

Studying and copying, I feel I'm adding a level of refinement, but Fatso isn't so impressed. Calling a halt to the proceedings, he lines us up once more. With a vague gesture to the other side of the field he says, 'Go run, fast.'

Mustering a modicum of enthusiasm, we sprint past the smouldering bonfire, touch the far wall and run back. It turns out that Shibu's squad are better at running too. The pack quickly spreads out with stragglers puffing back long after the leaders have casually romped home. Clearly this attempt to deal with the disparity in ability isn't going to work either, but our Shifu is not taxed for long. In an unprecedented moment of inspiration, he comes up with a new idea. Arranging us with partners of similar size, he indicates that one of the pair should get on the others back. Pointing to the other side, he again says, 'Go run, fast.'

Great, a Piggyback race! Reaching the ditch midway along the field, I make a quick calculation. Carrying VD, it's too wide to step over, I daren't try to jump it, and if I get into the trench I'll never get up the other side. Spotting a pile of broken bricks dumped further down the ditch, I head off at ninety degrees to the herd. I hear Shifu calling, 'No. What are do?'

My sudden stroke of genius hadn't factored the extra weight and suddenly the 'bridge' looks a lot further away than anticipated. I precariously totter over the discarded masonry as the other teams romp past on their return lap. It's pointless to continue. VD hops off and we slink back into line having scuppered another of Shifu's brilliant plans.

But all is not lost. Shifu has yet another idea up his sleeve. Splitting us into two teams, it's Go Run with a twist: competitive sprint relays. Seeing the results of a lap Fatso adjusts our positions in line so we compete against someone more equal for the next lap.

My routine is to wear trainers for the morning run and Feiyue shoes for training in the gym. Feiyues are thin and flexible, but provide little support. This novelty Go Run finds me unprepared and still wearing them. The dusty surface makes it difficult to find purchase with my toes and sprinting flat-footed on the hard-baked field is particularly unforgiving on the knees. Feeling every impact, I ease up and concentrate on rolling my feet. Shifu attempts to encourage me with a shooing motion and a call to, 'Go fast', but I know what's good for me and coast the rest of my races.

I haven't caught on quickly enough. The extra Go Run has already taken its toll. My knees are on fire and I'm all set to down tools by the time Shifu announces break. 'Twenty-minute go gym,' has never sounded so pleasant. Similarly unimpressed with the morning's activities, VD takes advantage of the break to make himself scarce.

The trouble with picking up a little injury here is that conditions make it difficult to recover. The Shifus reactions vary between two extremes, it's either, 'No train, three day' or to dismiss complaints as the excuses of lazy foreigners. No one wants to miss out on any real training so we work through our aches and pains, concealing all but serious injuries while simultaneously trying not to complicate our afflictions.

In desperation, I allow the tuck shop to furnish me with an exorbitantly priced pair of flimsy knee supports and lather my swollen knees in tiger balm (laohu you). On my last legs, I resolve to be more selective about joining in with things Shifu throws at us and gingerly make my way to the gym.

VD is not the only one to have made a sharp exit, but the absences go without mention. Shifu begins the lesson with the usual Jibengong. The standing punches and kick routines, are ok, but I'm in no condition for low stances. I move through the drills carefully without committing my legs to any stress. Luckily, the increased group size means we get longer rests between laps.

I'm just beginning to think I can make it through the session when we hit a complication. Pointing at the front of the line, Shifu makes the wavy arm motion and the lead guy sets off down the hall in a familiar fashion, but suddenly it's a whole new ballgame. Months ahead of our group, Shibu's students have extra moves in their repertoire. A manoeuvre I thought I knew has now evolved into craziness.

It begins with the circling arm movement that I had such difficulty getting the hang of in the first place. Happy that I can now windmill like a fury, I am distraught to see Shibu's students don't finish there. As their arms are returning to the starting position they drop into Pubu, slapping the ground with the leading palm and holding the other arm overhead. Body weight is transferred to the opposite knee and both palms push out to that side using the momentum to spin on the grounded heel, sweeping 360 degrees with the extended leg. Resuming the standing position, the whole thing is repeated to the other side.

After struggling with the first part of this movement, I am now in at the deep end. Never the most co-ordinated of people, I surrender the remainder of my dignity. Crossing the hall like this takes a lot of repetitions and my natural ability and tender knees ensure I make a complete hash of each one. It's apparent my evening training sessions are going to be occupied with practicing this for the some time to come.

Seeing the shambles, we make of this movement, Shifu splits us up to work our relevant forms. I'm glad of the break, but dividing the group is a further problem for Fatso as he finds it difficult to allocate his time between everyone. This works for me as, left unattended, I concentrate on the upright parts of Xiao Hong Quan.

Most of us train ourselves so aren't a problem for him, however, the slackers are now able to capitalise on his divided attention. As the volume of buffoonery increases, it's soon too much for our beloved Shifu. He gives it up as a bad job and my knees find their prayers answered with an early lunch.

While I have been crippling myself, VD has spent a leisurely morning hanging off the balcony, drinking tea and watching the Lion Dance teams. A traditional preserve of Kung Fu students, Xiao Long has several Lion Dance performance teams. We have done some dancing with lions ourselves over the years so are particularly interested in their practice. I can only marvel at their skill. It's a level of ability we can only dream of possessing.

In the canteen everyone is airing their dissatisfaction with today's training. Our usual jovial despair at the school is becoming less light-hearted as complaints rack up. The problem for western mentality is the lack of structure. Our timetable is little more than a rough guideline. There is no attempt to tailor lessons according to student requirements or ability. The school's love of organisation doesn't extend to the individual. There's no perceivable pattern to the 'one size fits all' training. It's whatever they can get away with.

It doesn't help that our classes are run by people who are little more than children themselves. The Shifus are barely older than their students, in our case considerably younger. I doubt they have had any teacher training, but have just gravitated into the role. None are interested in their job or their students. Rather than attempting to teach, they take the path of least effort and some try everything within their power to avoid exerting any effort on our behalf. Even if you are determined to learn, it's difficult to get anything out of them. They just saw Kung Fu as a means to an end. That end was to get a job. Now that they have achieved their goal, they don't feel the need to try any more. This is especially true of the Shifus who teach foreigners, they have won the life lottery by landing the job and think they will never have to work again.

The system relies upon its own weight to keep things rolling along but, with cogs like these fellows in the machine, it can easily head off course. Which is where we are today. This morning's activities have just been a waste of time.

While waiting for class, we exchange the universal banter of team-mates anywhere, but the little Korean reprobates have cottoned on. Some guys have been getting too friendly with them, cuddling them up and dandling them on knees. Taking advantage of the relaxed boundaries, the dastardly duo continually push the margins of polite society.

After lunch they demonstrate their grasp of the English language by pointing their fingers into people's faces and shouting, 'Fack you, muddah fackah'.

Most ignore the challenge until a caution from the fat American girl launches them into a tirade of expletives. Sticking to her guns, she again tells them to stop with the swearing. It's primarily her little clique who've been babying the twin terrors and, as she's been playing Mum, she now has to deal with the monster she's created. The chilblains know they are on to a good thing with that group and, not wanting to push it too far, one of them has a brainwave. Running to the tuck shop crowd, he drags a little Chinese kid back to the steps with him. The little kid is about four or five and hasn't a clue what's occurring. Korean Kid forces the junior's sticky little mitt into a fist, extends the middle finger vertically, and waves it at Fat Yank. The half-pint Korean laughs, we laugh, the tiny Chinese kid laughs and all is well. As humorous as the cheeky chappy is, I can see these playful high-jinks have the potential to get out of hand.

Lesson quality doesn't improve this afternoon. After the usual kitchen block laps, the amalgamated group heads for the back of school to drill up and down the dusty field. When Fatso motions for VD to join the line, he shakes his head, offers a few choice words and departs stage left. Mouth agape, Shifu is visibly shaken by the outburst and unsure how to react. With no one for support, he has little option but to let it go.

Now aware of the general lack of enthusiasm, Shifu attempts to keep us amused with a game of Touchy Knee. Immediately half the group opt out and sit in small groups on the side-lines. The remainder of us half-heartedly mark out an area in the dust and try to touch each other on the knee. It's not a devastating success.

Plan B sees Shifu appear with a football. Throwing it onto the field he motions us toward it. This approach to teaching takes me back to school games lessons as a kid. I wasn't keen then either. At least I don't have to suffer the indignity of waiting to be picked here. I leave them to it. The early afternoon sun is too much for my baldy head and I make for the shade of the wall to work on Xiao Hong Quan until Shifu calls time.

Twenty minutes later we are back in the gym doing the usual laps and stances. Perhaps realising Shibu's group requires more from a lesson, Shifu lines up, points to the threadbare carpet and says, 'Zaji.'

Acrobatics, just what my knees are crying out for. For the Chinese students, acrobatics takes place on the hard-baked field using a couple of old house-bricks for a take-off ramp. We fragile westerners get the luxury of doing it on the patch of disease ridden carpet in the gym. The briefest of glances is enough to tell me I ain't doing no acrobatics.

Not only are my weight and flexibility against me, but I have to go back to work when we get home. I'm already suffering with my knees and throat. I don't have the luxury of being able to support a real injury. Besides, it's pointless to spend my time training something I have no intention of maintaining. Given proper tuition, I could probably get the hang of the acrobatics, but it would be a long, hard task at the expense of my other training so it's just not practical.

At least half the class are of a similar mind. The remainder form a circle on the mat while I wander to the side and work on my form. From time to time I catch Shifu keeping an eye me, but, as I am actually training and not being any bother, he allows me the breach of etiquette. I suspect the other guys work ethic, and VD's sporadic absences, are making me look like a much more diligent student than I actually am. As we leave Shifu gets Mongolian Guy to ask me why I didn't participate in the acrobatics. It's far too complicated to explain through an intermediary so I just say, 'Wo nian ji da' (I'm old).

When it comes to Wushu, there's no denying this fact, so Fatso just shrugs and grunts, but Mongolian Guy tries to convince me that acrobatics would be good for my health. Under different circumstances I'm sure he would be right, but here and now we are going to have to differ on that one.

A previous Kung Fu teacher tried to warn me off training in China, saying, 'Everyone I know who's gone to China only learnt they couldn't do acrobatics'. I appreciate he was trying to say Chinese schools tend to teach Wushu rather than traditional Kung Fu. However, I already know I can't do acrobatics so don't intend to incapacitate myself to prove the point. All I have really learnt in China is that my levels of personal hygiene are far higher than I had been led to believe.

Unaccustomed to the lack of food and sleep, we foreign students tend to be in a permanent daze. Tired and hungry everything takes on a slightly surreal hue. My enflamed knees don't help. I'm so grumpy, I'm not inclined to go for dinner, but as part of the problem is my exhausted body doesn't have enough resources left to deal with an injury, I force myself to the canteen.

The atmosphere hasn't improved since lunch and the same old gripes rear their heads, but perspective makes all the difference. The camaraderie that stems from our common enemy is beginning to be seen in a different light. The schools disinterest in us means we are forced to rely on each other in times of need. Food and medicine for sick or injured students is provided by compatriots simply because there is no one else. Even in class we are really taught by other students. Everyone is happy to help out as there is the underlying appreciation that we are all in the same boat.

We are also our own primary source of information. The problem with this simple arrangement is the limited and random knowledge pool. Being taught by the other students isn't necessarily a good thing as I'm not convinced they have received enough tuition or have a thorough enough understanding to share. Similarly, without an official representative to turn to, the majority of our gripes don't get resolved.

As I force chopsticks of lukewarm mush into my face, the general discontent aired around me, doesn't help my disposition any. Unable to face any more of the food or grumbling, I rise from the table only to discover my knees have seized up. Hobbling out of the canteen is no mean feat on the slippery floor.

I can barely drag my aching limbs up the stairs. Putting the last reserves of energy into getting back, I find myself standing in unfamiliar territory. My room is nowhere to be seen. I'm so tired and dazed that it takes a moment to sink in. I have walked up an extra flight of stairs than necessary. Our room is on the fourth floor. The Chinese ground floor is called the first floor, as opposed to the European system where the first floor is the one above ground floor. So, while in the west our room 409 would be on the fifth level, in China it is the fourth level. I'm confused by my own explanation. I usually just stop at the floor with the Father Christmas picture stuck on the landing wall. As I've run out of stairs, and am Santa-less, I have clearly gone too far. Holding the bannister for support, I limp back down a level.

Much like the western thirteenth floor, some Chinese buildings, typically high-rises, omit the fourth floor, by numbering the floor above the third as the fifth. This is due to the Chinese word 'four' (si) being phonetically similar to the word for 'die'. Because of this superstition, fourth floor apartments have traditionally been cheaper to rent. At our school the fourth floor has been set aside for foreigners. This could be because foreigners aren't aware of the association or maybe because the authorities don't care if we die. I'm currently not in the mood to pander to social convention. If a homonym wants to kill me it's gonna have to be particularly polite about it because I'm feeling proper grouchy at the moment and not inclined to acquiesce to anything much.

Ideally, I would have liked to practice the windmilling, sweeping movement tonight, but there's no way I'm up to it. I'm beginning to wonder if, in the words of Danny Glover, 'I'm getting too old for this shit'. Taking the executive decision to skip evening training, I collapse on the bed and sleep through until morning.

It is all mystery inside.

Plaque outside Damo Cave.

A winding path leads to a peaceful Buddhist temple with
growing flowers and trees around.

Plaque along the trail to Chuzu.

I don't know whether I'm adapting to the dust and smoke fumes or am just getting used to a constantly inflamed pharynx. Either way it's bearable enough that I can now concentrate on my other ailments. Rather than making me fitter and healthier, this place is slowly crippling me.

Knees strapped tight, I take it easier on this morning's run up the mountain. As long as I'm careful to roll my feet and go at my own pace it's not bad, but I don't make it to the peak before heading back. Lined up at the crossroads, we are expecting a trip to the Breakfast Place, but things do not pan out the way our Shifu would like. Yuan Shifu has a brief discussion with Fatso involving stern tones and Fatso's Breakfast Place suggestion is effectively vetoed. I hadn't really appreciated the hierarchy among our Shifu, but it seems Yuan must outrank Fatso and his wheedling proves fruitless as, without Shibu for support, he is out-gunned.

'Hou men' or back door business is such a staple of Chinese life that Fatso is visibly put out at being denied a portion of his regular kickback. Sulkily, he orders us back to school and dawdles behind pouting like a petulant schoolgirl.

As we approach the canteen, Shifu grunts and motions us back. Joining him, we are made to line up in height order before being told, 'Go.' We then go back to where we were.

Tucking into my breakfast dose of rice and cabbage, I hear we can get signed out of school. Cue a mad scramble as word spreads.

Unlike certain Shifus one could mention, Yuan Shifu is actually in the DVD room at the appointed hour. We line up and hand him our slips, which he dutifully signs and returns. He signs both the slips I present without fuss, but then he goes and blows it by only handing one back. Retaining the other, he tells me VD has to collect his own. This is uncharacteristic of Yuan Shifu as he usually displays more acumen, but it's still nothing compared to Shibu's sign out procedure. Ironically, he has given me VD's slip so I have to ask VD to collect mine.

As our provisioning was taken care of Sunday, we are in a position to go on another excursion today. This week we have earmarked another local and key site in Kung Fu history, Damo Dong (Damo's Cave).

Damo began his life as a royal prince named Bodhidharma in Southern India. On receiving the Buddha's teachings he decided to give up his regal position to study Buddhism full time. After much perseverance his efforts paid off and Damo became so good at the old Buddhism that he was sent to introduce the Mahayana Buddhist teachings to the Chinese people. After an arduous trek over the Himalayan Mountains, Damo pottered around China's then capital of Luoyang, before arriving at Shaolin in AD527.

At that time, Shaolin practiced Hinayana Buddhism as taught by the founder Batuo and didn't appreciate being told they were doing it wrong. Further communication problems led to Damo refusing the monks invitation of accommodation. Instead, he climbed Wuru, the central peak of the Songshan Mountains, and make himself at home in a cave overlooking the temple.

For the next nine years he sat facing the wall in meditation. So long and hard did Damo meditate in his cave, that his shadow became engrained on the wall. This part of the rock has long since been cut out and installed within the Shaolin Temple to preserve the image. Ironically it was then damaged in the fire of 1928. We saw the rock a few weeks

254

ago and, through the distortion of its protective glass case, one can indeed make out a shadowy patch without much of a leap of imagination.

After nine years of meditating, Damo was hit with a sudden inspiration regarding the path to enlightenment. He realised that experiencing Buddhism for oneself was more important than theoretical knowledge. In an instant, Damo had invented Chan Buddhism and became China's first Chan patriarch. Chan Buddhism, also known as Zen, emphasises the attainment of enlightenment and direct realisation through meditation and Dharma practice. With this insight he rushed down the mountain to share it with the monks below.

On entering Shaolin, Damo noticed many monks were out of shape. The lifetime of studying texts and practicing long-term meditation had left them spiritually strong, but physically weak.

A member of the Indian warrior class, Damo understood the importance of physical exercise and developed a program of exercises to supplement the monks' meditation. The monks were likely to have been amenable to his ideas as China already had a long history of physical exercise for health. Indeed Huang Di, the famous Yellow Emperor, compiled a massive compendium of medical knowledge around 2500BC. Included in the Huang Di Nei Jing, along with treatments and medicinal recipes, are breathing and exercise routines.

The two sets of movements credited to Damo are now known as the Yi Jin Jing (Changing Muscle and Tendon Scripture) and Ba Duan Jin (Eight Section Brocade). Originally designed for stretching and strengthening the body, in time these exercises combined with indigenous Chinese fighting skills and evolved into a self-defence system known as Shaolin Temple Boxing. Later this martial training helped the monks defend against invading warlords and bandits, creating the legend of Shaolin Kung Fu.

The alleged birthplace not only of Chan Buddhism, but also Shaolin Kung Fu, Damo's cave supplies a double whammy in pilgrimage terms. It is further claimed that the majority of the world's contemporary martial arts are descended from Shaolin, giving rise to the expression, 'Tianxia wugong chu Shaolin' (All martial arts under heaven stem from Shaolin). While this claim may be a slight exaggeration, with this endorsement it's easy to see why Shaolin has become the Mecca of the martial arts world. If Shaolin is the Kung Fu Garden of Eden then Damo's Cave is the Buddhist equivalent of Jesus' living room.

With such a significant historic site right on the doorstep, it would be unthinkable to travel half way around the globe and not stick one's head in, even if it does involve walking to the top of a mountain. With Juha gone there are no takers for our jaunt.

It's a pleasant enough morning when we rock up and we are soon through the crowds and heading for the Pagoda Forest where a group of ramshackle vendors guard a fork in the road. Lessons learnt on our expedition to Sanhuangzhai find us more prepared for this outing. For a start we have an idea where we were going rather than just randomly wandering around and have also brought consumables for the journey. It's not that I necessarily object to paying through the nose for provisions along the way, more that I take exception when the supplier laughs at me for paying it.

We also decline the kind offer to use the tripod-mounted binoculars to view the statue on the peak. The asking price of 2Y is a modest enough sum, but it's really a service for the bus-tour day-trippers who run through the grounds without time to savour their surroundings. Being lucky enough to have the temple on our doorstep we are obliged to put in the honest toil of making it up the hill to visit in person.

Stepping off the surfaced road, a narrow dirt track leads off toward the trees where a flight of stone steps runs up the side of an earthen mound. Variously translated as the Sweet Dew Platform, or Manna Platform, Ganlu Tai is where Batuo, Shaolin Temple's founder, translated the Sutra of Ten Stages and gained immortality through his work. Sweet Dew and Manna being translations of the Sanskrit word Amrita meaning Nectar or Immortality. Amrita Hall was built at the site during the Ming dynasty in recognition of Batuo's achievement. Today nothing remains but traces of rubble poking through the weeds. I can see why he chose to work here. Handily situated, not too far to go back for dinner, it's just far enough removed from the main temple to be peaceful and offer a scenic solitude.

The well-maintained temple grounds are practically litter free, but as we get further away from the epicentre the jettisoned detritus increases. It's still negligible by Chinese standards so the regularly positioned concrete litter bins must be having an effect. Behind an overflowing bin, a small rise offers an enticing view through the trees. Clambering up the worn slope, I find the answer to the unasked question, 'What do they do with all the rubbish?'

The small valley is brimming with used wrappers, bottles and general waste. This method of refuse disposal typifies China's 'out of sight out of mind' attitude to problem solving. It's particularly galling as the litter bins have recyclable and non-recyclable sections, yet the rubbish is clearly just dumped all together and in a supposedly protected site.

Northwest of the main temple, we come to a fork in the path. To the right a narrow trail leads to the mountain while left, through the trees, is Chuzu (First Ancestor's) Nunnery, although the English translation on the sign proclaims it a Nursery.

Named in honour of Damo, the dedication on the gate sides roughly translates as, 'The 28th generation disciple of Sakyamuni in the West, the founder of Chinese Chan Buddhism in the East'.

Out of sight of the main tourist route, the nunnery is another of Shaolin's hidden gems. Tucked away in the woods, the area is completely deserted, giving an almost eerie sensation as we wander the ancient, barely maintained grounds.

Among the many trees is a lovely old Cypress planted in front of the Main Hall by the Sixth Patriarch, Huineng, the guy who invented Sudden Enlightenment. The legend is that Huineng carried the sapling in a bowl from Guandong in tribute to Damo.

For some reason the Nunnery got a proper kick-in during the Cultural Revolution and, just like the main temple complex, has mostly been rebuilt since the 1980s, although four buildings date back to the Song dynasty. The most impressive being the Main Hall also known as First Patriarch Hall. Originally built in AD1125, it retains some Song Dynasty architecture, specifically the 'bucket arches' supporting the roof and is amongst the oldest wooden construction in Henan province. The pillars are decorated with images of warriors, dragons, lotus' and cranes and the walls show selected highlights from the life of Damo and pictures of later masters. Behind the altar are statues of the first three Chan masters: Damo, Huike and Sengcan.

Overlooked by the day-trippers, Chuzu is a pleasant place to hang out and regain composure after the bustle and crowds. Time willing, it would be a nice meditation spot, but today is all about Damo's Cave.

Past the nunnery, traces of former walls and buildings are visible through the vegetation reclaiming its territory. Behind the back wall, amongst an overgrown pile of rubble, a decrepit Pagoda stands forlorn.

Against the green mountainside, we can make out the grey trickle of stone steps with the white marble Damo glistening at the peak. Our narrow trail meanders along fields of stubbly crops peeking through the parched earth. From the condition of the path, I'm guessing the cave doesn't see much foot traffic. Unlike the other mountain routes, there's no cable car to Wuru Peak. The physical labour of clambering up the steep, badly carved steps provides a sense of self-righteousness fitting for a pilgrimage route that I would have been denied in the comfort of a cable car. Although it would probably increase visitor numbers.

It's not as arduous as the climb to Sanhuangzhai, but the path is more hazardous. The steps are cracked and broken and in places overgrown. However, our training at school running up and down steps and our Sanhuangzhai trip serves us in good stead and we stomp steadily up the mountain. Prepared for the worst, we are pleasantly surprised about an hour later as the Memorial Gateway peeks over the rise. The few students who've visited Damo Cave had cautioned us against it due to the difficulty of the climb. They obviously haven't been to Sanhuangzhai. I'm glad we didn't do the trips in the other order as it would have given us a false sense of security for the Sanhuangzhai trek.

The Memorial Gateway, built in the Ming Dynasty, has the three Chinese characters Mo Xuan Chu engraved into the front which translate as 'The meditation Place'.

Just inside this impressive stone portal is a tatty little courtyard with a small plaque at the cave entrance. Upgraded since Damo's residency, the cave now sports a man-made façade over the natural entrance giving the mountain face a suburban aspect. The crude door is secured with a rusty length of chain and a padlock. The padlock and chain are so old they seem positively medieval, but are no less formidable for it. Even a casual glance makes it clear no one is going to steal this cave.

Our tired minds take longer than normal to assimilate this information as we stare dumbly at our wooden nemesis. Foiled again.

VD is the first to speak, 'I don't believe this!' Bizarrely, I don't really feel anything, but can see his point only too well. Conversations with the guys at school had prepared us for the cave to be an anti-climax, but this is something else.

It's typical of our journey that what should be a straight forward process merely brings further complication and frustration. The expression about 'eating bitter' really rings true as we have to work for every little thing here, making each day a constant battle. So, I shouldn't be surprised to be stymied by an antique door. It's blatantly locked, but, for the sake of appearances, I give the door a bit of a rattle anyway.

The hoary old timbers are only a rough fit into the entrance and leave a gap large enough to peer through. Eye jammed to the door, I can just make out vague shadows in the gloom. Purportedly, inside the natural cave are statues of Damo and his disciple Huike. Huike is the guy who cut off his own arm to convince Damo to take him as a disciple and subsequently created Shaolin's one handed salute. I'll just have to accept the word of the guys at school for the cave's contents. It's all getting a bit too Schrodinger's Cat for me. It's practically a gongan, 'What can you see behind the locked door?' Part of me was expecting a religious experience or epiphany at Damo's Cave. Presumably, I'm not ready for enlightenment; all I see is a locked door.

Tantalisingly out of reach, the cave must remain a secret to us. Yet there is consolation in the fact that, assuming a grain of reality in the tale, Damo may well have done his morning workouts in the very courtyard we are standing in. I would like to practice Yi Jin Jing or even meditate in the courtyard, but I'm not really in the right frame of mind for it at the moment. I content myself with the fact Damo may have walked the same path up the mountain we did. If so, we have, if only briefly, followed in his footsteps.

Denied the cave option, we mooch about the shabby little courtyard. Next to the memorial gate is a stone stele erected in 2006 by Shi Yong Xin (Abbot of Shaolin Temple) and Shi Yong Mei (Abbot of First Ancestor Nunnery) explaining the cave's relevance. One side in Chinese, the other in English, the stele version of the 'Dharma Hole' is markedly more surreal than the conventional legend.

> The first year of Da Tong of Nan Dynasty emperor Liang Wu (527 AD), Dharma left Jian Ye (Nan Jing), touring the Central China, came to Five Peaks of Song Shan Mountain, finding a hole beneath the central peak named Fire Dragon Hole where an immortal -- Fire Dragon had been practising. It is all mystery inside, 24-section main keel centres clearly with two dragons on both sides correspondingly protecting the doctrine, stars, moon, colourful clouds, The Yangtze River. The Yellow River, high mountains and flowing water all appear inside, looking like 'a mini-universe' The second-generation ancestor stands on the right. The Fire Dragon went up to the heaven after first ancestor Dharma came here who then faced the wall nine years, being in deep meditation. Inside the hole, he experienced 'trance' to 'conscious trance'; when in trance, birds nestling on his shoulder did not undulate him; Outside, he climbed up branches

and stretched body, and imitated monkeys, snakes, etc, forming a whole set each of 'Xin Yi Boxing' and 'Arhat Stick', becoming the founder of 'Shaolin boxing'.

Reading the stele everything slips into place. It all makes sense now. I simply can't imagine how I managed to make it all sound so complicated before.

The stone steps continue to the peak where sits a 12-metre-high, white marble, statue of the man himself. I'd seen pictures of the statue, but none included the back piece of golden flames. The mandorla, a halo of fire surrounding the body, is a traditional representation of divinity and is also incorporated in the new Shaolin logo. The Shaolin trademark for religious items is a stylised version of this statue whereas the registered logo for Shaolin cultural items shows 'San jiao he yi', China's three treasures of Buddhism, Taoism and Confucianism combined.

Constructed in 1997, his already cracked head silently watches over the valley. Somehow, it's less impressive up close than it was from the opposite peak, but he has got a good view. Standing next to the statue of our founding father, I look down on a scene that's hardly changed in 1500 years. The few differences are recent additions. I can only begin to wonder what he makes of the bustling coach parks and besieging sightseers. The conflicting aspects of the view tempt reflection and it's a more thoughtful pair that silently tromp back down the mountain.

My initial disenchantment has become philosophical. It's easy to find symbolism in the lack of care taken over the shrine to the founder of Chan Buddhism. However, much like our training routines at school, if you look hard enough it's possible to imagine significance in anything. While disappointment only exists in the mind, I'm sure I would have felt worse had the cave been turned into a Chan Disneyland. At least we got to see the outside of Damo's cave and experience the journey. On hindsight, maybe it's just as well it was closed for the day. It's fitting that our little pilgrimage to the birthplace of Chan Buddhism revealed nothing.

Let us get drunk today, while we have wine;
the sorrows of tomorrow may be borne tomorrow.

Traditional Chinese Proverb

Even though it's mid-week, the temple grounds are still too busy to comfortably hang around in. We are also becoming less tolerant of the crowds. It may be a case of familiarity breeding contempt but, as with everyone else at school, our primary objective is purely gastronomical. Some of Yuan Shifu's group recommended the Oux Café, assuring us that it's the closest thing to decent coffee that Dengfeng can offer. Picking up a cab at the visitor centre, we set off to test their claim.

Driving down Dayu Road we are forced to slow for a small crowd. A makeshift stage at the roadside features a traditional opera in full swing and the audience is gathered in the road.

Beijing opera (Jingju) developed in the Qing dynasty imperial court of Beijing. Compared to previous styles the simplicity of Beijing opera allowed anyone to sing along and the patronage of Empress Dowager Cixi cemented its popularity with the masses.

Female performers were banned by the Qianlong Emperor in AD1772, making Beijing opera an exclusively male pursuit. The Republican era lifted the ban in a drive for modernisation and equality.

However, during the Cultural Revolution, association with the imperial court caused Beijing opera to be denounced as 'feudalistic' and 'bourgeois'. It has since been reinstated as one of China's cultural treasures. Combining music, song, dance, acrobatics and martial arts, traditional Chinese theatre required a long and arduous apprenticeship beginning at an early age. It is from this background that many early Kung Fu movie stars hailed.

Although mainland China has a TV Channel dedicated to classic Chinese opera (CCTV-11), theatre audience numbers have been in steady decline over recent years. As a result, opera companies are giving free public performances in an attempt to garner interest. This may be one of those publicity shows, although a more pedestrian dense place, like the town square or in a park, may have given more exposure.

Our driver has never heard of Oux Café. Our directions begin at our regular supermarket, so I get him to drop us there. Pulling up, he offers to take us to the airport when we leave. We agree a price of 300Y. I'm sure the bus service to Zhengzhou would be far more economical, but we've heard such varied reports of its reliability that we're opting for the low-stress alternative. This guy is a gift. I gratefully accept his business card and squirrel it away.

Our directions may start at the supermarket, but they prove completely arbitrary and have us baffled within minutes.

Probably the best way to experience a city is to be lost in it and we do our best to experience Dengfeng to the full. Keeping an eye out for our elusive bookshop, we hunt high and low for the Oux Café. We look down narrow alleyways, investigate the mezzanine level of a strip of shops and peek behind the plastic sheets that cover so many doorways. We can rarely read shop signs, and many buildings don't have one at all, so we have to stick our noses in to work out what's happening. Behind one set of plastic slats is a fair-sized supermarket, which we would never have guessed from outside.

Dengfeng retail appears to be grouped into districts. We pass through Weapons Row, Stationery Street and Door District when we find ourselves in a narrow street lined either side by open fronted metal lock-ups. About two metres square there must be about forty of these units altogether and, apart from the few that are closed, are all identical. Each has a bored looking chap with a cleaver slumped behind an unidentifiable lump of raw flesh. The unimpressive cadaver is surrounded by enough flies to effectively double the amount of meat on the slab. I'm going to hazard this is Botulism Boulevard.

We must have wandered further afield than most foreign visitors to the city usually venture as there's visibly more commotion about our presence than is customary. We're used to a little nudging and pointing by the locals and calls of, 'Hello' or, in case I don't know I'm a foreigner, 'laowai'. It's another of those little things that are charming for a while, but just sometimes annoy, particularly when they're not even subtle about it. I've become so highly attuned to the word that I can pick up the hint of a whispered, 'laowai' at 200 meters.

My suspicion that we are attracting more attention than usual is confirmed when some old fellow walks up to me, looks me in the face and disdainfully sneers, 'Huh, laowai'. Standing directly in front of me he continues to stare.

Not a little affronted by his attitude, I take an exaggerated look around and ask, 'Laowai zai nar?'

Looking me up and down, he gives a disgusted snort and continues on his way. I guess I'm not the laowai he was looking for.

Apparently moving away from the retail centre, we turn about and take a shadowy, narrow alley hoping to shortcut back to consumerism. Surrounded by garish lights and balloons, I suspect we've inadvertently wandered into the Red-light district, but it's an entire street dedicated to wedding photography. Each store with an identical display. Creeped out by the avenue of floral arches, I don't pause for breath until I'm through the brooding marital madness. The alleyway opens up at the town square where I chance to look up at the large white letters of the Oux Coffee placed high on the front of a featureless brown building with a huge inflatable red and yellow arch at its entrance.

It's a complete fluke we found the place. It's nowhere near where our schoolmates directed us. Key elements like, 'in the square at the centre of town' were notably absent from their instructions.

Being a public space, the square has a collection of everyday folk practicing their hobbies. Among the parked cars is a guy flying a remote-control helicopter and a couple of groups of line dancing ladies, although the location may make them square dancers. Generally congregating in the early mornings and evenings at parks, town squares, car parks or anywhere they can find space, Guangchang Wu (public square dance) is all the go in China. Especially popular with middle-aged and retired women, known as Dama (great mothers), the participants are more colloquially referred to as Wu Nainai (dancing grannies).

As with everything Chinese, dancing for exercise has a long history. As far back as the Song Dynasty (960-1279) cities' public spaces were noted for their use in performance. More recently the 1960s Cultural Revolution emphasised collective use of public space and traditional Yangge dances, originally performed to mark important agricultural occasions, were adapted by the CPC for propaganda purposes before being banned altogether.

When Deng Xiaoping took over as CPC chairman and instituted a program of economic reform, 'socialism with Chinese characteristics', the pace of urbanization picked up and formerly suppressed trends, such as dancing, returned. Women who had lived through the Cultural Revolution, and the Yangge shows, began to reach mandatory retirement age and returned to dance as a way to stay fit, relieve boredom and socialise. They also embraced the new wave of Chinese Pop songs. The dancers received official encouragement when the government promoted fitness in anticipation of the Beijing Olympics. Due to its low cost and ease of participation, Guangchang Wu is now estimated to have over 100 million practitioners.

The dancing grannies are a delight and, even though they are often branded a nuisance by neighbours and pedestrians, I love the idea of old ladies repurposing public space in a way that urban planners hadn't designed. The mentality of remaking and adapting their environment is very Chinese. I've heard a lot about the 'real China' as if anything that doesn't conform to our postcard ideal isn't authentic. Traditional China is being washed aside as globalisation blends the world a shade of beige, but the people are the real China. And these gyrating geriatrics epitomise the Chinese spirit.

Also of note are a couple of Mao suited old guys practicing calligraphy. Using a three-foot long, sponge-tipped brush they write their characters in water on the paving stones, barely finishing a line before the previous characters evaporate into the midday air.

Calligraphy was once at the core of Chinese culture, a basic requirement of a well-educated citizen, but today the skill is losing significance to technology. Still appreciated by the populace, many passers-by stop to admire and seem impressed.

For the calligrapher, it's a philosophical pastime. Expressing oneself through the movement of brush and body is a Kung Fu in its own right. The process of creating being more important than the product, aptly demonstrated here in the impermanence of the writing. One guy is copying from a little notebook while the other, pausing occasionally, looks to be working from memory. Totally immersed in their activity everything else is forgotten; another example of Kung Fu and Chan in harmony.

I can see a difference in the two styles, but my untrained eye isn't unable to appreciate any intricacies. It all looks beautiful to me. I'm sure I'll appreciate the aesthetics much better when I'm on the outside of a coffee.

Oux Coffee's pneumatic welcoming arch is flagged either side by golden guardian lions. A cost-effective imitation of the old city gateways, these inflatables are hired for opening ceremonies and other celebrations. Maybe they are expecting us.

Inside a little wooden bridge trails over a pool of goldfish. The boardwalk to the stairs is so twee it might as well be paved with yellow bricks. It's mighty swish by Dengfeng standards. The restaurant obviously has delusions of grandeur. We choose a booth overlooking the square below.

There's something about VD and I that instils fear into Dengfeng serving staff. The Oux Coffee crew are no exception. We can see the fuwuyuan fighting over who is going to serve us and, as usual, the youngest and least experienced gets the rough end of the stick.

By the time they've finished arguing we've worked through the faux-leather bound menu salivating over the fabulously photographed offerings. As delicious as the food looks, the menu is another glorious train crash of cultures. I'm fluent in Wenglish, but the insane Chinglish diatribe makes my head hurt as my brain endeavours to wrestle the words into sentences. The opening page welcomes us with:

'Create a fine dining environment
You and I agreed common.......
To ensure food hygiene and safety, refused to
outer OUR food drinks!!!!
We will help you take good care of your children and to
prevent children fell cause unnecessaryharm, please
be assured Dining
If you always keep our casual elegance quiet
demeanor,your waiter will present the sweet s
mile
OUR pursuit of high-quality, all the apparatus

is designed specifically tailored to you drank
at the end was more
cautious can taste every bit if not cause
 losses to the price of your compensation.
I wish you a happy meal! !'

For a bear of little brain, like myself, it's all a bit much. I do hope it's not an indication of what's to come. Still holding her short straw, the office junior approaches in trepidation. Word of us must have spread through the local catering network.

Cheered by the thought of some quaffing and troughing, we attempt to put our waitress at ease by ordering most of the menu. Starting with a coffee each, VD has a couple of beers and I order a bottle of red wine. As a rule of thumb, it's good form to drink the wine of the country you're in. Local brew is designed for local cuisine, hasn't had the rigors of travel and is generally more economical. Given the ridiculous price of imported wine in China, it's a bottle of Great Wall for me.

After a commotion behind the bar, our waitress returns staggering under the weight of her heavily laden tray. Along with our booze and coffee she has also brought us two cans of Sprite and a large jug.

While she fumbles around, I get busy with the coffee. It's significantly smaller than the glossy picture implied and, despite the café's epithet, it's disgraceful. The characters in the café's name are Ou (European) and Xiang (style), so essentially the place claims European Coffee. I seriously doubt if it's even fulfilling the basic purpose of putting caffeine into my system.

It's not unusual to get a complimentary juice or similar in these places, but the Sprite is a new one on me. Intrigued, I watch her open the wine and pour half into the jug. She then opens a can of Sprite and proceeds to add it to the mix.

I hold up my hand to stop the sacrilege and release the jug before she can do any more damage. Filling my glass, I raise the crimson liquid to my lips eager for the fruity, alcoholic warmth. I'm no great wine connoisseur, but this tastes like it's been filtered through a horse's kidneys.

The horror on her face is incredible. She can't believe this savage is drinking neat wine. I must have looked like that when she tried to add the sprite. Although, having tasted it, I can't believe I'm drinking it either. As with most generalisations there's an exception that substantiates the rule. Chinese wine is vying for the unenviable position of libation that shouldn't even be drank in its own country. Chinese vintners must operate on the principle that, 'Its red and alcoholic, what more do you want?' For this price, I'd expect it not to have been fermented in a tramp's sock. However, even in these desperate times, I'm not prepared to dilute it with carbonated syrup water.

VD has more luck with his beer. A long, hard quaff is followed by a satisfied sigh, 'Now that is a tasty libation'. Beer or 'pijiu' was, brewed and consumed, in China as far back as 7000BC, but faded from prominence after the Han Dynasty (AD220) in favour of 'huangjiu', a low strength grain alcohol. Modern beer brewing was introduced to China in 1900, when Russians established a brewery in Harbin in Northeast China (formerly Manchuria) with other European firms following suit. The most well-known outside China is probably Tsingtao Brewery. Founded in Qingdao, Shandong province in 1903 by German settlers, the brewery became state-owned in 1949 when the People's Republic of China was founded.

Chinese beer has become increasingly popular since the 1980s, particularly since 2001 when the practice of adding formaldehyde to prevent sedimentation in storage was made illegal. Tsingtao is now China's second largest brewery with the brand sold around the world. The Chinese make a passable beer, and VD does his best to subsidise the industry, but its wine production has a way to go before getting my seal of approval.

Another couple of customers arrive and I watch them with interest. Reading of Japanese etiquette has made me realise that the Chinese outward appearance of civility is only skin-deep. The nouveau riche like to flaunt their wealth and possessions, but ultimately have no character to back them up. The pavements are a metaphor for the wider society. The polished marble is merely a thin veneer under which lies a jumble of building rubble. When the veneer cracks, the ramshackle foundations are all too visible.

To add to the images of spitting and urinating in the street, I cite the instance of today's waitress. A pretty, young girl wearing designer brands with bold labels takes the order from the other table while continuing her quest for gold. Knuckle deep in nostril, she only pauses her excavation to jot down an item or scrutinise her find and wipe it on her skirt. If that's considered acceptable as 'front of house', I dread to think what the backroom staff get up to.

It takes an age for our food to arrive, by which time the booze is starting to work its magic and our taste-buds are vibrating in anticipation. VD is in his element in any bar situation and is immediately more relaxed than he's been all week. And that's before the lubrication kicks in. We move the empties aside as the waitress slops a plate of brown goo in front of each of us.

Given the accessible alcohol, I should have numbed my senses more to better cushion the inevitable disappointment. Predictably, certain liberties have been taken with the menu. However, these illustrations far exceed artistic license, this is a clear case of false representation.

Fishing around in the gloop, I unearth some blackened sticks, which I presume to be chips. The larger cinder with a bone is probably the steak. No wonder the chef tried to hide it under a sauce. This hot sauce is right up VD's boulevard, but I am more dubious of the fiery goo. On the plus side, it does at least ease the taste of charcoal.

For a restaurant that supposedly specialises in European cuisine, they haven't the faintest idea. I'm guessing the chef has only ever seen pictures of the food he's making. I'm baffled as to why the place came so highly recommended. I shall be sharing a few choice words when we get back.

Sprawled over the seat, I survey the wreckage of empty bottles, cups and plates piled on the table. Despite paying a small fortune, and ordering half the menu, everything is wrong in some way. They've even managed to make a hash of the coffee. We would have been better off with the Chinese food we had last week. I suppose it's our own fault for having such high expectations. We should have learnt our lesson with the Dico's fiasco. Western food simply isn't a viable option in Dengfeng. Disappointed so many times the lesson is obvious: 'Ruxiang suisu' (when abroad, follow local custom.)

Bloated and unsatisfied, we stagger into a waiting cab. Feeling crappy, I'm reminded of last week's Chinese class. The lesson covered a trip to the doctor and we learnt several of the more common ailments that could befall us. I run VD through some phrases we learnt. As I get to diarrhoea, 'la dou zi', the driver explodes into hysterical laughter and swerves madly over the road. In any other country such erratic driving could have caused an accident, but in China it's a standard motor vehicle operational procedure. Besides I'm sure the guy would have got off scot-free for causing a multiple pile-up had he explained the mitigating circumstances of his actions to the judge. His court defence would go along the lines of, 'I had these two laowai in the car and one of them said poo'. I can just picture the jury rolling in the aisles.

At my Chinese language class, I heard a lot about the Chinese love of complicated wordplay and how Da Shang, the Canadian born Chinese TV presenter, is such a hit due to his grasp of classical puns. My experience is somewhat different. The comic appreciation I have witnessed has been solely based on the lowest common denominator. Physical humour goes down well and toilet humour is a guaranteed crowd pleaser. Our driver might be laughing his socks off now, but if he keeps driving like this he won't be so amused when he has to clean my la dou zi from the back seat later.

My turgid discontent has worn off by assembly, but I still feel obliged to share my views with the guys who recommended the place. Sitting on the steps waiting for the Shifus, I mention to Matt that we'd been to the Oux and that it was rubbish. He agrees, but before he can elaborate Knobby jumps in with his own complaints about Chinese versions of western food. On a roll, he continues to expand upon his theory.

I am embarrassed to say that for the greater part I must concur with him, but looking at the big picture, we've come to China to experience the place. The Chinese specialise in being Chinese and doing Chinese things. Expecting them to be anything else is a mistake. Be it food or mentality, the key is to enjoy the Chinese-ness.

My initial half-joking comment is taken out of my hands as the others are quick to jump in with gripes of their own. It's all the usual stuff until one of the guys complains about things missing from his room. I feel it's unlikely but, disturbingly, several others agree warning that we should lock our door as, 'The Chinese steal like ravens.'

I take the advice as it is intended, but am unable to follow it through. Even though I have now fixed our door so that it doesn't open of its own accord, we don't have a key to be able to lock it.

I can't really see anyone stealing from us. We are all so tired that the missing items are more likely to have been mislaid. However, rather than deal with the complication of anything important going astray, I decide to err on the side of caution. After class I reach for my trusty sword and set about making the lockers serviceable. There are four wooden lockers just inside our door. All of which are damaged. With a little imagination, I stick one back together with parts from the others. Clattering about replacing hinges and handles, I have a bit of a moan about the conditions here as, again, the lockers seem to have been deliberately smashed. VD responds by giving me a bit of gyp, 'Stop your moaning. You love it.'

It's not really the point I was trying to make, but it's a fair cop: I have turned into a low budget MacGyver. In my defence, it makes a welcome change to our routine and it's something to do other than read while VD is asleep, which is pretty much most of the time. A trait he shares with Adolf Hitler who was, purportedly, also an avid somnolist and probably not a big fan of bodge-job DIY either.

After the debacle of lunch, we are still not hungry enough to face school dinner. Skipping the bun fight at the canteen, I barge through the swarming ranks of pint-size germ mongers at the tuck shop and grab a dubious not-chocolate bar.

Knobby is already at the steps waiting for assembly. As the foreign contingent dribble forth, he desperately tries to get someone to join him playing hacky sack, but they all make polite excuses and stumble to the tuck shop.

The pair of pre-pubescent perils are in fine form and continue to test our limits. Unfortunately for Knobby he bears the brunt of their over familiarity today. I don't see the initial incident, but somehow Knobby managed to upset one of the little blighters. The first thing I'm aware of is Knobby huddled against the wall with his arms over his head while a tiny fury of tears goes medieval at him. The tearful, foul-mouthed, whirlwind kicks several barrels of bejesus out of Knobby before he's pulled off. Fair play to Knobby for not retaliating, but I hope he's learnt his lesson.

Alone again at evening training, I have to question the validity of coming here to train with no guidance. The idea of practicing what we have been taught in the day is fatally flawed when we haven't been taught anything during the day. I have enough experience to imagine I know what I'm doing, but I could be making it up as I go along, which is something I could have done at home.

When Fatso turns up for Tuck-in accompanied by Yuan Shifu I wonder if there's something afoot, but Yuan has merely come to share his interest in our visa situation, 'You need visa.'

'Do we?'

'How long your visa is? Show me.'

Further discussion reveals that school is offering to arrange visa extensions. China requires foreigners to have a visa (qianzheng) before they can enter the country. Longer stays require the visa be extended and have a Chinese sponsor. A complication we no longer have throughout the EU and which made navigating the Chinese visa application system seem particularly abstract. Just another obstacle we encountered prior to our journey. Our visas are up to date, so we're not concerned.

So much has happened since we last asked Shibu about our passports that I haven't yet had the tuneroppity to broach the issue with Yuan Shifu. As our visas are glued into our passports it neatly segues into the subject of their whereabouts. Yuan Shifu assures us that our passports are safe, but he can't return them as Shibu's room is locked.

More on the ball than the other Shifus, Yuan Shifu usually comes up with the goods, but his demeanour during the exchange doesn't inspire me with confidence. I get the distinct impression he's not being completely straight with us. My disappointment is nothing compared to VD's indignation. He's all for kicking through Shibu's door and ransacking the place this instant. At this rate Shibu will be coming back to an open plan room.

When they come to Shaolin, their behaviour changes.

Chen Tongshan

Any doubts as to the opinion of Shibu's squad regarding the training since his departure are answered at morning warming; less than half make it down the stairs. Waiting in the dark for Fatso, Yuan Shifu assembles our squad and, just in case anyone has had a change of heart, casually enquires as to our visa position, 'How is your visa?'

'Jolly good thanks, how's yours?'

'No, no! Your visa, where is?'

'Last night you told me Shibu had it.'

'Ah, ok ok.'

Meeting an equally interested response from my fellow students, he beats a retreat as Fatso arrives. Hardly bursting with alacrity himself, he appears unconcerned by the vote of no-confidence, Fatso doesn't even send Knobby to fetch the absentees. The number in attendance makes no difference to him, it's Go Run regardless.

Relying on the others to lead the way, I plod along behind. Running along the street I catch a scent of something unusual in Dengfeng; something pleasant. Following my nose, I almost pass the dingy doorway from which the delectable aroma leaks. With a shopfront no wider than a door, it's not surprising the other guys missed it.

The table blocking the entrance is mounded with fresh cakes hot off the stove. The beaming proprietor gestures to the golden domes and I waste no time in proffering her a 10Y note. Stuffed a bag with cakes, the cake-monger throws it on a scale and adds a brown cake from another pile on the top. I don't know if it's a treat for her most handsome customers or just to make up the weight. I shove the bulging bag inside my tracksuit and glance at my change. I've just spent 60p on about 70 cakes.

Cake in each hand, I sprint up the road taking alternate gulps of warm spongey goodness from either hand. They taste so good that I manage to expand my running repertoire to include eating at the same time.

When I catch up with the others it's clear I'm smuggling contraband, but with such economical goods I can afford to be philanthropic. The baked treats go down like hot cakes with my newfound friends. I've never been so popular. I may take up baking when I get home.

Not many of our missing comrades make it to breakfast. Those who do get to hear all about our wonderful morning of warming. I don't know what Shibu's squad were expecting, but they are clearly unimpressed by Fatso's pavement pounding workout.

An equally poor turnout at morning assembly doesn't improve the general disposition and Go Run around the kitchen block is even more lethargic than usual. Heading down the steps and out of view, we slow to a jog and practically stroll through the kitchen debris. Behind the kitchen, amongst the piles of ash and rotten food, a few Chinese students are hiding out. They've made themselves a little den with flattened cardboard boxes and are playing cards. The junior gamblers don't look up as we saunter past. In return, we don't acknowledge their presence. There are often little groups of kids ensconced around school. They are generally sleeping, eating or reading comics, but this is the most blatant breach of school rules I've seen to date. It's as if our dissatisfaction is contagious.

Rounding the last corner, we lay on a burst of speed for the benefit of any potential audience. Playing for the cameras proves pointless as Shifu has disappeared for a cigarette anyway. The facade merely makes me feel like a naughty child. How different to the skiving kids' card school is our half-hearted Go Run?

A dozen or so laps later Shifu returns all nicotined up and takes us to the gym for Power Stretching. We work basic stretches and kicks before getting down to business, but today's Power Stretching doesn't really cut the mustard. With no new students to laugh at, it lacks the usual excitement and the combined group means we get less of a turn each.

If we lack enthusiasm, its clear our Shifu's heart isn't in it either. While Fatso goes through the motions of mutilating us, some continue their own stretching, but the majority just sit and chat.

As ever, being left to lollygag merely gives the chance to air grievances. Today's theme centres upon our hosts attitude to foreigners, which tends toward ethnocentricity. It's a concept I'm familiar with. In Britain, we consider anyone from further afield than the next village to be a foreigner and there's nothing we like more than bemoaning how foreign they are. We even go to the next village just to see their foreignness for ourselves and to shake our heads in disbelief at their foreign antics. We are also very accommodating. We even built a dirty, great tunnel connecting Britain to the rest of Europe just so that we could bellyache about all the foreigners coming through. China, on the other hand, has a less whimsical view of its neighbours.

Traditionally, the Chinese considered themselves the centre of the world. The Chinese name for China, 'Zhongguo' even means Central Country, and regarded any non-Chinese as outsiders. The term 'waiguo ren' actually means 'outside country person'. The polite Chinese term for foreigner 'laowai' translates as 'old outsider'. The 'old' prefix suggests respect, however the term laowai is generally used with a hint of scorn.

Believing themselves to be the true 'civilised' people, the Chinese looked down on anyone else as 'yi' (barbarians) and built a great big wall to keep them out. Much of the 7000 mile long evidence still stands as a reminder of this conviction. As far as they are concerned, throughout history, anything any good has been invented in China or by a Chinese.

Mainland China closing itself to the outside world in the 50's and retreating behind the Bamboo Curtain did nothing to improve race relations and xenophobia was actively encouraged. Their experience of foreign influence meant the population didn't take a lot of convincing.

Following thirty years of isolation the recent opening of China has widened the minds of its populace, particularly those in search of commerce, but old habits die-hard. Not content with feeling superior to foreigners, Chinese nationals even look down on overseas Chinese calling them 'xiangjiao' (bananas: yellow on the outside, white on the inside), or worse 'chanza' (mongrels). The concept of racism being socially unacceptable has yet to catch on in China and our politically correct western minds struggle to come to terms with, and blanch at, the remnants of state sanctioned racism.

Everyone has tales to tell, but, living and working in China, Mason has a better understanding of the national psyche and is able to speak with authority. He cites tales of casual racism in the workplace. Openly racist to foreigners, the Chinese are particularly prejudiced against blacks and Japanese. In Britain to refer to someone as a 'foreigner' would be impolite, but as the distinction between locals and foreigners is more visible in China they see nothing wrong with stating something they see as so obvious.

From his observation, Mason believes the Chinese to have difficulty visually differentiating westerners' countries of origin and so use 'wai guoren' as an all-encompassing term for 'white people'. Koreans and Japanese are more easily identified and thus referred to by their specific countries while people of African descent are referred to as 'hei ren' (black person) regardless of their country of origin.

Whatever they choose to call us is academic. We are all in the same boat, which is currently a small one heading towards a stagnant creek without a manual propulsion implement.

Seeing how disaffected everyone is, Knobby wades into the conversation and attempts to endear himself to our brethren by asking the German guys if they are racists. Continuing to trample the golden rules of diplomatic relations, he mentions the war and follows with an addled synopsis of Nazi atrocities. From the proceeding ill-informed diatribe it's safe to assume twentieth century history isn't his forte. Not one to be taken in by cultural stereotypes, he proceeds to tell his roommates what exactly is wrong with their nation and its people. This is another of those times when I am glad to have disassociated myself from him. Fortunately, the German guys are cool. To their eternal credit, they laugh off his inanity and play along so an international incident is avoided. I thought these guys were good natured before, but they have now gone up in my estimation to the status of saints. I really don't know how they put up with him.

I know he means no harm, but he has inadvertently blundered into one of my pet peeves. Cries of racism, or any other 'ism', without grounds only serve to discredit real claims and belittle what some people actually endure. I can only hope he's not heard of Cultural Appropriation. Generally misunderstood, the term has been abused to such a ludicrous extent that it's lost the little validity it had. As a result, I'm never sure if I'm guilty of it or not. One thing the Chinese don't do is criticise us for being interested in their culture. On the contrary, I have always found them to be proud of their culture and delighted with us for taking an interest. A little surprised perhaps, but nevertheless delighted. And here are we westerners taunting each other's cultures and history.

Our missing compatriots are already at the canteen when we arrive and seem none the worse for missing out on the old Go Run and bit of a stretch. If anything, they seem more chipper than usual and the subject of visas is cheerfully raised. Some got so fed up with the impromptu visa-based spot quizzes that they went to the office only to be informed that a visa extension involves paying three months' school fees up front regardless of how long they wish to stay. Initially I suspected the denial of our passports was a ploy to prevent us absconding, but now I wonder if they will try to get us to fork out for another couple of months stay before miraculously finding them.

My post-lunch fruit acquisition routine ensures I'm early for afternoon assembly. The Chinese students' must have a different timetable and shorter breaks than us feeble foreigners as their classes are already underway when I appear. Also, their teachers don't keep them waiting, but get straight down to it. Sitting on the steps munching, I get to watch the classes in progress around the courtyard.

The class that takes place directly in front of our building is composed of about twenty children aged around four or five. This relatively small group is taught by a woman who they call Laoshi (teacher) rather than Shifu as we refer to our instructors.

She is also a lot stricter than our instructors and rules her dust mites with a rod of bamboo, which she isn't afraid to use. The kids clearly both respect and fear her. Having witnessed her teaching methods, I just fear her. Seeing her putting the kids into the splits is a real eye-waterer. She calls the command, 'Xia cha' and as one they stretch their arms out to the sides and swing their left leg up to the front. Dropping the leg, they let it follow through to the rear as they drop into position. Stick in hand, she goes around inspecting their efforts. If the stick passes under their groin she hits them on the outstretched hands with it. If they flinch they get hit on the head. Complainers are flogged into a happier state of mind.

One kid is a bit of a slow learner and gets a good going over with the stick before getting the picture. For the remainder of the lesson he blubbers away with his snotty nose dribbling down his grimy shirt front.

From my perspective it's difficult to watch the little kids taking a beating, particularly since they are as cute as buttons, but it's the way things work here. As they don't seem to take it personally, I fight back my self-righteous indignation.

Rachel is the first to surface and, having made her tuck shop purchases, joins me on the steps to watch the Grubby Monkey Show. The sobbing urchin is a tale she's familiar with, but despite being a Xiao Long regular, Rachel still isn't immunised to these teaching techniques.

As our bleary-eyed brethren begin to emerge, the stick-happy Laoshi calls break. She retreats to the mystical realm teachers inhabit between classes leaving the diminutive dirt mongers to swarm round their still whimpering brother offering moral support. Holding him on the ground between them they physically pull him into a front split position to spare him a further beating at their next lesson. Other than the beatings, the kids seem to enjoy the training and have a good work ethic and camaraderie. It's quite charming seeing them helping each other out like proper little Kung Fu brothers and sisters. In no time at all the kid is in the full splits with a great big grin on his face, which would be delightful if it wasn't also covered in dust and mucus.

To our delicate western sensibilities, it may seem a savage way to treat young children, but, for many of these kids, success at a martial arts school is their only way out of poverty. Often their parents sacrifice a lot to send them to schools like this. With such a massive population, the only way to stand out is to excel, which in turn requires discipline and hard work. There is a Chinese proverb that says, 'If you love your son, be liberal with your punishments; if you hate your son accustom him to dainties'. The parents of these children must really love them.

Traditionally, martial arts schools have been firm advocates of this 'spare the rod, spoil the child' policy and China's global success rate resulting from this strategy speaks for itself. The approach proved so effective that martial art schools, especially Shaolin, have a long history of taking in unruly children to be straightened out. So much so, it led some wag to coin the phrase, 'Shaolin Temple: Curing ADHD since AD495.'

Xiao Long continues this fine tradition with 80% of kids being sent here as problem children. Both amazed by this fact, VD sums it up best with the simple outburst, 'Dude, we've paid to go to Borstal!'

The kids may have been trouble before they got here, but there are no signs of any bother from them now. I guess being surrounded by three thousand people who know Kung Fu would put a dampener on the most rebellious streak.

Our Shifus, on the other hand, aren't so well regimented and we are subjected to another round of visa interrogation before Fatso arrives. It's like Ground Hog Day. At the beginning of each training session we are asked about visas. During breaks and at random points during the day we are approached individually and asked about our visas. Whenever the squads are assembled we are asked about visas. The management must be mad keen on this visa extension malarkey as I see the beginnings of a reoccurring theme. They must be on commission.

A victim of his own tardiness, by the time Fatso shows up, all the choice training spots are taken and he is again lumbered with babysitting Shibu's squad. Successfully hiding his delight, he marches us out the back of school, past the training field, and lines us up at the roadside. Pointing at the opposite kerb and back again, he explains the complexities of the exercise, 'Go run.'

Still wary of my aching knees, I think I'm doing well using my reach to advantage, but Shifu is less than satisfied with my performance, 'Noh!'

Getting us to stop, he demonstrates by throwing himself across the road, skidding across the surface gravel to the other kerb and scrambling back. Satisfied he has still got what it takes, he encourages us to follow his example, 'Fast, ok, go.' For all his skidding and flailing about, I don't think his efforts were any faster than mine.

The road may be quieter than at the front of school, but he is nonetheless encouraging me to play in the traffic. If I'm not exactly putting heart and soul into it, my efforts still far exceed the rest of the group. Shifu reconsiders the exercise.

Variations of Go Run and stance exercises on the pavement meet similar enthusiasm before Shifu gives up on us. Calling it quits, he marches us the long way around the block back to school.

Hotfooting it down the road, we meet a Chinese squad heading the other way and enjoying a good old singalong as they go. When marching in formation the Chinese students, particularly the younger ones, often chant little cadences. Just like the sort of thing I've seen in movies about US Marine boot camps. Although here the chants are generally based around the school song and work along the lines of, 'One, Two, Three,

Four. We are Xiao Long Martial School', but of course in Chinese.

Seeing these guys in full flow stirs something inside our Shifu who decides it's about time we got into the spirit of things with a gung-ho chant of our own. Nodding toward the other group he points at me saying, 'Hunh.'

I'm getting really good at decoding his grunts. This one means, 'Hey Welsh bloke. I'm not being racist, but you guys can sing, rustle us up a little number the like of which will put the other squad's chants to shame.'

I start with the standard, 'Zuo, zuo, zuo you, zuo'.

Delighted, our Shifu clamours for more. Had he counted on the result he would have quit while he was ahead.

'I don't know, but I've been told. Our Shifu weighs thirty stone.'

As I had the foresight to start this amazingly catchy ditty in English, the only word Fatso can understand is, 'Shifu'. Overjoyed with the compliment, his tired little piggy-eyes light up and a great big grin spreads over his dirty face. Puffing his chest out as we pass the other Shifus, he demands an encore. At this point I'm beginning to feel a little pang of guilt for picking on our Shifu, but I soon overcome any reticence as I remember the amount of Go Run he fobs us off with. Immediately I put my full creativity into further verses of this witty doggerel. Continuing the theme, my comrades are only too keen to chip in and we soon have the makings of a real chart topper.

Shifu is happy, we are happy, the sun is shining and all is right in the world. Just as the mood is finally picking up, Knobby's perverse streak kicks in. Through a combination of shouting and pointing, he gives Shifu the gist of what we've been singing. Shifu shrugs and pulls off an aerial (a no handed cartwheel) without breaking stride as if to say, 'I may be fat, skinny boy, but I can do this.' Which is doubly impressive considering his shape and effectively demonstrates his point.

Being overweight in China doesn't carry the social stigma it does in the west. A good appetite is considered healthy to the extent that the nickname Pangzi (fatty) is a perfectly acceptable moniker without a hint of fat shaming. Historically China often had difficulty feeding its expansive population and being fat was seen as a sign of success and contentment, which may be why many Chinese deities are portrayed as portly. Whereas the long periods of fasting mean most enlightened masters were more likely to have been on the skinny side.

The influence of western pop culture means carrying a few extra pounds is no longer considered de rigueur among modern Chinese. In the more cosmopolitan areas gyms and slimming clubs are springing up as the new generation aspire to images from TV and advertising. Our Shifu must be among those who subscribe to the old-school train of thought. It's nice to see someone sticking to tradition and not being swayed by the media and popular culture.

After break it's up to the gym for indoor Go Run. Laps complete, and in a change to the advertised programme, Shifu sits us in a large circle. Beckoning two people to come forward, he points his chubby digits to the centre and says, 'Shuai jiao.'

Most don't even know what he means, but, with his usual disregard for personal safety, Knobby is straight in there. Taken by surprise as his opponent grabs his legs he soon gets into the swing of things and has a good old flounder about on the threadbare carpet. Alternating between cuddling and physically abusing each other it's clear neither party has the faintest idea how to wrestle. At best they provide cheap entertainment, but as usual the majority are content to sit at the side in the guise of spectators.

Taking one look at the carpet based capers, VD purses his lips, shakes his head, says, 'Nope', and stomps off down the stairs.

VD's irascibility is making me sound like a far more tolerant individual than I really am. The fact is my snapping point is only slightly more robust than his and, were it not for him beating me to it, I'd probably be the cantankerous one.

I am, however, in accord with VD regarding a lack of desire to roll around on the floor with young men. I take myself off to the side and work on my form. I reason that at least I'm doing something productive and, as Fatso doesn't bother me, I can only assume he concurs. Maybe he's getting used to my eccentricities.

Catching a quick wash and brush up before dinner, I spot a new guy standing bewildered in the corridor. I can tell he's new because he's not covered in filth. Shiny clean Andre, from the U.S. is a cool guy. Just missing out on the grades required for his University of choice he's going to use the experience of a year at Xiao Long to make up the difference and get him in. We relay the very same advice we were given by Shaun a few weeks earlier.

Fortunately for Andre, the cavalry arrives and saves him from the benefit of our experience. Better organised than our mob, Yuan Shifu's group turn up en masse to escort their fresh recruit to the canteen and our advice proves unnecessary since he is now in more capable hands.

I'm heading to the Foreigner Seating Area with my rice and boiled cabbage when I pass the Shifus' table. I notice Fatso doesn't appear to be skimping with his meal. From his mounded plate it's clear that Knobby's comment hasn't phased him in the slightest. Although, there is always the possibility that he's resorted to comfort eating to ease the psychological pain of the hurtful remark.

Seeing Wouter sitting alone I make haste to plonk myself down opposite him. Wouter is always a delight. I've exchanged a few words with Wouter since he's been up and about and it's good to see him back to his old self. Ever the optimist, he isn't letting the present training situation get him down.

Having served his time in Dutch nightclubs, Wouter has had real world application for his Kung Fu and is used to a more practical approach to training. Unsatisfied with the level of instruction available here, he is dedicated enough to train himself and his good-natured outlook means he doesn't really get involved with the day-to-day complaints. Telling me about his previous career, I respond that he must have seen some interesting sights. He laughs, 'Ha, at end of night we clean up with fire hose. I turn hose on people to see if they dead.' I think he's joking, if not I hope there's something lost in translation.

After dinner the Tuck Shop Guy not only recognises me, but has a drink ready. I hate to be so predictable, but that makes it official: I'm addicted to Xiang Piao Piao. I don't know what it is about the sickeningly sweet concoction, but I am unable to pass the tuck shop without picking up a gaudy paper cup.

Evening assembly supplies unfortunate news. Proving my reservations regarding acrobatic class well founded, Knobby, who is much more flexible and acrobatically inclined than I, has nonetheless managed to break his leg. Ironically, he did this attempting the very move Shifu showed off with this morning. It looks like Fatso had the last laugh on that one.

Hobbling into line with his leg in plaster, Knobby complains he's spent the last of his funds on hospital treatment and will now have to stay at Xiao Long rather than move on to Wudang as originally planned.

Precious few people make it to the gym this evening. With my current level of motivation, it would be easy to start skipping classes myself, but this is the only chance I've had to get any real training today. I call it training, but without instruction, I'm doing little more than going through the motions as I understand them.

Another traditional expression adopted by Shaolin is, 'Shifu ling jinmen xiuxing zai geren ba', meaning, 'Teachers can show you the door, but it's up to you to enter.' This is interpreted as, 'It's up to you to practice and perfect what you have been shown'. Without the luxury of being able to train for the long haul, I need to train cleverly which means a few pointers and a little tweak here and there would make all the difference.

At bedtime Fatso barely sticks his head around the door to flick the light switch and his classic, 'Go sleep' is lacking much of its usual lustre. It seems we are losing ground with him again.

This sutra goes right for the heart of the matter, while mercilessly attacking all Ego trips that prevent us from waking up to our true heart.

Karl Brunnhölzl

With Knobby incapacitated and Julie convalescing from the Shaolin Slimfast, Fatso's squad is even thinner on the ground this morning. On top of that, Shibu's squad have chosen to vote with their feet. Dissatisfied with our man's performance yesterday, they likely saw their compatriots get away with not attending and decided to follow suit. I understand how they feel. Even under normal circumstances so much of what we do feels like an excuse to keep us occupied and it's especially true of our amalgamated squads at the moment.

If the combined squad makes for a poor show, our Shifu cares not a jot; it's all the more Go Run for us. At this rate of attrition there will be no one training by the end of the week, which I'm sure won't trouble Fatso in the slightest.

After breakfast, I take my laptop round for Knobby. I'm delighted to see his room hasn't changed since my last visit. It's exactly the same malodorous disaster area. His roommates have passed out after eating and, as a social animal, he's so starved of contact that he's pleased to see me. I have to admit lessons aren't the same without him.

While Fatso suffers no tardiness from his students, he is apparently allergic to punctuality himself. However, being fashionably late for assembly backfires on him today. By the time he turns up there's only VD and I left. Had he been earlier he may have been able to foist us on Yuan Shifu, and we would have been only too pleased to go, but Yuan has taken the other squads elsewhere and the opportunity has been lost.

So delighted is our Shifu at being required to occupy such a sparsely populated squad that he is unable to cope with the excitement. Thinking on his feet, he conjures up a cunning plan. Pointing to the back of school he says, 'Goh Pack.'

Flashing up a bunch of fingers he adds, 'Goh Fo xueke', which I take to mean, 'and you little scamps had better jolly well be back in time for Buddha Class.'

As we normally end up in the park on a Saturday, sending us there unattended is no more of a cop-out than usual. So, in an interesting role reversal, it's now my turn to give him a disinterested shrug, say, 'Ok' and saunter off.

His palm stops me in my tracks, 'Noh!'

Thinking I couldn't possibly have misunderstood such a basic instruction, I raise an eyebrow and give him one of my very best quizzical looks. His stern reply is to swing his arms and stamp his feet before emphatically gesturing at us and then the alleyway.

Always quick on the uptake, I gather he expects us to march to the park. My logic is that if he can't be bothered then he shouldn't expect me to be, but I've now learnt how to do things the Chinese way. 'Ok Shifu.' I nod and, with very little in the way of military bearing, go along with his request. No sooner are we through the gate than all pretence is dropped and we recommence sauntering. Along the training field, past the smouldering bonfire, out the school and up the road all without a single march.

Across the road from Wulin Park is a row of Xiaomaibu, small local shops. Nestled among the usual Wushu stores is a mini-mart. Taking up two ground floor units, the shop is practically a supermarket compared to the school tuck shop and, as such, warrants further inspection.

It's nice and cool inside and once our eyes adjust to the dimness we find the shop crammed to the gills with garishly coloured comestibles screaming to be compulsively purchased. Despite knowing better, we are unable to resist their lurid call.

We squeeze down aisles congested with boxes, crates and sacks to reach the shiny packets taunting us on the shelves. VD is in his element rampaging through the maze-like wonderland of artificially-hued snacks. Expressions regarding kids in sweetshops spring to mind, but I'm hardly any better.

Despairing at VD's purchases, the like of which I wouldn't normally give the time of day, I'm throwing similar items into the basket myself. Our bodies desperately crave energy and the ghastly provender is sending out all the right signals to get the metabolism excited. I have heard that one should never shop for food when hungry as the brain tends to over-compensate for the bodies urges. Ours must be working on overdrive. Even though I'm aware I am doing it, I find myself unable to stop and the Gruen transfer ensures we end up with far more than we really should.

The shopkeeper barely registers our presence as we mound our impulse purchases on the counter. Feeling our spree should at least warrant a raised eyebrow, I follow his gaze to the TV show that has him so riveted: a Kung Fu period drama.

Our exposure to Chinese TV has given me the impression there is never anything else on the telly. Logically, there's either one show on a continuous loop or all shows are exactly the same. I think I recognise one of the actors as Chen Xiaolong, our headmaster's son, but the characters are as interchangeable as the shows so I could easily be mistaken. Keeping one eye on the screen, the shopkeep shoves our haul into a molecule thin plastic bag.

Hauling our bulging bag of gaudily packaged poison across the road into the park, we follow the cutesy little path to a covered walkway. Hoping for a little peace and quiet in the shade we are thwarted by an agonised creature airing its complaints.

The tortured yowls of a wounded fox passing a kidney stone turn out to be a geriatric opera company limbering up. The small ensemble consists of a two-piece orchestra and a vocalist. A wispy-bearded old fellow wrings the life out of a jinghu (a small, two-string spike fiddle) while his lady friend with guban (a small high pitch drum and clapper) randomly add to the low budget improvisation of a piano falling down a flight of stairs.

Perched on the low wall on the side of the walkway, the musicians face their mate smiling encouragingly as she fills any space in the accompaniment with shrill nasal squeals. We seek sanctuary at the far end of the park and take up residence in an ornamental pagoda shaped like a sailing ship at the edge of an ornamental lake. Sitting ornamentally in the shade, we set about chemically enhancing our systems with the psychotropic carbohydrates.

Rooting through our cargo like a hyperactive bull terrier, VD opens the proceedings by tearing into a pack and tossing me what appears to be a Wagon Wheel. Visual examination passed with flying colours, I don't hesitate to commence the tasting round. My comrade's face tells me there is no need to mouth my verdict.

Looking for all the world like the spit of its European cousin, the brown disk serves merely to reinforce the old adage about judging books by covers. On seeing something that looks familiar the brain gears up for the associated experience, but in this instance is left unsatisfied.

The theme continues. Many of our purchases resemble products we are familiar with: Battenberg Cake, Twinkies, Wagon Wheels, Custard Creams and Fig Rolls. Others are more of a wild card for the sake of palette experimentation. The net result is the same. The seductive confectionary may look like products we know and love, but the similarity ends there. The stuff just doesn't deliver. At best, they could be described as flat.

My eternal optimism keeps telling me the next packet will be the golden ticket, but that merely makes each more disappointing than the last. When will we ever learn? As my expectations plummet, I begin to get excited by things being not bad. It's all relative I guess. Even so, most of our booty ends up in the bin as there's no point in eating poison that doesn't taste good.

Sampling on this scale soon adds up and it's not long before the combined E-numbers have my teeth and eyeballs vibrating so much that I have difficulty focusing. I sit quietly waiting for the seasickness to subside. Less taken by life on the ocean wave, VD quickly finds his land-legs and runs around the park taking photographs of his feet and fingers.

I've never really considered myself a nautical chap but, as long as I keep still, the near-boating experience is most pleasant. The multitude of Parkies do a fine job of keeping the place shipshape. Smaller and more relaxed than Songyang Park, Wulin Park is no less enjoyable. I've spent a lot of time sitting and watching life go by since being in China and Chinese parks are just the place for it.

Through my artificially stimulated haze, park-life unfolds around me. All the regulars are here: grandparents on babysitting duty entertain their charges, small groups practice their hobbies and oldsters out for a constitutional stroll.

Among the promenading pensioners is a respectably attired old guy rooting through the bins. Retrieving plastic bottles, he squashes them flat under foot, retightens the lid and pops them into his bag. I assume he's taking them for recycling and, if so, our school is missing a trick. With three thousand students, we get through a lot of plastic bottles a day. If this old guy thinks it worthwhile collecting a handful of bottles then our school is sitting on a goldmine.

Deflated with our breach of promise purchases, I'm now left buzzing from a gazillion artificial calories, but remain unsated. I've only been at this boating lark for half an hour and I know exactly how the ancient mariner felt. Hopefully a bit of Buddha Class can sort me out.

Ambling back, I spot a couple of our Chinese schoolmates hiding out at the back of school. There are a lot of Kung Fu schools in Dengfeng, yet whenever I see a kid skulking around in town or on the strip they are always wearing a Xiao Long tracksuit. It gives me a warm glow inside to be associated with such a proud and upstanding institution.

We are back at school just as I'm crashing from my sugar rush. Dazed and confused, I get into position outside the Buddha room where Andre has assumed the role of this week's new bloke standing behind me. All excited at the prospect of some Buddha'ing, he asks the procedure for when we get inside. I'm giving him a rough outline of the running order when he asks, 'How long until I get to light a joss stick?'

I can't help but raise a smile. It's exactly what I thought at our first Buddha Class. The high dropout rate means I am already approaching the front of the line and there's always someone new standing behind me, 'It comes around sooner than you might expect'.

I'm not sure what he thinks of the answer, but I understand his interest in the joss stick malarkey. Incense (xiang) is a staple part of Buddhism and commonly burnt at religious practice throughout East Asia. Chinese incense burning dates back to at least the Western Zhou Dynasty (circa 11BC) when scented grass was burnt to venerate deities. With the spread of Buddhism and Taoism, incense burning became central in Chinese society with incense offering (gong xiang) being an act of piety and prayer or to calm the mind for meditation. Stick incense (xian xiang) has a homophonic name meaning immortal scent. In the Song Dynasty they were referred to as incense inches (xiang cun) and used for time measurement. Burnt in ones, threes or nines, incense sticks are stood vertically to symbolise the prayers and messages being transported along the smoke. Ironically, while I remember Catholics go a bundle on it, I don't know much about incense burning in western religions.

Yuan Shifu stands at the Buddha room door monitoring us as we shuffle inside. Noticing my shiny, new beads he asks the obligatory, 'How much you pay?'

'Ten Yuan.'

He raises his eyebrows, 'Oh, you good at talk about price.'

Haggling or 'taojiahuanjia' is the national sport of China and possessing the slightest skill in the art, even by accident, has given me more credibility than I deserve.

With no one to help, Yuan Shifu takes control and leads the chanting in a much clearer fashion than Shibu does. I've converted the chants into pinyin, and am not struggling over the pronunciation now, but I'm very much a voice in the wilderness; the others are just humming along. My rough translation has given me a basic understanding it's just a shame this explanation isn't provided by the school for my classmates to share.

Thinking back to the mumbled explanation of the chants Shibu gave a few weeks ago, he may have been thinking of the five Buddhist precepts: Not killing or causing harm, Not taking things that are not-given, Avoiding sexual misconduct, Avoiding false speech and Abstaining from drink and drugs that cloud the mind. While that's a nice premise, it's not mentioned in the chants.

We use two chants at Buddha Class: the Heart Sutra and the Guanyin Praise Mantra. Composed in the 1st century AD, the Heart Sutra describes the nature of reality and the essence of Buddha's teachings. Summed up in the expression 'Form is emptiness, emptiness is form' the sutra encapsulates the philosophy of Chan Buddhism. Along with the Diamond Sutra, the Heart Sutra has become a Buddhist standard chanted at any relevant occasion.

The Bodhisattva Guanyin is closely associated with the Shaolin Monastery through its patron saint, Kimnara, who is an emanation of Guanyin. Also popular in Chinese folk belief, Guanyin is a source of unconditional love promising to answer the pleas of all beings and to liberate their karmic woes. The champion of the unfortunate, Guanyin is traditionally the protector of fishermen and sailors and, in recent years, has also become the protector of air travellers.

The meditation helps carry me through the sugar-crash of additive overdose, but I need some stodge to placate my system. For once I am looking forward to dinner for the food.

Filing out of the Buddha room, the Canadian girl behind me rolls her eyes and huffs in despair. Now I think about it, Julie doesn't come to Buddha Class so I guess it must be optional and fair play to her for voting with her feet. If this is the case, I have to wonder why some of these people attend. Although I'm baffled as to why some of them came to China at all. A few don't appear to be interested in the country, culture or the training.

Now we are all Buddha'd up Yuan Shifu lines us up for our weekly chastisement. Knobby inconsiderately breaking his leg neatly supplies the subject of this week's telling off which continues the on-going theme of, 'westerners are so stupid they keep making themselves ill.' The lack of instruction, adequate conditions and total absence of safety don't enter into the equation. The official line is that Knobby only has himself to blame for not being able to do something he came here to learn, 'If don't know how to do, ask you Shifu.'

I have to bite my tongue to stop myself saying, 'Have you met my Shifu?'

Mumblings from the group suggest this attitude isn't sitting well with them either. With dissent in the air, one of the Taiji students complains about the rubbish burning. Rubbish collected from the school is dumped on the exercise yard and burnt in a continually smouldering fire, with further tuck shop debris added throughout the day. The result is a permanent plume of black, toxic smoke which bleeds into our dormitory building like a malevolent ghost. Met with an empty expression, he presses on to query the environmental issues of this procedure. In bewilderment Yuan Shifu replies, 'No damage, is burn, all disappear.'

The group are awestruck by his statement. With this logic in play it's no wonder many of China's industrial regions are suffering horrific environmental damage and the more internationally visible cities, like Beijing, regularly make headlines with their smog attacks.

I vaguely remember a recent news feature about Western nations giving China large grants to encourage exploration of alternative fuels. It occurs to me that the money isn't the issue for the Chinese, it's their medieval attitude toward global impact. The official take on the situation runs along the lines of, 'You had an industrial revolution, now it's our turn.' With the west so reliant on China to produce low-cost consumables we are not in a position to kick up too much fuss for fear of upsetting our suppliers. Confronted by the row of dumbstruck faces Shifu repeats, 'No damage, is burn, all disappear.'

There's so much wrong with the statement that I can't begin to get my head around it. The others clearly feel the same. Providing us with another topic of conversation that will quickly devolve into more school criticism, Yuan Shifu takes tactical advantage of the silence to dismiss us for lunch.

Lunchbreak spent bellyaching, Shibu's squad have a pleasant surprise at afternoon training. They are the proud owners of their very own, brand new, substitute Shifu. He must be one of the 'First-class Kung Fu masters who have won the national level and the provincial level championship with rich experience and outstanding teaching achievement .... selected to the International Training Department.' All fresh-faced and shiny, he collects his excited group and takes them to the gym.

With our squad back to its core members, we have some good old Go Run before spending the afternoon doing the usual Jibengong out on the dust-patch optimistically referred to as a training field.

By dinner I'm not so much hungry as just glad to get away. VD is of a similar mind. Normally a dedicated trencherman, the catering hasn't been to his satisfaction. Unable to face another portion of rice and cabbage, he opts to self-cater from the tuck shop.

At the canteen Shibu's squad seem happier with their lot. Their new master is a young chap who they have taken to referring to as Little Shifu. His new epithet isn't ironic; the guy looks about twelve years old, but I'm guessing he's about seventeen. He must be a little sensitive about his age as his replies have got progressively older. Whatever he says now it's too late; 'Little Shifu' has stuck.

Back at the room, I find VD sitting up in bed, sporting a huge grin and a big pot of instant noodles. It's a strange state of affairs that this normally mundane product should now be considered the ambrosia of the gods.

Whilst at the tuck shop VD bumped into Wouter and got the news of the Zhengzhou competition. Outclassed in the stand-up fighting, Oli nonetheless managed to gain some credibility utilising his Judo skills to score a few takedowns. We have heard nothing about the event from official channels.

With time before training, I check on Knobby. He tells me Andre has taught him Wing Chun. I understand that Wing Chun was designed to be learnt quickly, but given that it's only taken them an afternoon and Knobby has a broken leg, either Knobby is extremely quick on the uptake or Andre is the best Kung Fu teacher in the world. I simply can't think of any other possible explanation. With this level of tuition on offer I would be a fool not to sign up for Andre's ad hoc Wing Chun class too.

Now that all the squads have their own teacher, it's back to business and evening training sees a record turnout. Shibu's squad mostly stand about chatting, but they are at least present and everyone is a bit more upbeat.

In an unusual turn up for the books, Yuan, Fatso and Little Shifu join us in the gym. Grasping the opportunity to prove himself in front of his captive audience, Little Shifu takes centre stage. Sensing a portentous moment, everyone stops to watch. Aware all eyes are on him, Little Shifu works through a complicated looking Taiji form.

He accepts the ensuing applause with an embarrassed grin, but it was clearly what he was hoping for. Personally, I don't think his display was that good. The mass-practiced Wushu version of Taiji, derogatively referred to as 'silk pyjama Taiji', is designed for performance and often lacks classical detail and basic principles. Still, the bloke's adopted squad are happy enough with him. However, it's difficult to share their joy. Not only am I jealous he gives a damn about his squad while our Shifu is busy dodging salad, but I wonder that now Shibu's replacement is suitably ensconced will Shibu be returning anytime soon?

My concern is not so much out of interest in his general location, but that of our passports. The way time moves here it's easy to lose track of what day it is let alone what's going on and Shibu being replaced has got me twitchy. We don't know how long Shibu will be away and whether he really has our passports or not. Until now the basic rule of thumb at Xiao Long has been: if you need something done, and you can't sort it yourself, go see Yuan Shifu, but his elusiveness on this issue has shattered my whole belief system.

Burden lifted, our Shifu is visibly happier at bedtime, but I still don't entertain the idea of asking him for help. Frustrated at our impotence, I'm also disappointed in him. I'm glad he doesn't linger. No sooner has Shifu flicked off the light than I'm starting to doze. My last waking thought is China is turning me into a sort of parrot.

LUOYANG, in the middle reaches of the Yellow River valley, has been occupied since Neolithic times and served as China's capital at various points from the Zhou through to 937 AD. While the drab modern city retains no atmosphere of past glories, there are two outstanding Buddhist sites nearby. Chief of these is Longmen Caves, one of China's three major rock art galleries, which rarely fails to impress with the scale and complexity of its giant figures and intricate miniatures.

China Rough Guide

With our daily routine so uneventful, I'm living for the weekends. The success of our excursions to date has imbued us with confidence and a full day off gives the opportunity to travel further afield.

Hailing a cab just outside school, the driver immediately asks, 'Shaolin Si?'

I'm prepared for this and give him my speech, 'Women yao qu Luoyang.'

'Ke yi'.

'Longmen Shiku duo shao qian?'

With no concept of a reasonable price we agree to the asked 230Y for the ease of getting underway. Particularly pleased with the negotiation the driver offers us a cigarette each.

The giving and sharing of cigarettes is an important social activity in China and until recently refusing could be perceived as being rude, but nowadays it's more admissible to say no. The accepted procedure is to smile and light-heartedly wave off the offer saying, 'Wo bu chou yan, xie xie', (I don't smoke, thank you). Even out in the sticks where attitudes aren't so cosmopolitan, foreigners can get away with slight social gaffs. Not being Chinese, we are obviously savages and therefore ignorant of social etiquette.

Our conversation has gone so well that our driver is under the impression I can speak Chinese. Unfortunately, the few sentences we exchanged have exhausted my repertoire. Also, my limited Chinese is text book, whereas the thick regional accent means I'm in the crazy situation where locals can understand me better than I them. As he rabbits away, I am forced to admit, 'Dui buqi, wo ting bu dong.'

This causes him to get a bit huffy and, with a final grunt, refuses to speak any further. He swings into a filling station in preparation for the mammoth journey to the next town. An oil-stained pump attendant hops to attention and sets about filling her up. Watching the dials on the pump, I notice it takes 40Y to fill the car. Suddenly our 230Y to Longmen seems like a lot, but our tight schedule makes the convenience of a cab essential as public transport just won't cut it in our timescale and it would be criminal not to take in as many sights as we can when they are on the doorstep. Henan province is regarded as the cradle of Chinese civilisation, dating from the Xia dynasty (2000BC), under the reign of the semi-mythical Yellow Emperor. As such there's a lot of history here and the Longmen caves are up there on the list of 'must see' wonders of the world.

Twelve kilometres south of China's former capital of Luoyang is Longmen Shiku (Dragon's Gate Grotto) a series of 1,400 caves carved into the steep limestone cliffs either side of the Yi River. Housing tens of thousands of Buddhist sculptures and calligraphy, the complex dates from the Northern Wei Dynasty when Emperor Xiaowen shifted his capital to Luoyang in AD493. Luoyang served as the capital for 13 dynasties with work on the grottoes continuing until AD1127. The late Tang dynasty rule of Emperor Gaozong and Empress Wu Zetian marked the peak of construction where an estimated 60 percent of the Longmen caves and temples were created.

Subjected to attack at several points, notably the 9th century anti-

Buddhist movement, the Ming and Qing dynasties (1368-1912) heralded a cultural revival and Longmen Grottoes received both national and international recognition. Changing fortune saw looting by the Japanese during the Sino-Japanese war and vandalism during the Cultural Revolution. Longmen has since been declared a protected national monument and added to the UNESCO World Heritage List.

The Zhengshaoluo expressway makes for an uneventful journey of around an hour, but getting onto the smaller roads our driver pulls over for directions. This is puzzling as there are signs for Longmen everywhere. Not only are the signs frequent and prominent, but the characters for Dragon and Gate are so common even I can read them. It's probably more a case of the Chinese urge to natter. Unable to converse for the duration of the journey, he's now feeling socially isolated and craves contact.

Passing a trio of security guards sheltering in the shade of a shrubby tree our man U-turns the car and asks if he is on the right track. Already lethargic from the warming day, a guard gestures vaguely in the direction we were going. The same direction the signs have been pointing. Spotting me in the cab, another guard gives a wave and says, 'Hello', but just grins when I reply in kind.

Navigationally reassured, we shortly pull up to the ticket office and our driver calls to the ubiquitous loafer propping it up. Disturbed from his cigarette break the loafer shouts instructions ref the entry procedure. Buoyant with his new information our driver repeats the instructions to us, but louder, and with more pointing.

The ticket station is for the electric coach across the river. The same sort of vehicle used at Shaolin. It's not far to the other side and, as we have been cooped up in the car for an hour, decide to walk. Paying our man, we set off toward the bridge only for him to call after us. Repeating the instruction with even more gusto, he points at the electric coaches, the ticket office and the opposite bank. There are other people walking on the bridge so I can't see that it's not the done thing. We just thank him again and continue on our way. He wanders away shaking his head at the crazy laowai who would prefer to walk over a bridge than ride in a glorified golf cart. It must conflict with his previous opinion of us as possessing more money than sense.

Within ten minutes we have crossed Longmen Bridge and follow the road through a coach park, to a tourist shopping street. The shops have all the usual tat we have come to expect, but as we are walking through one stall holder has a burst of initiative. Spotting the only two white people for miles, she points to us and calls, 'Hey, hey, hello, coffee.'

Not usually one to be swayed by such subtle, almost subliminal, manipulation I, nevertheless, feel the sudden urge for a hot, stimulating beverage. It feels an eternity since I've been caffeinated and we allow ourselves to be herded inside. I believe I've previously mentioned the Chinese ability to prepare western food and, sure enough, even an instant coffee is outside their remit.

Normally a sweet toothed chap, VD grimacing at his first sip of the anaemic concoction gives me a clue that all is not as it should be. Raising the lukewarm liquid to my lips reveals that during preparation the lack of coffee granules was compensated for with sugar. Will we ever learn? My teeth are vibrating as we get to the ticket office.

The 120Y ticket has four boxes printed along its edge relating to the four main sites within the Longmen complex: West Hill Caves, East Hill Caves, Xiang Shan Temple and the Tomb of Bai Juyi. Entering an archway under the bridge we just walked over gets the first box punched by a slouching youth.

The West Hill site (Longmen Shan) is the largest part of the complex and contains the more impressive sculptures, while the eastern bank (Xiang Shan) primarily served as residences for the monks.

The scale of the work is incredible and too much to take in at one go. Of the thousands of caves Guyangdong, commissioned by Emperor Xiaowen in AD495, is the earliest. The cave has three large images: a Sakyamuni Buddha flanked by Bodhisattvas. The slim features are typical Northern Wei style and still have traces of the paint that originally gave them life. Impressive now, these figures must have been visible for miles when painted. The walls have central Buddhas and three tiers of niches housing hundreds of statues along with inscriptions by the artists.

There are a fair number of people spread out along the route, mostly clustered around the more picturesque spots. Along the river bank VD spots a photo opportunity and, mounting a stubby, lotus shaped column, sits atop it in a cross-legged pose. The sight of VD in classic Buddha image causes much hilarity among the passing throng who form an orderly queue for some of the same themselves. The crowd at VD's inadvertently created photo-stop rapidly expands.

The ticket shows a route of the site and picks out three caves of note on the west bank: Wanfo, Bingyang and Feng Xian Temple. Wanfodong, or The Cave of Ten Thousand Buddhas, was commissioned in AD680 by

Gaozong and Wu Zetian. It houses 15,000 Buddhas carved in niches with the smallest being 2 centimetres tall.

Binyang Sandong (The Three Binyang Caves) were created in memory of Xiaowen's parents. Binyang Zhongdong, the Middle Cave, is said to have taken 800,000 men 24 years to complete. The three walls have Buddha figures flanked by Bodhisattvas representing Buddhas of the past, present and future. The canopy in the roof is carved in a lotus flower, but the two large bas-reliefs showing the Emperor and the Empress in worship have, reportedly, been stolen.

The Chinese Tourist Board never miss an opportunity to point a finger at Western nations destruction of Chinese cultural heritage, but little reference is given to their own peoples' acts over time. Warlords looting or local people scavenging for building materials is rarely referenced. The vandalism of the Cultural Revolution is especially conspicuous in absence of mention.

Other damage visible around the site rangies from the crude vandalism of disfigured faces to the evidence of looting of whole figures and heads. The damage is mostly limited to the lower levels because vandals and thieves are inherently lazy. The accident of being inconveniently positioned means many of the more impressive works have survived the ravages. Ironically, the modern concrete stairways and safety handrails now jeopardise the statues by making them more accessible.

Traversing the caves, one can see distinct differences in style, but we are not knowledgeable enough to make anything of it. Like the other attractions we have seen, Longmen isn't really catering for international visitors. Even the Chinese language signs are rudimentary so a guide book or some research beforehand is a must.

With so many internal sightseers eager to spend their newfound wealth, China isn't particularly interested in foreigners, especially outside the major cities so we rarely see any non-Chinese. However, when we do come across other westerners they tend to be loud, crass and very overweight and I'm vaguely uncomfortable by their presence. I'm embarrassed that they live up to the Chinese stereotype of us to the extent that I'm almost affronted by them. As they are equally determined to avoid eye contact, I can only assume the feeling is mutual.

Feng Xian Si (Ancestor Worshipping Cave) is the largest and most impressive cave and thus the classic postcard picture of the site. Constructed around AD676 for Empress Wu Zetian it is considered representative of Tang dynasty style and the 'quintessence of Buddhist sculpture in China.' The shrine inside the cave houses Longmen's largest Buddha statue the 17m high Vairocana Buddha.

The statue base credits the donors and artisans who worked here. Along with Emperor Gaozong, Wu Zetian donated 'twenty-thousand strings of her rouge and powder money' to complete this edifice. Just how much makeup did the woman wear? Vairocana's features are plumpish with a peaceful, natural expression which has led to the suggestion it was carved to resemble the Empress and has been referred to as the 'Chinese Mona Lisa'.

The sheer scale of Longmen is so overwhelming that it's impossible to take in the detail and appreciate the full extent of the work. I can't begin to comprehend the effort that must have gone in to this place. Confronted with so many notable caves it's difficult to pick out highlights. Many impressive creations don't get a look in as they are overshadowed by their bigger neighbour. A perfect example of this, and a cave I find particularly interesting, is Yaofangdong (Medical Prescription Cave). Dating from the Northern Wei dynasty and appended by subsequent dynasties the walls are inscribed with medical prescriptions ranging from the common cold to insanity. Allegedly many of these remedies are still used today. I'd love to be able to read them, but the ancient scripts are tantalisingly out of the scope of my knowledge and of the plentiful tat on offer at the shopping street there's nothing with any substance relating to the caves.

Crossing the Yi River via the Manshui Bridge we are back on the East bank at Xiang Shan where I spy a flatbed bicycle on the street corner mounded with green spiky footballs. The liulianguo (durian) has such a legendary reputation that I can't pass up the opportunity. At my approach, the seller cuts into the thick skin with a cleaver and pulls the fruit open. Tearing out half a dozen yellow, kidney shaped sections, he delicately places them into a plastic tray along with two toothpicks.

So odorous as to be banned on public transport in Singapore, it must surely taste fantastic. Otherwise why would you bother?

'Tastes like old socks.'

'I was getting more of a tramp's vest vibe.'

The dry, mouldy, sweaty taste has little to recommend it. I eat another couple of pieces, just in case I'm missing something, but it's a complete non-event. There's nothing about the taste or texture to compensate for the sensation of licking a locker room. As a foodstuff, it's simply not worth the unpleasant smell and lingering aftertaste. The boiled sweets I picked up in the supermarket to ease my throat now serve a secondary purpose in clearing the palette.

Not as heavily sculpted or as impressive as the West bank, this side is less popular with the visitors who seem to have reached carved cliff saturation on the first section. The three sites of note along this bank are Xiang Shan Temple, Bai Garden Temple and the Tomb of Bai Juyi.

Xiang Shan, the earliest of the ten temples at Longmen, was rebuilt around AD1707 during the Qing Dynasty. Located in the mid-section of the East hill, the name derives from the spices 'Xiangge' found extensively on the hill slopes. After the crowds it's nice to embrace the cool and calm.

Seeing us offering incense often attracts comment from other temple visitors. Generally, just raised eyebrows and knowing looks, but our actions here prompt an old lady to get her grandson in on the Buddha action. 'If those pair of funny looking buggers can manage it so can my boy'. Barely a toddler, he's oblivious to what's happening so his grandmother presses his hands within hers and bows him up and down at the altar saying, 'Amitabha, Amitabha'. He still probably understands what's going on better I do.

The grounds are relaxing after the hubbub of the West bank and even back down to the riverside the only other visitors in sight are a couple of grandparents with their little charge. They desperately try to get him to pose for photographs, but he's more interested in the two little plastic flowers he's carrying.

The riverside avenue is lined with statues of historical figures providing many photo opportunities for a pair of buffoons. One statue is of a Buddhist monk giving the Shaolin one armed salute attributed to Huike. The statues palm hanging in the air invites a hand slap and I get a picture of VD 'high fiving' him.

VD has clearly got an eye for a photo as it's the funniest thing the old folks have ever seen and lose all interest in their grandchild in order to take turns on the stone palm.

North of Xiang Shan, on Pipa peak, is Bai Garden Temple. Re-built in AD1709 by Tang Youzeng of the Qing Dynasty, the temple is surrounded by thick vegetation of pine and cypress trees and houses the Tomb of Bai Juyi. A government official during the Tang Dynasty, Bai Juyi is also a well-known poet. A devoted Buddhist, he felt great social responsibility and crafted his words to be accessible to the common man, even reworking them if his servants were unable to understand. Writing critically about what he saw in court led to an erratic career span and he was once exiled. Spending his last years at Longmen he referred to himself as the Hermit of Xiang Shan and requested a simple grave.

Exiting the Bai Temple grounds, we are confronted by a small group of young men hanging around on a bench. Looking to be about late twenties the spokesman of the group welcomes us by removing the cigarette from his lips. Throwing it to the ground, he advances toward me snarling, 'I hate America!'

I shrug, 'Don't go there then',

A little deflated he tries the same on VD, 'I hate America!', only to receive an equally interested response, 'You're barking up the wrong tree here, mate.'

During our stay we've become accustomed to being figures of interest for the locals. We are used to being pointed at and having random English words shouted at us, but this is the first time we have experienced anything resembling hostility from the natives. He obviously hasn't read the instructions on his ticket which clearly state, 'Everyone should live up to a civilized tourist. Please abide by regulations and keep clean in the tourist zone.'

In the winter of the 24th year of Jian'an reign of Eastern Han (219 AD). Guan Yu was murdered by the people of Sun Quan and passed away with righteousness. In January the 25th year of the Jian'an reign (220AD) CaoCao buried Guan Yu's head here in the ceremony of nobility and built this temple to memorize him.

More than 1700 years elapsed, the buildings of the temple were repaired many times, however the tomb remained well.

Nowadays Guanlin covers an area of over 200 mus and has over 180 rooms, over 50 paintings handed down from ancient times and over 200 pieces of sculptures, with lush and prosperous ancient cypresses and exquisite inscriptions. Solemn and dignified Guanlin is the only ancient classic building complex integrating forest and temple in China. As national key cultural relics protection unit and A4-class tourist attraction, Guanlin is also a tourist resort and saint place to worship Guang Gong (Guang Yu) famous at home and abroad.

www.Guanlinmiao.com

There are two taxis at the coach drop-off point, but the only person in sight is a well-worn old guy on the corner roasting sweet potatoes in an adapted oil drum. I've been so hungry lately that I struggle to pass a street vendor without sampling their wares. Time on our hands is time to eat and I make haste toward the vagabond potato man. Making an elaborate pretence of weighing the tiny dried-up spuds, he plucks an arbitrary figure out of the air, 'Forty Yuan.'

Making it clear he's in no mood to haggle, we pass up his extortionately priced offerings. If he's that attached to his produce he can keep it. Consummate grazers, the Chinese always have easily comestibles about their person and we have long since learned to follow suit. The gnarly old potato guy has misjudged us. No longer expeditioning unprepared, we are not desperate enough to be taken advantage of and break out our own provisions.

Munching Snickers, we are approached by a scruffy individual motioning toward the cab. Judging from the trademark leather jacket and half-buttoned shirt, I deduce he's a driver and open negotiations.

Asking to be taken to Guanlin only serves to confuse our man. Shaking his head, he explains we don't want to go there.

Insisting we do, I pull the old 'stroking a beard' mime out of the bag. It's a cheap shot, but his eyes light up and he launches into a mock battle using an invisible Guandao. Having established I do actually mean General Guan's Tomb, he again tries to talk us out of it. Digging a battered Luoyang tourist map out of his back pocket, he points out other attractions saying they are bigger or better.

Sticking to our guns forces him to change tack. Thinking on his feet, he informs us that the road is closed. In case I've misunderstood, he improvises a beautiful re-enactment of spade work. Obviously a frustrated thespian, this guy is wasted in his current position; he should be on the stage.

However, we haven't come this far without learning a trick or two ourselves. It's time for the old faithful 'shrug shoulders and walk away'. It's a close call as to who will cave first. Cabs seem a little thin on the ground, but the guy isn't exactly overrun with punters either.

It's a nail-biting few moments as both parties call the other's bluff. Ambling as slowly as humanly possible while still maintaining a semblance of movement, VD and I avoid each other's gaze in an attempt to remain poker faced. The tension is electric. I'm on the verge of giving in when the driver calls, 'Ok, ok.' Motioning us back he reluctantly agrees to take us to Guanlin.

Our little display of defiance must have earned us a modicum of credibility in his eyes as he offers us a cigarette each. Declining his kind offer we are soon underway.

Approaching Luoyang City, we come to a crossroads where the aforementioned highway renovation is taking place. Smack, bang in the middle of the road three workers are industriously hacking up the asphalt for no apparent reason. Wearing thin canvas shoes and army fatigues, the all-female team are laying into the road with picks and shovels amidst the traffic.

On top of our drivers warning, the scene catches my attention for two other reasons. In Britain it would be unusual to see an all-female group of council workers involved in heavy labour, it must be a side effect of the communist principle of equality. Secondly, European safety legislation means any council workers I see are covered in safety equipment. Cordons, barriers, high-visibility vests, hard hats, flashing lights and safety boots are just the beginning of a routine light bulb replacement. Strangely, without any expense spent on protection, these workers seem perfectly safe as the traffic just drives around them.

The trivial roadworks were a tenuous excuse, I wonder why our driver didn't want to bring us here. Maybe he didn't think we would appreciate it. There are bigger and more impressive sites around Luoyang, but none with the connection Guanlin has for martial artists.

Guanlin commemorates the iconic General Guan Yu. Easily identified by his trademark red face, long beard and guandao, a weapon he is now alleged to have invented, Guan Yu was born Guan Yunchang in AD160. During the Three Kingdoms period, he became a fierce warrior who wielded a guandao weighing 81 jin (about 40 Kilos). Fighting for the Kingdom of Shu, his skill in battle saw him rise to the rank of General. Further military success followed until he was captured and executed by Sunquan, the ruler of the State of Wu in AD219. Fearing revenge from Guanyu's blood brother Liubei, the ruler of Shu State, Sunquan sent Guanyu's head in a box to Caocao, ruler of Wei, seeking to deflect responsibility.

An admirer of Guan's loyalty and bravery, Caocao was not prepared to be framed for his murder. He had an eaglewood body carved to accompany the head and buried them with great ceremony outside the South Gate of Luoyang City. The temple built in his honour is now known as Guanlin.

Mausoleums of emperors were called 'ling', tombs of kings were 'zhong' and those of holy men and influential figures such as Confucius or Guan Yu were called 'lin'. Thus, Guanlin means 'Guans tomb'.

Tales of Guan Yu's bravery and faithfulness documented in the

302

classic San Guo Yan Yi (Romance of the Three Kingdoms) made him a legendary hero venerated in Shenism (Chinese folk religion), Confucianism, Buddhism and Taoism alike. In Shenism he is the god of law, fortune and war, in Confucianism he is the patron saint of brotherhood, for Taoists he is 'Wu Sheng' God of War, and for Buddhists a Bodhisattva and Dharma protector. At a time when many Chinese are losing touch with their history and traditions, Guan Yu is so ingrained in the national identity that he remains a folk hero nearly two millennia after his death. During the Lunar New Year pictures of Guan Yu are placed on doors to protect the home and he is honoured by fraternal organisations from police to gangsters. It is only polite that martial artists pay their respects when in the neighbourhood.

Luoyang has expanded considerably since Guan Yu's day and the old city gate, is now significantly inside the urban sprawl. The gate marker is composed of four columns forming three arches, the central beams of which often carry a place name or an inscription recognising the virtues or achievements of a 'local boy done good'. Used as gates or markers at the entrance to a town, building or administrative area, by the Song dynasty (960-1279) paifang had evolved into purely decorative, symbolic gateways. Following Guanlin road, our driver drops us at a public square. Even with the fairly negligible roadworks the ride has taken less than twenty minutes.

The midday heat is keeping the square pretty quiet. A few old guys are sitting at stone benches around the perimeter drowsily playing cards, smoking and chatting. There are also several grandparents with their charges, a common sight in modern China as both parents work to support their aspirations for their child. At the south end of the square, facing the gate of Guanlin, is the Wulou (Opera tower).

Fundamental to the performance and overall ambience of Beijng opera is the stage. Resembling a gothic cricket pavilion, traditional opera stages are square, raised platforms open at three sides.

Built in AD1791 the delicate Qing Dynasty architecture is grey and bleak compared with Guanlin's entrance. With the sun behind it, the stage is darkened by the buildings own shadow and the hazy mist of pollution serves to further blur the detail as passing traffic adds to the blackened exterior of the formerly red columns. A bit of spit and polish and I'm sure it would come up lovely.

I wish I could contact those opera guys we saw in the street the other day and tell them about this lovely Opera platform just going begging.

Dominating the view to the north, the bright red temple walls are emblazoned with four 10-foot-high characters. I can't read the ancient script, but apparently it says, 'Zhong Yi Ren Yong' or 'Loyalty, Righteousness, Benevolence, Bravery' the characteristics Guan Yu is famed for possessing.

One of China's three memorial temples to Guan Yu, Guanlin was originally constructed on the site of a Shenist temple during the Han Dynasty (206BC-AD220). By the reign of Ming dynasty Emperor Wanli in AD1595 it had expanded to more than 150 halls, covering 29 acres with thousands of cypresses inside. The temple's condition lapsed during the Cultural Revolution and the complex currently covers about 16 acres although excavations at either side suggest expansion. Restoration work in progress since 1994 has already seen Guanlin, the Opera Building and Marble Square renovated with donations from Guan Yu's followers.

The main gate now serves as a ticket office and a pair of majestic Ming Dynasty, white marble lions guard the automatic turnstile. Again, the turnstile isn't in operation so the lady who sells the tickets vacates her window and scoots around to check them manually before motioning us through.

Inside the compound, the bustle and pollution are left behind and we step into a timeless courtyard with a stone walkway around a central flowerbed. The period architecture houses an understated gift shop in the outer wall. The silver-haired proprietor looks up, nods and smiles kindly as we pass.

The tree-lined avenue follows the central axis toward the Qing Dynasty Yimen (Ceremonial Gate). Originally the main gate, Yimen was renamed when the temple was extended in the Ming Dynasty. The iron lion weighing 1.5 tons placed on guard at the same time, still stands proud 400 years later. The plaque above the central doorway contains the epigraph 'Wei Yang Liuhe' (Military Prowess known throughout the World) written by Empress Dowager Cixi (1835-1908).

As an example of the esteem in which Guan Yu is held, each of the three red doors are inlaid with 81 golden rivets, a symbol normally reserved for emperors and the temple is constructed along the form of a traditional palace befitting his status.

Suitably 'solemn and dignified' as per the sign, the brilliantly coloured buildings stand proud against the grey and green background of stone and twisted cypresses. As I have come to expect from a temple there are a lot of trees, many of which are draped in red ribbons. One ancient tree is round like an onion basket. In case the less observant miss this important feature the authorities have erected a sign pointing it out.

Integrated into the outer walls of this courtyard are the Drum and Bell Towers, 'gu lou' and 'zhong lou'. Placed side by side, horizontal to the centreline near the entrance of public buildings, Bell and Drum towers were historically used for declaring the time of day to the population. Since the Han Dynasty (206BC) most cities throughout China had 'morning bell' and 'dusk drum' towers. Silent today, the sober towers still command authority.

Through the central archway is Shi Shi Yu Dao a stone walkway lined with 104 posts topped with stone lions carved during the reign of Emperor Qianlong. In contrast to the grey stone the lions are all wearing cheerful red ribbons around their necks. Two large iron furnaces flank the walkway. Their soot-blackened openings evidence of their continued use for worshippers to burn joss items to their ancestors and make offerings to Guan Yu.

The First building, Qi Sheng Dian (Enlightened Sage Hall), is the grandest structure of Guanlin and where the memorial ceremonies are held. Built in the Ming Dynasty, it covers 760 square meters and the roof is covered with coloured glazed tiles and ornamented with pottery beasts. Tinkling bells hanging from the eaves sway in the breeze. Under the curled roof are plaques with inscriptions by Emperor Qianlong and Empress Dowager Cixi. Seated on his dragon throne, a statue of General Guan Yu looks down benevolently.

Kinder than the usual red-faced God of War incarnation, this golden-faced Guan Di wears an imperial crown with 12 tassels and an emperor's dragon robe with his followers at his side. On his left are Wang Fu and Guan Ping holding the official seal and on his right are Liao Hua and Zhou Cang holding Guan Yu's guandao.

Also known as Píngan Dian (Hall of Peace), this hall leads into a courtyard at the head of which are three Halls. The central building is Cai Shen Dian (Hall of the God of Wealth) with the smaller Wu Hu Dian (Five Tigers Hall) on the left and Niang Niang Dian (Goddess Hall) to the right.

One of the oldest buildings, Cai Shen Dian is where people pray for success in business. It holds a statue of Guan Yu standing proud with his glaring, red face and long beard moving in the breeze. His son, Guan Ping, stands on the left, carrying a sword while Zhou Cang stands on the right, with a guandao. Vivid paintings along the walls recount Guan Yu's valour from the epic Tales of the Three Kingdoms.

Niang Niang Dian is dedicated to Zhang Fei, Guan Yu's wife, who can be prayed to for medical issues while Wu Hu Dian honours Liu Bei's five great generals: Guan Yu, Zhang Fei, Zhao Yun, Ma Chao and Huang Zhong.

Running the perimeter of this courtyard is Shike Pianlang, a covered corridor displaying a collection of Luoyang's ancient stone works of over 2000 tablets and epitaphs related with important historical events.

Not so much an exhibition as a dumping ground for old stone works. The stuff is just jammed together with no accompanying material whatsoever. Apparently, notable pieces include the Eastern Han Dynasty reliquies, a Northern Wei Dynasty stone coffin and Sui Dynasty stone lions. It's difficult to tell which is what amongst the jumble, but I can't spot any of the mentioned items. It's a terrible feeling to have researched, turned up and still feel like a Philistine.

The final room along the centreline is Chunqiu Dian (the Hall of Spring and Autumn) built in recognition of Chunqiu (Spring and Autumn Annals) a Confucian classic favoured by Guan Yu, so his spirit could continue to read every evening. On the left a statue of the general reads by candlelight. Below the eaves three large paintings of Guan Yu in battle depict the well-known stories: 'Three Generals fighting Lu Bu at Hulao Pass', 'To Capture Jingzhou' and 'A Battle at Changsha'.

This room is also known as Qindian (the Bedroom Chamber) as the right side is dominated by a large bed holding a sleeping Guan Yu. Designed for the general's spirit to relax in, it almost feels as though we are intruding on his privacy. From this feeling I suppose the General to be buried here and I'm disheartened to see the musty room given so little attention and in need of a spruce up.

Leaving the chamber, I can still feel a presence and, as we continue around the building, the energy becoming stronger. VD turns to me, 'Woah, can you feel that?'

Reassured I'm not having a seizure, I take in the scene before me. A circular grassy hill with a supporting wall around its base. The energy here is palpable for a reason. This is where our man's decapitated head and wooden body were interred almost 1800 years ago. In front of the burial mound is the octagonal Feng Chi Pavilion which houses the Dragon Tablet commemorating Guan Yu's achievements. In front of the Pavilion is a stone paifang whose central arch is filled by an incense burner the size of a horse trough. Sitting next to this is an old lady selling incense. She has already grouped the incense into threes and obligingly points to the handmade 10Y sign on the table.

Offering up a 50Y note for two sets of joss sticks flummoxes her and she has to nip away to get change. It's a shame she didn't plan her cash-flow ahead as well. Transaction complete, she holds her hands together over her head and points toward the ding in the central arch.

It's fairly quiet here today, but I expect it gets much busier during exam periods and the like. According to the local tourism site, www.luoyangnianpiao.com:

'In the many lifetimes that have passed the Chinese people have revered GuanYu's, loyalty, humanity, bravery and spirit and aspire to act with his morality and integrity. Admired and respected by Monarchs, Military leaders and common people alike Guan Yu is honoured as the martial god, recognized by the people as a protecting spirit, ushering in wealth and prosperity by protecting merchants and managing good fortune and salary. The Cultural belief that he can assist in examinations, treat illness, avert calamities, drive away evil and judge and punish betrayers has become an important part of Chinese traditions.'

Taking turns at the paifang, we pay our respects. I don't know what the old dear thought we were going to do with the incense, but she looks satisfied when we are done.

Past the tomb, the grounds become unkempt parkland. According to the sign, Guanlin is the only temple complex in China to have a tomb, temple and garden like this. It certainly feels special as we walk around the tree covered mound. The scent of cypress trees mingles with the incense. The precious peace is a deserved resting place for a legend of a man who knew only war.

As with Zhongyue Miao, Guanlin has a great atmosphere. The visitors are a casual bunch, taking it easy, sitting around and enjoying the tranquillity. Mostly old folk who seem to be at home here, there are people practicing Taiji among the trees and meditating or just sitting around and chatting quietly.

It's a pleasure to sit in the shade and absorb the history. Dragging ourselves away from the serenity, we make for the exit via the gift shop. Even the gift shop is relaxed. The old guy smiles and nods again as we enter, letting us look around unmolested. Asking him about a Guan Yu statue, he is delighted we have some knowledge of the man and we wind up each clutching a statue as we stumble back out to the dusty heat of reality.

Outside, a couple of scruffy old beggars hang around the gate dejectedly. It's not a sight I'm accustomed to. Britain's social security system means we don't have many beggars back home. I understand that China doesn't have an unemployment benefit scheme, which I find odd for Communist country, although they do have a system for disability benefit. What's more, Chinese news recently reported on beggar gangs conning the general public and, even worse, people being deliberately mutilated to add authenticity to the scam. I seriously doubt that these old guys fall into either of these categories. Which puts me in a dilemma. It's hypocritical of me to give temple donations so that monks can have mobile phones and cars, or to buy incense and set fire to it to appease the gods, but not to give it to those who are in need and ask for it.

The unconditional giving of alms is a basic tenet of Buddhism and Taoism, as much to help others as to combat the illusion of greed and material possessions in the self. I've known people to act pious after making charitable donations, which goes against the whole premise, but all I feel is embarrassment at my relative good fortune. Seriously, anyone who is desperate enough to ask me for money must be really hard up.

My Buddhism teacher explained to me that our deeds determine our species in the next life and our charitable works determine our social position. Fortunately, I don't believe in literal reincarnation or I would be concerned about returning as an impoverished woodlouse. The pair are so grateful for the paltry sum I awkwardly push into their old paint pot that I must have done the right thing.

Having been so leisurely in our sightseeing, we don't have enough time left to visit Luoyang's other notable sites. I particularly wanted to see Baima Si (White Horse Temple), regarded as China's first Buddhist temple, but as it's been there since AD68, I guess it can wait a bit longer. Next time, maybe we can squeeze in the Ancient Tombs Museum as well.

We pick up a cab at the square without much ado, but once off the main road our driver asks for directions. Coming from the bustling city of Luoyang he is unfamiliar with Dengfeng and I end up directing him. There's not much at this end of town so my limited 'left', 'right' and 'straight on' get us where we need to be. In fact, our little excursion has gone so well that we are back in time for dinner.

With the prospect of lukewarm gloop hovering on the horizon I get the driver to take us past school and closer into town. Following the call of noodles, we head for a street which we know contains a row of Xiaochi Dian.

One of the best things about China is the food and the accessibility of it. VD wholeheartedly agrees. There's no shortage of quick bite shops and, selecting a noodle shop at random, we step into the tiled gloom to be welcomed by a wizened old lady. Everywhere we go there's a little old lady, I'm sure she's following me.

'Mian?'

'Liang wan, xie xie.'

She shouts our order through to the kitchen and resumes her seat on a folding chair next to a stack of brown earthenware jars. Sealed at the top with red cloth these jars are straight out of a period Kung Fu film.

VD clocked the winejars when we entered and is now desperately trying to play it cool. Worst poker face ever. He keeps glancing over as if the wine is calling him.

A grubby youth, wearing a once white chef's smock, shuffles from the kitchen and plonks two bowls of noodles on the table. Removing his thumbs from the soup he gives us a disinterested once over before disappearing.

Unable to bear the Sirens call any longer, VD cracks under the pressure, 'Dude we gotta got us some of that booze.'

Before I can respond he's on his feet and crossing the room. Normally content to test my limited Chinese, this is an occasion where VD is happy to get involved. The jars have the alcoholic strength and price on them in white paint which is all the information a connoisseur of fine liquor needs.

Pausing over the 70% alcohol, he puts his finger to his lips and furrows his brow. I know this to be his thinking face. Caught in a moral dilemma, he undergoes a slight pang of conscience as he reconsiders. Pointing to the 68% proof, he emphatically utilises his single Chinese phrase, 'Liang ge.'

Technically, it should have been, 'Liang bei' (two cups), but our hostess is more than happy to make the grammar concession. Telling him to sit down, she again calls for the kitchen monkey who brings a couple of the same bowls we have our noodles in. Holding the bowls for her, she fills them to the brim and he brings them to the table with a thumb in each. He's probably cooling his flabby digits down after sticking them in

309

our steaming noodles.

The syrupy liquid has a glossy, petrol-slick, sheen, which could be grease off the monkey's thumb. Almost thick enough to require chewing, the fruity bouquet belies the high-octane effect. I don't know what we are drinking exactly and perhaps it's for the best. Baijiu (white wine) is a traditional Chinese grain alcohol. Most Baijiu is made from sorghum although, like moonshine, it can also be made with any sort of crop that comes to hand. The local Mijiu (rice wine), tends to be a little more rustic than your average Baijiu and certainly lacks the sophistication of the stuff we got in the supermarket. The slightly nauseous smell of petroleum makes me wonder if this is the same 'sickly oily...Chinese rice-spirit' that Winston Smith referred to in 1984.

As my teeth dissolve, I realise allowing VD to make the wine selection may have been a fatal mistake. Out of the corner of my eye I see the old lady watching us. She can't believe we are drinking it either.

As a combination the booze goes down a treat with the noodles. She's visibly startled when VD orders another round. If I were capable of lucid thought I would be startled too, but find myself unable to formulate a protest. It's a strange intoxication. Along with the numbness of the Szechwan peppers, the rotgut has a stimulating effect whereby I feel my blood surging, but am still coherent. I'm wide-eyed and ready to take on the world which is probably not a good idea in a town full of martial artists.

Attempting to rise from the table, my legs fail to respond appropriately. To cover my inability to hold my drink, I feign a staggered-step and launch into a piece of a Drunken Kung Fu form. The old dear's face creases into a wry smile. She's not fooled, but you can't beat classic Jackie Chan.

Seated in the cool, dim light I wasn't feeling the full effect of the grog, but lurching out into the daylight is particularly disorientating.

I've just about recovered by evening assembly, but I'm still in no position for real exertion, so it's a shower and an early night for me. VD is already flat out, growling and snarling like a grumpy bulldog, so he must happy enough. I can only concur. We've expanded our range of exploration and visited another couple of 'must do' sites, VD had his booze and I'm beginning to regain my eyesight. All-in-all a successful day.

Feeling smug with success, I consider that perhaps our visits to Shaolin Temple were a bit mundane for our Shifu to find newsworthy.

General Guan's Tomb must surely carry more cache. When Shifu pops his head in for our evening catch-up I fill him in on our latest excursion, 'Today we went to Guanlin in Luoyang.'

A blank look is the only reply. In case my pronunciation is letting me down, I do the beard mime which has previously proved so successful. He gives a shrug, 'I know.' A metaphorical tumbleweed drifts past. After an eternity, my enraptured audience breaks the oppressive silence, 'Ok, go sleep'.

The light switch and the firm closing of the door put an emphatic end to the scintillating conversation. It's proving very difficult to excite a response from our glorious leader. I wonder does he perhaps think I'm showing off with my tales of wild adventure or is he really that uninterested?

To learn the forms for fighting is easy. It is possible for everyone to do
that in two or three months. To achieve serenity and endurance
however, this is difficult. One can always open the cage and let the tiger
out, but it is the tiger's containment that is the Tao. Everyone in the
position of Sifu or teacher should remember that it is not just the
fighting that is important, for anyone can learn to fight. It is the pursuit
of Tao that truly distinguishes the martial artist.

Hsu Hung Chi 1975

One who engages in combat has already lost the battle.

Traditional martial arts axiom

Today's formal assembly offers an uncharacteristic change in format. As
usual we join the rest of the student body at the main entrance and suffer
the same bewildering diatribe, but there's a twist. Instead of being
excused early, we tag on the end of a huge crocodile and march out the
front gate. With dawn breaking over the Song Mountains, the entire
student body runs in formation up and down Dayu road.

The Chinese students are in classes according to age, so members are
roughly the same size. However, size and ability vary considerably over
the age ranges so some groups move quicker than others which means

groups tend to collide. The result is our communal Go Run becomes a strange, staggered relay. We catch the group in front and are halted to allow them to gain distance before starting again. Similarly, as one group marks time at traffic lights, other groups pile up behind.

It's not an effective warmup, but despite the unconventional start to the day everyone is a lot more upbeat after breakfast. No doubt looking forward to training with their new teacher, Shibu's squad are out in force and Little Shifu has a full contingent for morning training.

Fatso is visibly relieved to be shot of Shibu's squad, but with Julie granted leave to visit the bank in town, he's not so keen to be landed with just me and VD. Taking us to the field, we drill Jibengong before he tires of our company and ambles off without a word. Unsure of how best to proceed, we break out the old Xiao Hong and bust a few moves.

Our audience in the Zhongguo Song Shan Shaolin Si Wushu Xueyuan are out in force today. Jammed up against the bars, their silent eyes bore into us, scrutinising every movement. It's a poor show if they are hoping to learn anything by watching me. Although, judging from the amount of time they spend at the windows, our neighbours get even less training than we do. Perhaps I'm the best source of information they've got. They are such a miserable bunch that they make us Xiao Long crew look like the Happy Gang. Maybe I've got it wrong and it's not a Kung Fu school but a juvenile correctional facility. I can't imagine how bored they must be to want to watch a pair of creaky laowai murdering Xiao Hong Quan. It can't be that much fun; we are not good enough to be instructive and not bad enough to be properly entertaining. I can only assume their telly is broken. Their blank stares and eerie muteness sit uncomfortably with me and we take advantage of our Shifu's absence to break for an early lunch.

At the canteen Shibu's former squad are in fine fettle so their new teacher must be working out for them. I wish we could trade ours in for a newer, more streamlined, model. One that was a teensy bit interested would be a start.

Just when my famous eternal optimism is beginning to tarnish, along comes the jolly cavalry in the form of a deranged Dutchman. Squeezing his legs under the tiny table, Wouter is a sight for sore eyes and is soon regaling us with a story of buying a suit. He needed a suit to take up a position in a nightclub and suffered no set-backs at all during its purchase, but is such a natural raconteur he has us in stitches. Wouter is so good natured that he doesn't see anything funny about his tale, which only serves to tickle my perverse sense of humour even more. The guy is an absolute delight and it's good to see he's no worse off after his bump on the noggin.

Never let it be said that I am stuck in my ways, for today I pick up an orange from the hole in the wall. It's one of those big-arsed oranges that have lost popularity in the west to the smaller, more user-friendly, varieties. Retiring to the front steps, I eat my lumps of sweetened sunshine while the little kids enthral me with Xiao Hong Quan. Part of the beauty of training here is the total immersion. We are constantly surrounded by martial arts and, as everyone else is better than me, I have plenty of opportunity to pick up a few tips. The kids growing up here must practically learn by osmosis.

Hands covered in sticky residue, I've not gone native enough to drop the peel on the floor. Getting strange looks from the Pink Overall girls, I cross the courtyard to deposit my peel onto the back of the garbage bike. While the orange tasted great it wasn't worth the faff. Another lesson learnt, I head to the room to wash my hands.

The lady, who I believe is supposed to be in charge of maintenance in our building, is still clad in the leather ensemble. She has now been wearing this outfit for at least four weeks. It can't be her uniform surely. Sitting on a low plastic stool inside the doorway, she holds court to the dozen Pink Coats seated in a semicircle around her.

Blocking the threshold, not a-one of them attempts to facilitate my entrance. Stonily avoiding eye contact, they manage to ignore the elephant in the room. 'Excuse me, coming through, watch your back, hot coffee, mind the doors', all fall on deaf ears as a six-foot white bloke clambers over them.

With Julie still away, Fatso spots further opportunity to get out of teaching us and catching up on his beauty sleep. Unable to look us in the eye, he mumbles, 'Go Sanda.' From his embarrassed mumble one might assume he was almost ashamed of himself. And this is my gripe. The Shifus know very well they are not doing their job properly. It's not a case of taking it easy on us because we are weak or old or foreign. They really are just on the skive and they know it. This is also why they don't like to be called on it; they lose Face when we rumble them. Yet here he is trying it again.

VD and I discussed this likely occurrence after our last Sanda lesson and agreed we had no desire to repeat the experience. It's not what we signed up for and it's time we could be spending on Kung Fu. I tell Shifu words to this effect, 'Bu Sanda, women yao lian Gong Fu.'

Firmer this time, he repeats, 'Go Sanda' and, putting his palm on my shoulder, attempts to shove me toward the Sanda line up. I twist my torso to deflect the push and continue to argue. I want him to teach me the Kung Fu he is supposed to and I tell him so. To reinforce the point, I gesture towards the Sanda class lined up next to us. As I turn Sanda Shifu erupts.

Waving his arms and shouting, he is clearly not amused. Little Shifu says something I can't catch, but it's obviously the wrong answer. Sanda Shifu goes ballistic. A single kick drops little Shifu to the concrete and Sanda Shifu is on top pummelling him. Recovering from the initial shock, Yuan and Fatso leap into action and pull the mentalist off the little chap.

As Little Shifu is being helped up Sanda Shifu grabs a wooden staff and breaks it over Little Shifu's head. Little Shifu is unceremoniously dumped as his rescuers attempt to restrain Sanda Shifu again. Not to be outdone, Little Shifu staggers to his feet and comes hurtling back with a stick of his own trying to hit Sanda over the top of Yuan and Fatso.

I'm spellbound by the shouting and posturing, but a few students are quicker off the mark and get involved trying to keep the two apart. Wouter puts his years of nightclub experience to good use. Crowding Sanda Shifu, he keeps him occupied while Fatso drags Little Shifu to safety inside the building.

Sanda Shifu is attacking the iron door with the splintered remnants of a wooden staff when a Security Guard turns up to investigate the commotion. A stocky guy in his early fifties, he more than fills his uniform and doesn't look like the sort of bloke who tolerates any hanky-panky.

Security work is a common occupation for martial arts school graduates so there's every chance this guy has some fight experience himself. He certainly looks handy. While I wouldn't fancy tackling the chap, Sanda Shifu's opinion on this matter must differ. He immediately squares up to the guy and an angry verbal exchange begins to escalate. Yuan Shifu gets between them and defuses the situation allowing them both to save the Face of backing down. However, the security guard isn't so easily placated and demands Yuan accompany him to the main building to make a report.

As the pair head across the courtyard, a seething Sanda Shifu orders everyone to the gym. Shell-shocked and Shifu-less, we are left with little option than to dutifully troop up the stairs under Sanda's glowering gaze. I decide to do what I'm told in Sanda class.

Predictably, the class is a bit of a non-starter. Once assembled Sanda Shifu tells us to stretch and turns to the sinks where he dusts down his tracksuit. He returns carrying a mean looking staff that he leans against the wall next to him. Thicker than the staffs we use in training this brute still has bark on it, so it's more of a log than a stick. It's also unlikely to break on impact.

Continuing to fume, he paces back and fore scowling. Out of nowhere his side-kick slams into the heavy bag. The bag swings back into place, but remains deformed in the centre. He's got a serious kick. A kick which I, for one, would not want to be on the receiving end of. VD gives me a raised eyebrow which I interpret as an echo of my thoughts. Seeing the way the land lies, everyone continues to stretch quietly while Sanda Shifu prowls the periphery occasionally smashing a kick or punch into a hanging bag. After nearly three hours of stretching Sanda Shifu lines us up to be dismissed and apologises for the lesson quality, 'Sorry I not teach you today.'

Personally, I didn't think it much different to his normal lesson, but we politely defer to his apology. Martin chips in, 'You are tiger Shifu.'

This is all the encouragement Sanda Shifu needs to begin his tale and explain the complicated social interplay that caused offence and triggered the altercation. Forcing the words through his gritted teeth, 'He kick me.' The very thought instantly has him seething indignantly again. He's so furious that he's unable to utter any coherent words through his shaking.

From the erratic machine gun stammering, I gather Little Shifu tried to get Sanda Shifu's attention by tapping him with his foot. Sanda Shifu, being senior, perceived this as a mark of disrespect that caused him a loss of Face (mianxi). Carefully considering his options, he decided the only possible retort to this social faux-pas was to psychologically urinate on the furniture by going bonkers on the little guy. I guess you don't get to be a champion Sanda fighter by being a calm and considerate individual.

It's another of China's paradoxes that a country that's tried to eliminate the concept of self through communism is still preoccupied with the egocentric concept of Face. Face is so fundamental to the Chinese psyche that it is summed up in the saying, 'ren hou lian, shu hou pi' (Men can't live without Face, trees can't live without bark).

Often difficult for westerners to fully appreciate, Face idiomatically refers to one's sense of social prestige, but in everyday terms it can be fairly straight forward. Although foreigners are not always expected to demonstrate the same exacting standards as locals, a general rule of thumb is to show respect to anyone older or of a higher rank especially in public or when asking for help.

Again, the influx of western culture into larger Chinese cities has led to more flexible etiquette and, of course, some Chinese are more conservative than others. Sanda Shifu is clearly a traditionalist when it comes to social interaction and not prepared to accommodate this new-fangled open-mindedness. Ironically, the outburst caused him a further loss of Face when he was unable to maintain his dignity in public.

Reports of Sanda Shifu's belligerence may not have been so exaggerated after all. I haven't learnt any Kung Fu today, but I have learnt a valuable lesson: don't mess with Sanda Shifu, he's a fruitcake of the highest order.

On tenterhooks throughout the afternoon, we are all relieved to get away. VD limps from the class having aggravated a previous injury by overstretching. Even more lugubrious than usual, the look on his face sums up how everyone feels.

Dinner sees moral at an all-time low. We've all suffered in Shibu's absence with the two classes lumped together, but today's fracas has given the atmosphere a turn for the worse. Just when Shibu's squad thought things were on the up they get the rug pulled from under them. While we are all astonished and upset by the incident Wouter is visibly traumatised. He handled the situation admirably, but this more than an adrenalin crash, 'You ok Wouter?'

'I'm ok. I just don't like see people like this, I'm ok.'

Unlike the steady diet of stylised, choreographed fights we are fed by the big screen, real violence is ugly and awkward. Far from seeming heroic the participants are, quite frankly, embarrassing.

I'd have thought Wouter's nightclub experience would have desensitised him to such brouhaha, but his good-natured outlook is clearly dented. He really is disillusioned in our teachers.

I've fallen for a similar thing with previous Kung Fu teachers. Believing their hype, I put them on a pedestal only to realise they were as fallible as the rest of us, in a few cases even more so. Even though our teachers here haven't been able to big themselves up, today's incident has still tarnished their image.

It was difficult enough to respect some teachers before this fracas. For those in Shifu Fatso's group the traditional Confucian etiquette of respecting teachers has always been a troublesome to demonstrate. At best, Fatso is lazy and disinterested. Not a winning combination in my book, but at least he's not mental. With our Shifus so fatally flawed, the expression, 'Yiri wei shi, zhongshen wei fu' (a teacher for a day is a father for a lifetime) just doesn't hold water here. Others are not so reticent with their comments. Having only just received a Shifu, they are now back to being Shifu-less and feel, some might say deservedly, aggrieved.

The recent complaints about the state of the timetable and training are just the beginning. Soon they are recalling all the wrongs inflicted on them during their stay. It's almost a competition. Tales that begin as harmless, humorous diversions soon lead to resentment and the overall feeling is that Sanda Shifu's explosion has been brewing for a while.

Historically, China emphasised a code of ethics which permeated all society. These ethics were embodied within martial arts as the concept of 'Wude', a martial virtue similar to the European Knights supposed code of chivalry. Still valued today, the International Wushu Federation's stated aims of Wushu are to cultivate health, develop self-defence and instil virtue. The esteem in which these martial ethics are held can be seen in traditional expressions along the lines of, 'Before learning Wushu techniques one has to know courtesy, before practicing Wushu techniques one has to know virtue.' Maybe it doesn't apply to Sanda teachers.

It's unfortunate for Little Shifu that his professional disagreement involved Sanda Shifu. This may have been his first teaching job and maybe someone else would have cut him a little slack. Hopefully, he's learned to keep his head down until he establishes the pecking order in future.

Evening assembly shows no sign of Little Shifu. It would seem that, in the competitive world of Kung Fu teachers, winner stays on. Being a man down, Shifu Fatso lumps the groups together and Little Shifu's mob, formerly known as Shibu's squad, are once again attached to Gimp Squad.

Summarily dismissed with a surly, 'Go train' the few who make it to the gym just sit around complaining. The wave of euphoria that accompanied little Shifu's arrival has proved short-lived and the general mood is even more despondent than before.

When Shifu Fatso doesn't come to tuck us in, I feel a little denied, but the fact he doesn't show his face speaks volumes.

Xiao Long Martial Arts School
The cradle of superstars, Kung Fu base
The example of famous schools. Train Kung Fu skill hard
Make body strong and keep fit, struggle hard
Compete for number one.
I am a member of Xiao Long Martial Arts school
I take each oath with solemnity
I formally abide by school rules and school discipline
Uphold the schools honour, Know good manners and honesty
Have civilised behaviour, Study diligently and train hard
Make a determined effort and win
Be determined to be a gifted scholar. Repay society

The Oath of the Xiao Long Martial Arts School.

Looking forward to being let loose at the old MW, I drag my exhausted carcase out of bed as VD hits the snooze button and mumbles, 'I ain't doing no Go Run.'

Blundering downstairs into the darkened courtyard reveals he is not alone in his decision for there is no Little Shifu and no Yuan Shifu either. It's left to Fatso to combine the groups and take us through the usual warming motions. I try to show willing, but it doesn't look like anyone is

319

feeling the love this morning. For all the effort injected we may as well have stayed in bed too.

Ever the trooper, after breakfast, Shifu Fatso begrudgingly continues his endeavours to hold things together by taking charge of all the squads. I'm pretty sure he didn't notice VD's absence earlier, but he is under the impression that Go Run hasn't sufficiently warmed us. Ironically for VD, this means Fatso takes the uber-squad out to the road for more Go Run.

The dusty, sleepy back roads are uneventful until we hit a pocket of civilisation. In anticipation of the heat Victorian Dad has worn shorts, but the good people of Dengfeng aren't prepared for the sight. Their consternation manifests in a range of physical comedy of which the Chinese are so fond. Absolutely everyone we pass stares at his tattoos while attempting to remain nonchalant. This results in a whole bunch of poker-faced people bumping into each other, walking into lampposts and falling off kerbs all for a glimpse at VD's illustrated limbs.

Once considered the preserve of gangsters and criminals, tattoos in China are another area being influenced by western trends. Becoming more popular with the cosmopolitan youth, they clearly still draw a crowd out in the sticks. Most adults attempt to be reasonably subtle with their gawping, but passing a primary school finds the little tykes less reserved. A troop of grinning, pint-sized heads jam up against the railings desperate for a glimpse of the strange foreigners. They are well impressed by VD's leg tattoo of a severed tiger head impaled on a fork, 'Wow! Look at that!'

I feel guilty about letting VD loose on these impressionable youngsters. In a few years these kids will be old enough to have tattoos themselves and I dread to think what the population of Dengfeng will look like when that day comes.

Plodding along the previously uncharted territory, it's a good job I've got people to follow otherwise I'd be completely lost. There's a lot more of Dengfeng than I had realised and regular signs of building work in progress mean the place is growing at a rate of knots. With nothing of note along the route, the foot-slog is boring and pointless. As I'm not the only one taking it easy, the others must feel the same. Bruce Lee subscribed to the theory that running was the 'king of all exercises', but I'm sure he would've changed his point of view after a week here. At least the extra generous allocation of Go Run means by the time we get back even VD has managed to work up enough of an appetite for lunch.

From the overall tone of canteen conversation, I deduce that no one is happy with the current training. The reoccurring conversational theme wearing thin, we adjourn to our room for a cuppa. A pleasant side effect of the lack of student interaction between classes mean we are not constantly exposed to the ill-informed bellyaching.

Tuck-shopped up and waiting for class, it seems there must be something in the air as it's obvious the little kids' teacher is also feeling out of sorts today. She has acquired a tiny plastic stool and alternately barks commands and sips from her tea flask. If she's anything like my primary school teacher then it's probably gin.

The look of thunder on her face scares the bejesus out of me. Having seen what she's capable of on a good day, I just hope the little urchins know well enough to keep a low profile until the malady lifts.

She does have a very nice tea flask though. It's much posher than the plastic jobby I picked up in the supermarket. It looks like the ones they had in a locked cabinet. Too rich for my blood, settled for the poor relation at 5Y. Not only are the flasks incredibly practical, but I felt obliged to get one as they're virtually compulsory in China and not being a native I wasn't issued with one at birth. I couldn't be without it now.

A cross between a thermos flask and a jam jar the 'cha bei' enables the constant swigging of warm tea or other herbal infusions. Topped up throughout the day, the interesting blends of leaves or flower heads make them look like portable aquariums. Carried by all walks of life from high-powered Business Execs to lowly Shoe-shines, I've even seen delivery boys with flask holders on their scooter handlebars. All of which is facilitated by the ever-accessible provision of hot water. The Chinese love drinking hot water. Recommended in the Huangdi Neijing for health, hot water is such a staple that airports, train and bus stations and public toilets all have hot water stations and some buses and trains have a guy who comes around with a big kettle.

Tea jars are so ubiquitous that they are barely acknowledged by Chinese airport staff. In Europe a ban on liquids over 100ml being carried on board was introduced in 2006 after an Al-Qaeda plot to use liquid explosives was uncovered. In 2007 China's Civil Aviation Administration introduced a similar rule for international flights, although passengers on domestic flights were permitted to carry liquids (excluding alcohol) not exceeded one litre providing they could be opened for inspection, thus giving tea flasks the green light. Even when the allowance was reduced to 100ml in 2008, tea bottles are such a common appendage that they go through unchallenged.

As my brothers dribble forth, I can see they're not looking forward to afternoon training. Shibu and Yuan were barely keeping us on track as it was, but now they are both AWOL, the training has gone to pot and I'm glad to get to Chinese Class. This week's lesson is a pleasant surprise as we get to learn the school song. I vaguely recognise some of it from the dirge mumbled, coughed and farted through at Monday morning assembly. I may be able to join in with more than the farmyard sound effects next week.

The song sounds very different with our teacher singing it. She has the voice of an angel and omits much of the accompaniment I'm familiar with. The class are stunned by her magnificent rendition, until someone stammers that she has a beautiful voice. With self-effacing modesty, she blushes, 'Thank you.'

She's fully aware she can sing well, but is uncomfortable with our recognition. Many Chinese are embarrassed by compliments and will deflect praise. Accepting compliments like this was, until recently, considered contrary to the ethic of humility. In Confucianism modesty is a virtue and a respectful manner a sign of an educated person.

The virtue of modesty influences Chinese character to show restraint, respect and be attentive to group-consciousness. This was especially true for women who were expected not to speak highly of their own merits and to downplay the achievements of family members in public. Even complimenting their children in front of others would be considered a lack of manners so a Chinese mum would praise her child indirectly by criticising them in order to receive a complimentary response from others.

The ideal is still prevalent today where a host will apologise for the quality of a meal before it's served and martial arts demonstrations begin with the performer asking the audience to excuse their poor skill. Typical traditional responses to receiving praise or gifts are humble disclaimers along the lines of 'na li' (literally 'where?', but means 'it's nothing') and 'guo jiang' (flattery) and may even respond by listing their deficiencies. This 'modesty' still permeates Chinese culture and, generally speaking, only the younger and more westernised would respond with a, 'Thank you'.

It's always a tough gig to follow a pro, but, having heard how it should be done, it's now our turn. Personally, I subscribe to the adage that, 'If you can't sing well sing loud' and go at it with gusto. I'd like to think the teacher appreciates my enthusiasm.

Collecting VD for break, I find the room full of flies. Hundreds of the little buggers cover the surfaces and swarm in the air. I give VD a friendly poke and question him as to his new friends, 'What on earth you have been doing?'

Still dazed he mumbles, 'Whah, where did they come from.'

'You know we're not allowed pets.' I light a joss stick from our temple stash and place it at the far end of the room hoping to drive the buzzing intruders out.

After break, it's out to the field. In an attempt to occupy everyone simultaneously with minimum effort, our Shifu concentrates on group activities. The Jibengong goes ok, but he's not providing the level of detail the other squads are used to. Their requests daunt Shifu Fatso so much he bails and resorts to Touchy Knee. Few join in and when they realise there's nothing else planned they soon lose interest and seep away too. Some work their own stuff, but most join the little groups sitting in the dirt and chatting.

We students seem to fall into two disparate groups: those who live in fear of missing a training session and those who will do anything rather than train. The current trend has seen a shift toward the latter group.

Touchy Knee being such a lack of success, Fatso gives up and leaves us to our own devices. This is fine and dandy for me. With Xiao Hong Quan under my belt, I am now able to look at another form. The next forms in the school's syllabus are Qimei Stick and Plum Blossom Broadsword. My style of Kung Fu uses versions of both these weapons, but Shaolin forms are performed so differently to the Southern forms I know that I am concerned about compromising the techniques I've spent so long developing. I decide to boycott the next forms in sequence and move on to a weapon that isn't included in my style.

Being a family style, Lau Gar Kuen has only a small number of forms, whereas Shaolin has hundreds. This gives me massive scope to experiment with the more unusual weapons. The school weapon shop is surprisingly limited, but a root through the low-grade selection in the dark hut, uncovered a nine-section chain whip (jiu jie bian).

Breaking out my new toy must pique Fatso's interest as he waddles over with his hand out, 'Hunh.'

Giving the weapon the benefit of his expert appraisal, he concludes it to be good, 'Hunh!' After an experimental swing, he is just about to get jiggy with it when SA guy comes along and hijacks his attention. Not usually such a conscientious trainer, SA guy suddenly feels the need to master the entire form right here and now with no detail omitted.

SA guy is a personable, almost charming, chap, but I find his self-centeredness trying. Receiving some personal tuition from Fatso, he is not content to practice, but continues to barge in on my session demanding limelight. Being told to wait or practice what he has just been shown only results in a tantrum. Fatso lacks Shibu's English and force of personality to deal with SA Guy, so gives in as a quick fix. This isn't as long-term solution. Just like training a puppy, all this does is encourage his behaviour.

Over the years I've suffered the same thing at home. I've been overlooked because of my lack of natural ability, fobbed off by teachers who favoured other pupils and stood on the side-lines while more vocal students dominated the time. These same people invariably dropped out and I still wasn't deemed worthy. Essentially, I was just forking out money for other people to be taught the things I wanted to learn. I ended up forced to steal Kung Fu by eavesdropping. Not that I'm bitter. Eventually I saw through the romantic nonsense indoctrinated into me from old movies and realised Kung Fu teachers are human and subject to human flaws. Shifu Fatso is no different, but I haven't come all this way to have the same treatment.

This afternoon's interruptions are so frequent that I believe him to be extracting the Michael. No sooner has Fatso returned from helping him than he asks for more help. After the umpteenth interruption, I give Fatso a look that isn't open to interpretation and he finally puts his foot down. Shoving the protesting SA guy back to his allocated piece of dry dirt, he tells him to wait his turn.

Weapon in hand, Fatso comes to life. Casually launching into action, he effortlessly loops and releases the whip from his arms, legs and head. Shown how it should be done, he indicates I should give it a whirl. For ten minutes I get the closest thing to quality time I've had with him to date. Unfortunately, while he can show how it should be done, he's unable to provide anything in the way of meaningful instruction and I just have to imitate the best I can.

It's just a shame we can't communicate effectively. Had I not believed the schools creative advertising, I would have been more diligent with my Chinese studies before I came. That said, my Mandarin is better than most of the foreign students and they seem to be getting by ok. Although many don't go out of school much and their Shifus have a better level of English than our Fatso, so it's not such a necessity for them.

Making the best I can from his advice, I set about endangering myself and those around me by copying what I've seen. I've never thought sado-masochism appealing and the novelty of whipping myself with a metal chain begins to wear thin very quickly. Fortunately, I'm using the light weight one or I would have beaten myself to death by now.

Loads of Chinese students play nine-section whip and I've noticed they've attached pennants near the pointy end of their chains. It makes the whip more visible when it's moving at speed and gives a satisfying sound as it does. It's the Shaolin equivalent of putting a playing card on your bicycle spokes.

On closer inspection, the pennants are actually any bits of rubbish the kids could get hold of. In a true Chinese 'make do and mend' philosophy, miscellaneous food wrappers, sheets of magazine, anything found lying around can be transformed into a pennant. I'll jump on the bandwagon and cut a piece of material from a shirt I've ruined.

At the canteen, VD comments my Chinese is improving. I wasn't especially happy with the way things were going, but I suppose I am using more Chinese these days. Shifu even seems to get the gist when I do. The combined result of immersion and necessity gives me confidence. Our Chinese lessons aren't a great help but, being constantly surrounded by Chinese speakers, I'm picking it up subconsciously.

I'd done some evening classes before we came, but I'm amazed by how many foreign students have turned up with little or no Chinese language experience at all. Those who don't speak much English either must surely struggle. Given the trouble we had finding the school, I don't understand how some of the guys managed to even get here. Those of us with English as a first language are in a much better position, but it does make us lazy.

Laughing the language barrier off, Marco, confides he says, 'excellent' when too tired to think and 'for sure', when he doesn't understand. I now realise Marco has understood very little I've said since we got here.

As usual, it's a subject the others guys have ready opinions about. They need no encouragement to air their dissatisfaction at the Shifus who spectacularly fail to live up to the advertised, 'The school's Shifus (masters) are all highly accomplished Kung Fu practitioners and those responsible for training international students can speak English.'

At assembly I ask Shifu how best to attach a pennant to my nine-section whip. He offers to take my whip and do it for me later. Overwhelmed with confidence in him, I pretend not to understand. I thank him and keep hold of my whip. This way I might have a bit of trial and error with the flag, but at least I get to see my whip again.

I give myself a break from the self-flagellation and work some basics in the gym before getting down to dervishly whirling my arms and slapping the floor. It's not great, but I'm getting there.

Fatso is not his usual cheery self at Tuck-in. With the weight of the world on his shoulders, he gives us a resigned, 'Ok go sleep.'

The fact he doesn't mention my whip or flag confirms I made the right decision.

The school has clean, neat, capacious and bright restaurants, and separating eating is offered for foreign students. The meal, with varied diet and agreeable to taste, can fully meet diet requirements of students from all over the world. Foreigners have the same dining hall with Chinese students but they can choose between numerous food.

Xiao Long Website.

With the timetable in disarray, the Shifus missing and Fatso struggling to give us any meaningful training, VD isn't the only one slacking off. I appreciate very well what's happening with the other groups, it's difficult to maintain motivation when the very people you rely on aren't delivering the goods. In a way, we are fortunate with Fatso; having such low expectations of him, he rarely lets us down. He doesn't seem to mind the declining numbers, probably because it reduces the pressure on him.

Returning from a particularly lacklustre morning warming, I attempt to jolly the old Grouch along for breakfast, 'Wakey, wakey, eggs 'n bakey'.

If I overcompensate for my real feelings in exaggerating the bill of fare, he remains unconvinced and growls, 'I ain't eating no more rice.'

Not a great success with the old jollying. In a complete reversal of our initial reactions to the school, I have docilely slotted into the school's mechanism while VD becomes ever more truculent in his rage against the machine. As it happens, he misses nothing; it is rice again.

After breakfast it transpires that Fatso can't be bothered with a small group either. I usually try to show willing and keep myself occupied, but when Fatso tells us to, 'Go Park', I opt myself out. Fatso must notice, but says nothing as I sneakily defect. Picking up a Xiang Piao Piao at the tuck shop, I infiltrate the other group and accompany them to Mandarin class while VD heads back to Bedfordshire.

Following yesterday's roaring success of the school song, our teacher continues the theme with a traditional folk song about a jasmine flower. Mo Li Hua gives her further scope to demonstrate her beautiful singing voice, but I'd like to think I give her a run for her money. Yet again my heritage shines through. While others may disavow my vocal talents, they cannot deny that I compensate with enthusiasm.

Mo Li Hua dates to the Qing Dynasty (18th century) and, used as a temporary national anthem by Qing Chinese officials touring Europe in 1896, became the first Chinese folk song widely known outside China. The tune is still played during Central Communist Party meetings and at international ceremonies like the handovers of Macau and Hong Kong, the 2004 Olympics closing ceremonies and the medal ceremonies at the Beijing 2008 Olympic Games. Mo Li Hua is so well associated with China that it has become 'a cultural symbol of China' and placed on the UNESCO list of recommended songs. There seems to be a UNESCO list for everything nowadays.

For all its fame, I only recognise the song because it's on a tape loop at the Temple. Having heard it so many times, it's nice to get the gist. I could even sing along now.

Mo Li Hua

Hao yi duo mei li de mo li hua
Hao yi duo mei li de mo li hua
Fen fang mei li man zhi ya
You xiang you bai ren ren kua
Rang wo lai jiang nai zai xia
Song gei bie ran jia
Mo li hua ya mo li hua.

What a beautiful jasmine flower
What a beautiful jasmine flower
Sweet-smelling, beautiful, stems full of buds
Fragrant and white, everyone praises
Let me pluck you down
Give to someone
Jasmine flower, oh jasmine flower

Unfortunately, it's all our teacher has planned for the lesson. After working through the translation, we spend an hour singing the song over and over. Relieved to get out for break, my heart sinks when the next session resumes where we left off. No one else seems phased by the prospect of spending the next hour and a half singing the same lines over and over, but I'm not so keen.

Last weeks muddled exchange with the bun flinger has encouraged me to become more sociable toward her and the ladle wallah. To this end, I ask our teacher for the names of the food served in the canteen. She takes no persuasion to change tack whatsoever, it's almost as if she didn't want to hear another rendition of Mo Li Hua either. Thus inspired, she bases the rest of the lesson entirely on foodstuffs. The only ones that are relevant in school are, 'mantou', 'mifan' and 'yecai' (steamed bun, boiled rice and cabbage). I could have done with this last week.

I'm still glad to get out for lunch. I spend most of my time here looking forward to meals which is strange because I'm usually disappointed by them. Dropping off my writing book, I again endeavor to entice VD to partake of a little repast, 'Grub up!'

'I'm really tired of this rice.'

It's like he's read my mind. I may have mellowed since my first impressions were made, but it doesn't follow that I'm overjoyed with the place and I'm rapidly coming around to VD's point of view regarding the food. Learning the entire menu in three words really brought the point home. Added to the ever-growing list of things I won't take for granted in future is home cooking. It's not that the meals here are particularly bad, they're just so repetitive and bland. Not only do we have the same meal three times a day, but it doesn't taste of anything. The main source of agricultural fertilizer means vegetables have to be boiled within an inch of their life for safe consumption. Thus, the tiny random vegetable portion we receive is little more than mush with no taste, texture or nutritional content.

Obviously no fans of the Fletcher theory of mastication, the kids just throw the food into their faces. Although our rations barely require any chewing. I suspect the reason everyone here eats so quickly is that there is no pleasure to be had from the process. It's just a case of trying to fuel the body out of necessity and shovelling the stuff in before the brain registers what's happening.

I'm not generally considered a picky eater. Of all the things that might spring to mind when thinking of Wales the cuisine doesn't immediately suggest itself. To compound the issue, I'm also from a culinary challenged family. My Dad's specialty is a deep-fried pork pie, although he actually cooks everything in the chip pan, and my Mam maintains that, 'You have to make sure it's cooked right through'. Subsequently, I was fifteen before I knew food came in other flavours than black. Nevertheless, the dearth of variation here is even beginning to take its toll on me. I'm finding it increasingly difficult to face meals. In spite of my hunger, I'm now struggling to finish a single serving. It's practically turning to ashes in my mouth.

If I'm not particularly enamoured with the canteen offerings, at least I am able to stomach the provender, whereas VD has reached the point where he can no longer force the stuff down his gullet. The food is so boring that his body has no interest in it.

We occasionally see kids at the canteen with food other than rice and cabbage. It's high time we investigated. By and by, we spot a kid with something on a stick returning from a small window in the far wall of the canteen.

Peering into the tiny cubicle reveals a limited range of optional extras consisting of Day-Glo cakes and nameless, batter-coated, lumps on sticks. There's no real sustenance on offer, and it all looks highly dubious, but at least it could offer some variation in texture or taste. It may even contain meat.

Normally Buddhists abstain from eating meat, however Shaolin warrior monks were granted exemption from this rule by the second Tang Emperor, Li Shimin, in AD625. This mixed blessing only applies to martial monks, 'Wu Seng' and not scholar monks, 'Wen Seng'. Although the average Buddhist also has a get out clause in the expression, 'Jiu rou chuan chang guo Fozu liu xinzhong' meaning, 'food and wine are not important as long as Buddha is in your heart.' A phrase eloquently delivered by a smiling Jet Li after eating his friend's dog in the Shaolin movie.

330

The actual content of the batter-coated products is ambiguous and the cakes are of such neon colours as to invite a migraine just looking at them. It's enough to give the European Food Standards Agency apoplexy. However, VD is so disaffected with our daily rations that he attempts to purchase the psychedelic offerings. A complicated process of shouts and gestures brings me to conclude that we are not welcome.

With the cake wallah singularly uninformative, we go in search of someone who can tell us the score. Bumping into Julie outside the tuck shop she informs us that canteen transactions require an electronic token which can be obtained at the canteen entrance. Why the Cake Obstructing Guy couldn't have told us this is beyond me. I understand his wanting to turn us into an SEP (Someone Else's Problem) rather than deal with us personally, but would it really have been any more effort to help rather than to flap?

We return to the canteen and queue at the meal token window for another round of arm waving. After much ado, we hand over 20Y deposit for the token and a further 100Y to top up the credit. We receive a pair of pink slips and are motioned to the adjacent window.

I've seen a lot of this labour intensive, task duplication since we've been here. I don't know whether it's a form of job creation, fraud prevention or simply bad planning, but there's often any number of people involved in a role which should barely keep one person occupied.

We queue for another ten minutes at the next window, not because they're busy, just that they take an eternity to carry out the simplest task. Not only could the staffing be streamlined, but if they were given an iota of training maybe they wouldn't find their jobs such a chore.

I present the pink slips at the second window. The occupant glances at them, shrugs her shoulders and motions the next person forward.

This is Chinese customer service at its best. Generally, I can make myself understood, but rely on the other party's patience. My Mandarin is limited enough that I have to formulate sentences in my head before I can say anything and then decode the answer making half-educated guesses around the few words I recognise. This shambolic process is not helped by being so tired and hungry that I'm essentially running on empty. If my conversation buddy becomes impatient, and asks another question while I'm still cogitating on the previous, it can force an infinite loop until one of us gives up. But that's not what's happening here; she just isn't interested and utilises her selective understanding to bypass the problem.

Not prepared to queue at the first window again just to make her life easier, I start badgering the woman. It's to no avail. She acts like she's doing her job properly by following the rules, but it's just going through the motions of her job description. Very few staff are willing or capable of thinking for themselves, as a result there's no quality in the service they provide.

Seeing that she's not the accommodating type, I resort to the old speaking English loudly trick. Pointing at the guy from the first window, who is sitting beside her, I say in English, 'Ask him, he's sitting right next to you.' She shrugs and points back to the first queue. This lady's clearly not for budging.

Tired and hungry, my tolerance levels aren't what they could be, but VD's are shot. Defeated by superfluous bureaucracy, he throws his arms in air and walks. I understand the despair only too well. Battling with Chinese jobsworths is a truly soul-sapping experience. The school's internal mechanism turns so slowly and needs so much encouragement that it's rarely worth the effort of getting the wheels in motion. It would be a lot easier and quicker to get things done if the organisation wasn't so overly complicated as to be chaotic. It's not surprising that, as a communist country, China has no shortage of Red Tape, but the strict demarcation of workers roles is a right pain in the proverbial. Maybe it's a cunning master-plan to discourage anyone ever asking for anything. It's certainly coincidental that shopkeepers and taxi drivers are able to understand me, yet school staff find me unintelligible.

Chinese customer service varies between two extremes: complete disinterest or rigidly sticking within the job description parameters. They opt for whichever will be easiest for them. Methods of choice for dealing with foreigners include: feigned ignorance, treating you like an imbecile and, the classic, pretending you don't exist. Choosing to argue or failing to disappear means digging in for a protracted battle of wits. They go through the motions of service, but haven't quite grasped the concept yet.

With this attitude I don't understand how they ever get anything done or manage to stay alive. They must be stationed behind these little hatches for their own protection as I could gladly rend anyone of then limb from limb.

Our trip was inspired in no small part by Antonio Graceffo. Others have written of training in China, but Graceffo made it sound accessible. Reading 'The Monk from Brooklyn' I was, at times, galled by his intolerance. However, experiencing the same situations myself, I can now perfectly empathise with his desire to run amok amongst them on a rampage of slaughter.

The Gods take mercy on our frustrated souls with an angelic vision. A Chinese girl from Berlin, Min Yi is the very person we need. As a group, we foreigners spend a lot of time relying on each other and everyone is always happy to help out. Min Yi has been looked down on by the locals for being a 'Banana' and just about reached saturation with their attitude. Being used to German efficiency must make it even more difficult to fathom the Chinese method of operating. For whatever reason, our tale touches a nerve and she feels obliged to take us under her wing.

While we have effectively given up, she is simply not having it. Marching us back into the canteen, she thrusts the form over the counter along with a generous dose of the old verbal. There's nothing as ferocious as a protective mother.

Thoroughly emasculated, and a little abashed, we hide behind our diminutive big sister while she lets rip. I have no idea what she says, but it certainly does the trick. Within seconds VD is sheepishly accepting his yellow plastic fob from a contrite hatch lady. It's probably just as well we can't make out what she mutters under her breath.

Min Yi gracefully defers our thanks. As I try to work out what just happened, she confides that she finds it particularly galling when the locals are deliberately obtuse. I reason that these people have had fifty years of indoctrination and are only just learning how to think for themselves. Regardless of my platitudes, she is another whose tolerance is wearing through.

Initially shell-shocked by her fury, I almost feel sorry for the fuwuyuan, until it occurs to me that if she could do it for Min Yi then she could have done it for us in the first place. This is yet another school procedure that should have been organised on enrolment.

Back upstairs, the grumpy hatch guardian acts like he's never seen us before, but we are un-phased. Pointing at everything in sight and saying, 'Liang ge' repeatedly, VD strives to burn through his fob credit in one fell swoop.

This is where the limit is revealed. The fob has limited expenditure of 15Y a day, 7Y a time. As very few items fall below the 7Y price limit, I can only assume that there is a scale of rations for students and teachers otherwise most items here would not be saleable. The school's inflated prices ensure our budget doesn't go far and within seconds we have spent the allowance on two pieces of cake and are hot-footing to the room to get the kettle on.

Predictably the cake disappoints. However, it was worth the rigmarole for the fob itself. VD now has options with his meals and settles down for his afternoon nap slightly more content than usual. Hopes dashed by the cake imposter, I seek solace with a banana on the steps.

I'm minding my own business and munching the potassium stick when a Korean kid starts kicking at me. Getting into an actual fight with a child would be a no-win situation so, instead of beating him like a red-headed step child as he so richly deserves, I'm left with little option but to stare down an eight-year-old. I console myself with the thought that it's what Caine would have done.

My sense of guilt is soon absolved as he moves on to one of the German guys and tries the same with him. Within seconds, the little blister has received a slap for his efforts and is wailing away with tears streaming down his face. The German guy is obviously contrite, but no one can blame him; someone was going to have to do it sooner or later.

At assembly, Fatso continues to manfully bear up under the strain of his burden. Pointing squadzilla to the kitchen block he mumbles, 'Go Run.' I must be particularly perspicacious today as I had a feeling he was going to say that.

Seeing that we aren't putting heart and soul into our kitchen circling, Fatso comes up with a new method of motivation. Picking up a section of a broken staff, he makes a pretence of chasing us while slashing wildly in our general direction. His aim is deliberately miles off as I'm sure even our beloved Shifu is aware our tolerance is at breaking point and that waving a stick around could very well get him turned into a lollipop.

Regardless of his big stick, I do a few laps before I peel off to stretch. Again, he clearly notices, but turns a blind eye, continuing to intimidate the others to, 'Go fast'.

It doesn't take a genius to see that their already frayed tempers aren't going to withstand much provocation. As the volume of grumbled protests increases, Fatso wisely quits while he's ahead and sends us inside.

In the gym, Fatso proves there's no end to his imagination by pairing us up for a Wheelbarrow Race. Already put out with today's extended Go Run and the canteen fob fiasco, VD has now had enough. Delivering a catalogue of choice expletives, he walks off in a huff muttering, 'No fat Shifu tells me what to do!'

Face like a kicked puppy, Fatso obviously understands VD's

sentiment if not the specifics, but what can he do? Asserting authority at the moment is likely to result in open rebellion. With a pained expression, he gives an awkward shrug and partners me with Mason.

As much as I've been trying to remain motivated, I'm aware the system has been wearing me down, but I hadn't appreciated how psychologically and physically drained I've become. I thought my body was adapting to the conditions, but clearly not quickly enough. It doesn't take many laps before my arm strength fails and Mason has to practically drag me down the hall.

Equally mundane exercises follow which convince me that VD had the right idea in opting out. Not only are we getting precious little tuition since Shibu left, but the activities Shifu Fatso dreams up to occupy us are getting in the way of practicing what we have learnt. I appreciate the need for strength and conditioning, but without a programme of increasing intensity this random, structureless training is pointless.

Having wasted the afternoon squandering my time and energy, I collect VD only for him to declare his intention to reject our usual rations and feed himself solely utilising his meal token.

As I'm tucking into my rice he reappears with his alternative fare in the form of an egg sandwich, or at least the Chinese equivalent thereof. Barely passing visual inspection, it fails the VD taste test miserably, 'That's disgraceful.'

His loss is my gain as he, once again, confirms himself to be the very bestest Dad of a Victorian persuasion by presenting me with his spare sandwich. He's right, it's truly a travesty. To even call it a sandwich is an affront to the Earl, however, as it's not rice and cabbage, it's most welcome just the same.

Few turn up for evening assembly and Fatso shows no concern. Never the most motivated, the stress of recent events has proven too much for our glorious leader and he has now given up all pretence.

Alone in the gym, I use the optional session to get some actual training in having frittered a whole day on filler material. Unfortunately, the daily grind is beginning to tell. I'm so weak and dispirited, the best I can manage is a token effort before deciding on an early night.

Downstairs I find the courtyard jam-packed with excited kids. On the building steps opposite a dim halo of light silhouettes a tiny figure squawking into a crackling PA system. By the time I get to our room, the vocal battle is in full flow with thousands of kids determined to mutilate each other's eardrums.

When Fatso turns up to tuck us in I ask what the deal is with the Dengfeng tune massacre.

'Ok, ok. Go Sleep.' With an awkwardly abashed grin he closes the door behind him. Characteristically loquacious, his elaborate explanation has left me in no doubt as to exactly what's occurring. Particularly well informed, I need to get my head down to better digest the expansive information.

Lapsing in and out of sleep, I can still hear the kids murdering the same song hours later.

All formations are transient; all formations are subject to
suffering; all things are without a self.

Guatama Buddha

If the world often seems unfair to people who believe in fate, this is
because fatalists can come to believe they cannot change or improve.
But if there is fate, it is fated that we make our own lives.

Monkey Magic

Living in such close proximity to a national treasure we risk becoming
immune to its charms. It's a phenomenon that many of our schoolmates
have succumbed to. Some are so indifferent about the surrounding sights
that they haven't explored further than the Breakfast Place. I wonder why
they came here at all. Their lack of interest serves to spur VD and I into
capitalising on the available opportunities. Agreeing that we simply
couldn't come to Shaolin and not see Damo's Cave, we prepare for
another assault of Wu Shan.

Events may have conspired against us until now, but I have my own perspective on, 'It's not meant to be'. Rather than choosing to see Fate trying to stop me, I see it as Fate making me work harder. The simple fact is Damo's Cave isn't going to come to me.

We may be suitably warmed by our morning run, but the day has yet to cotton on to the concept and is still reticent to brighten as we head toward the Breakfast Place. It's the wrong direction, but there's more traffic at the crossroads so more chance of getting a cab at this hour.

Dengfeng's commuter traffic is an eclectic variety of vehicles and it's not unusual to hear a honk when they meet. Chinese motorists love their horns and use them to navigate by echolocation, expecting others to make way by announcing their presence. As such, we have become a bit blasé about horn noise, but a screech of tyres alerts us one of Dengfeng's finest in action.

Amidst a cacophony of honking, a cab U-turns through two lanes of oncoming traffic, straight over the intersection and screeches to a halt in front of us. A smiling face sticking out the window pre-empts my request, 'Shaolin Si?'

We respond in the affirmative and, satisfied that negotiations have gone so well, he sparks up a fresh cigarette as we bundle into the cab. Our driver is particularly jolly and chuckles to himself between singing bursts of the Shaolin TV series theme. Although, he only knows the line, 'Shaolin, Shaolin', and hums the rest.

The cabs we've taken during our stay have been very samey, but I'm sure I recognise the pattern of the tape holding the window in place. It's the driver from our Louyang trip. No wonder he was prepared to risk life and limb to secure our fare; he must have another child he wants me to put through college.

Pulling up at the temple, he asks for 60Y. It's not the first time we've done this journey so he's not going to catch us out that easily. I hand him 30Y and a stern look.

He accepts the money with a cheeky grin which confirms my suspicion that he took us for a ride on the Louyang fare. I can't complain as it was only to be expected and we couldn't have done it without him, but I'm buggered if I'm letting him double this fare, even if it is only £3. Besides I'm sure he made enough out of us Sunday.

Another 100Y for a ticket and couple of quid for the electric coach have me wondering how many monks 4x4's I have personally financed.

It's still early enough that the stall holders are just setting up and the tripod-binocular guys aren't even here yet. Perhaps they looked out of the window this morning, saw the day was a bit grey and decided not to bother. However, it's brightening up nicely now and should be a good day for a trek up the mountain.

Taking a right before the Pagoda Forest, we get on to the dirt track that winds through the dry, scrub fields to Wuyi Mountain. Along the dusty trail we meet a little black puppy. Bobbing along in a bewildered, drunken fashion he is clearly out for an explore too. Chinese animals seem oblivious. In other countries animals might bark at one's arrival or beg for scraps, but these fellows are usually unconcerned by our presence. A quick tickle behind the ears is enough to confuse the poor hound's perception of reality and he staggers into the scrubby undergrowth.

As the jelly legged canine wobbles into the undergrowth a plaintiff cry breaks the silence, 'Excuse me sir.'

Slightly startled, I turn to see an exhausted young lady trudging up the trail. I do another look around to see who she might be so politely addressing. 'Excuse me sir.' There she goes again, it has me quite confused. She must be mistaking me for my dad.

'Can you tell me please where is Damo Dong?'

'Sure,' I raise my finger in the direction of the white dot on the horizon, 'There it is.'

'Ai yah!' Her expression speaks a thousand words, all of despair. Crestfallen, she stands with open mouth and slouched shoulders staring into distance. In her early twenties with long coat and cute bag she's already visibly fatigued and clearly doesn't relish any further exertion. Another, similar attired, young lady rounds the bend. As she catches her breath her mate, points to the mountain top and fills her in on the details.

Similarly thrilled at the prospect, her eyes bulge as mortification kicks in, 'Ai yah!'

Feeling charitable, I give them an easy out and point to the side trail, 'Chuzu Nunnery is just down there.'

It's a singularly brief discussion for the pair to make a decision.

Focusing on our goal, we skirt the Nunnery and head straight for the mountain. Cut into the side are, allegedly, a thousand steps, but the word for ten thousand, 'wan', can also be used to mean 'a lot', so it's probably not an exact count. I don't try to check.

Approximately a third of the way up the mountain we come to the first platform, which has transformed into a makeshift bazaar. Beneath a ramshackle construction of plastic sheets, a solitary monk greets us with a traditional, 'Amitofo'. Rather spoiling the effect, he gestures to his table of wares in the style of a game show assistant.

The rickety table supports an uninteresting collection of knickknacks, but the cheeky, baldy chappy isn't taking, 'No' for an answer. Failing to impress with his jumbled inventory, he changes tack. Proffering his hand to VD, VD responds as if to shake it, but the monk starts massaging the pressure points in his hand. When VD offers no resistance, he is gently pushed onto a tiny plastic stool where the process is expanded upon, working up his illustrated arm.

Tenderly escorting VD to an iron bedstead, the monk lays him down and gives him the full treatment. From the escaping sounds I'm not sure if I should render assistance or call a constable, but he assures me that all is good, 'Dude, you gotta have a go at this.'

Our new friend agrees, 'An Mo' (massage). Keen to get up the mountain, I say that I'll have one on the way back down. He's having none of it. Gently, but firmly, he sits me onto the low stool for a similar treatment. It's not as orgasmic as VD made out, but I'm still being massaged by a Shaolin Monk at Damo's Cave.

Producing a tatty old book, the monk indicates we should write our names along with an amount we would like to donate. After the vultures around the main temple our man's pleasant bedside manner is as refreshing as his massage. With this level of customer service, I don't care if we are being conned.

Physically and mentally rejuvenated, the mountain poses no obstacle to a positive mind. Warmer and brighter than our last visit it would seem that the Gods are smiling on us today. Everything is coming together and the climb is somehow more magical. It's such a perfect day that I'm not going to mind if no one is home when we get there.

About two thirds up the mountain is another platform with another makeshift stall under a tarpaulin sheet with the same selection of statues, beads and knickknacks. However, this fellow isn't a patch on our mate at the first platform and merely grunts as we pass through. He's never going to fill his commission quota with that attitude.

The steps continue, but seem less arduous than our previous visit and we are pleasantly surprised as the Memorial Gateway peeks into view. Built during the Ming Dynasty, the gateway has the three Chinese characters, Mo Xuan Chu, engraved into the front which translate as 'The Meditation Place'. Through the stone portal into the scruffy little courtyard the doorway in the cliff beckons, Damo's former residence is open for business.

There are already people inside the cave, and it's too small to hold any more, so we take a seat on the little stone bench in the yard.

As we wait, a monk appears on the platform outside. Swinging his legs as he walks along, he relaxes by sitting on the handrail in the splits. After a brief stretch, he launches himself into the air and summersaults along the terrace out of view. It's unbelievable what passes for casual behaviour in these parts.

As the pilgrims exit, we timidly take our turn in the hallowed hole. Inside a gnarly old lady sits huddled over a table in front of three statues: Damo flanked by his two disciples, Daoyu and Huike. To the right is a hole where the Damo Shadow Stone lived before it was removed to be preserved in the monastery.

We follow our now familiar routine of sticking money in a slot, lighting incense and bowing while an old lady rings a bowl. There's no space to linger in the cave so, respects paid, we step back out to the courtyard.

Returning to the bench, I take a seat to soak up the atmosphere. No sooner have I sat down than the old dear rushes out and hands us a big, yellow apple each. Damo's blessed apples no less. This day just keeps getting better.

With the exercising monk gone, the platform is free and I have the opportunity to exercise in Damo's front yard. If it's good enough for the monk, then it will do for me. I run through the Lau Gar Five Animal form. It's not flashy, particularly compared to the young monk's acrobatics I replaced, but it gives me a buzz to do it here at the source.

It's a short stroll to the mountain top where the white marble statue of Damo solemnly contemplates the view.

At the other end of Wuru peak is Xiyuan Pavilion built in 1984. Clustered at the pavilion are a couple of small family groups snacking merrily away. The Chinese are such consummate grazers that they always have snacks about their persons. So much so that the average Chinese family is a picnic waiting to happen. Showing ourselves no strangers to the lifestyle, we break out our apples and join the picnic.

The universal traveller guidelines, boil it, cook it, peel it or forget it, would prove a bit limiting here, so I just give the apple a good wipe on my shirt. Chock-full of Damo goodness, the apple tastes great.

The view is stunning in the clear, morning light. The landscape is virtually untouched since Damo's day and, along with the remoteness, the lack of embellishment somehow makes the site more authentic. The discommodious location is probably what's preserved the cave. Vandalism and renovations tend to target the most visible areas. The majority of visitors seem to skip the inconvenient parts of Shaolin. Being put off by a few steps is their loss and my gain.

Continuing the path around the peak, we are confronted with a steaming big shit in the path. Topped off with a square of tissue paper, it's clearly human and too big to be a child's. I understand there are times when needs must, but smack, bang in the middle of the path! We're on a mountain in the middle of nowhere, there are bushes and trees all around, but the perpetrator has not seen fit to step two feet away from the thoroughfare to lighten their load. Even a bear would have done it in the woods.

It's a tiny jolt back to reality, but we're so used to such things now that it passes without comment and only the briefest of exchanged looks.

On the way down, we are again waylaid by our new friend. Keen that we recharge our energy, he offers us our pick from his limited supply of ready comestibles. We opt for our old failsafe, the big pot of instant noodles. We are not really hungry, but it gives us an excuse to linger awhile longer. Approving of our selection, our man disappears under the tarpaulin to fill our pots with hot water. He places them on the rough bench in front of us.

'Xie xie', I say and reach for my noodles only to have him tap my hand away. Putting the lid back down, he jams it into place with the collapsible fork that accompanies the pot. Scolded like a naughty child by a Shaolin monk, priceless. Suppressing the urge to chuckle, I sit on the low stool with my knees under my chin. The plastic sheet overhead casually flapping in the breeze. I'm thoroughly content with my lot.

We sit in comfortable silence waiting for the noodles to soften. Perhaps feeling he should do more to entertain us, our host points at VD, gives him a thumbs up and says, 'Da bizi, hen hao.'

'What's that?'

'He says you have a big nose and it's good.'

I don't know why, but the Chinese like a big old hooter. Although I wouldn't have said VD has a particularly large conk, nor would I have suggested that it was an especially good one. However, not being a beak expert, I'm prepared to take the monk's word for it.

Unsure of the correct response, VD says nothing, but the monk is unconcerned. Having caught up on the latest snout related gossip, we continue to sit in quiet contentment. A few puppies spill from under the table and set to playing in the sunshine. Watching them rolling in the dust, the monk smiles, 'San zhi gou.' The profundity of this statement epitomises Chan.

Previously complaining about the extortionate price of provisions purchased en route, we are sitting in the shade on a warm day, looking down onto the Shaolin valley, eating instant noodles we didn't want with a Shaolin monk and enjoying every minute of it. It's about as idyllic as I could hope for. As timeless as the moment feels, the outside world eventually encroaches and we drag ourselves away.

At the base of the mountain we take the alternate fork at the Nunnery. The dusty trail leads from the Nunnery front door to a narrow, paved path dappled with sunlight peeking through the overhanging trees. Shaded and mossy, the path has stepped sections which remind me of the scene in Shaolin Temple where Jet Li carries water buckets from the stream. In this peaceful seclusion we pass a monk marching a bunch of young pupils to train out of the sight of distracting day-trippers. Just around the corner we are reminded why.

The maddening crowd jolts us back to reality. Denser and louder as we approach the Mountain Gate, we are shuffled along by the crowd to the automated turnstile where a surly young monk snatches my ticket. With lightening dexterity, he transfers it to his right hand and passes it over a panel on the turnstile. Shoving me forward with his left hand he holds the ticket in front of me like a carrot as the electronic voice of the turnstile chimes, 'Qing jin.' Clutching for the ticket, I stumble through the rotating limbs. Amidst the chatter, the electronic chant rings on, 'Qing jin, qing jin', as others follow similar customer focused humiliations behind me.

'Qing jin', means 'Please enter', but the onomatopoeia of coins bouncing in the temple coffers sounds more like, 'Kerching, kerching'. Like a singing cash register.

It doesn't take long for the noise and crowds to have their effect, and lead us to seek sanctuary in Ciyun Courtyard. Stepping through the archway, my path is blocked by a monk sitting at a table who demands we buy tickets. Since our last visit the courtyard has become a performance area. A sneaky peek through the window reveals the Kung Fu show is nothing we don't see at school all day long. I'm certainly not paying to see it.

Disappointment at being denied our favourite courtyard, supplies today's lesson: the transience of things. I'm learning a lot of lessons at Shaolin.

By this time, the mass of people is just too great to be able to enjoy the temple. Resistance is futile as I'm swept along. Stepping over the threshold of the Medicine Courtyard, I realise I've missed Chuipu Hall. The courtyard with the Eighteen Luohan Statues and scenes was closed on our last visit and I was hoping to see them this time. A palm prevents my turn and a stern-faced monk pushes me forward. A graduate from the Vogon school of Diplomacy, there's clearly no reasoning with the scowling mendicant. The only way back is to go up to the tourist centre, buy another 100Y ticket and enter through the front door again.

I appreciate they want to keep people moving, but this is ridiculous and just another tarnished image of the monks here to take home and treasure. Still, it's been a good day overall and, with another Shaolin must-see ticked, it's time for our other priority: provisions.

In the cab, I show the bookshop address to the driver, after all he should have the knowledge of Dengfeng. He identifies it immediately and takes us straight there. I can just as quickly tell that it's not our badger.

One could be forgiven for thinking it was a public library. Teenage loafers are sprawled all over the floor reading comic books. Gingerly stepping over the prone forms, ten seconds inside confirms my doubt. It is, indeed, a bookshop, but it is not the one we asked CITS for. Again, we have simply been palmed off with any old bookshop, rather than the specific one we wanted.

Walking around the corner to our original destination, a passing pedestrian dredges the contents of their mucous membrane and spits it onto the pavement in front of us. In a wave of exasperation all the minor tribulations we've dealt with well up to a flash point. Not a patch on some social hygiene misdemeanours we've witnessed, it's the straw that broke the camel's back and Dengfeng's quirky charm is washed aside by an explosion as VD vents his spleen, 'For crying out loud.'

It's a phenomenon I'm choosing to call China Fatigue. The little idiosyncrasies that go towards making China to fascinatingly exotic suddenly overwhelm. VD's frustrations and tiredness bursting forth makes me long for the clean and simple familiarities of my dreary existence back home.

Speaking of which, I'm going to give up on the bookshop and mail order the books when I'm back in the UK. It would be nice to buy them at their source, but it's just too much like hard work over a task that can be achieved so easily in my natural habitat.

My reverie is broken by a chorus of shouts. We have subconsciously wandered into a noodle bar. It's almost as if our sole concern is food. The shouting women are pointing back at the door. Seeing my confusion, other patrons join in. Causing such consternation, I guess that the place is closing or that they don't want us there. Used to not being welcome, I move to leave, but the old lady drags me to a hand-written sign pasted to a pillar by the door. The small piece of paper has three items and prices so I assume it's the menu. From what I can work out there are three dishes on offer: a small something at 5Y, something at 6Y and a large at 7Y. I guess the middle one is a medium but, other than the prices, I can only read two characters and that doesn't really help. On impulse, I point to the top item, 'Liang ge da wan' (two big bowls).

The old lady creases up. Pointing at me she announces to the clientele, 'He said two big bowls!'

The place erupts into hysterics and I sheepishly join VD at a table.

'What was that about?'

'I just ordered two big bowls.'

'Lovely. What of?'

'Dunno, but if it's that hysterical we may not want to eat it.'

I bear the brunt of the continued hilarity as we await our mystery fare. Watching the other restaurant patrons slurping big bowls of noodles it looks like I needn't be concerned; big bowls are all the go.

There's a fairly rapid turnover of customers in this joint. If evening meals are a social event, the customers here have a more functional attitude toward lunch. People arrive individually, sit alone, throw noodles into their face and scram.

Cousin It, wearing a formerly white apron, shambles from a back room. Greasy nose poking through his greasy fringe, he doesn't register us as he slops two huge, steaming bowls of noodles on the table. Removing his asbestos thumbs from the bowls, he shuffles back to continue his shift in the grease mine.

The wide flat noodles swimming in a dark sauce are kept company with random fragments of anything the chef could lay his hands on. Despite coming in the appropriate sizes, the culinary delight doesn't resemble anything the three bears would recommend.

Rallying from the consternation of our entrance, the fuwuyuan isn't pleased with me experimentally nibbling the noodles. Already concluded that we are a pair of retards, she shouts something I can't catch. When I don't respond she exhales loudly, stomps over to the table and snatches the chopsticks from my hand. 'Aiya!' she jabs them into the steaming mound and mixes up my noodles before handing my chopsticks back.

Among a certain class of Dengfeng eatery these noodle soups are a staple. 'Chow fen' are made from rice flour, corn-starch and potato starch and most agreeable. I furiously shovel the noodles into my face as the old lady continues to point me out to any new customers and tell them the Tale of Two Bowls. It's better than some names I've been called.

The noodles are the very fellows for a quick bite. Rustic it may be but, yet again, the local cuisine has not disappointed. There's a peppercorn in the mix that, without being particularly spicy, has a mild anaesthetic effect. By the time we are finished I am pleasantly stuffed, can no longer feel my face and feel slightly intoxicated. I consider it 7Y well spent.

Having got ourselves on the outside of some food, there's still enough time left on the clock for some supplies. I would like a bigger chain whip and VD is after a Taiji style training suit he saw last week in the 'Wealth Bringing Martial Monk Performance Clothing Wholesale Department' on Shaoshi Road.

It takes some time for my eyes to adjust to the gloomy interior before I notice the little head grinning at us from behind the counter, 'Ah, ni hao!' She's absolutely delighted to see us. She must remember our last visit. Unless we get better at this bartering lark we are going to be the most popular guys in Dengfeng.

The shop walls are covered in display items that appear to have been there since Damo was a lad. Pointing at a filthy suit, VD asks if she has one in stock. Looking him up and down, she rummages into a mound of clothes. Holding the suit to his ample frame she tells him that it's the one he wants. Not so convinced, he tries the suit on. Her professional eye hasn't let her down. Expertly smoothing the cloth into position while admiring the snug fit she rubs her hands over his beer belly. Her wizened old face cracks into her silver-toothed grin as she chuckles, 'Pang pang!'

The Chinese are traditionally great fans of the fuller figure and our ancient friend obviously clings to those values using 'Fatty' as a term of endearment. The time and money spent cultivating his rotund physique is paying dividends with the old lady.

Diverting her attention from his waistline, VD makes chopping motions at his arm, 'Do you have one with short sleeves?'

Quickly grasping the concept, she nods, 'Ke yi.'

Two quick snips with her scissors are all it takes for VD to be wearing a short-sleeved jacket. Undressing him like a bossy matron, she settles herself at an equally antique sewing machine and deftly finishes the job in a matter of seconds. You've got to hand it to the old lady. The ninja seamstress exhibits a level of professionalism far beyond the rest of Dengfeng's workforce. She literally has a 'can do' attitude and is so personable that it would only make me feel churlish to haggle. So again, we don't.

Seeing her throw the off-cuts into a sack, I have a lightbulb moment and ask her for a couple of bits of shiny cloth for my chain whip. The old Dear catches on quickly, pulls a piece of orange polyester from the sack and trims two square-ish pieces from it with her big scissors. I love it when a plan comes together. Deferring my cash reinforces the idea that we pay her far too much, but she's so lovely she's worth every penny.

'Xie xie ayi', I believe it's acceptable to call ladies over a certain age 'Aunty'.

'Mei shi, mei shi' (No problem), her gap-toothed chuckle confirms no offence has been taken.

Around the corner we approach our favourite weapon shop just as our eight-year-old neighbour emerges. The shop keeper didn't feel it necessary to wrap the purchase, so the young man from Uzbekistan is walking down the street with a loaded crossbow. The huge grin on his face belays the fact that he is a catastrophe waiting to happen. Realising it's not a stick-up, I lower my hands, 'Woah! Careful where you're pointing that thing.'

'Is ok, was good price.'

'Either unload it, or carry it point downward.'

'Is ok, is good. Look', he pokes the crossbow into my face for my inspection.

Neatly sidestepping the proffered projectile, I palm the weapon downward, 'Carry it like this ok.'

'Ok.' Still beaming, he marches up the street pointing the crossbow directly in front of him.

My experience with Chinese children to date hasn't led me to believe they are any more sensible or less accident prone than your average western child. I find it hard to believe that the shopkeeper has sold him this crossbow, let alone allowed him to load it. Maybe it's a kind of natural selection in progress.

The shop is an impressive array of low quality Wushu weapons, most of which aren't covered in my Kung Fu style. Rooting amongst the vast mounds of shiny, pointy things, I unearth a heavy duty, nine-section whip. At least five times the weight of the Wushu version used at school, a novice could seriously damage themselves with it. We get ourselves a couple of these bad boys in order to prove that we are far more sensible than the average eight-year-old Uzbekistani.

Evening assembly sees the reappearance of Yuan and Shibu. While we are waiting for Fatso to dismiss us, Shibu casually saunters over and wordlessly hands us our passports.

After training, I see that Amateur Night at the Karaoke Kindergarten has packed out the courtyard again. I can't make out any detail in the dark so it's not really a spectator friendly sport. In a tweaking of last night's event, tonight participants are invited onto the step individually in a tournament to see who can maim and mangle the tune into the most contorted and hideous wreck. There's stiff competition and it sounds like they are going to the death. It's one instance when we are glad to close the door. I don't recognise it as the school song, but I have to wonder if there is a link between what's occurring downstairs and our recent Chinese lessons. I guess I'll never know.

Physical discomfort and suffering are not the same. We suffer in our minds and the mind creates the conditions that we find unsatisfactory.

The second of the Four Noble Truths.

Xiao Long Wu Yuan is not only one of the largest Kung Fu schools Dengfeng, it's also the cheapest. US $450 a month covers room, food, Chinese class, and training. Six days a week, twelve plus hours a day.

www.Shaolin-wushu.de

Shibu is at morning warming to reclaim his squad, but doesn't receive the heartfelt welcome he may have expected. If he was looking forward to the joyous reunion of a prodigal returned, he is to be sadly disappointed. In his hiatus the damage has been done. There's no need to take a survey to see that customer satisfaction has hit an all-time low.

As sole attendee of our group, I get to join their malcontent company just in time for Shibu to work his way around the squad making polite enquiries to visa requirements, 'You visa?'

Sadly, any commission opportunities have sailed without him. The relentless push for extensions during his absence has ensured that we are all fed up to the back teeth with visa talk and he's not doing himself any favours in the popularity stakes.

Further endearing himself to his estranged brood, Shibu supplies a half-baked morning warming no different to one of Fatso's finest. Many were counting on Shibu's return to turn things around, but his efforts so far have left them more jaded than a Han dynasty burial suit.

It's a right morbid bunch sprawled on the steps after breakfast. The cumulative effect of recent incidents has led to increased dissension in the ranks and we now move into the autumn of our discontent. With plenty of complaints already in hand, the deterioration in training, the Shifus fighting and the latest spate of food poisonings are the last straws for many. Some students are giving up and going home, while others are investigating different schools.

With no Fatso in sight, I slot back into Shibu's squad. After some mandatory kitchen block, it's time for Power Stretching. Again, the waiting time to be pulled about offers plenty of opportunity to grumble and the talk is all of making a break.

There is no shortage of Kung Fu schools around the area, Dengfeng had approximately eighty at last count. However, the majority of these schools are not authorized by the Chinese Ministry of Education to recruit foreign students, which rather limits the available options.

A laid-back chap in general, Mason's China know-how equips him to better deal with the current situation than the rest of us. While we rage impotently at our treatment, he is currently in negotiation with rival school, Tagou. They charge about $700 a month compared to our schools $450, but Mason is no walkover. Working in Shanghai has given him a good enough grasp of Chinese language and culture that he has managed to get Tagou to match the fees for the cache of getting a defecting foreign student.

As a frame of reference, the Chinese students at Xiao Long pay for a year approximately what we do a month. They get the same food as us and better training, but spartan accommodation with a lot more beds to a room. Despite the quality offset we are still a nice little earner for the school who primarily sees foreign students as a form of bonus. They charge us a premium and don't feel obliged to provide anything extra in return. It's also highly coincidental that they prefer payment in cash wherever possible.

Once the readies have changed hands the school's attentiveness tails off significantly and, contrary to their prepayment assurances, there are no refunds for early leavers. The general consensus of opinion, especially for those who paid several months up front, is that they wish they'd seen the accommodation and training before coughing up.

Despite making a financial killing from us, the schools aren't particularly keen to accommodate foreigners. We are just too much bother, especially when a less demanding clientele is clamouring on the doorstep. This may be why they don't advertise outside China. My initial research into studying Kung Fu in China involved serious effort as most schools simply weren't interested. It's the modern-day equivalent of the fabled student selection process but, rather than of standing outside the temple gates for days to demonstrate determination, I sat trawling internet sites and magazines for months. I eventually unearthed contact details for four schools around Dengfeng namely: Epo, Xiao Long, Tagou and Zhengzhou. Of the four, only the first three replied but, as Tagou replied twice with conflicting information, the numbers averaged out nicely. Also, Zhengzhou not responding wasn't a great loss as, being much further from the temple than we wanted, the school was a wildcard choice anyway.

Xiao Long was by far the best represented care of the German website www.Shaolin-wushu.de. Piecing the limited reports together led me to believe that Xiao Long was, at least on paper, the best all-rounder. The size and expense of Tagou and Epo served to put me off both. Tagou apparently has 18,000 students which must make it a Kung Fu factory. The prices involved may not be a great deal by western standards but, as a notorious skinflint, the economics of Xiao Long immediately appealed to me. Actually, Xiao Long comes out quite well in comparison to its competition and I'm not convinced there's anything to be gained by paying more at another school.

Listening to the other guys confirms my conclusions. They also mention another school in the area, Shaolin Wushu Guan. Situated next to the Shaolin Temple, it's apparently ridiculously expensive, has poor standards and limited training facilities with only four hours training a day, four days a week. On the plus side their foreign students get to stay in a real hotel.

Although our current information tallies, everything here is so subject to change that it's only valid for about ten minutes. Schools' standards fluctuate with staff and student turnover and even premises are demolished and rebuilt at different locations at the drop of a hat. As a result, our already limited reports are out of date before we get them. Even the official websites are not reliable as it is not unknown for schools to use pictures and information from other institutions and pass them off as their own.

Access to data sources around Dengfeng is also confounded. Interschool rivalry previously resulted in student confrontations in town so the larger schools now coordinate their days off. Preventing Dengfeng from being swamped with rampaging teenage martial artists has a side-effect. Combined with not being allowed out of an evening, it limits our opportunities for contact with students of other schools. It's difficult to form any real comparison when most information we get is hearsay.

Before long, any useful info has been covered and the conversation deteriorates along a familiar path. I ooze away from Les Miserables and stretch against the wall for the remainder of the lesson.

Waiting for afternoon assembly I notice an addition to the classes already in progress. Three new Chinese kids have appeared and they are fat. Boy, are they fat. They would fit right in at a Sumo school. So fat, that they don't participate in a Kung Fu class, but just run laps around the flowerbed. The flowerbed, and I use the term hesitantly to describe the three-metre square patch of dry earth, is in front of our building so I have a good view of their progress.

At a cursory glance they fit the profile of China's new generation of problem children. The Little Emperor, 'Xiao Huangdi' or Little Princess, 'Xiao Gongzhu', syndrome is an aspect of China's one-child policy where single children receive excessive attention. With both parents working and two sets of doting grandparents, the family unit's spending power and general desire for their child to experience the benefits they themselves were denied often result in extravagant pampering.

While over-compensating on material goods, the parents also put immense pressure on these children to succeed academically. The combination of stress and pampering is reported to have resulted in a stunting of social and emotional growth. A phenomenon that is so widespread as to be considered problematic and there is concern that it is creating a future behavioural time bomb. Unsurprisingly, some of these Little Emperors rebel. Some wind up in places like this. Broadening its borstal status, it appears our school has embraced the concept of Fat

Camp.

One of the salad dodgers has a beaut of a black eye. It's probably what you should expect for pushing your weight around in a Kung Fu school.

My brothers slowly emerge and as they regain consciousness notice the new school members. Martin offers his trademark, 'Jiao you!' and others offer their own forms of encouragement. Nikolai shows his solidarity by joining them for a few laps before throwing his arms in the air as if he's won. The poor fellows must be pleased to see the back of us when our Shifus stop giggling and line us up.

Fatso and Julie are back so, after a communal Go Run, the squads are split. Fatso takes us to one side for Jibengong while Shibu's squad set about some acrobatics.

As we are back-ing and fore-ing, one of Shibu's guys wanders over and joins in. Shifu tells him to get permission first. In response the interloper suggests that Shifu go and do something distasteful to his own mother. As one, the room holds its breath. Shifu gives him the opportunity to take back his comment by asking the kid to repeat himself. When the same answer is delivered, he pulls out his mobile phone.

A very brief exchange with an anonymous confidante, sees Fatso take the kid by the arm and escort him down the stairs closely followed by Shibu.

Left standing around like lemons, some of us attempt to occupy ourselves but, when it becomes apparent they are not coming back, I make an executive decision, 'Early dinner it is then.'

Heading to the canteen I see the fat kids are still trying to wear a groove into the concrete. They won't be fat for long here. In the month I have been at Xiao Long, I have lost over a stone in weight already. The laps may be an unimaginative diet plan, but it's bound to have the desired effect. Although I can't image it catching on in the west; burn more calories than you consume, isn't complicated nor gimmicky enough.

After dinner they are still running. Maybe they don't get to eat until they lose some weight. Seems a bit extreme, but I bet it's effective.

I drop by Knobby on the way back. A source of constant amazement, he proves that his finger is still on the Xiao Long pulse by bringing me up to speed on the incident he wasn't present at, but knows more about than those who were.

Dennis, as Knobby informs me is the lad's name, is gone. Apparently, he was a former occupant of our room and, having previously been caught smoking, has been living on borrowed time. I've only seen him around a few times and, as he was so rarely at training, hadn't clocked that he was one of us foreign students. I only recognise him at all as he once came around to borrow toilet paper.

In fairness to our Fatso, he dealt with the situation with considerably more aplomb than I would have credited him with. Perhaps the Shifus were prepped following the latest Sanda Shifu fracas.

Newsworthy as the Dennis incident was, Knobby's primary concern is that the internet is down. The connection is poor at the best of times so it's not unusual for it to drop out, but after checking the settings, testing the cable and scratched my head, I find it's disappeared completely. I nip next door and ask our neighbour if he's having any trouble with the connection.

Kai reveals that the leather-clad housekeeper turned off the internet access for the whole building when she left for her hols. She just shut everything down and went. As far as she's concerned the entire building ceases to exist when she turns her back. Perhaps she thinks we all stop whatever we normally do and sit around with heavy hearts waiting for her to come back and return the brightness to our lives. Actually, this may well be the case for the Pink Overall Posse as manifest in their attitude toward keeping the floors clean and emptying the bins, for they no longer keep the floors clean or empty the bins. Although, they weren't exactly diligent in the first place.

The conspiracy theorist in me finds this denial of internet service highly coincidental considering the amount of traffic to other schools' websites at the moment.

Not even a fractured limb can keep a good man down and Knobby joins us on the steps before evening assembly. He was due to move on to a school in Wutang but, having been warned that it's even worse than here, was unsure of his next move. Breaking his leg has forced his decision and he will wait here until healed. This will buy him time to research a hot-tip in Qingdao or, failing that, will return to his previous school.

He is also trying to convince some guys to wait until he's fit and accompany him. His prime target being Wouter who, having paid six months up front, has a couple of months left, but has started researching other schools in preparation.

Starved of attention during his enforced absence, Knobby's diatribe continues when we line up, but he somehow manages to avoid any press-

354

ups. I guess his broken leg is a 'get out of jail free' card, but I wouldn't like to bet on it. It's more likely that Fatso can't be bothered.

Upon being dismissed everyone heads back to their rooms, but Shifu motions VD and I to him. Pointing to the gym he tells us, 'Go Yuan Shifu.'

As there is no one at the gym, it looks like evening training has died a death. So I'm a little startled when I turn on the light and a little voice calls out of nowhere, 'Nick?'

Surprisingly, Yuan Shifu was expecting us. Even more surprising is that he is hiding in a cupboard. Squeezing through the jammed door he joins us in the gym. Standing us, in turn, against the wall he takes our photographs.

I'm not particularly photogenic at the best of times, but the Xiao Long weight loss plan, coupled with Yuan Shifu's over-exposed, amateur photography make me look like a startled corpse with a hangover. VD has more of a grumpy axe murderer vibe going on in his photo, so at least Yuan Shifu captured a good likeness there. Seeming pleased with the resulting mugshots he motions us to the ajar door, 'Come, come.'

Unable to fully open the door, we lever ourselves through the gap. Once inside I realise that this is Yuan Shifu's crib. Probably intended as a storage room, Yuan Shifu has managed to cram a bed into a space little bigger than a cupboard.

Squashed together on the bed, VD and I revisit the same old list of questions that we answered when registering via email, again on enrolment with Shibu and at reception with Idiot Boy.

Curious about the spot quiz and makeshift modelling. I ask what the craic is. Yuan Shifu explains he wants to put our photos in the school brochure because we're English. Personally, I am Welsh, i.e. a person from Wales. I was expecting the Chinese not to understand this point and had braced myself in preparation of being referred to as English. However, putting it in print is another thing altogether; if my mam sees it, she'll go ballistic. I point this out only for Yuan Shifu to retort, 'It's ok, you in China now.'

We then run through a list of European countries that Yuan Shifu knows. To be fair, he does manage a more comprehensive list than anyone else so far. However, I don't really feel that he's getting my point with the whole geographic origin thing. Coming up with a cunning plan I ask him, 'How would you like it if I called you Japanese?'

Incredulous, he cries, 'I am Chinese!'

Clearly, my clever, role-reversal psychology was lost on him. I just won't tell my Mam about the Xiao Long website. The chances of her stumbling across it on her own accord are pretty slim. In parting, Yuan Shifu asks about our visa situation.

Crossing the courtyard, night three of karaoke madness is just setting up. I don't know what it's all in aid of, but the kids sure seem excited about it. At our room, I peer over the balcony at the amorphous, red-suited, mass as thousands of twilight figures ooze into position, but can't see anything to give me a clue as to why.

History has proved there's no point in asking Fatso. All I know is the once charming and quirky night-time serenade is now royally getting on my baps. Despite VD's complaints, the conditions seem to be affecting him not a jot as he is spark out as usual.

Fatso visits have been considerably shorter of late. He's always been a bit up and down with us. Initially his lingering was awkward, but I at least felt like he was trying. Then he had a period of going through the motions. Now, just like everyone else, he seems to have given up altogether. I turn off the light and close the door, but stop short of telling myself to, 'Go sleep'.

I'm tired enough that not even a few thousand caterwauling chilblains can keep me awake for long.

The number one illness for travellers in China is diarrhea, which can be caused by viruses, bacteria, or parasites, which can contaminate food or water. Infections may cause diarrhea and vomiting (E. coli, Salmonella, cholera, and parasites), fever (typhoid fever and toxoplasmosis), or liver damage (hepatitis).

Centers for Disease Control and Prevention

It's generally a little nippy in the morning, but normally warms up quickly. Today the mercury has taken a plunge and the sun takes much longer to get into the swing of things. It's an unwelcome sign that winter is on the way. The German guys warned that the weather was about to take a turn, but I hadn't anticipated such a sudden shift. Yesterday I was training on the field with a rag tied around my head to prevent sunburn, this morning it's minus 3C. It would appear that the Communist Government even make the seasons run on time, albeit without the customary politeness of a transitionary period to ease us in. (Actually, in Beijing, the Government cloud seed before major outdoor ceremonies to ensure the events are not marred by inclemency.)

Winters in Henan province can be cold, temperatures fall well below freezing and there's often heavy snow. Outdoor training continues in all but the most extreme conditions. With no heating in the gyms or rooms, anyone planning a training trip to the area should probably avoid November to February.

Everything here is an uphill battle at the best of times, but lately things have gone from bad to worse. We really don't need to be cold on top of everything else.

The number at assembly is atrocious. Out of the twenty or so foreign students, there are four on parade: Julie, Martin, Mason and myself. Lumped together, we make the best of our run. The coolness dampens the dust and pollution making the air fresher, and more user-friendly, than I'm used to. Although the sudden drop in temperature also means morning warming takes longer to have its desired effect and I'm particularly looking forward to my brekky.

I am disappointed to see my food-serving friend conspicuously absent from the canteen. I attempt to exchange pleasantries with his replacement, but he's not interested. All fingers and thumbs, his serving skills suggest that he is merely a stand-in and not a professional ladle operator. In fact, this grease-stained fellow looks like he's straight from an oil field. Struggling to get to grips with the oversized spoon, the kitchen amateur is not about to waste time on friendly banter with a funny looking laowai. The slop has little in the way of redeeming features, but he somehow manages to make it even less appetising than usual. It's not even warm which would have made it slightly palatable. I just hope he's had nothing to do with the preparation.

The day has brightening nicely by morning assembly but, despite the temperature picking up, attendance hasn't improved. Having gone through the effort of straining its way through, the feeble sunlight finds a pitiful sight. Apparently, we four are the only ones well enough to make it down the stairs. As Shibu and Yuan Shifu also fail to appear, it looks like Fatso drew the short straw again.

Inspecting the walking wounded that barely passes for a squad, Shifu notices that Mason really doesn't look well. Leaving us in line, Shifu escorts him to the doctor's office at the side of the courtyard. From behind the plastic curtain we can hear Shifu complaining that foreign students always get ill. He goes on to blame the canteen saying that, with the money we pay, the school should at least feed us properly. I appreciate the sentiment, but I'm quite sure the good doctor isn't responsible for catering quality. Nevertheless, he agrees that Mason looks peaky and sends him to rest. Wan Shifu's amalgamated super-group is now a trio.

The pathetic remnants of three classes march to the back of school where Fatso points to some hilly scrub, 'Go run.'

There's no visible route, but the ever-cheerful Martin confidently leads the way up the scruffy slope with Julie and I dutifully trailing behind. Less pleasing to the eye up close, this little piece of cross-country is particularly unforgiving underfoot. Dumped building materials and household refuse poking through the dusty earth cut into my flimsy Feiyues and trip my feet. Dry and stunted shrubbery snags my trousers and scratches my legs. China really has it in for me today. It's a relief to get back to the pavement frolics. The cracked and uneven paving is a bowling green in comparison. After a session of the usual Jibengong, Fatso comes up with a grand finale, 'Wa tou'. Squat jumps down the street.

About halfway back, I experience painful stomach cramping. Assuming I've overworked a neglected muscle, I stand up and stretch backward, but to no avail. I drop back and, rather than continue jumping, slap my feet heavily as I walk behind Shifu Fatso.

Being Saturday, there should be Buddha Class after break. Today it's not to be. Casually slinging a basketball at Martin, Fatso points to the hoop in the courtyard and retreats around the corner. Predictable plumes of smoke follow.

I normally enjoy Buddha class and I'd be happy to go to meditate on my own, but I know it's pointless to suggest it. Even if Fatso had taken the class it would have been worse than usual, so it's not like we are missing much. The old joke about Kung Fu being a way of getting young men to meditate just doesn't hold water here. Similarly, there has been no sign of the Chan and Kung Fu union that is the defining feature of Shaolin.

We perfunctorily pass the ball around and shoot a few lacklustre hoops. In a burst of unprecedented enthusiasm, I attempt a layup shot only for a spasm of pain to halt me mid-launch and bring me to the ground. Accepting that the short-term will have to consist of not exerting myself, I return to the spiritless passing. When Fatso fails to return, and unable to muster any dynamism of our own, we dismiss ourselves early and I check on my bedbound buddy.

Working on developing bedsores has left VD so bored with the same four walls that he deigns to forsake his fortress of solitude and accompany me to lunch.

The catering imposter hasn't been rumbled yet and is still randomly splashing soggy vegetables around the kitchen. Despite his ladle technique, some slop manages to make it onto my tray.

The Chinese students are being given a bulging carrier bag with their meal. We don't get one, and I think little of it, until one of the canteen staff dumps a couple of these bags on our table and stomps off. The pink and white striped bag contains eight packets of various junk food. Some are identifiable as crisps and biscuits, others just mysterious. I don't understand why we've been given them. I'm not aware that today has any special relevance, but it's a pleasant novelty nonetheless. I wouldn't have considered buying any of the products myself, so this way I at least have a chance to try them.

Gingerly eyeing-up the comestibles, I decide the biscuits may be a fitting accompaniment to a cup of tea, but am less convinced by the remainder. Setting them aside for later consideration, I repack my goody-bag. Looking up, I see VD has already sampled half his treats.

Munching away like a bull terrier with a house brick, he offers up what I presume to be a crisp, concluding, 'That ain't no 'tater.' VD's meticulous taste challenge takes no prisoners and all the products meet similar disapproval. The goody bags' brief interlude into our otherwise featureless existence proves a non-event and the conversation returns to the current situation.

VD has effectively given up training altogether. I've been attempting to put on a brave face, but am unable to project much positivity into my reports to encourage him otherwise. Caving to popular opinion, I have to concede VD's point of view. There's no getting around the fact that, in real terms, it's a waste of time being here. Deprived of the training the place is just miserable. With no sign of any improvement on the horizon the time has come to be gone. It's difficult for me to admit defeat, but suddenly I want to leave Mr. Han's island.

I sniff out Yuan Shifu and give him the news. Unconcerned by our announcement, he asks if we require a taxi to Zhengzhou. Informed that we have arranged one, he asks the obvious question, 'How much you pay?'

If I was pleased with our quote of 300Y, Yuan Shifu thinks otherwise, 'That too much, I get cheaper one.' Considerably more astute than the other Shifus, he must notice the expression on my face, so reinforces his statement, 'I get taxi, you know same bring you.'

'We weren't picked up from the airport. No one turned up to collect us so we found our own way here.'

Now it's his turn to express surprise, but he quickly recovers.

Ignoring my revelation, he returns to his favourite subject, 'How much you pay?'

I really don't think he's getting the point here. I understand well enough by now not to expect an apology from the school. 'Sorry', is simply not an expression one hears in China. The Chinese concept of an apology implies they were at fault in the first instance. Thus, to apologise means a loss of face as it admits a mistake. So, like petulant children, they accept no responsibility for anything. I know exactly what his response will be, but I tell him anyway, 'Four hundred Yuan',

'That too much, you should not pay.'

It's all very well to say what we should have done, but at the time we had little option. The taxi driver was actually very good to us and I am perfectly happy with his fee. It could have been a lot worse. While we are on the subject, we 'should' have been met at the airport as promised. It's a little late in the day to complain now and I'm really not in the frame of mind.

My stomach is cramping so much that I wimp out of afternoon training. I daren't stray too far from the porcelain throne in case of impending disaster. I don't even go down to make my excuses. As no one comes to get me, I guess they are equally interested. Maybe no one else turns up either. Whatever happens, I can guarantee I miss nothing. Instead, I use the time to sedately sort my stuff out. Packing my case, I realise all my training gear is hideously filthy beyond redemption. I had thought I was relatively presentable compared to everyone else. Turns out I was covered in shit too.

The indigenous population must Teflon coat their clothes. In spite of being permanently surrounded by swirling dust and pollution the majority of everyday folk are generally spic and span. We are not. Evaluating what is worth taking home soon has the corridor bin overflowing.

Someone must notice the brimming bin. As word of our impending departure spreads, we have a steady stream of visitors come to wish us well. Some of whom we've never met. A brief exchange of pleasantries invariably culminates in them pointing at some random item and asking, 'Are you leaving this?'

Our discards are sifted through like a slum level, jumble sale. We have never been so popular with our fellow students. Some even take furniture and the room is picked clean in short order.

Hearing that we are about to make ourselves scarce, one of the German guys decides to tag along. Marco, originally intending to stay much longer, is now thoroughly disillusioned with the whole experience. He was expecting to learn how to fight and, after spending six weeks learning a section of a form, was told it would take another eighteen months to get to the end of it. Shaolin Kung Ku is an all-encompassing art, and designed to be learnt slowly. However, perfection achieved through constantly polished repetition doesn't work without intensive training from an attentive teacher and that simply isn't on offer here. It's just taught badly, with the onus on the student to find their own sense of it the best they can.

This may work for full-time students, but not for us Kung Fu tourists. Staying for such a relatively short time emphasizes the need to train smart or one could easily go away having learnt nothing.

Marco has already agreed to Yuan Shifu's minibus, so it's easier to go together. If we can't get flights to Beijing, we can stay in Zhengzhou. Or there's always the train. We had previously decided against the train journey, due to time restrictions. It would be nice to have seen some scenery and lived the experience, but there's negligible financial saving verses the massive time difference of flying. Although anything that gets us away from here is a bonus.

Our neighbour Kai also sticks his head in to wish us bon voyage. Being a long-term student, he has already fully accoutred his room and disdainfully turns up his nose as he pokes through our tarnished remnants. As he leaves, he adds, 'Make sure you get your certificate, it's very nice.'

I saw mention of these certificates on the Xiao Long Website. It's a nice thought, but I won't hold my breath. More optimistic, Marco is determined to get his certificate and is off to the office like a shot.

Feeling decidedly dodge, I skip evening assembly in favour of a couple of precautionary Imodium and curl into a foetal position trying not to move. Barely semi-conscious, I ignore any further visitors and let VD deal with the circling vultures.

During the night, I'm the most violently ill I have ever been in my life. I don't know what upset my system so much, but my body isn't taking any chances ejecting the miscreant. Projectile vomiting and dry-retching with well-defined abs is a serious event, and that's not to mention the diarrhoea of a madman.

Being so desperately ill without it being self-inflicted runs against my sense of fair play. Had I spent the previous evening binge drinking rotgut at least I would have felt a sense of universal justice in action. As I've been so careful, I don't feel I deserve this.

Cuddling the toilet, I get a flashback to Dr. Jones' surgery. Having researched the area to check jab requirements, the good Doctor discovered, that on top of China's recent Bird Flu and SARS scares, Dengfeng was hit by a typhoid outbreak last year (2007) and several foreign students at the school succumbed.

Looking me in the face, he earnestly enquired, 'Why do you want to go there exactly?'

I'm awakened by an unpleasant, cold sensation on the side of my face and a throbbing skull. It takes me a while to focus, and longer to put the pieces together. I have vomited so aggressively that I passed out. As the realisation dawns, I jolt from horizontal to vertical with nothing in-between. Of all the bathroom floors, in all the world, this is not one I would have chosen to regain consciousness on.

Face frozen in a silent scream, I stagger the length of the hall to the shower room. Stripping off my clothes, I throw them in the bin outside. Lucking out on an old box of washing powder, I frantically scrub myself with handfuls of clumpy blue granules. The cold shower rips me out of the initial adrenalin surge. As I regain composure, I realise I don't have any clothes or a towel. It's a good job Yuan Shifu isn't here to see me limping back to the room.

Huddled under my sheet, I eventually shiver myself to sleep. By morning, I'm just about sentient. I'm sure a lesser man would have died.

When a driver finds another driver's driving skill poor or
operation incorrect he should inform the second driver of his
error in a timely manner so as to avoid an accident.

The Chinese Peoples Official Booklet
of Motoring Rules and Regulations

It's cold enough to force my aching corpse out of bed just to put on some clothes. It's an hour later than my usual roll out, but still gloomy outside and the temperature is equally reticent about rising. My nocturnal antics have left me in no condition for training, so it's just as well I had no intention. I couldn't bear the thought of morning warming let alone a Go Run. I'm also not sorry to miss breakfast.

I can't even face a cup of tea and, waking VD, he says he would rather wait until the airport than eat any more rice and cabbage. Moving as quickly as my fragile disposition will allow, I pack the remainder of my serviceable belongings and bin the rest. It's fortuitous we got ourselves sorted yesterday. Even at a snail's pace, the task takes it out of me.

I'm still catching my breath when Marco turns up to say that our carriage awaits. Thwarted by the school's machinery yesterday, he is going to the office to get his certificate and will meet us at the side gate.

With impeccable timing, Shifu turns up just after Marco has left and asks if we have collected our certificates. Pulling a dog-eared scrap of paper from his pocket he motions for our addresses so that our certificates can be posted on to us. We have already given the school our addresses at least five times, but I dutifully endorse his document with my very bestest writing anyway. I won't hold my breath on my local Postie being encumbered by any correspondence from China, particularly as there is no mention of a surcharge.

Squinting at the supplied details, Fatso points to me and grunts. I deduce he's asking my name. Why he doesn't ask me in Chinese I don't know. I tell him my name and he points at VD with another grunt.

'Whuhuh!' Only now we are leaving does he realise VD and I have the same first name. It just goes to show how much notice he has taken of us. Pointing at VD and then back at me, he asks if we are brothers. Unsatisfied by the response, he crumples the paper into his pocket and wanders off. The view that my calligraphic endeavours were another fruitless exercise cements itself firmly in my mind.

Finding the ransacked room depressing, I'm keen for some air. As we quietly make our way down the stairs, it's clear none of our comrades have emerged yet and are not about to do so. The ghostly hush combined with the general shabbiness feels like trespassing in an ancient crypt.

The courtyard is a whole different world on a Sunday morning. A few small groups of vacant looking kids stand around aimless and silent. It's downright eerie. The only sound my wheeled hold-all rattling and bumping along the uneven concrete.

At the side gate I'm surprised to see Shibu, Fatso and Sanda Shifu all sitting in the open doorway of a battered, old mianbiao. I wouldn't have expected them to be up at this hour and I'm pretty sure this wreck is not the school's official minibus. It must be another backhander for the boys and thus spurred their rise.

As usual, Sanda Shifu is scowling and spitting. None of them acknowledge us or attempt to move so that we can get on board. Taking a pew on our cases, we join in with the waiting.

Half an hour later Marco ambles towards us giving a resigned shrug. He has abandoned all hope. Given that he couldn't get his certificate organised when present, I feel there is little chance of us ever seeing ours. Or of it ever blinking into existence.

As the Shifus show no sign of moving, I advance my case like a battering ram until they begrudgingly budge aside. Jamming our luggage into the back seat, I look around just in time to see Shifu Fatso sloping off without so much as a, 'Bye'. I'm disappointed that we were unable to express ourselves better toward someone we could have become close to. VD is not so fussed as his tolerance reached saturation with Fatso some time ago. Marco is annoyed he couldn't get his certificate. For all sad words of tongue and pen... It's a miserable trio that cram into the mianbao. None of us feel the need to speak.

Sensing we are ready to depart, our driver slams the side door only to have it slide open again. Fourth attempt works a treat and he climbs aboard to begin his cockpit drill. Cigarette check completed satisfactorily, the engine is less obliging and protests with a series of coughs and splutters before cutting out. Evidently even the cars spit in China.

This must be a familiar turn of events for him. Unfazed by the vehicles lack of cooperation, he tries the engine again with the same result. A dozen or so false starts later I would be getting annoyed and trying the old impact maintenance, but our man is made of less volatile material and continues to repeat the same action over and over.

Just as I'm thinking we are going to have to push the van to Zhengzhou his persistence pays off. The engine splutters into life and every warning light on the dashboard flashes in sympathetic alarm. I've seen Christmas trees with fewer illuminations, no wonder he's a cheap ride. I, for one, have an idea that he will never bring this journey off.

With many a squeal of engine and a grinding of gear, we hit the road. Rather than risk the rust bucket on the new highway, and pay the toll, the groaning crate is taken along the back roads cunningly locating every pot-hole and boulder along the way. It's just as well I'm empty and VD is jammed full of Imodium as this method of road navigation isn't doing us any favours.

Chugging and creaking our way forth, I undergo a mixture of emotions. Saddened by the anticlimax of the farewell, at the same time I'm glad to be underway and my weakened body is looking forward to a bit of pampering. Fragile at the moment, I'm nonetheless pleased with our performance overall. I had been expecting to struggle much more than we had, not that it was easy, but we certainly gave some of the younger guys a run for their money.

Perhaps our visit was unfortunately timed and we didn't experience the best of Xiao Long. It's an awkward time for China in general. The economic explosion has left the infrastructure and mentality of small towns struggling to keep up and many of the population are out of whack with the current society. Xiao Long is caught up in this confusion and still recovering from the enforced move from Shaolin village. On top of this, the International Kung Fu Department was left in disarray when Shi Yanlin absconded. All this compounded to culminate in the fracas between the Shifu. The vicious cycle is likely to continue until someone with a personality takes the helm.

A particularly large pothole shakes me from my reverie. Considering the van is on its last legs, the driver isn't being particularly gentle about coaxing it along. I thought we were conditioned to Chinese motoring, but this fellow's erratic driving has me reaching for the seatbelt. It's not there. All that remains is a ragged, sawn-off stump. It looks as if the seatbelt has been cut away in order to facilitate the fitting of seat covers. Given the condition of the threadbare, moth-eaten protectors this wasn't done in recent history.

With the haphazard driving, glaring warning lights and complaining engine, I'm not holding out a great deal of hope for our vehicle surviving the journey. If our cranky mianbao were a horse it would have been put out of its misery years ago and our driver jailed for cruelty.

Staring out the window, I see that our dilapidated transport isn't particularly out of place. Aging, rickety vehicles without lights or indicators that can't possibly maintain safe road speeds are a common sight. This is partly because Chinese drivers have never been particularly well regulated. Before 2004 vehicle traffic laws were purely administrative and actual road regulations were little more than guidelines. Even now many motoring conventions are often disregarded altogether. Motorists drive too fast, too slow, on the wrong side of the road, cut people up, talk on mobile phones, ignore red lights, don't have licenses or drunk drive. In fact, many drivers should never have been given a license in the first place.

Currently the world's largest motor vehicle market, China has over a million new cars on the road every month, but the road network hasn't kept pace and driving etiquette is developing much slower than their appetite for motor vehicles. As a result, traffic is often chaotic and right of way and other courtesies are generally ignored. Cars and buses in the wrong lanes frequently hit pedestrians and cyclists. Not even pavements are safe. According to the World Health Organization, China has one of the worst fatality rates per metre of road in the world.

Traffic issues, along with the growing pressure of modern life, have been accused of degrading people's emotional wellbeing with road rage cited as one of the visible symptoms. John Fletcher Moulton claimed that the greatness of a nation resided in its abiding by non-obligatory conventions. I can't imagine the depths of despair to which Chinese motoring would bring him.

Alongside the dusty road, dry fields of yellow crops droop forlornly and every now and then a smattering of squat, grey buildings breaks the view. These small clusters of civilisation are all variations on a limited theme. An old lady sitting on a doorstep, a child playing in the dirt, a dog, a chicken, sweet corn or chilies drying. All have a scooter repair shop with its contents vomited onto the roadside.

Tired and battered after a night worshipping the porcelain, the petrol fumes and uneven road surface aren't doing me any favours so I insulate from the rigours of the drive by withdrawing into myself. Barely conscious, my senses shrink around me until I am in my own little cocoon.

I'm shaken out of my self-imposed bubble as I am thrown across the van. An industrial truck has tried to overtake us into the face of oncoming traffic. Unable to move forward or back in time, he forces our driver to swerve off the road to make way.

I'm still pretty much out of it, but VD sticks his head through the open window to better eyeball the trucker, unwittingly breaking one of the cardinal rules of Chinese etiquette. In many parts of the world drivers use nods or hand gestures to defer right of way. The opposite applies in China, where people actively avert their gaze so as to communicate their intention to proceed regardless.

Eye contact established, the truck driver glowers back. Gunning the engine, he closes the gap between us until he is right on our tail. Glancing into the rear view mirror our driver is panic stricken. Glaring at the road ahead, he forces every ounce of power from the straining vehicle rather than be crushed by the behemoth behind.

Chinese truck drivers are infamous throughout their country. China Daily ran an article about the tragedies they've caused by drunk driving, nodding off or just their idea of road ethics and cited instances of even experienced truck drivers having difficulty obtaining licenses outside China. Bearing down on us like a scene from a Stephen King movie, this trucker has certainly given our driver cause for concern.

Not knowing what to expect from a mentalist Chinese truck driver VD, rummages through his bag and retrieves a heavy-duty chain whip. I'm running on empty here, if the bloke messes with me I'll have to go for one all-out attack. Marco has gone into shock. He grips the seat in front with white knuckled paralysis.

Fortunately, this quarry haul truck is as ancient and battered as our mianbao. Spewing black smoke, it struggles to keep up, but is so close that our driver dare not slow. It's a real battle of will power as I'm sure its only determination keeping their vehicles alive in the first place.

This is the second time today I have caught the attention of the Grim Reaper and I'm not in the frame of mind to put up with any more of his nonsense. Forget riding to Samarra, at this rate that scythe is going right where the sun don't shine.

As if sensing my mounting displeasure, we are granted a last minute reprieve when our pursuer slows and turns down a dirt track. Our driver eases off and the agonised engine screech lowers to a whine. There's an audible drop in cabin pressure as we simultaneously breathe a sigh of relief and our driver reaches for a cigarette. I suspect he will need to change his underwear early this year.

I've had it with the sticks. I now crave civilization and the beckoning luxury of a Beijing two-star hotel can't come soon enough.

Appendix

The Praise Mantra for Bodhisattva Guan Yin
Guanyin Pusa Zan

Guanyin Pusa miao nan chou
qingjing zhuangyan lei jie xiu
sanshier ying bian chen cha
bai qianwan jie hua yan fu
ping zhong gan lou changshi sa
shou nei yangliu buji qiu
qian chu qiqiu qian chu xian
kuhai chang zuo du ren zhou
Namo putuo liuli shijie
da ci da bei Guanyin Pusa.

Bodhisattva Guanyin repays disaster with wonderful stately peace.
Gathering calamities to cultivate the 32 responses
Transform countless calamities
Willow disregards the autumn
One thousand respectfully appeal
'Namo'(Buddhist salutation)
World greatest compassion
Greatest sadness Guanyin

Song of the Shaolin Temple Little Dragon Martial Arts School
Xiao Long Wu Yuan Xuan Shi Ci

Xiao Long Wu Yuan
Ming xing yao lan
Gong fu ji di
Ming xizo feng fan
Ku lian wu yi
Qiang shen jian ti
Nu li pin bo
Yong zheng di yi

Wo shi xiao long wu yuan di yi yuan
Wo zhuang yan xuan shi
Jian jue zun shou xue xiao xiao gui xiao ji
Wei hu xue xiaorong yu
Ming li cheng xin
Xing wei wen ming
Qin xue ku lian
Fa fen zheng you
Li zhi cheng cai
Hui bao she hui

Xiao Long Martial Arts School
The cradle of superstars, Kung Fu base
The example of famous schools. Train Kung Fu skill hard
Make body strong and keep fit, struggle hard
Compete for number one.
I am a member of Xiao Long Martial Arts school
I take each oath with solemnity
I formally abide by school rules and school discipline
Uphold the schools honour, Know good manners and honesty
Have civilised behaviour, Study diligently and train hard
Make a determined effort and win
Be determined to be a gifted scholar. Repay society

Shaolin Temple Generation Poem

The names for all Shaolin monks and disciples are taken from this poem written during the Sung Dynasty by the Shaolin abbot Xueting Fuyu (1203-1275).

Fu Hui Zhi Zi Jue
Liao Ben Yuan Ke Wu
Zhou Hong Pu Guang Zong
Dao Qing Tong Xuan Zu
Qing Jing Zhen Ru Hai
Zhan Ji Chun Zhen Su
De Xing Yong Yan Heng
Miao Ti Chang Jian Gu
Xin Lang Zhao You Shen
Xing Ming Jian Chong Zuo
Zhong Zheng Shan Xi Xiang
Jin Zhi Yuan Ji Du
Xue Ting Wei Dao Shi
Yin Ru Gui Xuan Lu

Only the holy person can understand the way, then one may attain wisdom and bliss. Using the whole to see the principles, you may understand the way. We must spread Chan like rays of sun all over the world. All the branches of Buddhism celebrate the same root. Clarity and stillness are deep as the sea. When you abandon attachments, your true face emerges. Only virtue is never ending, your pure heart never changes. When your heart is still, its brightness will dispel the darkness. Your true nature is the highest. If you are loyal, upright and kind, you will receive happiness and peace. Always remember your Buddha heart. Following the spirit of Huike, this is the way to Buddhahood.

The Heart Sutra
Ban Ruo Bo Luo Mi Duo Xin Jing

Guan zi zai pusa, xing shen ban ruo bo luo mi duo shi,
zhao jian wu yun jie kong, du yi qie ku e. She lizi,
se bu yi kong, kong bu yi se, se ji shi kong, kong ji shi se,
shou xiang xing shi yi fu ru shi.
She lizi, shi zhu fa kong xiang, bu sheng bu mie,
bu gou bu jing, bu zeng bu jian.
Shi gu kong zhong wu se wu shou xiang xing shi.
Wu yan er bi she shen yi, wu chu sheng xiang wei hong fa,
wu yan jie nai zhi wu yi shi jie.
Wu wu ming yi wu wu ming jin, nai zhi wu lao si yi wu lao si jin.
Wu ku ji mie dao. wu zhi yi wu de.
Yi wu suo de gu, pu ti sa duo,
yi ban ruo bo luo mi duo gu,xin wu gua ai.
Wu gua ai gu, wu you kong bu,
yuan li dian dao meng xiang, jiu jing nie pan.
San shi zhu fo yi ban ruo bo luo mi duo gu,
de a nou duo luo san miao san pu ti.
Gu zhi ban ruo bo luo mi duo shi da shen zhou,
shi da ming zhou, shi wu shang zhou, shi wu deng deng zhou,
neng chu yi qie ku, zhen shi bu xu.
Gu shuo ban ruo bo luo mi duo zhou.
Ji shuo zhou yue jie di jie di.
Bo luo jie di. Bo luo seng jie di. Pu ti suo po he.

Bodhisattva, Guan Yin coursing deeply in meditation, perceived the five Buddhist aggregates to be empty, and thus overcame all suffering and calamity. Sariputra, form is no different from emptiness; emptiness is no different from form. Form is emptiness; emptiness is form. Feeling, thought, activity, consciousness are also thus. Sariputra, all phenomena are empty of characteristics: non-arising, non-ceasing; non-defiled, non-pure; non-adding, non-subtracting. Thus in emptiness, there is no form, no feeling, thought, activity, consciousness. No eye, ear, nose, tongue, body and no mind. There is no form, sound, smell, taste, touch or consciousness. There is no realm of eye consciousness nor realm of intellect consciousness. There is neither ignorance nor end of ignorance, neither old age and death nor end of age and death. There is no suffering, no cause, no cessation, and no path. There is no wisdom and no attainment. With nothing to attain, a Bodhisattva relies on Perfection of Wisdom and the mind is without hindrance. Without hindrance, there is no fear. Far beyond all delusions and dreams, perfect nirvana is attained. Thus there is no attainment whatsoever. As such Bodhisattvas have no obstruction of the mind. All Buddhas of past, present and future rely on Perfection of Wisdom, to attain unexcelled perfect enlightenment. Therefore know that the Perfection of Wisdom is a great divine mantra, a great mantra of enlightenment, an unsurpassed mantra, a mantra that has no equal. It is able to eliminate all suffering and is true, not false. Therefore we recite the Perfection of Wisdom mantra; The mantra that says; 'Gone, gone, gone over, gone fully over, awakened, so be it.'

Printed in Great Britain
by Amazon

51041289R00228